D1234510

HORROR INTERNATIONAL

CONTEMPORARY APPROACHES
TO FILM AND TELEVISION SERIES

*A complete listing of the books in this series
can be found online at http://wsupress.wayne.edu*

General Editor

Barry Keith Grant
Brock University

Advisory Editors

Patricia B. Erens
Dominican University

Lucy Fischer
University of Pittsburgh

Peter Lehman
Arizona State University

Caren J. Deming
University of Arizona

Robert J. Burgoyne
Wayne State University

Tom Gunning
University of Chicago

Anna McCarthy
New York University

Peter X. Feng
University of Delaware

HORROR
INTERNATIONAL

EDITED BY
STEVEN JAY SCHNEIDER
AND TONY WILLIAMS

WAYNE STATE UNIVERSITY PRESS   DETROIT

© 2005 by Wayne State University Press,
Detroit, Michigan 48201. All rights reserved.
No part of this book may be reproduced without formal permission.
Manufactured in the United States of America.
09 08 07 06 05   5 4 3 2 1

Library of Congress Cataloging-in-Publication Data

Horror international / edited by Steven Jay Schneider and Tony Williams.
        p.   cm. — (Contemporary approaches to film and television series)
    Includes index.
    ISBN 0–8143-3101–7 (pbk. : alk. paper)
    1. Horror films—History and criticism.   I. Schneider, Steven Jay, 1974–
II. Williams, Tony, 1946 Jan. 11–   III. Series.
    PN1995.9.H6H73 2005
    791.43'6164—dc22

                                                                                    2004017352

An earlier version of Tony Williams's essay, "Hong Kong Social Horror: Tragedy and
Farce in Category 3," appeared in *Post Script* 21, no. 3 (2002). Revised version reprinted
here by permission of the publisher.

∞ The paper used in this publication meets the minimum requirements of the
American National Standard for Information Sciences—Permanence of Paper for
Printed Library Materials, ANSI Z39.48-1984.

Dedicated to the memory of
Harry Nadler
(1940–2002)

Contents

ACKNOWLEDGMENTS

For their support, encouragement, and assistance throughout the development of this project, the editors would like to extend their sincerest thanks to Barry Grant, Jane Hoehner, Frank Lafond, Kim Soyoung, and all of the contributors.

Introduction

Steven Jay Schneider and Tony Williams

Until fairly recently, analysis of the horror genre tended to concentrate on entries from the Western world, whether the American horror film, British examples such as Hammer horror, or the Italian *giallo* tradition of Mario Bava and Dario Argento. Although this may appear to reflect Western prejudice (which, to a certain extent, it does) the main reason for this restricted focus has been difficulties accessing films from other parts of the globe, as well as the relative lack of interest shown by several national cinemas in this genre until the last decade or so. Certainly, up to 1950 it was possible for most critics and scholars to claim a knowledge of world horror cinema based on the admittedly limited theatrical distribution of various examples in the art or popular entertainment fields. Thus it was left to marginal publications such as *Oriental Cinema, Video Watchdog, Fangoria, Cinefantastique, Asian Trash Cinema* (now *Asian Cult Cinema*), and *Necronomicon,* along with developing video distributors and specialized mail-order houses like Midnight Video, Sinister Cinema, Something Weird Video, and Video Search of Miami to furnish and champion hard-to-come-by examples for those enthusiastic explorers seeking something different from what was then provided by the relatively limited distributions venues.

Another factor in the critical bias against non-Western cinematic horror has been the tendency of most reviewers and academics to avoid dealing with the disparate nature of popular culture, concentrating instead on those works that qualify as art cinema or else analyzing certain isolated examples within narrowly defined parameters. In her important and timely book, *Cutting Edge: Art-Horror and the Horrific Avant-Garde* (2000), Joan Hawkins persuasively argues that "paracinema" fanzines and mail-order companies like the ones listed above "challenge many of our continuing assumptions about the binary opposition of prestige cinema

1

... and popular culture," highlighting through their categories, selections, and reviews "an aspect of art cinema generally overlooked or repressed in cultural analysis; namely, the degree to which high culture trades on the same images, tropes, and themes that characterize low culture."[1]

Hawkins goes on to claim that "paracinema consumption can be understood . . . as American art cinema consumption has often been understood, as a reaction against the hegemonic and normatizing practices of mainstream, dominant Hollywood consumption."[2] The trouble with Hawkins's argument is that, even while problematizing the opposition between art cinema and the so-called trash film, she effectively recasts it in terms of an ideological and equally misleading dichotomy between Hollywood and non-Hollywood filmmaking practices (whether alternative, experimental, "underground," or simply foreign). As recent scholarship has endeavored to show, however, the relationship between Hollywood and its various "Others" is every bit as complex, evolving, and mutually influential as that between trash (cult, "psychotronic," etc.) filmmaking and the cinematic avant-garde.[3]

This is especially true when it comes to the horror genre. The dominance of American film production and the ready availability of U.S. films from all periods may have gone a long way toward engendering the disproportionate critical focus on this nation's cinematic horror. But at the levels of style, technique, and narrative form, the influence of U.S. horror filmmaking practices, formulas, and (sub)generic conventions has by no means been unidirectional. Indeed, more than ever before, the horror film traditions of other national and regional cinemas are engaged in a dynamic process of cross-cultural exchange with American mainstream, independent, and underground horror alike.

One obvious and oft-cited example of such cross-cultural horror exchange is the impact of German Expressionism on the aesthetic of classic ("Universal") U.S. horror. Less well known is the case of Italian *giallo* auteur Mario Bava, whose *Sei donne per l'assassino* (*Blood and Black Lace*, 1964), and *L'ecologia del delitto* (*A Bay of Blood*, 1971), anticipated by some years the key formal and narrative conventions employed in the popular American "stalker cycle" of horror films, a cycle initiated by John Carpenter's indie sensation *Halloween* in 1978.[4] Then there are those big-budget U.S. remakes of such foreign horror hits as *Spoorloos* (Netherlands/ France, 1988; remade as *The Vanishing*, 1993) and *Nattevagten* (Denmark, 1994; remade as *Nightwatch*, 1998) by their original European writer-directors, only with the unasked for "assistance" of studio-assigned Hollywood script doctors. Both of these films failed miserably among critics as well as fans in their shiny new "Americanized" forms.[5] In sharp contrast is the case of *The Ring* (2002), DreamWorks' big-budget remake of *Ringu,* the 1998 film that stands at the forefront of the horror genre's current resurgence in Japan.[6]

The situation over the last ten or so years has changed drastically due to the effects of the new global economy, the decline of rigid national boundaries, and the transcultural phenomenon affecting virtually all sectors of cinema, from Hollywood to Hong Kong and beyond. However, even a book such as *Fear Without Frontiers: Horror Cinema across the Globe* (2003) contains a preface by Kim Newman that states "the dominant strains of any given genre (including horror) are American, with only the martial arts movie providing a non-American alternative to the Western." To be fair, Newman does mention other traditions such as Mexican horror, Italian horror, the international vampire movie, and the 1973 hybrid *The Legend of the 7 Golden Vampires,* which combines Hammer horror with Hong Kong's Shaw Brothers via the teaming up of Peter Cushing and David Chiang.[7] But even acknowledging the very few book-length exceptions—*Cutting Edge, Fear Without Frontiers,* Cathal Tohill and Pete Tombs's *Immoral Tales* (1995)[8]—and with a nod to Phil Hardy's broad-based *Film Encyclopedia: Horror* (1986), it is not inaccurate to claim that scholarly interest remains focused primarily on the American horror film, as recent studies by Carol Clover, Paul Wells, Rhona Berenstein, Isabel Pinedo, Judith Halberstam, Cynthia Freeland, and Harry Benshoff (among others) reveal.

Although the sporadic work that has appeared in the past decade has helped to rectify this imbalance, a great deal more research needs to be undertaken in the field so as to give the international perspectives and cross-cultural dynamics of world horror cinema its due. In an era defined by the blanket terms "post-modernism" and "global economy," it is increasingly difficult to distinguish *any* cinema according to exclusive national and sociocultural parameters. Every nation, region, and cultural artifact is now influenced by forces outside its geographic boundaries. But recognizing this undeniable fact does not mean proclaiming the definitive victory of American culture, whether in a cultural imperialist or "end of ideology" sense of the term. As Toby Miller points out, the 1990s have seen the emergence of truly global film distribution cartels, representing "a possible new international division of cultural labour."[9] In the present case, what it tells us is that characterizations of the nature of horror films (narratively, thematically, stylistically, and economically) from various geographical and cultural locations are more fluid and transitional than ever before.

Furthermore, recognition of this fact does not mean denying the existence of national features that affect and are reflected in particular horror films, whether from an artistic or reception standpoint. Instead, we must respect and seek to identify the diversity of factors bearing on specific works, as well as draw attention to neglected social, cultural, and ideological aspects of the horror genre's appearance in its various national cinematic contexts. While Italian, Japanese, Mexican, Spanish, and Hong Kong horror films have been accorded a modicum of critical recognition in recent times, the areas of Russian, Belgian, Scandinavian, Dutch, Canadian (besides Cronenberg), and Thai horror (for example) all still need—in fact, demand—some attention.

For reasons of space, it was impossible for us to assign coverage of *every* horror film–producing country and territory on the map. But it is our hope and anticipation that this study will stimulate more critical interest and work in these neglected areas, and that additional approaches to the regions examined herein will be developed and tested by others. The essays collected in this volume both express goals to be reached and bring much-deserved attention to issues that have received relatively limited attention to date. They not only examine new material but also focus on different conditions of audience reception, thereby stimulating fresh readings. These in turn shed new light on the original cultural production of many works as well as their subsequent "translations" and meanings in different national contexts. The realities of the present era may complicate any attempts to read horror films exclusively against their original historical and cultural background. But at the same time, such realities can spark efforts to analyze the disparate nature of multicultural factors, resulting in diverse and illuminating readings such as those collected here.

The first section of *Horror International* examines in a variety of different contexts the dynamics of cross-cultural horror exchange. Raiford Guins's "Blood and Black Gloves on Shiny Disks: New Media, Old Tastes, and the Remediation of Italian Horror Films in the United States" deals specifically with the new conditions of reception of Italian horror films as a result of new technologies. Although works such as Riccardo Freda's *I Vampiri* (1956) and Mario Bava's *La maschera del demonio* (1960) have been well known over the past forty years, Guins describes the manner in which contemporary discursive practices and new media formats produce different forms of readings from those in the past resulting from theatrical exhibition, fan magazine discourse, and video circulation. This essay engages not only with transcultural issues of reader reception but also with the technological roles of transformation that often result in new forms of signification both in terms of their previous cultural histories in the United States as well as their contrast with current American examples involving a different reception within a new national context.

Transcultural reception issues also concern Andrew Syder and Dolores Tierney in "Importation/Mexploitation, or, How a Crime-Fighting, Vampire-Slaying Mexican Wrestler Almost Found Himself in an Italian Sword-and-Sandals Epic." Noting the manner in which various Mexican horror films were hideously cut and dubbed for American distribution, the authors believe that this transcultural movement is "too complex to be simply disregarded because of a belief in the 'purity' of the Mexican originals and the 'impiety' of the American adaptation." Like Guins, Syder and Tierney examine the original stage of their films' reception in the United States and their subsequent revival as cult movies in the 1980s by "psychotronic" viewers. Noting the original status of these films as "bad objects" whose production and consumption represent a legitimate form of resistance to mainstream Hollywood, the authors see not only a dialogue occurring between the foreign and the local, particularly with respect to the project of constructing a national identity, but also a more flexible mode of spectatorship playing a key role in the formation of cultural identities.

Most representations of the serial killer appear to follow an Americanized model. As Steffen Hantke demonstrates, "the trope of American uniqueness has established itself as an indispensable part of the public discourse on serial murder," as illustrated by the success of *The Silence of the Lambs* (1991). Hantke interrogates two German films from 1995: *Der Totmacher* and *Der Sandmann,* both featuring Götz George. While the first film exhibits a mainstream Hollywood aesthetic representing a postmodern narrative universe commodifying and denying Germany's own history, the second example evinces a different cinematic strategy reminiscent of the cinema of Rainer Werner Fassbinder, Werner Herzog, and early Wim Wenders, one which emphasizes the historical specificity influencing German culture past and present. But while *Der Totmacher* superficially uses American genre conventions before inverting them in order to expose the ideological and pragmatic agenda behind such conventional perceptions, *Der Sandmann* develops the previous film's theme

of the accomplished post-modernization of Germany spatially as well as
temporally. For Hantke, both films interrogate the dictum of American
exceptionalism, seeing it as dystopian and challenging Hollywood genre
cinema to rethink its status as global cultural vanguard.

Section 2 focuses on haunting histories and regional gothics, starting with Jyotsna Kapur's essay, "The Return of History as Horror:
Onibaba and the Atomic Bomb." In the traditional Japanese horror film
the past haunts the present, invariably taking the form of the supernatural, of ghosts or spirits. As Kapur reveals, Shindo Kaneto's *Onibaba* (1964)
is a radical reworking of this genre into a political allegory of survival in
conditions of scarcity amidst class antagonism ruled by war. Told from the
perspective of two women who manage on their own in a world of men,
Onibaba is also a feminist rendering of this genre, one in which Shindo
follows his mentor Mizoguchi. Shindo's powerful visualization portrays
history as nightmare, tracing the roots of nuclear war not in some external catastrophe but in history itself. Nowhere in the film is the A-bomb
mentioned explicitly, nor is the film a visual translation of a political parable; rather, Shindo's cinematography, mise en scène, sound, and narration
create a throbbing, unstable world filled with opposing energies that
evoke the "political unconscious" (to use Fredric Jameson's term).

In "'Terror Australis': Areas of Horror in the Australian Cinema,"
Jonathan Rayner examines the location of the abhorrent and the definition of fear within Australian film, despite the apparent absence of the
generically pure horror movie from the output of this country's national
cinema since 1970. Rayner's analysis of some notable examples of the
Australian feature film, including *The Cars That Ate Paris* (1974), *Long
Weekend* (1979), *Bliss* (1985), and *Incident at Raven's Gate* (1988), reveals
the ubiquity of horror motifs and subtexts within a variety of genres, from
science fiction and fantasy to coming-of-age narratives and period dramas. Particular attention is also given to the categorization of Australian
Gothic, and the hybridization of pop cultural forms within its style and
tone of black comedy. Rayner's recognition of the pervasiveness of the
gothic highlights the popular generic basis and specific cultural relevance
of the Australian cinema.

As Ian Conrich points out, a dominant image of New Zealand is of
a pastoral paradise, a country of harmony and tranquility with a landscape
of natural, primordial beauty. Yet if New Zealand can be regarded as an
Eden, there can also be observed to exist within this overgrown garden
excess and disorder. In places of isolation, in communities geographically

and psychologically "on the edge," individuals appear trapped within a landscape that is both enchanting and seemingly "alive." In his contribution, Conrich discusses the characteristics of what is arguably a distinctive New Zealand cinema of fear he terms "Kiwi Gothic." Claiming that there is not a singular form of the Kiwi Gothic, but rather multiple variations, Conrich analyzes such short films and features as *The Scarecrow* (1982), *Trial Run* (1984), *Death Warmed Up* (1984), *Mr. Wrong* (1985), *Kitchen Sink* (1989), *Moonrise* (1992), *Braindead* (1992), *Jack Be Nimble* (1993), and *Possum* (1997) in order to explicate the differences between the urban gothic, rural gothic, the psycho-drama, and gothic horror.

Meanwhile, Brian McIlroy looks at how the films of Neil Jordan—including *The Company of Wolves* (1984), *High Spirits* (1988), *Interview with the Vampire* (1993), and *The Butcher Boy* (1997)—interweave elements from the horror genre, the psychological thriller, and the Anglo-Irish Gothic. Tracing Jordan's interest in the gothic and the fantastic to his early fiction, McIlroy argues that the director is a natural inheritor of the Irish gothic literary tradition (which claims writers such as Bram Stoker, Charles Maturin, and Sheridan Le Fanu) and explores why an Irish-Catholic educated writer and filmmaker should find the (Protestant) gothic of particular force. Making the case that Jordan appreciates the release of the supernatural because it allows for ready discussion of race, gender, and nationality issues in a culture that finds these matters especially difficult to confront, McIlroy also notes that such themes allow for a sensational treatment of sexuality in an atmosphere of sexual repression both remembered and real.

In "Thailand Haunted: The Power of the Past in the Contemporary Thai Horror Film," Adam Knee investigates three recent examples of a marginal genre within Thailand. These films investigate the paradoxical status of women in Thai society and the need to come to terms with Thai tradition and history in which the past and the feminine function as sources of anxiety. Perhaps the most interesting example, *303: Fear/Faith/Revenge* (1998) deals with potentially explosive facts involving students in the 1960s and the present. It also deals with the continuing attempts to assign guilt and come to terms with university uprisings of the mid-1970s and the bloody coup attempt of 1992.

Section 3, beginning with Andrew Willis's essay, "The Spanish Horror Film as Subversive Text: Eloy de la Iglesia's *La semana del asesino*," focuses on horror in the social realm. Concentrating on de la Iglesia's 1972 film (a.k.a. *Cannibal Man*), Willis discusses the specific circumstances defining a popular work made in the Franco era. He also looks at how a low-budget Spanish horror film managed to subvert national issues and concerns in a manner similar to the way that Britain's Hammer horror films reflected the dark underside of its own cultural context. By analyzing how the director uses the generic conventions of the horror film alongside social realism to challenge the beliefs of mainstream society, Willis shows how *La semana del asesino* is a striking example of radical, popular filmmaking in Spain in the early 1970s.

Focusing on two highly regarded films made in Holland during the next decade—Paul Verhoeven's *The Fourth Man* (1983) and George Sluizer's *The Vanishing* (1988)—Steven Jay Schneider and Kevin W. Sweeney argue that the primary source of negative emotion in these and other Dutch horror-thrillers is not a hyperbolic return of the socio-culturally repressed in the form of a monster. Rather, "such emotion—be it horror, terror, dread, or what have you—is generated largely via *the protagonist's dawning realization that such repression is impossible to overcome.*" This is in contrast to Robin Wood's influential formula for the American horror film, according to which, following Freud, that which is repressed always strives to return, threatening "normality" in the form of the monster.

In "Hong Kong Social Horror: Tragedy and Farce in Category 3," Tony Williams examines the social relevance behind such Hong Kong "true crime" graphic exploitation films as *The Untold Story* (1993), *The Untold Story 2* (1998), *Dr. Lamb* (1992), *Underground Banker* (1994), and *Ebola Syndrome* (1996). Despite their gruesome nature, these films often contain indirect social commentary on human exploitation in a post-capitalist society that has passed from the status of colony to incorporation with the motherland figure of Mainland China in 1997. Set in the colonies of Hong Kong and Macao, *The Untold Story* satirizes an uncaring bureaucratic police force as well as containing some degree of sympathy for the brutal killer played by Anthony Wong. While both the British colonial administration and the current Hong Kong special administration region operate a rigid form of censorship, these exploitative Category 3 films reveal the dark underside of a dehumanizing society affecting both law enforcement officials and criminals.

According to Christina Stojanova, the study of Romanian cinematic horror must be based on examples scattered over genres and years, since horror films in the Western sense have not been made in Romania. Following Freud's discussion of the uncanny, which attributes terror to the collapsing of the psychic boundaries of self and other, life and death, reality and unreality, Stojanova explicates the peculiarities of horror representation in Romanian cinema with reference to tensions between traditional Eastern awareness (predicated on irrational beliefs and collectivism) and the modern Western one (promulgating rational individualism). The first section of Stojanova's essay, "Beyond Dracula and Ceausescu: Phenomenology of Horror in Romanian Cinema," analyzes the Dracula/Vlad Tepeş controversy, locating it with respect to the historical idiosyncrasies of Romanian culture. The horror motifs in interwar literature are then linked to the mounting frictions between traditional Romanian ways of life and modernization. Finally, Stojanova reflects on the abundance of horror motifs in post-communist Romanian cinema, seen as attempts at diffusing old as well as emerging tensions between tradition and (post-)communist modernity.

In "Snapping up Schoolgirls: Legitimation Crisis in Recent Canadian Horror," Suzie Young posits the "multiple figuration of the schoolgirl as the *mise-en-abyme* in Canadian cinema that expresses the 'structure of feeling' in contemporary Canada. Analyzing in detail Vincenzo Natali's *Cube* (1997) and John Fawcett's *Ginger Snaps* (2001), Young shows how the depiction of the schoolgirl in Canada's recent horror cinema achieves an "expressionistic allegory of the real," expounding a Canadian ethos that remains mostly repressed in normal life. In the former film, a naïve schoolgirl is betrayed and brutally victimized by a trusted adult, exposing a world of patriarchal hysteria, treachery, and legitimation crisis. In the latter film, meanwhile, the quotidian becomes "thoroughly obnoxious, inviting the schoolgirl's transgressions as well as the audience's sympathies."

The fourth section of *Horror International* looks at a number of contested horror traditions around the world. First, Jan Uhde examines the "implicit horror" in the distinctly non-generic films of Czech animator and visual artist Jan Švankmajer. One of the most accomplished film artists working today, Švankmajer is little known internationally, although this is slowly changing. As Uhde reveals, Švankmajer's pessimism, dark humor, and concern for the human condition reflect the historical experience of his own country and that of Central Europe. Working with horror, "but remaining outside the conventions of the genre, he does not attempt to shock or scare his audience by assaulting their emotions; instead, he uses indirect, implicit horror to stimulate viewers' minds, forcing them to contemplate the darker side of reality beyond the film screen."

Viola Shafik's "Egypt: A Cinema without Horror?" investigates a rare national cinema in which the horror genre appears wholly absent. Considering reasons for this phenomenon, Shafik notes the absence of a Western gothic tradition that could have facilitated the adaptation of horror to the big screen and other significant cultural factors as well. These involve a cinematic commitment to the perspective of a materially cornered petit bourgeois that left little space for the type of Western generic conventions we understand as horror. Instead, Egyptian films tend to ignore such concepts "in order to confirm a strongly modernist and/or scriptural Muslim ideology" which does not objectively deny dominant values. Shafik's analysis ultimately seeks to explain why those Egyptian films that come closest to qualifying as "horror" have more interest in rationalizing than in demonizing, or more precisely, in depicting "social reality" rather than its people's psyche.

In "Burn, Witch, Burn: A First Look at the Scandinavian Horror Film," Rebecca A Umland and Samuel J. Umland begin by observing that, in contrast to their American and Japanese counterparts (for instance), Scandinavian horror movies do not readily invoke images of marauding monsters or supernatural creatures. Although a few isolated if unusual examples can be named, such as Carl Theodor Dreyer's *Vampyr* (1932), no distinct horror tradition has been identified in Scandinavian cinema to date. Surveying a number of films from Denmark, Sweden, and Norway, by several different directors, the Umlands proceed to offer some defining characteristics of Scandinavian horror. In their view, what distinguishes such horror from that of other nationalities is "the tension between paganism and Christianity, revealing a deep-rooted cultural fear, or at least preoccupation, with the opposition between a Norse heroic code of life and the Christian values that drove this system of belief underground, culturally and psychologically."

Belgium appears to be a country particularly hostile to producing horror films, much less having a critical community favoring the genre itself. In "*Man Bites Dog* and the Critical Reception of Belgian Horror (in) Cinema," Ernest Mathijs investigates why Belgian critics have not dealt appropriately with its own horror genre, contrasting the international reception of films such as *Daughters of Darkness* (1971) and *Man Bites Dog* (1992) with their reception at home. As well as engaging in a dismissal of popular genres, most Belgian criticism has remained immune from advances in international film interpretation such as psychoanalysis, post-structuralism, and feminism that have led to new readings of films and genres often neglected in the past. Although the release of *Man Bites Dog* led to Belgian critics viewing the horror film as culturally relevant, Mathijs's research shows that most of the country's reviewers focused on the relationship between horror and culture rather than extending the debate to address the wider (and neglected) parameters of the horror genre itself.

Finally, in "Exorcising the Devil: Russian Cinema and Horror," Josephine Woll describes the pre- and post-Soviet cinema in terms of its structure as an industry, its audience, and its genres, with particular reference to horror films. She also looks at the Soviet period, 1917–86 (technically 1991), discussing several issues: the tension among competing functions for cinema as an arm of the state and the relevance of that tension to genre film production overall; the ideological reasons the Soviets excluded horror as an acceptable genre; the categories that replaced Western generic designations in Soviet cinema; the practical and related aesthetic reasons to exclude horror; and the use of "horror moments" in other kinds of films, including literary adaptations. Finally, Woll returns to the post-Soviet period, analyzing such films as *Mr. Decorator* (1989), *Daddy, Santa Claus Died* (1992), and *Of Freaks and Men* (1998).

All of the essays in this collection represent new approaches and attempts at developing further work geared toward understanding the different ways the horror genre operates within different national contexts. Although Hollywood influences are often unavoidable, many of the films looked at here employ its formulas while adopting novel approaches to changing them in order to reflect both artistic concerns and reader-reception strategies. The Western horror film has received due attention and recognition over the past twenty years. Now is the time for voices from different cultural and national contexts to be heard.

NOTES

1. Joan Hawkins, *Cutting Edge: Art-Horror and the Horrific Avant-Garde* (Minnesota: University of Minnesota Press, 2000), 3. Hawkins quotes Jeffrey Sconce on "paracinema": "this is 'an extremely elastic textual category' and comprises 'less a distinct group of films than a particular reading protocol, a counter-aesthetic turned subcultural sensibility devoted to all manner of cultural detritus. In short the explicit manifesto of paracinematic culture is to valorize all forms of cinematic 'trash' whether such films have been either explicitly rejected or simply ignored by legitimate film culture,'" 14, from Sconce, 372. See also Jeffrey Sconce, "'Trashing' the Academy: Taste, Excess, and an Emerging Politics of Cinematic Style," *Screen* 36, no. 4 (1995).

2. Hawkins, *Cutting Edge*, 7.

3. See, for example, Graeme Harper and Xavier Mendik, eds., *Unruly Pleasures: The Cult Film and Its Critics* (Guildford, UK: FAB Press, 2001); and Xavier Mendik and Steven Jay Schneider, eds., *Underground U.S.A: Filmmaking beyond the Hollywood Canon* (London: Wallflower, 2002).

4. See Ian Conrich, "La mort n'est pas une fin: La série des *Vendredi 13* et la fonction culturelle d'un grand guignol moderne," in *Cauchemars Americains: Fantastique et horreur dans le cinéma moderne*, ed. Frank Lafond (Liege, Belgium: Les Editions du CEFAL, 2003); and Reynold Humphries, "Just Another Fashion Victim: Mario Bava's *Sei donne per l'assassino* (*Blood and Black Lace*) 1964," *Kinoeye* 1, no. 7 (2001), online at http://www.kinoeye.org/01/07/humphries07.html, accessed September 5, 2003.

5. See Steven Jay Schneider, "Repackaging Rage: *The Vanishing* and *Nightwatch*," *Kinema* 17 (Spring 2002): 47–66.

6. See Ramie Tateishi, "The Contemporary Japanese Horror Film Series: *Ring* and *Eko Eko Azarak*," in *Fear Without Frontiers: Horror Cinema across the Globe*, ed. Steven Jay Schneider (Surrey, UK: FAB Press, 2003).

7. For more on this film, see I. Q. Hunter, "*The Legend of the 7 Golden Vampires*," *Post-colonial Studies* 3, no. 1 (2000): 81–87.

8. Tombs also authored the bulk of *Mondo Macabro: Weird & Wonderful Cinema around the World* (New York: St. Martin's Griffin, 1998), although this popular read includes under its purview (as the subtitle implies) "action pics … sex exploiters and monster movies," 7, along with horror films "proper."

9. Toby Miller, "Hollywood and the World," in *Oxford Guide to Film Studies*, ed. John Hill and Pamela Church Gibson (Oxford: Oxford University Press, 1998), 377.

I

THE DYNAMICS OF CROSS-CULTURAL HORROR EXCHANGE

Blood and Black Gloves on Shiny Discs:

New Media, Old Tastes, and the Remediation of Italian Horror Films in the United States

Raiford Guins

Eager to capitalize on Asia Argento's prominent role in the Vin Diesel vehicle, *Triple X* (2002), the Virgin Megastore in West Hollywood, California, erected a display to showcase its "Euro-Horror" collection. Here the DVD versions of Dario Argento and Mario Bava films are presented to onlookers as "masterpieces" of horror. DVDs from Anchor Bay's "Dario Argento Collection" and Image Entertainment's "The Mario Bava Collection" contain original movie poster artwork. The plastic cases are neatly arranged on red velvet. Bava and Argento's enigmatic black-gloved psychopath, whose shiny blades often drip the red hue of blood, contrast starkly with the black cases of shiny DVDs that, today, comprise the prevailing media-object relation between Italian horror "films" and U.S. audiences.

Italian horror cinema has an incredibly rich lineage. Its modern incarnation stretches back to Riccardo Freda's *I Vampiri* (a.k.a. *The Devil's Commandment*, 1956) and Bava's *The Mask of Satan* (a.k.a. *Black Sunday*, 1960); has produced a distinct subgenre known as the *giallo* (an obvious influence on the U.S. slasher film); has blurred and exploited generic conventions (e.g., Aristide Massaccesi's *Emanuelle and the Last Cannibals* [a.k.a. *Trap Them and Kill Them*], 1977); and has generated a global following (most notably in the United States, United Kingdom, France, the Netherlands, Germany, and Japan). Today's international fan community greatly benefits from online mail-order companies specializing in world horror, cult, schlock, camp, splatter, sleaze, mondo; or what Jeffrey Sconce defines as "paracinema"—"less a distinct group of films than a particular reading protocol, a counter-aesthetic turned subcultural sensibility devoted to all manner of cultural detritus."[1] Media superstores, ever diligent in subsuming niche audiences through sheer quantity of available titles, have also dedicated their profit-making practices to include not only mass but also micro-paracinephilic tastes. For example, Italian titles long sought after in uncut versions—including *Stage Fright* (Michele Soavi, 1987), *Torso* (Sergio Martino, 1973), *Shock* (Mario Bava, 1978), *City of the Living Dead* (Lucio Fulci, 1980), *The Beyond* (Lucio Fulci, 1981), *Cannibal Ferox* (a.k.a. *Make Them Die Slowly*, Umberto Lenzi, 1981), *Profondo rosso* (a.k.a. *Deep Red*, Dario Argento, 1975)—are now available on DVD and can easily be found at superstores such as Virgin and Tower Records, online companies like Shockingimages.com and DiabolikDVD.com that specialize in paracinema, and "cult" video stores like Los Angeles' Mondo Video.

Despite recent availability and temporary high profile, or perhaps on account of both, the Italian horror film continues to experience a peculiar reception beyond Roma. This peculiarity invokes a deceptively simple question: How are Italian horror films known in the United States? In considering this question, it is first imperative to stress that film is *not* the medium through which Italian horror is best known in the United States. This is by no means a trivial point. Prior to videocassette and its large-scale "home penetration" in the mid-1980s, Italian horror "films" (when distributed and shown on U.S. screens) were exhibited in limited release, or found on the midnight movie circuit, or at paracinema festivals, or at drive-in cinemas after their post-War glamour period had run its course. Tim Lucas's liner notes for the DVD version of Mario Bava's *Twitch of the Death Nerve* (a.k.a. *Carnage*, *Bay of Blood*, and *Last House on the Left—Part II*) explains how the film was exhibited in the United States. According to Lucas, it became "a perennial drive-in favorite, playing for years in support of such films as Wes Craven's *Last House on the Left*."[2] The Argento-Lamberto Bava film *Demons* (1985), perhaps on account of its heavy metal soundtrack that featured the then-popular groups Mötley Crüe, Accept, and Saxon, played U.S. theaters in the mid-1980s, as did its sequel *Demons 2* (1986). More recently, Michele Soavi's *Dellamorte dellamore* (1994, released in the United States as *Cemetery Man*) introduced a younger generation, or at least those who frequent independent cinemas, to Italian fantasy-horror in the mid-1990s.

If one were to accept Susan Sontag's claim that "To see a great film only on television isn't to have really seen that film,"[3] then perhaps in the last twenty-plus years only a select few have actually *seen* Italian horror films in the United States. This seems unlikely given that it is within the home theater, made possible by the VCR and more recently by DVD players, that Italian horror can boast of nationwide exhibition in the United

States. That said, I want to foreground the media that Sontag would dismiss, and focus on how Italian horror films have been seen and understood during two specific periods. The first period (roughly the mid-1980s to 1997) is marked by the availability of Italian horror on videocassette, while the second period is distinguished by DVD's elevation to the preferred medium through which to experience Italian horror cinema.[4]

The dominant discourse that defined Italian horror during the first period was fan writing in the form of fanzines and fan-authored books. This social discourse and Italian horror's reliance on the videocassette as "the" medium through which to meet U.S. audiences created, I argue, the Italian horror film as "gore-object." The necessary sub-question is: How did the poor quality of adaptation and transfer to videocassette (e.g., cut footage, dubbing, new titles, and packaging) and fan writings on Italian horror films affect the popular conception of these films during the period in question? In the second period, Italian horror metamorphosed into an "art-object." Reliance on the new medium of DVD remediates how the Italian horror film is known and forces one to ask: How are Italian horror films reconceived through the restoration process promised by DVD (e.g., digitally remastered and uncut prints)?

Each period, I am claiming, has produced distinct ways of knowing Italian horror. As such, the Italian horror film—like any other genre—is not a stable category. This essay attempts to articulate how discursive practices work on and through videocassette and DVD in order to produce knowledge about, and define, Italian horror within U.S. cinema culture. My use of the term "remediation" is dependent on what I consider to be a productive tension between Jay David Bolter/Richard Grusin and Paul Levinson.[5] Levinson regards the term as a process of reform. New media can be said to "repair" or "correct" a presumed deficiency found in existing media. Bolter and Grusin, however, are hesitant to adopt an "evolutionary" or "progressive" approach to remediation. As such, and as a way to avoid the dangers of linear progression, they urge that remediation be used as a process of *refashioning* rather than repair and/or replacement. For the purposes of this essay, both definitions are relevant to foster an understanding of the Italian horror film during each of the aforementioned periods.

Cut and Dubbed: Italian Horror as Gore-Object

"In 1980," Douglas Gomery demonstrates, "only two of every one hundred homes in the United States had a VCR."[6] The years 1983 to 1985 hailed the beginning of the peak in sales for home video recorders. In 1983 alone, 11.8 million home units were sold in the United States. By the end of 1986, it is estimated that "the proportion of TV-owning homes with video machines was expected to reach nearly 45% in America."[7] Accompanying unit sales, pre-recorded videocassettes also began to emerge as a prosperous industry. The initial rise began in 1983, when figures charting the U.S. market illustrated 11.0 million cassettes sold. 1987 saw this number multiplied by seven to reveal 72.0 million in sales.[8] During this period the acquisition of videocassettes for rent was through independent merchants such as "Mom & Pop" stores, and through emerging regional chain retailers. At the same time, the gap between VCR households and TV households in the United States began to shrink. Figures indicate that in 1988 between 51.7 and 56.2 percent of a million households possessed a video recorder in relation to 56.9 percent of a million households that had televisions.[9] The early 1990s saw a further closing of the differential. By 1992, 70.0 million is the estimated number of VCR households in the United States.

As is well known, pornography took to video with industrial zeal. X-rated videocassettes were the most prominent pre-recorded features for early video sales and rentals.[10] The inclusion of porn had repercussions for the video store's image. Owners began to position porn away from Hollywood features. For example, as James Lardner reports, one video storeowner in Washington, DC states: "Unless you ask us, we don't tell you we've got 'em."[11] In addition, the problem of porn visibility while in the store (explicit videocassette covers) was dealt with by separation: "We've built a separate room—our adult room. No one under eighteen permitted."[12]

Exploitation films (in this case "women in prison," Nazi atrocity, and cannibal films) along with horror films of the period appearing for the first time on videocassette often shared space with porn in the forbidden "separate room." On account of limited funds for marketing, the videocassette box cover had to communicate its contents in a blatant (and sometimes vicious) manner. Due to their provocative cover art, Cesare Canevari's *L'ultima orgia del III Reich* (released on video in the United States as *Caligula Reincarnated as Hitler* and *The Gestapo's Last Orgy*, 1976), Sergio Garrone's *Lager SS Adis Kastrat Kommandantur* (U.S. video title, *SS Experiment Camp*, 1976), Massaccesi's *Emanuelle and the Last Cannibals*, and Lenzi's U.S.-titled *Make Them Die Slowly* all shared shelf space alongside porn.[13]

VHS cover art for *SS Experiment Camp* (1976)

The influx of titles that began to fill the shelves of American video stores by 1987 included a number of Italian horror films, many of which were new to the medium. This marks the first time that Italian horror cinema became readily accessible (i.e., available to rent) in the United States by means other than bootlegged tapes, copies recorded from European formats, or Japanese laserdiscs. The video recorder is a time machine in two ways. Its time-shifting capabilities, as marketing campaigns boasted, permitted the user more control over "when" and "how" broadcasting was programmed. At the same time, though not ordinarily recognized as part of the VCR's temporal capabilities, film history became manageable. During the late 1980s one had access to more films from different historical periods and national regions than any time prior to the VCR's welcome into the domestic sphere. Viewers gained access to Bava and Argento's *gialli* from the 1960s and 1970s, as well as to films most likely never, or only rarely, exhibited nationally in the United States by the likes of Massaccesi, Fulci, Ruggero Deodato, Lenzi, and Antonio Margheriti.

The common adage of "new on home video" can, at this time, also be read as "new to U.S. audiences."

Major studios were not the giants behind the distribution of Italian horror. If a film did not predate the video release, then the poster art did not necessarily reacquaint the renter. Box covers relied on film stills or, if an older title was reincarnated for videocassette, artwork from the original production or newer artwork designed to appeal to the current horror cycle was transposed. The U.S. release of *Profondo rosso* as *Deep Red Hatchet Murders* is a good example. The front cover contains an isolated still of the film's eerie doll having its head smashed apart. "HBO Video" appears in the left hand corner; its white and black logo clearly not part of the poorly reproduced still. The film's title appears in the lower half of the cover in red lettering offset by white to produce a lighting effect. Absent from the title is the director's name. In addition, an image of David Hemmings (the film's star) peering into darkness is poorly inserted onto the cover scene, but boxed to indicate another scene that is separate from the one provided to onlookers. The back cover offers a cursory plot synopsis. This treatment marks a drastic understatement for a film that many feel is one of the greatest Italian horror films ever made and Argento's best work.

Like the videocassette covers crafted to target a supposedly nondiscerning audience, poor dubbing became synonymous with viewers' first experience of Italian horror on videocassette. Voices were often rerecorded to change accents and in certain cases dialogue was changed. Tim Lucas has demonstrated the changes in dialogue between the Japanese laserdisc version of *Demons* (presumed by Lucas to be the closer translation to the original Italian version) and the U.S. videocassette version.[14] In a scene where the punk gang is cruising around doing cocaine, the character Ricky cuts Nina while attempting to remove cocaine from her breasts with a razor blade. Lucas points out that Nina's response to Ricky's cruelty changes from "Wait'll I get near your prick, Ricky!" (Japanese version) to the U.S. version that shifts the threat of castration to name-calling: "You're a prick, Ricky!"[15] The poorly dubbed print, aside from its appearance and changes to the narrative, can also signify a statement of value. Antje Ascheid's work on film dubbing argues that, "Considering a film an artistically valuable 'authored original' seems to suggest the use of subtitling, whereas films categorized as short-lived, mass-produced entertainment products ease the distributor's way into employing the dubbing technique."[16] As Ascheid's argument suggests, a mark of value is ascribed to the film bearing subtitles as opposed to the dubbed version that is marked as being one of lower quality, cheap, and popular.

In addition, processes of videocassette release generally disregard the honorific notion of "authored original." For example, the name "Dario Argento" is in smaller print than the synopsis that accompanies HBO Video's *Deep Red Hatchet Murders*. And Mario Bava's *Gli orrori del castello di Nuremberga* (*Horrors of Nuremberg Castle*), released in U.S. theaters as *The Torture Chamber of Baron Blood* was given similar treatment when appearing on videocassette, also through HBO Video. Bava's name did not even appear on the Video Treasures 1990 release of *Beyond the Door II* (rereleased in 2000 as *Shock*). Claims of "authored original" status are obviously stretched by the likes of *peplum*, western, sci-fi, horror, and porn director Aristide Massaccesi (whose many aliases include "Joe D'Amato," "Alexandre Borsky," "David Hills," "Robert Duke," and "Steven Benson"!). It was also fairly common during this period for Italian horror films to be retitled when appearing on video in the United States: Argento's *Tenebre* was released in 1986 as *Unsane* (the cover art color was changed as well), Bava's *La frusta e il corpo* (*The Whip and the Body*, 1963) was first released on videocassette as *What*; and Massaccesi's *Rosso sangue* (exported as *Absurd*) was released as *Monster Hunter, Grim Reaper II*, and *Buried Alive*.[17]

It is fair to wager that most Italian horror films to reach American shores as videocassettes were cut to satisfy MPAA censorial policies. This is perhaps the most marked example of Italian horror being positioned as an object of low quality, low value, and further removed from any claim of authorial intentions. In addition to retitling, poor dubbing, and non-"original" cover art, it should be stressed that any judgment as to the quality of a particular film was a judgment passed on an incomplete and severely cut print. A few well-known examples will suffice to illustrate this point: Fulci's *The New York Ripper*, released in 1987 by Vidmark, did not contain two sex scenes found on European prints. When released in 1985 by Media Home Entertainment, Argento's *Phenomena* (released in the United States as *Creepers*) was cut by twenty-eight minutes. *Tenebre*'s U.S. videocassette title *Unsane* was without ten minutes of footage. Anchor Bay's new release of *Deep Red* is claimed to be a complete uncut print at 126 minutes. This is in great contrast to *Deep Red Hatchet Murders*' running time of only 100 minutes.

The emphasis on cut footage, a major challenge to any claim of "authored original" status especially when the cuts are for a videocassette, segues into a much-needed address of Italian horror fandom. For it is here that the said technological processes affecting Italian horror on videocassette couple with a distinct social discourse to produce Italian horror as gore-object. In his study on horror film fanzines, David Sanjek argues that these amateur publications are broad in scope, ranging from the puerile in form and tone to the studious and archival. "The fanzines," Sanjek writes, "constitute an alternative brand of film criticism, a school with its own set of values and virtues. They aim not only to *épater le bourgeois* but also to root out obscure marginalia of the horror genre and revel in the private consumption of outrage for outrage's sake."[18] Scores of fan-published texts available during the period, as well as the glossy likes of *Fangoria* and its off-shoot *The Gore Zone,* are best represented by two writers' articulation of the Italian horror film on videocassette: John McCarty and Chas Balun.

McCarty's books, including *Splatter Movies: Breaking the Last Taboo of the Screen, The Official Splatter Movie Guide,* and *John McCarty's Official Splatter Movie Guide: More of the Grossest, Goriest, Most Outrageous Movies Ever Made,* along with Balun's *Horror Holocaust, The Gore Score, More Gore Score: Brave New Horror,* and his fanzine, aptly named *Deep Red,* have served as a definitive voice corresponding to "its own set of values and virtues," as well as producing "values and virtues" for its objects.[19] I stress the word "definitive" here because, as V. Vale and Andrea Juno make apparent in the first few lines of their 1986 volume *Incredibly Strange Films,* paracinema in academic circles was at the time of their writing a "territory largely neglected by the film-criticism establishment."[20] Italian horror too has been only marginally positioned within the officiating discourses of academic film criticism.

This should come as no surprise if one considers that Pierre Leprohon's *The Italian Cinema* and Peter Bondanella's *Italian Cinema: From Neorealism to the Present* virtually ignore the genre.[21] Nonauteur-based academic research references Italian horror only briefly, as part of a larger project dedicated to the study of the horror genre;[22] horror as part of a national cinema other than the United States tends to be subsumed into a larger consideration of the genre as not nationally specific, that is unless the "American Horror Film" is singled out.[23] More developed critical considerations of Italian horror within academic research have adopted the article as their main literary form of engagement with Italian horror.[24]

The voice attributed to fan writing, meanwhile, is of a specific tone that subsumes the Italian horror film into a larger project concerned with redefining (and recreating) horror movies as "splatter" movies. The neologism, as outlined by McCarty, emerged as a subgenre with a different agenda than that of the more tame horror film: "Splatter movies, offshoots of the horror film genre, aim not to scare their audiences, necessarily, nor to drive them to the edges of their seats in suspense, but to *mortify* them with scenes of explicit gore."[25] The emphasis on gore as a defining quality of the splatter movie by proxy is then applied to Italian horror. Already positioned as "low" on account of its inception on videocassette, Italian horror was further implicated in the category of "lowbrow" when described by McCarty as "Spaghetti Splatter." Whereas directors were ignored or given scant attention by videocassette cover credits, here Bava becomes known for "overtly realistic horror films with lots of graphic violence," Argento is cited as "the poor man's Mario Bava," and Fulci is declared "Italy's reigning King of Splatter."[26]

Balun too adopts the neologism of splatter to discuss Italian films, albeit in a tone that Sanjek would regard as "sophomoric." The challenge taken up by Italian directors according to Balun is to "GROSS US OUT— AT ANY COST!" (emphasis in original). A disclaimer of sorts that celebrates the "in-the-know" allegiance of fandom begins Balun's chapter on Italian directors in *Horror Holocaust:* "Unfortunately, most films made by these pioneering gut slingers could only be loved by unrepentant gorehounds; wandering, curious critics; or by someone who might be sicker than even *he* could ever imagine."[27] In fact, Italian films have a prominent place in all of Balun's writings, and are often elevated to the status of splatter par excellence. The cover designs of his fanzine *Deep Red* constantly paid tribute to the likes of Fulci and Argento. The entire cover of issue 7 is filled with the famous scene of Betty's (Cristina Marsillach) torturous abduction from Argento's *Opera* (1987); while issues 1 and 2 contain printed stills from Fulci's *The Beyond* and *City of the Living Dead.* If cover art is not a satisfactory homage, accompanying captions like "Foreign Gore" assure readers of ample coverage.

It may in fact be incorrect to regard the types of Italian films that I have discussed above as actual horror films. "Splatter," "gore," "foreign gore," and such were the adjectives that actively created an understanding of Italian films during this period (after all, the prefix "sub" in subgenre does imply "below," or "lower" than horror). According to McCarty, Balun, and others, the films in question possess certain qualities that distinguish them from the more conventional films that one may point to as normative representatives of the horror genre. This observation is further evidenced by both writers' decision to "score" or evaluate the splatter offered by potential candidates. Balun rates films according to two different sets of criteria: skulls are attributed to films that work within the conventions of horror (e.g., four skulls = "hard core horror," whereas two skulls signify an "ordinary horror film"). "The Gore Score" ranges from "0" to "10" and deals "with nothing but the quantity of blood, brains, guts, and assorted precious bodily fluids, spilling during the course of the film."[28] It comes as no surprise that Italian films often score highly. Andrea Bianchi's *Burial Ground* (a.k.a. *Zombie 3*, 1980) rates three skulls while it scores a perfect 10 for gore: "Forget the plot, just enjoy the gore! . . . It's all here . . . maggot infested corpuses, entrail munching, heads decapitated and blown off, nudity, incest, etc."[29] The "treats" that award Argento's *Suspiria* (1977) an 8 in the same issue include: "a maggot infestation, a girl getting dropped into a room of barbed wire, and some open heart surgery via butcher knife, etc."[30]

The fan discourses active in enunciating Italian films as splatter and gore coupled with the low quality associated with Italian films on videocassette together work to define and position them as gore-objects. Like the visceral effects so prized by "gut slingers," the visceral of the videocassette—its dubbed and cut prints, along with its butchered surfaces—mark Italian films in ways that have only recently begun to shift on account of another set of discursive practices, as well as a new medium.

Own It on DVD: Italian Horror as Art-Object

In beginning to consider how Italian horror films are being remediated by DVD, it is valuable to work from a few ideas posited by Joan Hawkins in her recent book *Cutting Edge: Art-Horror and the Horrific Avant-Garde*.[31] Hawkins's account is particularly useful for its thoroughness, shared subject matter, and the careful consideration it gives to fanzines as well as the media through which paracinema reaches its discerning audiences. When discussing the importance of trash aesthetics and the celebration of affect within paracinema culture, Hawkins claims that "the designs of the catalogs also enforce a valorization of low genres and low generic categories."[32] The means of production and distribution that I have discussed in relation to videocassettes can also be said to emulate a low status. However, this is not as intentionally contrived as those video mail-order catalogs (e.g., *Something Weird Video*) that embrace a fanzine aesthetic in promoting their "affect-ive products" as well as communicating low-cultural capital to their learned audiences. According to Hawkins, such catalogs "look like something that anyone with access to a computer and photocopier could produce. They certainly don't look like the publications of companies that—to a certain extent—depend on sales to the upscale end of the video market and cater to European art house fans."[33]

Despite writing in a period already experiencing DVD penetration, Hawkins barely considers DVD in her text. The discs of which she speaks are laserdiscs. As such, "the upscale end" that she refers to is largely assigned to titles available in the Criterion Collection. When considering how Italian horror films in particular have been remediated through DVD, I would suggest that many of Hawkins's claims regarding paracinema value do not immediately account for this change. In fact, the remediation that is currently underway is one that stresses *both* the "repair" and the "refashioning" side of the tension I spoke of earlier. Italian horror films on DVD mark an attempt to repair the low status (and low quality) afforded their initial presence on videocassette as well as an effort to exchange the "sophomoric" fanzine nomenclature that overdetermined the object during its initial mass mediation.

DVD players were first introduced in the United States in 1997. In the same year, according to Anne Friedberg, it was estimated that 89 percent of U.S. households had been penetrated by VCRs. By 2000, 12 million homes were reported to have DVD players.[34] The dramatic fall in prices between 1997 and 2002 may account for the rapid growth and acceptance of DVD players (some of which enter the home as computer drives or video game systems) within the domestic setting. In conjunction with the growth rate of DVD players, the availability of DVD titles has grown tremendously. Friedberg claims that "In 1997, in the United States, 900 titles were available on DVD; in 1998, 3,000. By the end of 2000 there were over 10,000 titles available on DVD in the United States."[35] The sheer availability of older titles being rereleased and remediated on DVD, as well as out-of-print, restored, and debuting titles, has prompted new sections to be housed in media superstores. The same Virgin Megastore proudly displaying its Euro-Horror collection now has a massive "Cult Film" section dedicated to paracinema from companies such as MGM's new-to-DVD "Soul Cinema" label, New Horizons' "Roger Corman Classics" series, Something Weird Video, Anchor Bay, and Image Entertainment. To make titles easily locatable and still appealing to paracinematic tastes, new categories like "Euro-Horror" have emerged in superstores to account for the numerous Italian films available on DVD as well as to other European horror films.[36]

Expanded disc storage enabled by compression technology allows for a more elaborate presentation of the main feature, as well as the inclusion of additional information commonly regarded as "extras," "features," or "special features." For example, on most horror DVDs today we now have access to American as well as European trailers for the accompanying feature; a variety of subtitle choices; photo, poster, and stills galleries; deleted scenes; and alternative endings. Anchor Bay's release of *Opera* on DVD includes the following two-disc set:

Disc 1
Widescreen Presentation (2.35:1) enhanced for 16 x 9 TVs
Conducting Dario Argento's Opera (36 minute documentary)
Theatrical Trailers
Daemonia Music Video
Dario Argento Bio

Disc 2
Original Claudio Simonetti Soundtrack CD

In addition, it has become common to find extensive notes (mini essays) that detail the history of the film, director, and associated subgenre. Unlike the poorly designed HBO Video release of *Deep Red Hatchet Murders,* Anchor Bay's DVD release of *Deep Red* includes a booklet that provides a short history of the film and its famous director.

The covers, liner notes, and booklets radically remediate how Italian horror films are known through digital media. Whereas previously director's names may not have appeared at all, or received only marginal treatment on releases, titles on Anchor Bay and Image Entertainment correct this oversight. Directors like Bava and Argento are hailed as "auteurs" and "masters" of their respected works (which have also shifted from "splatter" to "horror," a shift in semantics as well as a shift in value). Image Entertainment's *Twitch of the Death Nerve* is part of the "Mario Bava Collection" and Tim Lucas provides an exhaustive account of this film's unique history. Anchor Bay's release of *Deep Red* seems to want to avoid any confusion with its U.S. videocassette predecessor. Part of the "Dario Argento Collection," the title *Deep Red* is introduced as "a film by Dario Argento." The back cover continues to sing Argento's praises. His name appears six times and the synopsis begins with "Dario Argento's Masterpiece." The criteria of "authored original" attributed to subtitled films by Ascheid can now perhaps be applied to a number of Italian horror films appearing on DVD in uncut, letterboxed, and of course subtitled versions. The packaging layout and design for many DVDs today assists in creating a new product from an old film. In this case, older horror films—some never originally released in the United States at all, some cut beyond comprehension, some degenerated from repeated play on video-cassette—are repaired and refashioned for mass consumption.

The Italian horror film on DVD is not the same film, and does not command the same set of meanings, as it did when first released on video-cassette. Its status has shifted. A set of meanings has been refashioned through DVD technology and the aesthetics of its new design (packaging, liner notes, booklets, etc). Equally, this refashioning made possible by a new medium attempts to "correct" prior meanings and values associated with the medium of videocassette and the discourses first speaking of a relationship to Italian horror.

The command first issued by the Blockbuster Entertainment Corporation to "Own it on DVD" specifies a certain relation to DVD that differs from videocassette. The disc prompts a different sense of appreciation to its user than does the videocassette. Charles Tashiro explains this romance for cinephiles and collectors: "They are disposable in a way discs are not, and if one expression of my 'love' of a film is my desire to have a copy of it, that love is never fully expressed until it can sit as a disc, congealed into aluminum and plastic, glued in place as a designer object, with no power of transformation, no ability to adopt new programming whenever I feel the need to erase."[37] The sense of permanence attributed to a disc (and here it must be pointed out that Tashiro is referring to laserdiscs, not DVDs, which according to one source have a less than eternal five-to-seven-year lifespan) elevates the disc as an object that is, according to Tashiro, a "self-contained art work." Permanently locked in as an "authored original," the Italian horror film on DVD ceases to be a gore-object: an object known by its incompleteness, a "disposable" object (in that dubbing connotes a marked mass product), an object rented and watched from bootlegged copies in search of a complete print, and an object "scored" for gory content. Italian horror on DVD is thus remediated as an art-object. Even the fan voice is repaired and refashioned; it returns not as a fan but as an authority and critic. Its vocabulary has changed: the "gut slingers" have become maestros. The full-color booklet is a far cry from the photocopied, cut-and-paste (I don't mean via computer application) images and Courier fonts common to fanzine reviews. The voice articulating the Italian horror film now has a historical tone, one that is educational and premised on informative criticism and genre

Anchor Bay's DVD cover art for *Deep Red* (1975)

knowledge rather than shock-value descriptions, prose littered with exclamation points, and the masculinist propensity to demarcate taste hierarchies through the construction of ratings.

Given the current remediation and the lineage I have tried to explicate in this essay, it is possible to disagree with Hawkins when she claims that paracinema fans differ from the likes of connoisseurs of the Criterion Collection. "For the most part," Hawkins writes, "paracinema companies do not attempt to package an event or a complete film experience the way the Criterion collection does."[38] Companies such as Anchor Bay have begun to market their products, especially "affect-ive products" that are nearly impossible to distinguish from Criterion titles available on DVD. The best possible original prints are sought for digital remastering onto DVD. "Extras," digital transfers, widescreen/letterbox, subtitles, original soundtracks, and attractive packaging easily close the gap between the highbrow cinema attributed to Criterion's restoration process and the lowbrow aesthetics once associated with tattered videocassette covers, dark prints, poor dubbing, and cut-up releases. Even the "Not Rated" classification accompanying paracinema on DVD today is closer to a category of exemption attributed to art than the outlawed "NC17" or nostalgic "X" afforded to filmic licentiousness. The companies promoting the likes of Argento, Bava, and even Fulci on DVD, selling a title as part of a "collection," place their directors on the market as auteurs in order to invoke value statements that valorize the director's work as an art-object, an "authored original," and a masterpiece of Italian horror cinema.

Both Sconce and Hawkins agree that films of the paracinema variety signify a tone of "opposition" and/or "reaction against" the doldrums of mainstream Hollywood product. The period that marked the prominence of DVD and Italian horror beginning to appear in this format also marked a commercial high point for U.S. horror films, such as *Scream* (1996), *Scream 2* (1997), *Scream 3* (2000), *I Know What You Did Last Summer* (1997, sequel 1998), *The Faculty* (1998), and *Scary Movie* (2000, sequel 2001). Commenting on the all-too-familiar generic conventions of horror conformed to by *Scream* and films of similar ilk, Sanjek claims that many new U.S. horror films appear not "to be interested in critiquing or subverting those parameters. Instead, they merely call attention to them in the most blunt and obvious fashion."[39] The Italian horror film as art-object can also double as a reactionary-object. The video generation who had to endure poor prints, not younger audiences snacking low-cal on the banal pastiche of clean-teen horror, is the generation consuming Italian horror on DVD.

Appealing to a restoration process that privileges cinema's past and all of its detritus as "worthy" of restoring, the remediation of Italian horror returns a film unlike those currently occupying screen spaces. The reincarnated films—much like the zombie hordes overtaking cities in so many Italian films (Soavi's *Dellamorte dellamore* actually prefers "returner" over zombie to describe the body's indeterminacy)—are vicious, grotesque, brutal, atmospheric, stylish, painful, not overtly comedic, shocking, perhaps willing to transgress parameters and now digitally remastered to flesh out these qualities in their uncut entirety. Whereas the lowbrow has been remediated into a highbrow aesthetic—or at least works through conventions afforded to highbrow sensibilities—the highbrow form now provides the reactionary-object through which paracinephilia may oppose the "no-brow" horror film geared toward the deep pockets of millennial teens. This "return" also speaks to a rejection. Old tastes return via a new medium: hints of opposition are generational taste preferences and part of the polysemy determining the new medium-dependent object.

By way of conclusion, it is worthwhile to end—like so many horror films—with a portentous question: will the remediation of Italian horror films place them outside of paracinema culture? As work on paracinema culture insists, part of the attraction when evoking a "particular reading protocol" resides in the "outlaw," "sub," or "marginal" status attributed to the interpellated object. What happens when the same reading protocols are brought to bear on a different object: an object officially and legally placed on the market and now dependent on mainstream modes of promotion? When Italian horror undergoes a restoration process it ceases to be the object it was previously. This remediation also reveals the historical contingencies through which paracinema articulates its many objects. Where the integrity of a print has been restored or perfected by DVD technology, where a new voice enunciates a different relation to the object (a relation it must be said that does not alienate as did its predecessor), where the object itself signifies a new status, perhaps any loss suffered is a loss to the very claim of opposition.

Notes

1. Jeffrey Sconce, "'Trashing' the Academy: Taste, Excess, and an Emerging Politics of Cinematic Style," *Screen* 36, no. 4 (1995): 371–93, quote on p. 372.
2. Tim Lucas, Liner notes on *Twitch of the Death Nerve* (directed by Mario Bava, Image Entertainment, 2000), paragraph 10.
3. Susan Sontag, "The Decay of Cinema," *New York Times Magazine*, February 25, 1996, 60–61, quote on p. 60.
4. Related considerations that exceed the scope of this project and its context within the present volume include: a larger historical focus on horror culture and fandom; relations between Hollywood and the international film industry; and, I would argue, a fastidious consideration of how Italian and U.S. culture(s) dialogue through popular culture, especially cinema.
5. See Jay David Bolter and Richard Grusin, *Remediation: Understanding New Media* (Cambridge: MIT Press, 1999); and Paul Levinson, *The Soft Edge: A Natural History and Future of the Information Revolution* (London: Routledge, 1997).
6. Douglas Gomery, *Shared Pleasures: A History of Movie Presentation in the United States* (London: BFI Publishing, 1992), 279.
7. Ben Keen, "'Play It Again, Sony': The Double Life of Home Video Technology," *Science as Culture* 1, no. 1 (1987): 6–42, quote on p. 35.
8. Figures taken from *Video World-Wide: An International Study*, ed. Manuel Alvarado (London: John Libby, 1988).

9. Figures for pre-recorded videocassette sales and the comparison between video and television ownership are taken from Michael Wiese, *Home Video: Producing for the Home Market* (n.p.: Michael Wiese, 1986).

10. See Gomery, *Shared Pleasures*, 1992; James Lardner, *Fast Forward: Hollywood, the Japanese, and the Onslaught of the VCR* (New York: W. W. Norton, 1987); and Janet Wasko, *Hollywood in the Information Age* (Cambridge: Polity, 1994).

11. Lardner, *Fast Forward*, 184.

12. Ibid.

13. The decision to relocate certain titles, whose cover art relied on the enticement of seminude women, away from the safe and legitimating boundaries of horror and most likely away from young eyes was not exclusive to Italian films. The *Ilsa* series, as well as the long forgotten "big-box" graphics from companies such as Continental Video, Comet Video (the company that first released H. G. Lewis's films on videocassette in the United States; the cover for Lewis's *Color Me Blood Red* [1965] is a perfect example of cover art as surface for appeal!), Super Video Inc., and Wizard Video (the last two were responsible for introducing numerous international horror titles to the U.S. market in the 1980s), all had a strained relation to the placement of the horror genre in video stores.

14. See Tim Lucas, "The Cutting Room Floor," *Video Watchdog* 8 (1991): 48–54.

15. Lucas, "Cutting Room Floor," 54.

16. Antje Ascheid, "Speaking Tongues: Voice Dubbing in the Cinema as Cultural Ventriloquism," *Velvet Light Trap* 40 (1997): 32–41, quote on p. 34.

17. At "Eurofest 95," a horror/exploitation film festival held annually in London, Aristide Massaccesi was the guest of honor. During the interview, the question of his aliases and the process of retitling were raised. According to Massaccesi, his most well known alias, "Joe D'Amato," was an attempt to play off of the success and popularity of "Brian De Palma." The decision to change titles for world markets, Massaccesi claimed, is often orchestrated to financially benefit from current horror cycles.

18. David Sanjek, "Fans Notes: The Horror Film Fanzine," *Literature Film Quarterly* 18, no. 3 (1990): 150–59, quote on p. 153.

19. John McCarty, *Splatter Movies: Breaking the Last Taboo of the Screen* (New York: St. Martin's, 1984); McCarty, *The Official Splatter Movie Guide* (New York: St. Martin's, 1989); McCarty, *John McCarty's Official Splatter Movie Guide: More of the Grossest, Goriest, Most Outrageous Movies Ever Made* (New York: St. Martin's, 1992); Chas Balun, *Horror Holocaust* (New York: Fantaco, 1986); Balun, *The Gore Score* (New York: Fantaco, 1987); Balun, "*Suspiria*," review of *Suspiria*, directed by Dario Argento, *Deep Red* (December 1987): 45; Balun, "*Burial Ground*," review of *Burial Ground*, directed by Aristide Massaccesi, *Deep Red* (December 1987): 43; Balun, *More Gore Score: Brave New Horrors* (New York: Fantasma, 1995).

20. V. Vale and Andrea Juno, *Incredibly Strange Films* (San Francisco: Re/Search, 1986), 4.

21. Peter Bondanella, *Italian Cinema: From Neorealism to the Present* (New York: Frederick Ungar, 1983); Pierre Leprohon, *The Italian Cinema* (New York: Praeger, 1972).

22. Carol J. Clover, *Men, Women and Chainsaws: Gender in the Modern Horror Film* (London: BFI Publishing, 1992); Barbara Creed, *The Monstrous-Feminine: Film, Feminism, Psychoanalysis* (London: Routledge, 1993); Steven Shaviro, *The Cinematic Body* (Minneapolis: University of Minnesota Press, 1993); Wheeler Winston Dixon, *The Second Century of Cinema: The Past and Future of the Moving Image* (Albany: State University of New York Press, 2000).

23. See, for example, Gregory A. Waller, ed., *American Horrors: Essays on the Modern American Horror Film* (Urbana: University of Illinois Press, 1996); Tony Williams, *Hearths of Darkness: The Family in the American Horror Film* (Madison, NJ: Fairleigh Dickinson University Press, 1996); Andrew Britton, Robin Wood, and others, *The American Nightmare: Essays on the Horror Film* (Toronto: Festival of Festivals, 1979).

24. See, for example, Leon Hunt, "A (Sadistic) Night at the *Opera:* Notes on the Italian Horror Film," *Velvet Light Trap* 30 (1992): 64–75; Adam Knee, "Gender, Genre, Argento," in *The Dread of Difference: Gender and the Horror Film,* ed. Barry Keith Grant (Austin: University of Texas Press, 1996): 213–30.

25. McCarty, *Splatter Movies,* 1.

26. Ibid., 121–22.

27. Balun, *Horror Holocaust,* 56.

28. Balun, "*Suspiria,*" 42.

29. Ibid., 43.

30. Ibid., 44.

31. Joan Hawkins, *Cutting Edge: Art-Horror and the Horrific Avant-Garde* (Minneapolis: University of Minnesota Press, 2000).

32. Hawkins, *Cutting Edge,* 4.

33. Ibid., 12.

34. Anne Friedberg, "CDs and DVDs," in *The New Media Book,* ed. Dan Harries (Berkeley: University of California Press, 2002), 38.

35. Friedberg, "CDs and DVDs," 38.

36. Image Entertainment also has "The EuroShock Collection" to promote films by the likes of Jean Rollin (France) and Jess Franco (Spain).

37. Charles Tashiro, "The Contradictions of Video Collecting," *Film Quarterly* 50, no. 2 (1996–97): 11–18, quote on p. 12.

38. Hawkins, *Cutting Edge,* 46.

39. David Sanjek, "Same As It Ever Was: Innovation and Exhaustion in the Horror and Science Fiction Films of the 1990s," in *Film Genre 2000: New Critical Essays,* ed. Wheeler Winston Dixon (Albany: State University of New York Press, 2000): 111–23, quote on pp. 113–14.

2

Importation/Mexploitation, or, How a Crime-Fighting, Vampire-Slaying Mexican Wrestler Almost Found Himself in an Italian Sword-and-Sandals Epic

Andrew Syder and Dolores Tierney

In the mid-1960s, a large number of Mexico's most popular horror, fantasy, and science-fiction films were dubbed into English and released onto drive-in and television screens in the United States. Almost entirely responsible for importing these "mexploitation" movies were two North American producers: Jerry Warren and K. Gordon Murray. Warren was a hack filmmaker who adapted several Mexican pictures for the drive-in circuit and, later, for television. He held no qualms about inserting his own footage or splicing together parts from entirely different films, and the results of his butcher knife include *Curse of the Stone Hand* (1964), *Attack of the Mayan Mummy* (1964), *Face of the Screaming Werewolf* (1964), and *Creature of the Walking Dead* (1965).[1] By far the more significant of the two, Murray was a Florida-based mini-mogul who released more than two dozen imports, mostly through the television arm of American-International Pictures (AIP). Somewhat more faithful and respectful to the original versions than Warren, Murray supervised the U.S. distribution of such classics as *El vampiro* (*The Vampire,* 1957), *La momia azteca contra el robot humano* (*The Robot vs. the Aztec Mummy,* 1957), *Santa Claus* (1959), *El barón del terror* (*The Brainiac,* 1962), *Las luchadoras contra el médico asesino* (*Doctor of Doom,* 1962), and several El Santo movies.[2]

The principal focus of this essay will be these K. Gordon Murray releases, particularly the series of horror/wrestling pictures he imported. However, rather than simply dismissing these dubbed, often recut U.S. versions as abhorrent and loathsome bastardizations of the Mexican originals, as many fans and critics have, this essay will examine the transnational implications of the American importation of mexploitation—not least because this was how many Americans were first exposed to Latin

Original poster art for
*La momia azteca contra
el robot humano* (1957)

American cinema. Indeed, the transcultural movement across national borders, in both directions, seems too complex to be simply disregarded because of a belief in the "purity" of the Mexican originals and the "impiety" of the American adaptations.

Following a consideration of how critical studies of Mexican horror and wrestling films might be situated within broader Latin American national cinema discourses, which perhaps too often tend toward abstract theoretical paradigms, this essay will offer a case study of the international circulation of mexploitation. It will first examine the films in relation to their original Mexican context. It will then focus on two distinct stages of reception among Anglophonic audiences in the United States: their initial distribution by Murray in the mid-1960s, and their subsequent revival as cult movies by "psychotronic" viewers since the 1980s.[3]

Mexploitation and National Cinema Debates

Issues pertaining to the international circulation of films have long been central to critical debates about national cinemas. The capital-intensive nature of the motion picture industry requires films to reach a large (i.e., international) market if they are to recoup their production costs. These economic imperatives, however, are often antithetical to the ideological concerns of national cinemas, since making films with international appeal invariably involves a process of cultural homogenization that runs counter to projects of national specificity. As Paul Willemen argues, "a cinema positively yet critically seeking to engage with the multi-layeredness of specific socio-cultural formations is necessarily a marginal and a dependent cinema: a cinema dependent for its existence on the very dominant export and multinational-oriented cinema it seeks to criticise and displace."[4]

Historically, these debates have tended to focus on the international circulation of a particular type of film: not lowbrow/trash/cult films, but art or auteur cinema, that is, the type of cinema that gets subtitled rather than dubbed. In his groundbreaking essay "The Concept of National Cinema," Andrew Higson argues that discussions of national cinema are more often prescriptive than descriptive, citing what the national cinema ought to be rather than describing the actual cinematic experience of popular audiences:

> The concept of a national cinema has almost invariably been mobilised as a strategy of cultural (and economic) resistance; a means of asserting national autonomy in the face of (usually) Hollywood international domination. . . . The discourses of "art," "culture" and "quality," and of "national identity" and "nationhood," have historically been mobilised against Hollywood's mass entertainment film, and used to justify various nationally specific economic systems of support and production.[5]

Such concerns have been particularly pronounced in studies of Latin American film, which have been inextricably tied to the analyses of the functions and viability of a nationalist cinema in the face of the aesthetic, economic, and ideological hegemony of the Hollywood industry. Not surprisingly, given the massive sociocultural impact of colonialist domination in both the region and its film industry, greatest importance has been granted to the explicitly anti-imperialist, often militantly political New Latin American Cinema movement of the 1960s and 1970s. Although many scholars over the last decade have started to examine the popular appeal and resistive possibilities of melodrama, from the Golden Age to contemporary *telenovelas*, horror and fantasy films remain conspicuous in their absence from mainstay histories of Latin American cinema.[6] As a result, questions about how the study of mexploitation might be placed alongside existing discourses and histories of Latin American film have yet to be adequately answered.

One of the dangers of discussing the international circulation of national cinemas in this way is the endorsing of essentialist or monolithic ideas about the nation. Indeed, as noted by Amaryll Chanady, many scholars have criticized monological discourses and strategies of nation building in Latin America, instead favoring the conceptualization of Latin American identities in terms of plurality, hybridity, and heterogeneity.[7] Higson notes: "Cinema never simply reflects or expresses an already fully formed and homogeneous national culture and identity, as if it were the undeniable property of all national subjects."[8] However, by routinely neglecting horror, wrestling, and churro/action films on grounds of taste, critical accounts of Latin American cinema risk being guilty of precisely that, placing sole focus only on those genres they think the national cinema ought to be: that is, the militant New Latin American Cinema, which represents a highly regarded opposition to Hollywood, or the potentially less reputable melodrama, which is seen to transcend issues of taste by being the genre that "personalizes the political" and "unifies" Latin America.[9] In other words, not considering the whole spectrum of filmmaking activity risks constructing monolithic conceptions of national cinemas—which in turn risk the development of monolithic ideas about Latin American identity, since what people watch is an important part of the construction of that identity. Therefore, care needs to be taken with how mexploitation cinema is approached because of its potential importance to issues of nationhood.

Some of the recent studies of melodrama, however, do perhaps offer a model for the study of mexploitation, given that they have had to address similar issues regarding how to historicize the role and function of popular culture in Latin America. Scholars such as Ana Lopez, Laura Podalsky, and Dolores Tierney have been acutely sensitive to the colonialist implications of hybridity in popular forms, underlining the differing cultural meanings both between Latin American and Anglo-American manifestations of melodrama and between manifestations of melodrama within Latin America from different historical periods. These scholars have demonstrated that in hybrid cultures like those of Latin America, the inescapable specter of colonialism does not mean that the popular cultural forms associated with colonialist domination inherently embody colonialist ideology, or that embracing those forms is necessarily speaking in the voice of the colonizer. For example, in a recent essay in *Screen,* Tierney identifies strategies within 1990s melodramas like *Danzón* (1991) to mobilize popular forms from the Golden Age, which are traditionally associated with patriarchy and machismo, and redirect their ideological implications toward sites of cultural/feminist resistance—reinscribing the genre's conventions and iconography with sites of female pleasure.[10]

Recent critical work reassessing the terms on which American exploitation cinema has been analyzed in the past seems to provide another potential model for the study of mexploitation. Rather than simply dismissing them as "bad" objects or failed attempts at technical competency, scholars such as Eric Schaefer and Jeffrey Sconce have begun to develop more sophisticated understandings of the aesthetic, institutional, and cultural implications of American exploitation films—films that often, in both their production and consumption, represent a legitimate form of resistance to mainstream Hollywood.[11]

Indeed, this interface between texts and sites of consumption seems crucial for understanding the international circulation of mexploitation cinema. Higson argues that the context of consumption is as important to the discussion of national cinema as the site of production, that we should focus our attention more on the activities of national audiences and the conditions under which they make sense of and use the films they watch. Paulo Antonio Paranaguá has argued that this is particularly important in the study of Latin American film: "in Latin American societies, the only permanent relationship with film is that of reception. Dependency made us film consumers and only exceptionally film producers."[12]

The case of the international circulation of mexploitation films, therefore, also provides a rare instance of a Latin American country managing to produce a cinema with considerable appeal outside the region. Indeed, as David Wilt has speculated, more mexploitation films have probably been exported to the United States than any other genre of Latin

American film.[13] The specifics of the transcultural movements across borders that have ensued, however, demonstrate the difficulty facing national cinema incentives if they aim to fix the nationalist meanings in texts that go on to enter the international market.

South of the Border

Although most critics have ignored or dismissed mexploitation cinema, labeling it evidence of an era of decline in the Mexican film industry, the decade following the release of two films by Fernando Méndez—*Ladrón de cadáveres* (1956) and *El vampiro* (1957)—constituted something of a Golden Age for the mexploitation film. During this period, horror, fantasy, and *lucha libre* pictures accounted for approximately 20 percent of the national industry's output.[14] What is striking and widely noted about these movies is the extent to which they utilize the conventions and iconography of the horror movies made by Hollywood during its own classical period of the 1930s and 1940s, including mad scientists, vampire bats, gothic castles, and chiaroscuro lighting. Many even explicitly poach whole scenes or scenarios from established classics. For example, *Ladrón de cadáveres, Las luchadoras contra el médico asesino,* and *Santo en el museo de cera* (*Samson in the Wax Museum,* 1963) all copy sequences from *Frankenstein* (1931). The last of these also draws heavily on *Mystery of the Wax Museum* (1933) and provides a nice metaphor of this process of cultural appropriation through its waxwork replicas of famous monsters like Frankenstein, the Phantom of the Opera, and Jekyll & Hyde.

A number of institutional roots can be traced to classical Hollywood horror cinema as well, dating back to when a Spanish-language version of *Dracula* (1931) was shot simultaneously with the Bela Lugosi version, filming at night on the same sets. Also during the 1930s, Fernando Méndez served as an assistant to one of the godfathers of American exploitation cinema, Dwain Esper, the creator of *Maniac* (1934) and *Marihuana* (1935).[15] In the 1950s, Abel Salazar self-consciously modeled his production company, ABSA, on Universal Studios because of their success with horror films in the 1930s: "That was what sustained Universal. Therefore I decided to make a horror film and I chose *El vampiro.* I basically made *Dracula,* located on a Mexican hacienda."[16] And in the 1960s, a number of horror veterans were enlisted for roles in Mexican projects, including Boris Karloff, Lon Chaney Jr., and John Carradine.

At first sight, this dependency on popular Hollywood forms and institutions seems problematic with respect to post-colonialist discourses

A publicity still from *Samson in the Wax Museum* (1963)

of imperialist domination and cultural hegemony, suggesting that Mexican horror producers had no interest in developing and sustaining an autonomous national film industry. This, however, would be to present only half of the picture. More than simply duplicating Hollywood horror movies to exploit their popular appeal with audiences, there seems to be a dialogue between the foreign and the local taking place within most mexploitation films—particularly with respect to the project of constructing a national identity. For instance, alongside the elements borrowed from Hollywood, many mexploitation films seek to incorporate more indigenous themes, characters, or settings, including such homegrown monsters as the Aztec Mummy and *La llorona* (the crying woman), the Mayan pyramids, and local versions of vampire mythology. In the many films featuring the Aztec Mummy, for example, the Mummy embodies a specific cultural threat quite different from that of its Egyptian cousin in Hollywood: a threat to Mexico's present from its own pre-Columbian past, particularly the association of Aztec culture with human sacrifices. As Podalsky has argued, such films can be seen to be using horror movie conventions to engage in Mexico's nationalist project of modernization by highlighting the sensationalist, unsavory, and potentially embarrassing underside of Mexico's patrimony, aspects that might otherwise have been brushed under the carpet by official state histories.[17]

Arguably the most significant variation of this strategy of national specificity, however, was the fusion of these horror tales with *lucha libre* wrestling to create a hybrid form in which famous fighters do battle with all manner of supernatural villains and monsters. *Ladrón de cadáveres* was one of the earliest examples of this generic hybridization, telling the story of a mad scientist's scheme to create a race of Aztec Warrior supermen by transplanting gorilla brains into wrestlers. The popularity of such movies led to a number of wrestlers (*luchadores*) developing successful film franchises, including Neutron, Blue Demon, Mil Máscaras, and, most famously, El Santo. A popular wrestler and comic book hero, Santo appeared in more than fifty movies, including two that Murray released in the United States: *Santo contra las mujeres vampiro* (*Samson vs. the Vampire Women*, 1962) and *Samson in the Wax Museum*. Alongside the *luchadores* there was also a series of films starring *las luchadoras* (female wrestlers), of which *Doctor of Doom* and *Las luchadoras contra la momia azteca* (*Wrestling Women vs. the Aztec Mummy*, 1964) were imported by Murray.

Hollywood-inspired horror narratives characterize these horror/wrestling hybrids that are punctuated with wrestling sequences at the Arena Mexico. These films often make little effort to integrate the wrestling bouts into the ongoing narrative. Santo, for example, is just as committed to his day job as a professional wrestler as he is to crime fighting and vampire slaying, often abandoning the main narrative to fight a regularly scheduled bout at the Arena. The wrestling sequences are clearly included to provide a source of spectacle for audiences, and, as spectacle, they are of a very local sort: spectacle very much tied to the lives of the films' audiences. Indeed, the wrestling sequences serve to bridge the fictional narrative and the real world. The above-mentioned wrestlers all play themselves in their films, providing a sense of continuity between their onscreen and offscreen exploits. Moreover, most of the wrestling bouts in these films were not shot specifically for the film in question but were comprised of actuality footage of real fights—allowing film audiences to see footage of wrestling events at which they themselves may have been present. (This use of actuality footage is particularly noticeable because cutaways to characters in the crowd rarely match the fight footage.)

The wrestling bouts at the Arena are also very striking because of their lack of integration into the ongoing horror narratives. They feel very much like padding, an inexpensive way to fill the running time—which of course they are—and they severely disrupt the fictional story line by containing little or no plot development. This is compounded by the sheer length of the sequences, which usually last more than five minutes—with Santo's first bout in *Santo contra las mujeres vampiro* running close to ten. The segues into the wrestling sequences also tend to be rather flimsily motivated, given only perfunctory narrative justification, such as characters remarking that they had better wait for Santo to finish his bout before they approach him.

Most critics have been quite dismissive of these bouts, seeing them as little more than "gratuitous *lucha libre* matches tucked into the narratives like awkward dance numbers."[18] However, the sequences seem to be more than just failed attempts at mimicking the codes of Hollywood cinema. The manner in which they interrupt the horror narrative suggests that the sequences offered audiences pleasures of a different sort. Rather than adhering to Hollywood conventions, such sequences frustrate desires for narrative economy and demand that the viewer alternate between fictional/narrative and nonfictional/nonnarrative passages. Indeed, the wrestling sequences seem to demand that the viewers "unsuture" themselves from the horror narrative, thus encouraging a more flexible reading protocol than that promoted by the Hollywood cinema model on which they drew.

Seen in the light of cultural studies–oriented debates within Latin American cinema about the ideological implications of Hollywood forms and their perceived pacification of the spectator, these mexploitation films are particularly interesting. The formal construction of the texts suggests a dialogue between Hollywood viewing codes and a set of disruptive, counter-viewing codes. Rather than simply duplicating their Hollywood models, the strategies of incorporating local elements into these films seem to have opened up a space not only for national concerns but also for a more flexible mode of spectatorship. In this sense, mexploitation cinema perhaps offered another instance of strategies within Latin American film to reappropriate, but ideologically redirect, popular forms in a manner similar to that described in accounts of 1990s melodrama—and from a pre-1968 moment in national cinema at that.

This more flexible mode of film spectatorship seems to have played a key role in the formation of cultural identities since it appears to derive from the social function of *lucha libre*. After being imported from the United States in the early 1930s, *lucha libre* emerged as a very popular sporting and social event, especially for working-class families. It developed its own nationally specific myths and conventions, with regular battles between *técnicos* (good guys) and *rudos* (bad guys) providing inexpensive catharsis for the stresses and strains of urban life. One of the central ways in which *lucha libre* fostered this sense of community was through the high degree of physical and verbal participation it demanded of the spectator, including touching the wrestlers as they enter the ring and the trading of insults with the *rudos*. Indeed, when *lucha libre* first appeared on television in the early 1950s, this collective and interactive mode of spectatorship was maintained. For example, those families who could afford a television set would invite their neighbors (often charging admission), and bars would screen wrestling events to attract clientele.[19] Likewise, the transition of wrestling to the big screen provoked similar viewing habits among cinema audiences, evident in Carlos Monsiváis's description of spectators at a *lucha libre* film screaming and shouting at the screen as if they were in the Arena Mexico itself.[20]

A question remains, however. If *lucha libre* already attracted large audiences and was successfully able to generate a sense of community and identity using its own more flexible reading protocols, why did these films feel the need to borrow from Hollywood models in the first place? Is it further evidence of Hollywood's cultural hegemony being so deeply ingrained that the hybridization of forms seemed a "natural" choice? Perhaps. However, a closer examination of the history of *lucha libre* reveals a more specific cultural engagement with Hollywood generic forms that needs to be considered, central to which was the government banning of televised broadcasts of *lucha libre* in the mid-1950s—a ban not revoked until 1991.

The official reason why *lucha libre* was banned on television was because of its influence on children, with sports arenas also pressured at the time to prohibit the attendance of children at live events. However, as Heather Levi has argued, alongside the ostensible fears about children's safety implicitly lay more politically motivated reasons for outlawing wrestling on television, particularly with respect to President Ruiz Cortines and Regent Ernesto Uruchurtu's attempts at controlling the cultural expressions and social geography of Mexico. In the 1950s, the primary audience of *lucha libre* was working class, and the *luchadores* themselves hailed mostly from working-class backgrounds and were promoted as proletarian heroes for the masses. Moreover, the very structure of *lucha libre* reinforced an anti-authoritarian worldview:

In the interactions between apparently suffering *técnicos* and apparently underhanded *rudos, lucha libre* dramatized and parodied common understandings of the post revolutionary system and their place within it. It reflected a political system in which people who appear to be opponents are really working together. It paralleled an electoral system in which electioneering took place behind closed doors and elections ratified decisions that had already been made. Ongoing dramas in the ring demonstrated that loyalty to kin and friends is more important than ideology, and that arbiters of authority are not necessarily on the side of the honest and the honorable.[21]

The banning of *lucha libre* broadcasts on television proved to be a very effective way for state officials to control and contain the sport, stifling its growth in popularity among the middle and upper classes: "It situated *lucha libre* as a neighborhood-based and class-specific practice."[22] By the late 1950s, unless one could attend a live event, the only way to see *lucha libre* was at the movies.

It does not seem coincidental that the first horror/wrestling films should happen to emerge in the mid-1950s, at the same time as the ban on television. With this in mind, the use of horror conventions appears to have served a very specific function of enabling the films to circumvent the censorship inflicted on television. Much of the wrath of that censorship had been directed toward the villainous behavior of the *rudos*, which tainted the image of Mexico that Cortines and Uruchurtu wished to promote. Shortly before it was banned on television, for example, the heads of *lucha libre* organizations were charged with drawing up a new list of rules that, as Levi has remarked, would have "made it impossible to perform the *rudo* role at all. And really, without the *rudos*, there is no *lucha libre*."[23] Had the films focused primarily on bouts between *técnicos* and *rudos* in the Arena, they would surely have met a similar fate to that of televised *lucha libre*. What the fusion of wrestling with horror achieved was to enable the mexploitation films to direct attention away from the *rudos* somewhat and onto clashes outside of the ring with vampires, mummies, and mad scientists.

The monsters that Santo and his friends battle, however, are well trained in the acrobatic conventions and moves of professional wrestling, and it seems quite clear that these fantastical creatures really serve as stand-ins for the traditional *rudo*. This is taken to its logical conclusion in

Santo contra las mujeres vampiro when one of his fights with a *rudo* at the Arena turns out to be actually a battle against a werewolf. This kind of iconographic coding should be familiar to fans of horror and science-fiction cinema: during the same period in the United States, giant insects and alien invasions served as metaphors for fears about atomic energy and communist infiltration. By borrowing from Hollywood horror conventions and iconography, mexploitation films were able to carry on, in a coded fashion, the social functions of *lucha libre* outlined above. State officials and even film scholars may have simply dismissed mexploitation as cheap, silly exercises in fantasy, but their formats facilitated a covert continuation of both the communal pleasures and the anti-authoritarian structures of traditional *lucha libre*—with Santo and others remaining no less proletarian than in real life. However, as an examination of the films' reception in the United States demonstrates, the preservation of such potentially liberating strategies of engagement with Hollywood forms and reading protocols—and potential for critiquing and/or circumventing governmental attempts at fixing the parameters of national and cultural identity—is far from guaranteed in the actual circulation of the films on the international market.

North of the Border

Historically, the majority of foreign films released in the United States have played through art cinema circuits. This was particularly true during the 1960s when the institution of "the art cinema" solidified itself as a highbrow exhibition space for elite audiences, different from that of the mainstream picture palace or the drive-in. This was achieved not only through the choice of movies shown (notably European auteur cinema) but also through the cinema architecture and through their treating of the art film as a cultural event similar to that of the theater—such as requesting block purchases of tickets, as one might for a season of plays or operas.[24] With the viewing of foreign films in such a space, it is not surprising that a concept of national cinema equated with "art" and "quality" developed along the lines described by Higson.

The sites of exhibition of lowbrow mexploitation cinema in the United States were quite different, however, contributing to a different set of cultural meanings from those of foreign art film imports. The drive-in, for example, had acquired a name for itself during the 1950s as a less reputable exhibition space. Because the major studios would not supply drive-ins with first- or even second-run films, an affiliation was formed with exploitation companies like AIP, who furnished drive-ins with inexpensive double bills aimed squarely at the teen audience—with a number of mexploitation films released in this way (especially by Warren).

Although Murray distributed several movies to theaters, principally for Saturday matinee audiences,[25] his imports were principally released directly to television under the aegis of AIP-TV. Just as AIP had been founded on successfully exploiting the new market offered by the drive-in circuit, they sought to capitalize on the emergence of late- and all-night broadcasting on U.S. television when it became a growing trend in the mid-1960s. Because this "fringe" programming was initiated by local affiliations and independent stations rather than the major networks, audiences were relatively small, as were advertising revenues. Therefore, a primary way in which this time slot was filled was through the showing of cheap horror and science-fiction films, provided by the likes of AIP. In order to provide "new" movies for TV, for example, AIP commissioned Dallas-based filmmaker Larry Buchanan to shoot a series of ultra-low-budget, color remakes of their own old movies (thus economizing by not having to commission new scripts). Another method of saving money was to import foreign films and sell them as packages, such as Murray's 1964 "Spookies" package of two dozen mexploitation films. In other words, and in contrast to the exhibition of art cinema, the incentive for importing mexploitation films into the United States was primarily *economic*, with fidelity to national or cultural considerations clearly being of secondary importance at best—which was evident also in the willingness to dub and recut the films.

It can be argued that these sites of consumption in the United States—the drive-in, the Saturday matinee, and especially late-night television—significantly altered the cultural meanings derived from the texts. Nick Browne argues that "The schedule determines the form of a particular television program and conditions its relation to the audience. Just as important, the positioning of programs in the television schedule reflects and is determined by the work-structured order of the real social world."[26] This seems applicable to all the above spaces of exhibition to suggest mexploitation films served a different cultural function in the United States than in Mexico.

In the Mexican context, as noted earlier, *lucha libre* functioned as a leisure activity that sought to unite working-class spectators, with children only being able to experience it covertly. Each of the exhibition

spaces for mexploitation in the United States, however, was a site of consumption geared toward those people outside of the work-structured
order of society; in particular, children and adolescents who do not have to
work. The drive-in circuit, for example, specifically tailored its advertising
toward youth audiences by stoking the fires of the generation gap between
children and their parents. Similarly, the Saturday matinee was a place for
parents to dispose of children for a precious couple of weekend hours. The
same is even truer of the scheduling of Murray's imports on late-night television. As Sconce has noted, following Browne's lead, the only type of
person who could watch all-night television were those outside rhythms of
the workweek and the household: "Broadcasters designed the 'creature feature' to attract this very narrow demographic of younger viewers who, after
a week in school, were allowed to stay up later on weekends and yet, by and
large, were not allowed (at least in the sixties and seventies) to pursue entertainment outside the home after a certain hour."[27] In other words, the
sense of working-class community encouraged in the Mexican context of
viewing seems to have been translated away from issues of class unity and
toward a generational splintering within the family.

This shift in audience and context of consumption also appears to
have affected the films' perceived engagement with Hollywood conventions, with the classical horror elements seeming to be the reason why they
were imported in the first place. This was evident in Murray's calling the
collection of films the "Spookies" package, a direct reference to Universal's own "Shock" package of classic horror films. The early 1960s was
marked by a significant interest among American children and adolescents with horror monsters; in particular, the very same 1930s horror and
monster films from which the mexploitation movies borrowed in the first
place. Much of this interest was spearheaded by the release of fifty-two of
Universal's vintage horror movies to television in 1957, giving a whole
new generation access to the likes of Dracula, the Mummy, the Wolfman,
and Frankenstein's monster. As one article in *Look* magazine remarked—
following an account of more than 13,000 nine- to twelve-year-old boys
overrunning the Philadelphia WCAU-TV studios at a horror open
house—"After a postwar diet of giant insects, psychotic vegetables and
vicious blobs, the kids went wild for the veterans."[28]

This interest in vintage horror continued to grow throughout the
early 1960s. "Make-your-own-monster" hobby kits and horror-themed
games became among the most popular gift items for Christmas.
Fanzines like *Castle of Frankenstein* and *Famous Monsters of Filmland*

(both founded in 1958) grew ever more popular. And Colgate-Palmolive even produced a line of "Soaky Spooks" soap featuring Frankenstein and the Wolfman, guaranteed to "scare you clean." The year in which the majority of Murray's releases first aired, 1964, saw a particular boom in vintage monsters. For example, within two weeks of each other in the fall of 1964, monsters invaded the sitcom market with the premieres of *The Munsters* and *The Addams Family*. *Life* magazine proclaimed it to be "TV's Year of the Monster"[29] and a similar article in the *New York Times Magazine* examined the year's monster craze, arguing of children's fascination with vintage monsters: "It seems highly probable that the monster craze perpetuates itself because it can turn an inarticulate child into a raconteur. Children have always loved to tell the tales they see on television, and a monster tale is by far the juiciest."[30]

This all seems to suggest a significant difference in how audiences might have used these texts in each national context. Mexploitation films engage with classic American horror films through a very particular negotiation and dialogue that opens up a space for local concerns and reading protocols. In the movement of these films north of the border, however, this nationally specific engagement with Hollywood conventions seems to have been inflected quite differently, with the emphasis shifted away from the Mexican elements and back onto the familiar horror ingredients. Rather than identifying with the *luchadores* or Mexican settings, it seems that American children's sympathy was placed instead on the monsters. Indeed, a number of accounts in the popular press note the concerns of parents, teachers, and psychiatrists about children's fascination with horror monsters. The article in *Look* magazine, for example, offers its own pop-Freudian explanation by arguing, "They think of him as another child. He is not responsible, as an adult is expected to be....[Monsters are] bloody but blameless creatures."[31] Thus, again, mexploitation seemed to contribute to a fostering of the generation gap in American households.

Perhaps more significant, however, was the impact of this on the films' quest for national specificity, as the move north of the border appears to have involved an attempt to erase or at least neutralize the foreign, Mexican elements—of which the emphasis placed on familiar horror conventions was a factor. In other words, the international circulation of these texts involved a substantial adaptation away from their original national function, a strategy evident both in their new sites of distribution and consumption and in the changes made by Murray and his collaborators to the actual texts themselves.

The manner in which these films were marketed and packaged, for example, clearly sought to play down their Mexican heritage, quite opposing the tactics employed by art cinemas to attract a particular audience on the grounds of their product's foreignness. The same policy can be seen in AIP's importing, recutting, and redubbing of films from foreign countries other than Mexico during the same period, including Italy, Japan, and Russia. Moreover, alongside the "Spookies" package, AIP also sold networks a film package of Italian sword-and-sandals epics titled "Epicolor '64," among which were a number of bona fide Samson movies. Because Santo was renamed Samson in the United States, from titles alone it is very easy to confuse the two sets of movies—again blurring origins and erasing national specificity. Indeed, only the most dedicated trash film buff could tell the difference between *Samson and the 7 Miracles of the World* (1961), *Samson in the Wax Museum* (1963), *Samson vs. the Vampire Women* (1962), and *Samson and the Slave Queen* (1963).

These attempts to neutralize national differences are most notable through the changes made to the actual film texts. For example, Murray has noticeably used the opening credits of the films he released to place greatest emphasis on his own involvement, using approximately the same title design formula for each film. While all the other credits for cast and crew appear in generic horror movie lettering, "Soundlab" at Coral Gables, Florida (where Murray rerecorded the soundtracks), is given a particularly prominent titlecard and Murray's own "Supervised by" credit has his name flamboyantly rendered like a handwritten signature, setting it apart from the rest of the names, as though he is the author signing his own work. Indeed, Murray seems to have been selling himself as an American brand name that unifies the imports, as is also suggested by Michael Weldon's somewhat exaggerated remark that "At the time, his name was as well known as Walt Disney or William Castle, thanks to saturation television promotion. The youngsters didn't know they were seeing substandard Mexican films that K. got for a few pesos."[32]

More significant still were the alterations Murray made to the films' soundtracks, such as dubbing them into English or, in the cases of *Doctor of Doom* and *Wrestling Women vs. the Aztec Mummy*, gratuitously adding a piece of American rock 'n' roll music to several fight sequences. Beyond the obvious erasure of the Spanish language, the effect of this dubbing has particular implications with respect to the horror genre and issues of national specificity.

As Robin Wood and Andrew Tudor have noted in their work on the genre, the vast majority of U.S. horror films from the 1930s and 1940s were set in foreign, mostly European locations, thus coding the source of horror as exotic and Other.[33] It was not until the 1960s, following *Psycho* (1960), that American horror movies began to be mainly located in America, identifying the source of horror as indigenous to the country. Although they used the classical American horror film as a model, Golden Age Mexican horror films differed crucially by being very specifically set in present-day Mexico, not Europe or America. This seems vital to their nationalist project in that it narrativizes a threat to modern Mexico deriving from either Mexico's own past or from Europe/America—threats that often seem coded to be analogies of the threat of imperialism (with the *luchador* hero becoming a symbol of modern, working-class Mexico overcoming and destroying imperialist aggression). The figure of the mad scientist in mexploitation films, for example, is frequently represented as a foreigner, such as the villain of *Santo en el museo de cera*—a European who lost his sanity after being interned in a Nazi concentration camp and is now driven to destroy Mexico's beauty.

In the majority of the dubbed U.S. versions the location is not specified, but one can assume that the average viewer might identify it as Mexico, if only because all the written text within the diegesis is in Spanish. However, with an English-language soundtrack in this new context of consumption, Mexico becomes coded as yet another exotic, foreign locale, like Europe. In other words, rather than the setting being coded as indigenous and functioning within a process of nation building, that project is neutralized and the mexploitation film is subsumed back into the Hollywood conventions it sought to deviate from in the first place. For example, the high percentage of Aztec Mummy films to be imported into the United States no doubt stems from the popularity of the culturally different Egyptian Mummy in Hollywood. Moreover, one of the few films to have a setting specified in the dubbed version is *Samson in the Wax Museum*, but the location is identified as America, not Mexico—thus erasing the ideological implications of the metaphor of a European savaging the beauty of Mexico.

Psychotronia and Beyond

What this seems to suggest is that the nationally specific strategies within mexploitation were largely disregarded when these films were exhibited to Anglophonic viewers in the United States in the 1960s, due to several factors: the differing sites of consumption fostering differing uses of the texts among differing audience demographics; a cultural emphasis placed more on familiar horror than unfamiliar wrestling elements; and a physical alteration of the texts themselves. In more recent years, mexploitation has acquired a growing reputation in America among fans of cult and psychotronic cinema who in turn have their own sites of exhibition and sets of reading protocols. Although they still crop up occasionally on Spanish-language television in the United States, the primary source of these movies for Anglophonic Americans is now through video labels that specialize in psychotronia: most notably Something Weird, Rhino, and Sinister Video. Several of Murray's releases have also been selected for derision on the cable television program *Mystery Science Theater 3000*: namely *The Robot vs. the Aztec Mummy, Santa Claus,* and *Samson vs. the Vampire Women.*

Much of this psychotronic embrace of mexploitation can probably be related quite closely back to their screening on late-night TV in the United States. Sconce has argued that the scheduling of low-budget horror and science-fiction films on late-night television, and the antics of the "horror hosts" who introduced, derided, and frequently interrupted the screenings, formed a basis for later manifestations of ironic reading protocols and a psychotronic cinephilia that emerged in the early 1980s through fanzines like *Psychotronic Video* and *Zontar: The Magazine from Venus.*[34] (The former provided reviews of late-night movie broadcasts overlooked by the *New York Times* television guide, while the latter was named after one of Larry Buchanan's AIP-TV movies.) Indeed, most of the Web sites on mexploitation exhibit just this psychotronic bias.

This embrace of mexploitation films as cult items by psychotronic fans seems to be based upon a disregarding of the films' nationally specific strategies by emphasizing instead their formal similarities to other types of cult cinema, as is evident in at least three ways. First, psychotronic cinephilia has long cherished low-budget rip-offs of Hollywood cinema, such as those that dominate the Italian horror film industry. Therefore, when divorced from their original cultural contexts, the negotiations between American conventions and indigenous elements in mexploitation films might appear instead to be simply failed attempts at imitating Hollywood cinema—which is one of the highest orders of merit among many psychotronic movie buffs.

Second, Sconce has noted that the ironic reading protocols of psychotronic fans often involve the pleasure of seeing attempts at constructing a fictional diegesis fail so miserably that all that remains is the

profilmic event: "the action on the screen becomes but the trace of an isolated moment of desperate human activity, a farcical attempt at 'art' taking place on a particular day many years ago in someone's garage, on a
Dallas parking lot."[35] Given this propensity of psychotronic fans to move
between the fictional and the nonfictional, the diegetic and the profilmic,
it is perhaps not surprising that mexploitation films have been embraced.
Without identifying the national specificity of the aesthetic strategies
being used in the integration of wrestling scenes into horror narratives,
the alternation between fictional and nonfictional footage seems like a
failed attempted at obeying dominant cinematic codes of storytelling—
and is therefore befitting of psychotronic reading protocols.

Third, Schaefer has described the aesthetics of exploitation cinema
as involving a "hodgepodge of cuttings and splicings," characterized by
textual incoherency and the use of gratuitous padding and spectacle that
violate dominant norms of narrative economy.[36] Once again we can see
that the lengthy nonnarrative content of footage from real wrestling
matches in mexploitation films approximates the textual features of U.S.
exploitation when divorced from its original site of consumption. Likewise, the hybridity of wrestling and horror seems bizarre and incongruous when viewed from outside of Mexico, further endearing the films to
ironic psychotronic reading patterns.

Interesting proof of this is perhaps the 1986 rerelease of *Wrestling
Women vs. the Aztec Mummy* by Rhino Video, retitled *Rock 'n' Roll
Wrestling Women vs. the Aztec Mummy*, which seems explicitly geared
toward psychotronic reading protocols. Whereas Murray's import of the
film ran for approximately seventy-seven minutes, the Rhino release cut
the film down to under an hour in length, mostly excising talky exposition
scenes with an apparently gleeful disregard for narrative logic. What
remains of the film is an incoherent collection of wrestling and horror
sequences, made even more incongruous by the addition of several spe-
cially recorded, deliberately cheesy rock 'n' roll songs to jazz up the
action—further removing the wrestling scenes from the realism of the
Arena, making them play more like kitsch MTV videos. Even though
most cult audiences actively despise the show, a similar tailoring of mexploitation films for cult audiences is clearly also evident in the inclusion of
several of them on *Mystery Science Theater 3000*, where the films' cultural
origins are ignored and their aesthetic strategies explicitly mocked and
derided.

Conclusion

This translation of nationalist textual strategies into ironic psychotronic readings, based on formal similarities between mexploitation and U.S. horror exploitation, is perhaps not entirely inappropriate, however. As Schaefer stresses throughout his recent study of American exploitation cinema, the films' aesthetics are inseparable from their institutional position and modes of production. Although made under often quite different cultural circumstances, some aspects of the production of mexploitation films are comparable to their gringo cousins. Both are invariably low-budget films made with an eye on exploiting popular topical trends. Both are often characterized by the piecing together of footage from disparate sources or the recycling of footage across films. And both are often constructed like serials (in the United States to circumvent censorship; in Mexico because of strict union restrictions on feature film production). Moreover, many of the same reading protocols developed among American psychotronic fans have cycled back around to fans of mexploitation in Mexico, such that these new practices of consumption are now also occurring in the place of national origin. Perhaps all the instances of exhibition and consumption analyzed here are equally legitimate, with none inherently more authentic or inauthentic than another. Although the specificity of the films' roles within nationalist projects may have been disregarded and signifiers of Mexicanness systematically erased, the 1960s and 1980s consumptions of mexploitation in the United States still constitute valid cultural experiences for people.

There are two possible implications that this case study of mexploitation might have on theories of national cinema within Latin America that we would like to address here by way of a conclusion. First, the example of mexploitation amply demonstrates the futility of attempts to control or fix the cultural meanings that will be attached to works of national cinema when they enter the international arena. Therefore, theories, strategies, and policies need to keep in mind this very slippery process of flow and inscription across cultural borders. Second, if theories of Latin American cinema and identity are to embrace post-structuralist or post-modernist models of cultural hybridity and heterogeneity (such as prescribed by the likes of Chanady and Homi Bhabha), something of a paradox seems to exist. If textual representations of that identity are hybrid and heterogeneous, they will inevitably invite equally pluralistic (mis)interpretations when circulated internationally, precisely because their hybridity and heterogeneity opens them up for audiences to read what they want into the texts, making any attempt at trying to fix their meaning at the site of production a fruitless endeavor. If there is no "center" in a post-modern world, the "play" of textual signifiers (at the site of consumption) becomes the place at which issues such as nationhood and identity are inscribed. Indeed, the appropriation and alteration of mexploitation by Anglophonic American distributors and audiences can only really be viewed as a bastardization and debasement if one clings onto homogeneous, essentializing, and monolithic notions of Mexican national identity—that there was a "pure" Mexican center or core to be lost in the first place.

Notes

The research for this essay, a version of which was first presented at the 2001 Society for Cinema Studies conference, was funded in part by a grant from the Roger Thayer Stone Center for Latin American Studies at Tulane University. We would like to extend particular gratitude to our SCS co-panelists Laura Podalsky and David Wilt for their assistance.

1. We have only given the English language titles because all of these films are amalgams of footage from a variety of sources, so to think of an "original" Mexican version in most cases seems somewhat futile.

2. Due to the different versions of many of these films, we have adopted the following system for citing titles: when first mentioning each film we have provided both Spanish and English language titles; in subsequent references that pertain specifically to the original Mexican version, we have used the Spanish language title; and in subsequent references that pertain specifically to the dubbed U.S. version, we have used the English title.

3. The term "psychotronic" refers to the realm of cinema that includes cult, trash, sleaze, camp, exploitation, and B movies. The name derives from Michael Weldon's cult movie fanzine, *Psychotronic Video*.

4. Paul Willemen, *Looks and Frictions: Essays in Cultural Studies and Film Theory* (London: BFI Publishing, 1994), 212.

5. Andrew Higson, "The Concept of National Cinema," *Screen* 30, no. 4 (1989): 37, 41.

6. See, for example, John King, *Magical Reels: A History of Cinema in Latin America* (London: Verso, 2000); John King, Ana López, and Manuel Alvarado, eds., *Mediating Two Worlds: Cinematic Encounters in the Americas* (London: BFI Publishing, 1993); Paolo Antonio Paranaguá, ed., *Mexican Cinema* (London: BFI Publishing, 1994); Chon Noriega, ed., *Visible Nations: Latin American Cinema and Video* (Minneapolis: University of Minnesota Press, 2000); Michael Chanan, *The Cuban Image* (London: BFI Publishing, 1985).

7. Amaryll Chanady, ed., *Latin American Identity and Constructions of Difference* (Minneapolis: University of Minnesota Press, 1994), introduction.

8. Higson, "Concept of National Cinema," 44.

9. See, for example, Jesús Martín Barbero, *De los medios a las mediaciones: Comunicación, cultura y hegemonía* (Mexico City: Ediciones G. Gili, 1998), 181.

10. Dolores Tierney, "Silver Sling Backs and Mexican Melodrama," *Screen* 38, no. 4 (1997).

11. See Eric Schaefer, *"Bold! Daring! Shocking! True!": A History of Exploitation Film, 1919–1959* (Durham, NC: Duke University Press, 1999) and Jeffrey Sconce, "'Trashing' the Academy: Taste, Excess, and an Emerging Politics of Cinematic Style," *Screen* 36, no. 4 (1995): 371–93.

12. Paulo Antonio Paranaguá, "Of Periodizations and Paradigms: The Fifties in Comparative Perspective," *Nuevo Texto Crítico* 11, no. 21/21 (January–December 1998): 32.

13. David Wilt, "Horror Films from South of the Border," *Cinefantastique* 27, no. 10 (1996): 40.

14. David Wilt, "Masked Men and Monsters," in *Mondo Macabro: Weird & Wonderful Cinema around the World*, ed. Pete Tombs (New York: St. Martin's Griffin, 1998), 144.

15. For a detailed discussion of Mexican horror cinema during this decade, see Gary D. Rhodes, "Fantasmas del cine mexicano: The 1930s Horror Film Cycle of Mexico," in *Fear Without Frontiers: Horror Cinema across the Globe*, ed. Steven Jay Schneider (Surrey, UK: FAB Press, 2003), 93–103.

16. Quoted in Wilt, "Masked Men and Monsters," 142.

17. Laura Podalsky, "Aztec Mummies and Vampire Women: Pinning Down the Other in the Mexican Horror-Wrestling Film," presented at the 2001 Society for Cinema Studies conference.

18. Heather Levi, "Masked Media: The Adventures of Lucha Libre on the Small Screen," in *Fragments of a Golden Age: The Politics of Culture in Mexico since 1940*, ed. Gilbert Joseph, Anne Rubenstein, and Eric Zolov (Durham, NC: Duke University Press, 2001), 337.

19. Levi, "Masked Media," 336.

20. Carlos Monsiváis, *Los rituales del caos* (Mexico City: Ediciones Era, 1995), 131.

21. Levi, "Masked Media," 344.

22. Ibid.

23. Ibid., 339.

24. For an account of art cinema practices of exhibition, see Barbara Wilinsky, *Sure Seaters: The Emergence of Art House Cinema* (Minneapolis: University of Minnesota Press, 2001).

25. Murray had particular success, independent of AIP, annually rereleasing the children's fantasy film *Santa Claus* in theaters. Michael Weldon also notes that a double bill of *El ataúd del vampiro/The Vampire's Coffin* (1957) and *The Robot vs. the Aztec Mummy* played at some theaters as part of a "Giant Scream Show."

26. Nick Browne, "The Political Economy of the Television (Super) Text," in *Television: The Critical View*, ed. Horace Newcomb (New York/Oxford: Oxford University Press, 1987), 588.

27. Jeffrey Sconce, "Programming the Fringe," in *Trash Cinema*, ed. Eric Schaefer (Austin: University of Texas Press, forthcoming), n.p.

28. "Those Clean Living All American Monsters," *Look*, September 8, 1964, 50.

29. "TV's Year of the Monster," *Life,* August 21, 1964, 54–57.
30. "Why They Love Monsters," *New York Times Magazine,* October 25, 1964, 109.
31. "Those Clean Living All American Monsters," *Look,* September 8, 1964, 52, 54.
32. Michael Weldon, *The Psychotronic Encyclopedia of Film* (London: Plexus, 1983), 147.
33. See Robin Wood, "Return of the Repressed," *Film Comment* 14, no. 4 (1978) and Andrew Tudor, *Monsters and Mad Scientists: A Cultural History of the Horror Movie* (Oxford/Cambridge: Blackwell, 1989).
34. Sconce, "Programming the Fringe."
35. Sconce, "'Trashing' the Academy," 390.
36. Schaefer, *Bold! Daring! Shocking! True!* The quotation refers to the title of Chapter 2, "'A Hodge-Podge of Cuttings and Splicings': The Mode of Production and the Style of Classical Exploitation Films," 42–95.

—————— 3 ——————

The Dialogue with American Popular Culture in Two German Films about the Serial Killer

Steffen Hantke

The Trope of "American Uniqueness"

Ask any scholar or journalist who has studied the statistical record of serial murder, and you will hear that serial killers are as American as apple pie, barbershop quartets, and televangelism. Michael Newton's 1990 study *Hunting Humans,* for example, claims that the "United States boasts 74 percent of the world total of serial killers. Europe claims 19 percent."[1] These numbers are so impressively disproportionate that other critics come to the same conclusion as Newton. Serial murder, Jane Caputi states, "is an overwhelmingly Western capitalist phenomenon."[2]

This is an odd conclusion because it ignores the vast statistical discrepancy between Europe and America. Is Western capitalism a sufficient common factor for thinking about the social, political, and cultural origins of serial murder? If so, then why does Europe fall behind America by such a dramatic margin? Questions like these tend to disappear if we assume, together with Caputi and Newton, that America provides the defining category for theorizing serial murder. If Europe is essentially like America, then we do not have to wonder about discrepancies any longer: we can safely add up the two numbers. Consequently, Americans can—with a perverse kind of national pride—"boast" that they own serial murder. Obviously, Caputi (after Newton) uses the term "boasting" ironically, aware of the fact that "to be first" is not necessarily an accomplishment; that "to be first" is an empty category, the value of which is only determined at the moment when it is given content in a concrete situation. Caputi's irony skewers a tendency in American culture or, for that matter, in any culture that is driven by competition, to strip the accomplishment of "being first" of its content. Even when discussing something as alarming, reprehensible, and condemning as serial murder, Caputi reminds us, some will take pride in the fact that America, once again, leads the way.

What Caputi explicitly perpetuates, however, is the idea, supported by Newton's statistics, that America produces serial killers more effectively than any other country. Not even her use of irony undermines this belief. The numbers, however, should be taken with a grain of salt, as others have suggested. In his book *Using Murder,* Philip Jenkins phrases these reservations in the most coherent and convincing way. Serial murder, Jenkins argues, is a phenomenon enmeshed in a variety of conflicting economic, political, and ideological interests, all vying for the power to define it. The ones granted this power of definition are those most deeply invested in it—law enforcement, in particular, whose funding rests, to a large extent, on the seriousness of the threat that a certain type of crime poses, or is at least perceived to pose to society. Law enforcement, as the major compiler and distributor of statistical information on serial murder, is therefore prone to exaggerating the threat, both in its seriousness and in its prevalence. "American uniqueness," Jenkins therefore concludes, "may thus be exaggerated."[3]

In order to demonstrate that American uniqueness is a result of social construction rather than empirical truth, Jenkins produces an impressive list of German serial killers: Georg Karl Grossman, Karl Denke, Peter Kürten, Bruno Ludke, Adolf Seefeld, and Rudolf Pleil, to name but a few. The sheer number alone demonstrates how a country that most Americans probably associate with law and order has not been exempt from the phenomenon of serial murder.[4] Similarly, most of these cases go back to the era of the Weimar Republic, the 1920s and 1930s. The killers' names are on record, and if they have been forgotten, then studies such as Jenkins's are doing their part to reintroduce them into the discussion. The "German experience," Jenkins writes, "confirms that in historical terms, there is little that is truly novel about the phenomenon of multiple murder in the contemporary United States."[5]

Despite these well-founded reservations, the trope of American uniqueness has established itself as an indispensable part of the public discourse on serial murder. A film crucial to the formation of genre conventions like Jonathan Demme's *The Silence of the Lambs* (1991), based on the equally successful and popular novel by Thomas Harris, is not overtly concerned with Americanness as a theme. Yet it continuously writes the figure of the serial killer into a specifically American iconography of crime. Nicknamed Buffalo Bill by the Kansas City Homicide Squad, and

psychologically disfigured by the Vietnam War, the film's killer functions
as a dark double of the American hero, a rugged individualist gone bad.
Demme uses him as a figure exemplary of what Richard Slotkin has called
"regeneration through violence," a culturally specific response to the American frontier, the maintenance of its ideological significance, and its
historical disappearance.[6]

Even more striking is the insistence on American uniqueness in an
HBO film titled *Citizen X* (1995) because this film, at first glance, seems
to assert that serial murder exists not only outside the United States but
also that it flourishes even in a political and economic system other than
Western capitalism. The film is based on a series of murders committed
by a man named Andrei Chikatilo (Jeffrey DeMunn) in the final years
before the collapse of the Soviet Union. Criticizing the Soviet bureaucracy for dismissing the killings as a symptom of American capitalist
decadence, and thus for refusing to take action, the film plots a detective,
Victor Burakov (Stephen Rea), lacking all conventional resources of law
enforcement, against a resourceful killer. Since his superiors are unwilling
to prevent further murders, Burakov is forced to consult (without their
explicit consent) the FBI's databases on serial killers. Only here, the film
suggests, can he find reliable information on serial murder. Unlike the
Soviet Union, America is primed in its fight against serial murder, partly
because of past experiences, partly because of the willingness to confront
its problems head on, without ideological blinders. "The Soviet Burakov's
desire to talk to the American FBI, which the film later uncritically poses
as the climactic answer to all of Burakov's problems, underscores the
degree to which the FBI's theories of serial murder have been canonized
by the popular media."[7]

Citizen X features a scene that overtly addresses what Jenkins calls
the social construction of crime. During a brief stay in the hospital,
Burakov watches William Friedkin's *The French Connection* (1971) on television. Obviously, the same narrative universe that contains Rea's
lugubrious Russian detective cannot hold Popeye Doyle (Gene Hack-
man). Perhaps what we see in this scene is a reflection of what Wendy
Lesser sees as a recurring theme in the non-American perception of
American crime; namely, that "America ... stands for the absence of moral
rules, or perhaps rules of any kind."[8] Since Rea's character is offered to the
viewer as a point of identification, Friedkin's fictitious Popeye Doyle is
severed, in the eyes of the viewer, from any connection with the realities

of crime or law enforcement. The scene ironically dismisses the cop movie as an ideological fabrication, a move that, conversely, confirms the FBI database as a faithful reflection of American crime. The existence and factual accuracy of such a database reinstates America as the proper site, the vanguard even, of serial murder.

Citizen X concedes that serial murder exists outside of the United States, and thus, that it may constitute an extreme variant of a transcultural, perhaps even universal, human pathology. Serial murder, in short, can happen anywhere. However, the lack of expertise with which law enforcement in the Soviet Union confronts the phenomenon recuperates serial murder as "properly" American. In an ideological maneuver analogous to the American rhetoric on free trade, the definition of serial murder as an intrinsically and indigenously American phenomenon extends American jurisdiction into spaces beyond the boundaries of the United States. Wherever serial murder occurs, someone unequipped to confront the problem may call on the FBI to step in and help. Invited to step across lines of national sovereignty, American law enforcement fulfills a complex and potentially far-reaching obligation to address a problem that is somehow always its own. And yet the difference between a moral obligation and a political prerogative is sometimes as murky as the question of whether *The French Connection* on Soviet Russian TV is harmless entertainment or cultural imperialism.

These two examples are American productions, and may thus show a bias that is hardly surprising given their origin. However a British production, the BBC's *Prime Suspect* series, confirms this attitude. *Prime Suspect* Episode 3 (1993) features, as the temporary love interest of British detective Jane Tennison (Helen Mirren), an American "profiler" named Jake (Michael Shannon). He is an expert on serial murder, although it remains unclear whether he is, or was, a journalist, writer, or member of the legendary Behavioral Sciences Unit of the FBI. In fact, he is a combination of all three—a self-promoting entrepreneur weaving a number of professional identities into one product. At this point, he is on a promotional tour through Britain for a "true crime" book on serial murder he has written. When we see him delivering a lecture to a rapt audience, his face above the rostrum juxtaposed with a series of photographs of crime scenes and mutilated bodies, his voice is calm and sober as he seriously recounts the familiar tropes of serial murder. Yet his status as expert is compromised by his failure at producing a bestseller. He encourages Tennison to take

Captured serial killer
Andrei Chikatilo
(Jeffrey DeMunn) in
Citizen X (1995)

more than one copy from a whole stack of his books. "Serial killers are a big business," he muses, "at least they were last year. I might have missed the gravy train."

Jake and Tennison, the American and the British detective, each represent a different type of murder. Jake is concerned with serial murder, while Tennison's investigation hinges crucially on the single violent death. Jake's hybrid profession as writer, journalist, and public speaker connect him to the transfer of violence into cultural discourse. While Jake works at the commodification of violence, Tennison's police work involves her only marginally in the profits made from crime. While he transforms actions into words, she disentangles actions from words in search of the single story that tells the truth. His presentation erases the names of the victims, while her investigation aims at recuperating the victim's identity and reclaiming it in the name of dignity. Jake stands for a new kind of murder, while Tennison stands for a well-established convention, the police procedural based on the classic form of the murder mystery.

The question these examples raise is how serial murder comes to be committed in the Soviet Union and in England if it is a distinctly American crime. *Citizen X* offers the explanation that serial murder is a symptom of Western capitalist decadence. Although it is likely that serial murder lurks more in the heart of man than in the heart of Mother Russia, the official explanation—that it is a uniquely American phenomenon—is never fully discredited. Hence, it appears perfectly reasonable within the narrative and thematic logic of the film to assume that the Soviet Union has somehow been "contaminated." The same goes for *Prime Suspect*. Serial murder is not Tennison's problem in Episode 3, but it does appear as a crime in the show's first episode, and thus as one that a British deviant is perfectly capable of committing. England, and perhaps (in keeping with Newton and Caputi) all of Europe along with it, is not exempt from the virus of serial murder. Unlike its occurrence in America, however, where it is (after all) indigenous, its occurrence outside the United States constitutes an anomaly, one which immediately calls for explanation. Not so much the question "How can this possibly happen?" that routinely accompanies, and largely drives, the discourse on serial murder in the United States, but the question "How can this possibly happen *here*?"

The shift in emphasis may be slight, but its consequences are significant. No longer is the mystery of serial murder primarily a psychological one, confronting us with early childhood traumas or else slow, gradual processes by which the individual psyche comes unglued. No longer is it a social mystery, confronting us with a society that rewards aggression and cultivates violence as a form of entertainment, art, or business. The trope of American uniqueness creates a position from which the United States itself suddenly becomes the focus of attention. The "here" presupposes America as a "there," a point of reference or a frame of inquiry. Serial murder committed anywhere outside the United States needs to be measured—whether in its psychological or in its social dimension—against the United States itself as its distinct, though sometimes remote, point of origin. This is not a choice on the viewer or reader's part, and thus is not subject to individual or collective sentiments or prejudices for or against America. Rather, it is a theme written into the discourse of serial murder, where each new contribution is able to use it for the purposes it sees fit.

What these specific purposes can be is something I would like to examine through the lens of two German serial killer films, both from 1995. One is Romuald Karmakar's *Der Totmacher*, the other Nico Hofmann's *Der Sandmann*. Both films feature Götz George (son of Heinrich George, star of many UFA silent films), a German stage and film actor of considerable star status, in the role of the serial killer.

Der Sandmann

Made for German television, Nico Hoffman's *Der Sandmann* is a slick mainstream production that largely follows the stylistic, narrative, and thematic conventions of American serial killer films.[9] In Hofmann's film, the celebrated and notorious true crime writer Henry Kupfer (George) is about to release a new novel, titled *Der Kannibale*. As enfant terrible of the literary scene, Kupfer owns up publicly to his personal predilection for, and expertise in, matters of excessive, gruesome sexual violence. Having spent eight years in prison for murdering a young woman when he was a teenager, he has subsequently succeeded in forging a literary persona in which the ex-con and the hard-hitting author have merged into one fascinating, ambiguous, media-savvy celebrity. Kupfer is already a fully formed post-modern media fabrication before the plot takes off, a self-made man, a simulacra of the *poet maudit*, who satisfies the public's unsavory appetite for gore. Even the character's name testifies to Kupfer's status as media fabrication: "Kupfer," German for copper, does not so much point to the slang word for policeman as to the material of money— albeit of the smaller, less valuable coins in the German currency. Ironically, Kupfer's name stands for small change and not for big bucks.

The name of Kupfer's nemesis is equally significant. Ina Litmann (Karoline Eichhorn) is the junior reporter sent by the reality TV show *Auge in Auge* (*Eye to Eye*) to manipulate Kupfer into making an appearance on the show. Her surname ("Lit" is a trendy abbreviation that strips "Literature" of its metaphysical grandeur and demotes it to the status of post-modern commodity, while "man" stands for "male" or "masculine") points as much to the business of literature as to the masculine assertiveness and determination with which she begins to pursue Kupfer as a surefire ticket to career advancement. While Kupfer strings her along, endlessly equivocating on his decision, Litmann's job is to ferret out as much personal background information about the author as possible. Her research, however, quickly leads to the suspicion that Kupfer may be responsible for the murders of a number of prostitutes. The press has already nicknamed the killer "der Sandmann." As the world-weary, elderly Inspector Stolpe (Jürgen Hentsch) explains to Litmann, the killer is "always the last customer . . . he rocks them to sleep gently, like the Sandman usually does."

While Litmann follows Kupfer around during the promotional tour for his new novel, the serial murders—which begin as part of the media noise in the background of the plot—gradually take center stage. As the suspicions against Kupfer begin to solidify, Litmann's bosses decide to stage the revelation of the writer as serial killer on the air. The television show, an aggressive one-on-one interview during which the subject is confronted with the evidence Litmann has compiled, constitutes the climactic scene of the film. This climax, however, fails to deliver. Increasingly uneasy and erratic, Kupfer finally gets up and leaves instead of breaking down and confessing on air to the murders. His public behavior, however, appears sufficiently revealing to warrant questioning by the police. Five minutes before the film is over we are firm in our belief that Kupfer's final apprehension is just a matter of time and persistence.

In the final sequence of the film we watch Kupfer enter Litmann's apartment while she is asleep. She wakes up to find herself tied to the bed, helpless in the exact same position in which we, the audience, have already seen earlier victims of the serial killer. After enacting the verbal routines of the Sandman (most notable among them the line "you can kiss me if you want to"), Kupfer suddenly stops and unties Litmann. His behavior shifts from the frenzied demeanor of the Sandman to cool, professional detachment. He admits that the clues tying him to the murders have been planted, some even fabricated, in order to generate public attention for his new novel. "But we don't want to complain now, do we?" He goes on:

> Each one of us got what he wanted: you got the ratings you dreamed of, and I finally got a decent advertising campaign. Basically, we're even. But I wonder if you can tell me why I still feel like shit? ... How did you like me in my role? ... Come on, why are you looking at me like that? We're both in show business, whether we like it or not. Or did you forget about that? ... I'm sure I'll be hearing great things about you. And if you can't sleep at night, well, then you can dream of me ...[10]

The plot has been straining so hard, just like Litmann, to convince us that Henry Kupfer is the Sandman that we have willingly gone along with the idea. Now we learn that clues have been fabricated or planted, Kupfer's behavior was the result of deliberate deceit, corroborating external sources were really accessories to the deception (a woman who appeared earlier as a prostitute turns out to be Kupfer's girlfriend), and that supposedly neutral characters have been conspiring with Kupfer to pull off the media stunt (the production assistant Volker [Martin Armknecht], a colleague of Litmann's at the station, is seen paying off Kupfer). In the end the film is infuriatingly indifferent toward the question of who committed the murders. It is never addressed, and never resolved. What appeared to be a fable of detection, seen from Litmann's point of view, turns out to be a conspiratorial narrative from Kupfer's and some of the other characters' perspective.

Which narrative genre the director's audience is dealing with is of crucial importance here, not just for Litmann, who represents the viewer's point of view, but also for Kupfer, who leads Litmann (and so the viewer) to believe that this is a story of serial murder (which it isn't). Erroneous genre expectations lead Litmann to misread the clues. These expectations are heightened by Kupfer, who skillfully manipulates the generic inventory of the serial killer narrative. In Jenkins's terminology, Kupfer is an expert at the "social construction of serial homicide." To a viewer familiar with serial killer films, most of the crucial details of *Der Sandmann* are uncannily reminiscent of *The Silence of the Lambs,* as the following list reveals:

1. The killer's private space holds the key to his true identity: Litmann wants to see Kupfer's house, assuming that she will catch a glimpse of the murderer behind the mask of the writer. The house previously belonged to Karl Friedrich Hansen, another killer.
2. The serial killer is himself an expert on serial homicide: Kupfer is writing a book on Hansen, and is knowledgeable about everything concerning serial murder, lecturing to Litmann and others who are willing to listen.
3. The serial killer is the double of the detective figure: Litmann becomes uncomfortably intimate with Kupfer throughout her investigations, and the ending reveals that each is using the other for the advancement of their respective careers.
4. The serial killer takes trophies from his victims: Litmann finds bones in Kupfer's house, and later discovers newspaper clippings of the prostitute murders in his bag.
5. The serial killer wants to be caught: Kupfer's readiness to open up to Litmann, to come on the show, and to write about killings that resemble the prostitute murders, all seem to indicate that he craves public attention to such an extent that he is willing to give himself away.
6. The serial killer is created through childhood trauma: Kupfer describes abuse by his father, establishing the possibility that he may have killed his sister when they were both children.
7. The serial killer, in his paternal role toward the female detective, is doubled by a second father figure: Inspector Stolpe takes on the role of Litmann's "good father"; unlike Kupfer, he is not interested in her sexually, and poses no threat.

8. Relationships between the characters are subject to excessive doubling: see 3 and 7 (above).
9. The series of murders is potentially open-ended: with Hansen as Kupfer's inspiration, and the mental scenario in Kupfer's mind unattainable (recuperating or punishing his sister from/for her early childhood death), there is no reason why he would ever stop killing.

The list of similarities among the characters, themes, and plot of the two films could be extended into even smaller details. But this brief outline should be enough to demonstrate that Kupfer's fabrication of himself as serial murderer would come across as convincing to anyone familiar with the conventions of the genre.[11] Litmann falls for it, and, if the ending strikes us as at all surprising, so do we.

Hofmann's film posits the post-modern media—which draws books and television into the same Baudrillardian system of endless circulation and exchange—as based on mutual manipulation and exploitation. Kupfer may still "feel like shit" after having pulled off his media stunt; Litmann may have had scruples all through her voyeuristic snooping in and around Kupfer's life; and we as viewers may feel a little bit uneasy about our desire (revealed through our disappointment at film's end) to see violence and gore. In short, everyone involved may have acted against some remnants of ethical integrity, and in the end no one walks away with clean hands. Characters talk incessantly about selling out, but only a few of them seem to really mind. Early on, one staff member of *Eye to Eye* resigns, calling the program "the ultimate peep show for dangerous psychopaths"; Kupfer tells his TV audience that "obscenity is a state of shamelessness, and shamelessness is the only word I can use to describe the world and all the people in it right now"; and Litmann is framed underneath a sign on the wall that reads "Lower Your Standards." Apart from these isolated examples, however, cynicism rules, especially among Litmann's colleagues at the TV station.

Der Sandmann's critique of a mass media that celebrates the serial killer at the expense of his victims, and willingly ignores ethical and professional standards in pursuit of higher ratings, is a convention of the serial killer genre. Serial murderers, so the thematic rule goes, kill for attention, and the media inspires and rewards their crimes. Philip Simpson, for example, demonstrates how director Michael Mann in *Manhunter* (1986) sets up a psychological dynamic by which viewer and detective form an uneasy alliance in wanting to see tabloid reporter Freddie Lounds

(Stephen Lang) punished for his transgressions, just as audiences of Oliver Stone's *Natural Born Killers* (1994) are rooting for "sleaze-journalism schlockmeister" Wayne Gale (Robert Downey Jr.) to meet his deservedly violent end.[12]

Hofmann is well aware of these generic expectations on the part of his audience. Although the media is undeniably criticized for its lack of ethical standards in *Der Sandmann,* it is not specifically singled out for its high degree of cynicism. Hofmann associates lack of authenticity with a larger public sphere that is dominated by the media. What makes this sphere all the more hostile and inhuman is its voracious appetite for the personal, the private, and the intimate. The film's interiors reflect this distinction. The commercialized, high-tech environment of the television station stands as the epitome of insatiable public space—extreme close-ups of human faces in all their vulnerability projected onto large walls of TV sets; transparent office spaces; the simulation of genuine human emotion for economic benefit. In her role as investigative journalist, Litmann participates in the penetration of secrets that is characteristic of this public sphere. Her goals and ambitions are shaped by it, and her activities push its boundaries out into every available space commonly designated as private.

Hofmann, however, offers his audience the prospect of a haven in this heartless world. Against Litmann's post-modern space of total transparency and simulation, he presents Kupfer's private space, an old house in the country with a deep, gothic history of its own. As Kupfer explains to Litmann, it is a building free of all modern technology. It is also a building marked by the non-alienated, authentic labor of the writer, and as such stands opposed to the compromised activities of TV journalism taking place at the studio. Litmann comes here to catch a glimpse into Kupfer's mind. Extending that same promise of seeing Kupfer for who he really is, the film also offers viewers another space exempt from transparency, the basement of the house where he spent his childhood. Kupfer invites Litmann and her camera crew in, hinting at the possibility that this is where the childhood trauma that made him a serial killer occurred. Litmann enters these spaces hoping to find clues, and if the rules of the serial killer genre did in fact apply here, she would certainly have reason to be optimistic.

Both spaces, however, are revealed to be shams. Kupfer's house merely masquerades as an antique; Litmann eventually discovers the phone and television Kupfer claimed he did not own. Similarly, the whole "childhood home" trope—the house and its gothic basement underneath—is part of an elaborate scheme to attract Litmann as unwilling accomplice in Kupfer's media stunt to promote his new book. In both cases, the killer's space is merely a stage set, concealing his complicity in the public sphere. Kupfer is a post-modern celebrity: there is no self behind the mask. The absorption of his private spaces into the public sphere, therefore, cannot really be considered a result of his selling out, just as Litmann's corruption cannot be considered a result of her getting involved with Kupfer. Privacy as the ontological foundation of the self is an illusion before the film even begins. Kupfer may evince traces of something resembling guilt for having manipulated Litmann ("Basically we're even. But I wonder if you can tell me why I still feel like shit?"), but the film attaches no negative consequences to these traces. Kupfer walks away to collect his reward, his admission of a guilty conscience possibly just another layer of deception. Litmann's sense of victimization appears marginally more genuine, though, again, the end of the film does not allow for narrative substantiation of this impression.

Hofmann makes sure to steer clear of the kind of nostalgia made possible by the story at this moment. Remnants of an earlier time appear to exist only in this post-modern narrative universe. It would not be difficult, for example, to think of the writer as counterforce to the TV journalist, the representative of an older technology, an older form of communication that still possessed integrity and authenticity. But Hofmann allows his viewers no such sentimentality. The book business is only part and parcel of the post-modern media, integrated into the larger mechanisms of celebrity culture, and thus not essentially different from television or tabloid journalism. The economic and cultural post-modernization of Germany in the mid-1990s has reabsorbed traces of its own prehistory, reproducing them today just like any other commodity. It denies history by turning itself, in effect, into a process without discernible historical origins. A final diagnosis of *Der Sandmann* reveals that there are no spaces left in contemporary Germany that have not been colonized by the economic rationale and cultural sensibility represented through the figures of Litmann and Kupfer.

Der Totmacher

The same year (1995) that Götz George starred as Kupfer in *Der Sandmann*, he played a very different kind of serial killer, in a very different kind of film: Romuald Karmakar's *Der Totmacher*. For this austere, minimalist production, scriptwriters Karmakar and Michael Farin read through the transcripts of interviews conducted between August 18 and September 25, 1924, by a psychiatrist in Göttingen with convicted serial murderer Fritz Haarmann (1879–1925). These transcripts provide the film's dialogue between Haarmann (George) as he awaits his execution and the court-appointed clinical psychologist sent to study the mystery of his violent nature. Driven by this dialogue, the film restricts itself to scenes in the interrogation room, and to just a few characters—Haarmann, the psychiatrist Ernst Schulze (Jürgen Hentsch, who incidentally plays Inspector Stolpe in *Der Sandmann*), and an unnamed stenographer (Pierre Franckh).[13]

In this deliberate austerity, *Der Totmacher* differs significantly from Hofmann's film with its mainstream Hollywood aesthetic. The film has virtually no physical action. It is driven exclusively by dialogue. Camera work and editing draw little attention to themselves. The film limits itself to one locale and few characters. There is no love story. It leaves the final mystery of Haarmann's personality unsolved. By withholding a final explanation of his mental state, the film makes it difficult for viewers to position themselves emotionally with respect to the characters. Apart from Haarmann, the other characters are two-dimensional and insufficiently developed to provide sources of identification. Narrative suspense is not generated via an uncertain outcome; Haarmann has already been apprehended, and there is no doubt that he will be executed.

The film violates the rules of commercial mainstream cinema and also ignores some of the crucial conventions of the serial killer genre. The series of murders committed by Haarmann is not open-ended, for example. Haarmann is already in prison for his crimes, and the film does not provide any of those signals by which viewers will come to understand that the "virus" of serial murder has been passed on, that is, that someone else will continue the killer's grisly work.[14] There is also very little of the doubling in Karmakar's film so characteristic of the serial killer genre. Haarmann and his interrogator, Professor Schultze, may have a few moments when they seem a little too close for comfort (e.g., Schultze's figurative opening of his patient's skull to look inside it is reminiscent of Haarmann's literal cracking-open of some his victims' skulls), but their approximation of each other always remains unambiguous. Schultze has moments of sympathy with his patient, but he never wavers in his moral condemnation of his actions. He calls Haarmann back to his position on the opposite side of the table when Haarmann excitedly begins walking around the room. And he refuses to accept Haarmann's expression of

Fritz Haarmann (Götz
George) under interroga-
tion in *Der Totmacher*
(1995)

gratitude after presenting him with a cigar. By contrast, the attraction
between Clarice Starling (Jodie Foster) in *The Silence of the Lambs,* or
between Detective Will Graham (William Petersen) and Hannibal
Lecter (Brian Cox) in *Manhunter,* is far more subversive and ambiguous.[15] In the end, though, the small number of characters in the film
makes it technically impossible to create the elaborate network of corre-
spondences, analogies, and similarities that generate the ideological complexity present in such films as *Manhunter* or *The Silence of the Lambs.*

George, under Karmakar's direction, succeeds brilliantly at keeping
Haarmann a mystery, thus injecting a surprisingly strong element of non-
closure into a story that is headed for its historically determined ending.
Haarmann goes from moments of self-aggrandizement to dejection and
depression, to tenderness, joviality, and calculation. He displays signs of
arrested development, adopting the attitude and language of a small
child. The curious term "totmacher," a synonym for "killer" or "murderer"
that literally means "dead-maker," is an example of this type of diction; it
is a word a child would use, curiously lacking the rich social and moral
connotations of adult language. Karmakar often associates Haarmann's
real or contrived childishness with his lower-class background and the
psychological damage it inflicts in a society where class differences are
essential. Haarmann is shown reveling in his public notoriety, viewing
himself as a celebrity whose fame rubs off even on his antagonists and
captors, a victim of self-delusions, potentially a victim of childhood
abuse, a homosexual whose violence is a product of brutal external and
internal repression.[16] Reviewers have commented on the oppressive
effect that being in the same room with Haarmann, and with George, an

aggressive, confrontational actor, for 110 minutes has on the viewer. There is something simultaneously austere and overwhelmingly assaultive about the film, reminiscent of the verbal barrages and relentless bleakness that David Mamet's audience must at times endure. Karmakar's direction manages to give the viewer, at the same time, too much and too little—an appropriate strategy considering the theme of the film, the exploration of a personality outside the bounds of human imagination. The film's willingness to ignore the rules of mainstream cinema, which also makes it specifically non-American in the eyes of German viewers, is reminiscent of earlier German auteur cinema, such as that of Fassbinder, Herzog, or early Wenders.[17]

Karmakar's turning away from the mainstream also manifests itself in his choice of subject matter. Unlike the fictional Kupfer in *Der Sandmann*, Haarmann is a historical figure, and an extremely well known one at that. Rainer Marwedel, in his foreword to Theodor Lessing's essay about the trial, calls the Haarmann case "a piece of entertainment history of the Weimar Republic."[18] Fritz Lang's 1931 film *M*, for example, opens with a group of children skipping rope to the song "Warte, warte nur ein Weilchen / Bald kommt der schwarze Mann zu dir / mit dem kleinen Hackebeilchen / macht er Schabefleisch aus dir" ("Wait, just wait a little while / Then the Black Man will come to you / With his little axe / He'll make minced meat out of you"). In German popular culture, "Haarmann" will come to replace the more generic "Black Man" (today, most Germans are probably familiar with the later version).[19] Most of Haarmann's contemporaries were paying close attention to the case in the media: "While the name Haarmann … does not appear in the standard cultural histories of Weimar Germany, it can be found with astonishing frequency in newspapers of the time. … When Lang released his film in 1931, and Döblin published his novel in 1929 [*Berlin Alexanderplatz*], both could count on general familiarity with the case of Fritz Haarmann, a serial murderer executed in 1925."[20] Karmakar's film, though based on historical events, cannot help fictionalizing the serial murderer. But the Haarmann in the film is a fictional character deeply embedded in Germany's history and collective cultural memory. Karmakar can therefore assume a certain degree of familiarity with the figure and his story, not so much based on exact historical records, but on the history of fictional representations set in motion by the events themselves, and their records.

At the expense of the popular and the sensational, Karmakar points his audience back toward history. We are supposed to remember Haarmann not as a generic monster adaptable to such totalizing abstractions as "pure evil," but as the product of specific historical and social circumstances. Some reviewers have remarked on the conspicuous absence of the Haarmann song ("Warte, warte nur ein Weilchen") in the film. A reference to the song would have established Haarmann as a more fictional figure, a fabrication either of modern folklore, or, more specifically, of a cinematic tradition that begins with *M*. Karmakar fails to provide the intertextual nod, instead opening the film with the Ludwig Uhland song, "Der gute Kamerad." The song opens with the words, "Ich hatte einen Kameraden, einen bess'ren findst du nicht" (I had a comrade, you won't find a better one"), a line that accomplishes precisely the opposite of the "Black Man" song, emphasizing Haarmann's humanity rather than demonizing him.

These small gestures signal Karmakar's intent not to de-historicize Haarmann, but to claim him as a uniquely German phenomenon. In the beginning of the film, George's appearance is highly reminiscent of Adolf Hitler. In later scenes, Haarmann's street clothes have been replaced with a prison uniform, and his head has been shaved, all of which makes him look like a concentration camp victim. Whereas Haarmann's mixture of murderous insanity and cold methodical premeditation makes him resemble the Nazis, his homosexuality would have cast him among their victims. He served his time in the German Imperial Army, learns some of his violence from books (he uses an ax, "like the Indians do it"), and regrets his murders after committing them, even to the point of making himself physically sick by remembering their details. Schultze's questions, aimed at establishing his patient's connection to the real world, refer to the river Rhine as a German border that has been heavily contested since the Versailles Treaty, and to the disappearance of the German emperor and the subsequent government under Fritz Ebert. Haarmann, in turn, compares himself to Napoleon in exile, or to Jesus Christ, whose sacrifice is demanded by the Jews. The specific nature of these questions and the answers, random as the former and delusional as the latter may be, point toward a historical background that makes Haarmann an uncanny prefiguration of Germany's future descent into fascism. Again, the film does not provide easy answers in constructing these parallels. Haarmann alternates between delusions of grandeur and moments of genuine vulnerability, while there is always the possibility that either response, or both, are just fabrications. The only fact the film establishes beyond the shadow of a doubt is that his victims are dead.

The subtle differences between Haarmann as historical figure and Haarmann as Karmakar's film constructs him are of great importance here. The psychologist Theodor Lessing, a contemporary witness to the police investigation and subsequent trial, sees Haarmann as the product of a modernity specifically defined by the inhumanity of World War I and its aftermath. Writing in 1925, before the massive rise of fascism in Germany, Lessing notes that "in order to comprehend [Haarmann's] atrocities by looking at their external circumstances, we must remember in which condition law enforcement was in all of Europe at the end of five years of slaughter; in those days when, in plain view of 'cultured society,' over a million people starved to death."[21] Haarmann simply "reenacts on a small scale what five heroic war years already presented us with on a large scale," which is why Lessing diagnoses Haarmann as an exemplar of modernity: human beings as "wolves with radios and electricity, cannibals in nice underwear and elegant clothes."[22] Writing with historical hindsight, Marwedel adds the following:

> It is possible, Lessing said back then without much prophetic grandeur, that a time is coming when mass murderers of Haarmann's caliber won't attract much attention any more but may be considered mere amateurs. On the day the verdict was announced, anyone buying the evening edition of a newspaper could read, next to the headline and commentaries about Haarmann's death sentence, two special bulletins: "Hitler Released" / "A New Mass Murderer?"[23]

Contrary to this characterization of Haarmann as a prototypical modernist (Lessing) or fascist (Marwedel), Karmakar's allegory aims at entering the public debate concerning the Third Reich. *Der Totmacher* is not primarily concerned with German fascism; it is concerned with how Germany after 1945 conducts the debate about fascism. Or, to be more precise, how this debate may still be conducted after fifty years have yielded a vast array of positions, arguments, and confrontations. Establishing Haarmann as a radically ambiguous character, *Der Totmacher* is a film that suits the Germany of the mid-1990s particularly well because it neglects the question of what Haarmann's motivation for his murders could have been.[24] To address this question in the hopes of arriving at a satisfactory answer seems to strike Karmakar as a somewhat anachronistic endeavor. Why even raise the issue when sixty years of public discussion have buried the possibility of resolving it under their crushing weight? By the 1990s, most commentators would probably agree that the question is better seen as an end in itself, useful because it sustains an important continuing debate, not because it will eventually yield a final answer. Hence, the answer to this question is identified as unattainable from the outset. The serial killer remains a mystery, and all attempts at explaining his pathology must fall short of our expectations, either because he is endlessly duplicitous and unreliable, or because his reasons are inaccessible even to himself. After sitting through the entire film, we know as little about Haarmann's motivation as we did in the beginning. What we are left with is the discussion, having witnessed the transcription of narrative accounts into the historical record. "Er hat eine schöne Hand" ("He has a beautiful hand" or "He has beautiful handwriting"), Haarmann comments with predatory ambiguity on the handwriting of the stenographer at one point. Haarmann has become a story, fascinating or horrid. The film is not about determining the motive for excessive violence; it is about living in continued ignorance, and about how to rescue from absurdity a debate conducted in ignorance in the presence of millions of dead.

The dialogue of *Der Totmacher* opens with these words, spoken by Haarmann: "Das wissen Sie doch" ("You know all that already."). The words are spoken during a scene of the interrogation in which the interrogator is not visible; later he is revealed to be Schultze. Haarmann is compelled to answer to the bodiless voice of authority, which has not yet been identified for the viewer as either that of a doctor, police officer, or psychiatrist; an interrogation reminiscent in equal parts of Kafka and Althusser.[25] Placed in such an exposed position within the film, the statement is programmatic in several different ways. In terms of the historical allegory mentioned previously, the challenge is issued by a voice demanding a moral account of history. But it is also a statement addressed to an audience that is familiar with the serial killer as the hero of a popular genre. It presupposes that viewers going to see *Der Totmacher* will arrive with a set of expectations formed by mainstream cinema and its conventions. A film dealing with a figure like Fritz Haarmann must operate and define itself inside the boundaries of such a cultural field. The unusual balance Karmakar strikes between genre conformity and genre violation is a creative response to this familiarity, simultaneously bearing out the genre and revising it.

Not only in terms of historical allegory does the statement address the audience as specifically German, affirming the status of this story as a shared cultural memory. Obviously, the presence of Fritz Haarmann alone does not suffice to make this a specifically German film; after all, *Citizen X*, the HBO production discussed earlier, features a serial killer in the Soviet Union, yet still manages to be a uniquely American production. In fact, it would be quite easy to imagine an American film about the Haarmann case, staffed with Americans, budgeted as any big Hollywood production, and following a mainstream aesthetic.

The Germanness of German Serial Killer Films

Since the aesthetics of mainstream cinema are no longer exclusively American, as Hofmann's *Der Sandmann* makes clear, a more intertextual approach in reading these films is needed to bring out what makes them so uniquely German. This intertextual approach is all the more important because neither one of the German films I am discussing here actually features the theme of American uniqueness. Neither *Der Sandmann* nor *Der Totmacher* makes explicit reference to America as the source or proper place of serial murder. Karmakar presents Haarmann, the butcher from Hanover in the 1920s, anchored firmly in his time and place, while Hofmann shows us a contemporary Germany that may look like America, but only to the degree that most industrial nations around the end of the twentieth century look alike anyway—slick, sleek, post-modern. If my initial observation about the trope of American uniqueness is true, and this trope indeed constitutes an essential part of the serial killer genre, then it should be articulated differently in these two films.

These films must be seen in the context of a German culture in the postwar period that, especially since the late 1960s, has been struggling with its relationship to America and American popular culture. Beginning with the Marshall Plan, and reaching into the present with the GATT negotiations in the second half of the 1990s, America has imported its popular culture into Germany at an astonishing rate.[26] Despite some minor fluctuations, massive political changes, and individual acts of consumer disobedience, German audiences on the whole tend to embrace U.S. pop culture.[27] This results in a competitive situation for German producers, which, especially for the German film industry, is a race they cannot possibly win without some sort of government regulation. A number of the people involved in the films discussed here, especially Götz George, have made no secret of their skepticism toward Hollywood's ability, and intention, to dominate the German market. George has openly advocated establishing a quota for American films, following the French model. He has also proposed granting American films access to the German market with a temporal delay, so that German productions have a better chance of attracting the attention of audiences. Director Hofmann rejects the quota model, but after issuing a general endorsement of open competition ("as long as a film is any good, it'll do well"), he adds the following reservation: "Of course, the Americans are trying to occupy the German market. They deliberately started *Saving Private Ryan* against us [i.e., Hofmann's 1998 film *Solo für Klarinette*, featuring George in the lead role once again], and as a result we postponed our release by one week. For that, they're now having problems getting *Small Soldiers* (1998) into the theaters because we're already in there."[28] It is hardly far-fetched to assume that this same attitude, which manifests itself in such logistical maneuvering and strategic thinking, must also play a part in the selection and handling of filmic genres, especially when they are specifically marked as "American" (and thus as "Hollywood").

This economic and political context plays itself out as an ongoing public debate that also reaches the broader film audience and influences its responses to the films in question. The effect of this context on such an audience may be attenuated in comparison to that on German directors and actors, yet it constitutes one crucial factor in the individual and collective perception of movies. Although German filmmakers do not collectively reject, or even express hostility toward, American pictures (as *Der Sandmann* and many other German productions demonstrate), the question of a uniquely German cultural identity is inextricably linked with how a film looks and how it tells its story.

The challenge of representing the figure of the serial killer, then, raises the question whether there even is a distinctly German cinematic tradition for directors like Hofmann and Karmakar to fall back on. As Jenkins demonstrates, there is certainly a history of serial murder in Germany, with cases such as those of Grossman, Denke, Kürten, Ludke, Seefeld, Pleil, and Haarmann. And all of these cases have provided the media with ample opportunity to invest the murderer with that fascination and mystique familiar to most American audiences. There are also German films about serial killers, ranging from Lang's *M* to Uli Lommel's *Die Zärtlichkeit der Wölfe* (*The Tenderness of the Wolves*, 1973; this latter one dealing with Fritz Haarmann as well). In short, popular culture—theoretically speaking—provides the material necessary for construing an indigenous cinematic serial killer genre.

What is absent from the two films I have been discussing is the sense that they are elaborating on the figure of the serial killer as a foundational element of a specifically German tradition, that is, of a genre other than the American one. With the decision not even to include an intertextual link to Fritz Haarmann's cinematic precursors, Karmakar explicitly steers away from genre signals altogether. He sacrifices Haarmann's popular perception in order to increase his historical specificity. To the degree that genre is always, overtly or not, intertextual in nature, Karmakar cuts himself off rather dramatically from the option of conceiving of *Der Totmacher* in generic terms at all, turning his film into an exploration of German (discursive) history that may be quite difficult to grasp for an American audience.

Hofmann conforms superficially to American genre conventions, but then inverts them in order to expose the ideological and pragmatic agenda behind such conventional perceptions. The agenda he discovers concealed behind the serial killer genre is that of moral bankruptcy and economic exploitation as established facts of contemporary German society. That these conventions are borrowed from a genre of American cinema, which, to boot, internalizes them in the trope of American exceptionalism, is hardly a coincidence, given the perception that "America leads the way" when it comes to economic progress and its social consequences. Hofmann's film reiterates the dictum of American exceptionalism but, seeing America in largely dystopian terms, strips it of its characteristic perverse sense of pride. *Der Sandmann* picks up on the theme of the accomplished post-modernization of Germany, exploring it not only temporally but spatially as well. Germany's past, which might otherwise have provided models for an alternative present, has been reabsorbed into the post-modern flow of commodification; with the globalization of American popular culture, alternative spaces have also been absorbed. There is no longer "a different time" or "a different place." In one sense of the term, American exceptionalism becomes absurd when American culture has successfully gone global; every place will in fact be like every other place. Feeding the trope back into the genre after it has been pushed to this point of absurdity, Hofmann's film denies the cherished status of global cultural vanguard to its American precursors. Such belligerent lack of respect issues a challenge to American genre cinema to rethink itself along these lines, hopefully with the result that the formula in question will begin to undergo change.

Notes

1. Quoted in Jane Caputi, "American Psychos: The Serial Killer in Contemporary Fiction," *Journal of American Culture* 16, no. 4 (1993): 101–12. The statistical record has

likely been adjusted since then to match a changing national and global reality. I would argue, however, that whatever the changes in the statistical record may be, the image of America as cradle of serial murder remains unchanged. Richard Slotkin, in his *Regeneration through Violence: The Mythology of the American Frontier, 1600–1860* (New York: HarperCollins, 1996), makes this extraordinary resistance to change a distinctive feature of myth. While "the [mythical] images may readily exhibit changes in response to the play of social and psychological forces," Slotkin observes (and, I would add, to historical and political changes as well), "the narrative or narratives which relate them to each other have or acquire a certain fixity of form," 9.

2. Caputi, "American Psychos," 112.

3. Philip Jenkins, *Using Murder: The Social Construction of Serial Homicide* (New York: DeGruyter, 1994). "In addition," he writes, "contemporary American rates are not that unusual compared with some past societies with high rates of serial homicide, most notably Germany in the early twentieth century," 42–43.

4. Historical events and their social effects, Jenkins suggests, have been to the killers' advantage ("The chaos of the war years allowed [Georg Karl Grossman] to kill unmolested," [Jenkins, *Using Murder*, 43]).

5. Ibid., 44

6. For a detailed discussion of Demme's use of American iconography in *The Silence of the Lambs*, see Steffen Hantke, "'The Kingdom of the Unimaginable': The Construction of Social Space and the Fantasy of Privacy in Serial Killer Narratives," *Literature Film Quarterly* 26, no. 3 (1998): 178–96.

7. Philip Simpson, *Psycho Paths: Tracking the Serial Killer through Contemporary American Film and Fiction* (Carbondale: Southern Illinois University Press, 2000), 124. The political subtext here requires little effort to decode. Simpson adds acerbically, "For the American television audience, at least dimly aware of the political transformation of the Russian nation a few years before and certainly aware of the United States' self-congratulatory assumption of total political credit for that change, *Citizen X* centers on the former Soviet Union's communist bureaucracy as the ideal ethnocentric metaphor for man's hatred of his own need of organizational existence. The system is the enemy. The heroic profiler is its redeemer," 123.

8. Wendy Lesser, *Pictures at an Execution: An Inquiry into the Subject of Murder* (Cambridge: Harvard University Press, 1993), 117. Lesser's comment is made specifically in reference to Dostoyevsky's *Crime and Punishment*.

9. In 1995, the film was one of the most successful productions for its commissioning channel, RTL2. Both George and Hofmann were awarded the Adolf Grimme Award in 1996; the film won the Golden Lion Award for best made-for-TV movie, best director for Hofmann, and best actor for George; Karoline Eichhorn won the Silver Lion; Hofmann also won the Bavarian Television Award in 1996.

10. This translation from the original German, as well as that of other primary and secondary sources to follow, are the author's own.

11. Which also means that there is not going to be a sequel. For a more detailed list of genre conventions, see Hantke, "The Kingdom of the Unimaginable," 1998.

12. Simpson, *Psycho Paths*, 89.

13. Three other characters make brief appearances in the film, but their significance (as far as the present discussion is concerned) is very minor. *Der Totmacher*

earned George another award, this time at the 52nd Cannes Film Festival, for best actor.

14. For a more detailed discussion of seriality as a form of biological, social, and textual reproduction, see Steffen Hantke, "Murder in the Age of Technical Reproduction: Serial Killer Narratives as 'Seminal Texts,'" *theory@buffalo: an interdisciplinary journal* (Fall 1996): 89–107.

15. Karmakar leaves one small narrative opening for ambiguity, however. In the last interview shown in the film, Schultze tells Haarmann that he will come to visit him one more time before his execution. Since he has demonstrated that he is a man of principle, there is no reason to assume he does not keep his word. This encounter between the two men is not a part of the film, nor does the film make reference to it in dialogue. Placed at the very end, it haunts the narrative as a crucial absence. The film's reticence to reveal anything about this final encounter seems atypical enough to suggest its significance.

16. Karmakar and his star George borrow some of these strategies from Fritz Lang and Peter Lorre. In their depiction of Hans Beckert, the serial murderer in *M* (1931), they incorporate the same contradictions George invests Haarmann with. These contradictions can have unforeseen consequences. Maria Tatar, for example, in her *Lustmord: Sexual Murder in Weimar Germany* (Princeton: Princeton University Press, 1995), mentions that a shot of Jewish actor Lorre's "panicked response . . . to his capture" was "spliced into a piece of Nazi propaganda," 170–71. Stripped of their essential humanity, criminals were inflated beyond all reasonable proportion by the Nazis, and with it the evil they represented. Criminals were superhuman and thus warranted increased fear and paranoia, and, at the same time, less than human, opening the door to cold-blooded extermination. Lang's film also features a scene in which Beckert has the opportunity to defend himself, and in this dramatic monologue he makes himself out to be the victim of his own pathological urges. This ability to declare the perpetrator of violence a victim, Tatar explains, was also a welcome addition to German fascism's political rhetoric: "For the Nazis, it was easy enough to take advantage of the demonizing discursive strategies surrounding criminality, just as it was possible to tap into notions of bloodletting (in this case, not their own blood but the blood of the Jews) as a kind of purifying ritual that turned the murderer into a paragon of heroic self-sacrifice," 172.

17. An online article by Sibylle Peine ("Ich habe es nur für mich gemacht" [September 19, 2000], http://mainz-online.de/freizeit/kino/film/totmacher/kitotmac.html, accessed September 5, 2003) mentions George admitting to the risks that the film takes in alienating its audience. The consensus among journalists that the film successfully negotiates the possibility of complete financial failure is echoed in George's statement that his own enormous investment of time and energy into the project—Haarmann's role in *Der Totmacher* is a veritable tour de force—was basically just to prove to himself that he still "had it in him."

18. Rainer Marwedel, "Von Schlachthoefen und Schlachtfeldern," in Theodor Lessing, *Haarmann: Die Geschichte eines Werwolfs, und andere Gerichtsreportagen*, ed. and intro. Rainer Marwedel (Munich: Deutscher Taschenbuch Verlag, 1995), 7.

19. Although Lang's version does not mention Haarmann by name, a subsequent version does, replacing "the Black Man" with "Haarmann." Both versions go back to

the 1923 operetta by Walter and Willi Kollo, titled *Marietta*, where the original verse is: "Warte, warte nur ein Weilchen / bald kommt auch das Glück zu dir / mit dem ersten blauen Veilchen / klopft es leise an die Tür" ("Wait, just wait a little while / Soon, love will come to you, too / With the first blue periwinkle / It will knock upon your door"). The reference to Haarmann "making minced meat out of you" is due to the police's well-founded suspicion that Haarmann, a butcher by trade, actually used some of his victims' bodies in his products. Apart from having become a staple in the pop pathology of serial murder in subsequent years (e.g., "Hannibal the Cannibal"), the cannibalism reference also goes back to the fictional Henry Kupfer in *Der Sandmann,* whose latest book about a German serial murderer is called *Der Kannibale.*

20. Tatar, *Lustmord,* 3.
21. Lessing, *Haarmann,* 77.
22. Ibid., 180.
23. Marwedel, "Von Schlachthoefen und Schlachtfeldern," 12.
24. "Let's leave aside all questions about 'legal sanity,' 'responsibility,' and 'madness' for the time being," Lessing reminds his contemporaries. "All readers must be cautioned not to mistake things that are complicated for simple ones, and simple things for the complicated ones that clinical psychology inevitably must resort to, being obsessed with fitting everything into neat clinical 'types' and working with quickly found words of wisdom, often derived from Greek and Latin, that are often as quickly outdated again," *Haarmann,* 80.
25. *The Minus Man* (USA, 1999), based on a novel by Lew McCreary, elaborates on the theme of interrogation. The police force the serial killer into a dialogue that is such a powerful constituent of his actions that he actually imagines them, filling them in voluntarily as long as the police fail to catch up with him. If we see these scenes of dialogue as forms of Althusserian interpellation, then they are in fact as necessary as the killer thinks, integrating his actions into a larger symbolic order where they finally acquire significance.
26. See, for example, the 1996 Foreign Trade Barriers Report, online at http://www.usinfo.state.gov/journals/ites/0496/ijef/ej24a.htm, accessed September 5, 2003.
27. Consider the protest against John Milius's 1984 film *Red Dawn* on grounds of political disagreement with U.S. cold war politics (the stationing of nuclear short-range missiles in Germany in the mid-1980s as part of a hastening of the arms race, and the general dissent within NATO about cold war politics); or of protests against Tom Cruise films as part of the German debate about the legality of Scientology.
28. The full text of these interviews can be read at the following Web sites: George's comments at http://rheinzeitung.de/freizeit/kino/galerie/solofuerklarinette/ interview-george.html, accessed September 5, 2003, and Hofmann's comments at http://www.s-trip.de/html/www/kino/151098/klarinette/interview.htm, accessed September 5, 2003.

II

Haunting Histories and Regional Gothics

4

The Return of History as Horror:
ONIBABA AND THE ATOMIC BOMB

Jyotsna Kapur

Japanese filmmakers have struggled with the question of how to represent a nuclear war since Hiroshima and Nagasaki, a question whose relevance extends to the challenges of depicting the unprecedented human slaughters of the twentieth century. The quest is fundamentally radical since it combines formal innovation with political content as opposed to the simplistic notion that formal radicalism is in itself politically radical. This essay concerns one particular text and its reworking of the horror film genre to represent the atomic bomb: Shindo Kaneto's *Onibaba* (1964). The power of this film lies in Shindo's transformation of the conventions of cinematic horror into a political allegory of war as an outcome of class conflict and patriarchy.

Shindo uses allegory, the power to visualize a figurative expression, to invoke the past as horror, as layers that are only slumbering under the present. The ghosts and spirits that haunt the Japanese horror film in the guise of the supernatural are refigured in *Onibaba* into creatures of this world. Thus, a form based on superstition and fate is turned into a rallying cry for changing the present, specifically Japan in the 1960s, caught between an imperial past and a post-industrial future. Close reading of the film offers a convincing lesson about the barbarism of history, the possibilities of the horror genre as a political allegory, and the importance of allegory within a Marxist tradition of filmmaking. Allegory, if made historical, can be a profoundly powerful turn of speech, used evocatively by Karl Marx (for example) to describe capital as a "Juggernaut" that drove the peasantry into factory labor and arrived "dripping from head to foot, from every pore, with blood and dirt."[1] Shindo's experiments with both allegory and a popular genre like the horror film are significant for a discussion of socialist cultural practices, since the Left has largely tended to reject popular forms. In this discussion, Shindo's continued involvement with the Japanese Left film movement will prove helpful in contextualizing his work within a socialist aesthetic politics, and more specifically in the continuities and departures between the postwar Left and the 1960s Japanese New Wave.

The Japanese Left Film Movement

The Japanese Left film movement thought of itself as part of a larger socialist movement, and its growth corresponds with this movement's ebbs and flows. The earliest Japanese leftist film group, Prokino (The Proletarian Film League), was founded in 1929, bringing together artists from film, literature, and theater. Although the group disbanded in just a few years, interest in its activities was rekindled most strongly with the coming of the Japanese New Wave, which, as David Desser has demonstrated, was grounded in the mass protests against the renewal of the U.S.–Japan Mutual Security Treaty in 1960.[2] In the 1920s the thrust of the Left was against the feudal regime of the emperor, while in the 1960s it was against U.S. Occupation, under which those who had led the country to war—both in the military and industry—were seen as returning to power. Ironically, it was the political reform process initiated by the U.S. Occupation in 1945, including the legalization of the Communist Party and the right to form labor unions, that enabled socialist politics to emerge as a public force.

Such reforms were short-lived, however, and were reversed in the summer of 1948 under the Red Purge, which included the withdrawal of the right to strike and the dismissal of union activists from their jobs.[3] Subsequently, a strong socialist party emerged out of the protests against the signing of the security treaty between Japan and the United States in 1951, which made Japan dependent on the American military and ensured a continued U.S. military presence in Japan. The protests peaked in November 1955, when the Japanese government allowed the United States to extend the runways at the base in Sunakawa to accommodate new and larger jets, thus displacing the farmers who lived in that region.

The 1960s saw another mass resurgence of political protest (unmatched since) against the renewal of the U.S.–Japan treaty—a protest in which Oshima Nagisa and Hani Susumu, among other New Wave filmmakers, directly participated. Desser has argued that the aesthetic of the Japanese New Wave "repudiated individualist tragedy and encouraged alienation—alienation from the specific characters in this specific film and alienation from the culture at large."[4] Such an aesthetic makes sense only in light of the betrayal experienced by the filmmakers of Oshima's generation of liberal humanism and communism to bring about any substantial change inside Japan, and the failure to prevent the return of imperialism. The treaty was signed in 1960 and so, at its very outset, the Japanese New Wave was marked by a deep sense of failure and self-introspection.

Shindo Kaneto's career spans the old Left and the New Wave with the atomic bomb remaining a major theme despite censorship and the difficulties of the subject itself. In examining Shindo's representations of the bomb, we can see a shift from the realist aesthetic of the old Left to the formal distanciation of the Japanese New Wave. While the latter movement, as Desser has shown, strove to break away from preceding generations, Oshima acknowledged Shindo as an old master who continued to be "furiously creative."[5] What has remained consistent throughout Shindo's career is his passionate engagement with the atomic bomb theme, and a particular understanding of distanciation according to which he seeks audience identification using well-known genre conventions without allowing viewers to escape from the real world into the fictional world of the story. It is through allegory that Shindo follows Bertolt Brecht's dictum to leftist artists to be ever-mindful that while the spectator sits in the theater, that theater sits in the world; that the work of art is ultimately to make the audience want to change the world, not escape it.

Shindo's Early Work

Born in 1912 in Hiroshima, which partly explains his involvement with representing the A-bomb, Shindo has continued to speak out against war, seeing it as an outcome of imperialism among nations and internal class warfare. After the September 11 tragedy in New York, Shindo reiterated his views on the cold-blooded use of Hiroshima and Nagasaki as testing grounds for imperialistic warfare:

> Hiroshima and Nagasaki happened during wartime, but Hiroshima and Nagasaki were not battlefields. Atomic bombs were dropped without any warning where people were going about their daily lives. There was an outcry after the terrorist attacks in New York that five thousand people had died. But in Hiroshima and Nagasaki two hundred thousand people were killed without warning. Atomic bombing is a crime. The US bombers loaded with the atomic bomb and

fuel were promised a year off in Tenyan. When the Enola Gay was
to take off, a war pastor prayed to God for the mission to be successful . . . for the plan to kill two hundred thousand people without
warning. When President Truman was in wild joy after hearing that
the mission was completely successful Hiroshima was a hell.[6]

Shindo's first film effort was a script for *Nagasaki no Kane* (*The Bells of
Nagasaki,* 1950), directed by Hideo Oba. It was based on the life of a
Christian nuclear scientist, Dr. Takashi Nagai of Nagasaki, who died of
radiation at the age of forty-three, while his wife had died in Hiroshima.
The Civil Information and Education Section censored the original
script, making it necessary for Shindo to rewrite it two times. According
to Kyoko Hirano, Shindo had to include a lengthy opening statement that
blamed the bombing on Japanese militarism, omit the scenes depicting
Nagai's wife's death after the bombing, and Nagai's efforts to save her.[7] In
the completed film, the bombing was merely suggested in a scene in which
Nagai's children see the mushroom cloud in the sky over the city from
which they have been evacuated.

     Notably, Shindo made the first Japanese film on the atomic bomb—
Children of Hiroshima (1953)—to be released after the end of U.S.
Occupation. He was commissioned by the Japan Teachers Union, a
communist-leaning group, to make the picture. In keeping with the pre-
dominant Left aesthetic of the 1950s, *Children of Hiroshima* was a realist
docudrama in which Shindo cast actual survivors of the bomb. It follows
a young teacher (Nobuko Otowa) who returns to Hiroshima seven years
after the bombing to find that only three of her entire kindergarten class
has survived. She finds the first mourning the death of his father, the second celebrating his sister's wedding but whose parents were killed, and the
third on her deathbed from radioactivity. She ends up adopting the grandson of her father's former employee, who is now blind and survives by begging. In order to make his grandson leave with the teacher, the man sets
himself on fire asking that his body be given for research. The Union
rejected the film, calling it a tearjerker that negated the political implications of the bomb.[8] In my view too, the film sentimentalizes the middle-
class teacher's concern for the children and provides cathartic resolutions,
such as the teacher's eventual adoption of the survivor's grandson.

     Shindo's next effort was *Lucky Dragon No. 5* (1958), which drama-
tized the radioactive contamination of the crew of a Japanese tuna boat
following the 1953 explosion of the hydrogen bomb in the Pacific by the

United States. This film was made on the heels of large-scale Japanese protests against the tests and the use of Japan as a testing ground even after the American occupation had officially ended. With *Onibaba,* however, Shindo abandoned realism. His subsequent film on the A-bomb, *Honno* (*Lost Sex,* 1966), tells the story of a young man made impotent by the bomb who is restored to manhood by his housekeeper. We thus see that not only did Shindo move from realism toward an aesthetic of distanciation, he also combined a political critique of class and imperialism with one of gender and sexuality—a move that Desser has identified as particular to the Japanese New Wave. In fact, a fundamental critique the New Wave filmmakers made of the old Left was that its revolutionary imagination was poor when it came to questions of sexuality.

Children of Hiroshima had tried to approximate the documentary form. Besides the casting of actual survivors, the film is clearly located in time and space—in Hiroshima, seven years after the bombing. Right after the end of the Occupation, Shindo and his crew spent forty-nine days on location in Hiroshima filming parts of the city that were still in ruins. The central character, an ordinary schoolteacher who is also a survivor, stands in for the everyday person. As she returns to Hiroshima, her voiceover introduces us to the city and the film's subject: "This is Hiroshima, where the first victims of the atomic bomb died on August 6, 1945. Her beautiful rivers flow just as they did on that fateful day. Her beautiful sky is just as big as it was on that fateful day. Children of that time are now grown and the devastated city rebuilt." For most of the film, spectator identification with the bomb victims is encouraged through realist representation. We are given details of the ongoing suffering of the survivors—emotional trauma, physical deterioration due to radiation poisoning, an inability to bear children, and the courage of the surviving children and adults.

However, the film's realist aesthetic is rejected in the portrayal of the actual bombing. Shindo shows the moment of bombing by juxtaposing the sound of a clock with children doing their morning exercises in the schoolyard and a bomber in the sky. The sound of the clock changes to slow, sad music rendered by a female chorus (composed by Akira Ifukube, better known for scoring *Gojira* [1954]) over an image of people moving in a manner akin to the Japanese underground dance known as Butoh.[9] The stylized dance movements are violent and sexual, depicting human bodies weighed down by gravity, like corpses standing upright. In *Onibaba,* by contrast, Shindo eschews realism throughout, moving the narrative away from a specific location and individuals to talk about history in more allegorical terms. The conventions of the horror genre are particularly effective here since history can be embodied in the external world surrounding the characters, creating an atmosphere that rustles and pulsates with antagonism.

Onibaba

The film begins with a long shot of reeds swaying in the wind with the following text: "This story based on an old legend is of war and tragedy, of the primitive beneath the civilized veneer." The next shot is from the bottom of a dark hole toward the light, the text reading "Black hole, deep and dark. Since ancient times its darkness has lasted." What follows is a dynamic example of graphic montage foreshadowing a story of horror, energy, and barbarism. To the sound of cries and drumbeats, the reeds come to life as the camera changes direction between shots—the reeds move from right to left in one shot and left to right in another. Movement is also emphasized by changes in distance (from a long shot to an extreme close-up) and lighting (from lighter to darker tones). The reeds overwhelm two figures on horseback who charge at each other from opposite ends. This is intercut with close-ups of their faces, one young and the other old, both samurai. As they collapse from sheer exhaustion we see a point-of-view shot of the open sky. This moment of stillness is suddenly pierced by three arrows that kill both samurai to the loud beating of drums—taking the viewer as much by surprise as the samurai. From an extreme low-angle shot that make the reeds appear claustrophobic and prison-like, we see the feet of two women as they circle their prey and tear apart their clothes. The next few shots of the women removing the samurai's armor and throwing their corpses into the dark hole are intercut with a shot of vultures on the dried-out branch of a dead tree and the opening shot of the hole from outside.

Onibaba's plot centers on two peasant women, a mother (Nobuko Otowa) and her daughter-in-law (Jitsuko Yoshimura), who survive a medieval war by killing lost and wandering samurai and selling their armor for food. After killing them, they dump the bodies into the large black hole—the same one that opens the film. While the businessman who buys and sells the samurai armor thrives on war, the two women barely survive it, literally clinging to life amidst the harsh and barren reeds. Their partnership is threatened with the arrival of a young man, Hachi (Kei Sato), friend of the older woman's son and the younger woman's husband, whom he tells them is now dead. Upon his arrival Hachi demands food and soon afterward the younger woman as a sexual partner. As the two begin to have sex, the older woman fears being abandoned and threatens Hachi with death; she also offers to have sex with him. Nothing works until one day a strange figure comes into the old woman's hut while the daughter-in-law is away. It is a samurai wearing a frightening mask. The samurai asks her to show him the way through the reeds, and obsessed with the desire to see his face she cunningly leads him to his death in the dark hole. In one of the film's most stunning moments, the old woman removes the mask only to see the face of a bomb victim, or *hibakusha*.

The old woman then begins to wear the mask so as to waylay the daughter-in-law on her nightly visits to Hachi. During the day she tells the younger woman horrific tales of severe punishments meted out to those who have extramarital sex. The daughter-in-law, terrified of the mask, begins to believe the woman's tales of divine punishment but is burned by the desire to see Hachi. One dark, stormy night she forces her way to Hachi's house, leaving the masked woman alone and defeated. In another of the film's more terrifying moments, the old woman finds that the mask is now stuck to her face. Upon her begging and pleading, the younger woman breaks open the mask with an axe. What she unmasks is the bleeding, tortured face of an alive *hibakusha,* from whom she flees in revulsion. The film ends with three repeat shots of the old woman jumping over the black hole behind the younger woman, crying "I am not a demon, I am a human being."

Onibaba's mise en scène is constructed around two motifs—the mask and the reeds. The reeds are a character in themselves, filling the screen with the opposing energies of an extremely hostile and savage external world and the throbbing human desire for an end to economic scarcity and sexual oppression. The tension is heightened by moments of stillness when the reeds stand motionless in suspense—as witness to this human drama and the unpredictability of the outcome of the struggle. Sometimes watching and waiting, at other times swaying fiercely, the reeds transform the narrative from being character-centered to an allegory about history. The morning after Hachi first visits the women, the reeds stand still in the bright sunlight. So does the water where the daughter-in-law washes clothes. The light reflects off of the young woman's face while Hachi approaches her and eyes her lustily. A long shot reveals the older woman at the end of the pier eyeing the pair suspiciously. This

Mother (Nobuko Otowa) and daughter-in-law (Jitsuko Yoshimura) remove their victims' bodies in *Onibaba* (1964)

moment of stillness is dramatically interrupted by the arrival of two samurai and a loud beating of drums, during which time the three act quickly to kill the two samurai in unison. The peasants act together against the samurai but an uneasy truce exists among them—for three cannot survive in this hostile environment.

The reeds also echo sexual desire. The first time the young woman goes to meet Hachi at night she runs through the reeds in dead silence. However, as she tears through the reeds the sounds of their rustling accentuates the urgency of her passion. The camera alternates between long shots to extreme close-ups of her feet and the reeds. The dynamism of sexual energy is further heightened through a change of direction. In a trio of quickly edited shots, the woman first appears to come to the foreground from the center, then from left to right, and then in a jump-cut from screen left to right. The next shot is back inside the hut, where the straw door sways in the wind—evoking the young woman's absence—and the camera pans to reveal the older woman waking up. The sexual energy of the young couple, dramatized by the swaying reeds (each lit almost as if from within), is contrasted with the threadbare curtain woven of the same reeds, now unable to guard the old woman's helpless isolation. While the empty shots in Yasujiro Ozu's films serve as a means of evoking *mono no aware*—a meditative detachment that is supposed to underline the transient nature of this world—in this instance such shots serve to both heighten tension and emphasize the world in which the characters are trapped, thus locating their psychological motivations in a historical context.[10]

The mask is the second motif around which *Onibaba*'s mise en scène is constructed, Shindo here taking a page from the conventional horror movie. But the demonic mask is transformed in this film into a cover for the disfigured face of the *hibakusha*. This is a brilliant move, for the burnt faces of the *hibakusha* were stigmatized in Japan and thought of as subhuman, faces that their owners hid or masked and from which the younger generation fled. As John Dower elaborates, in the years after World War II the most desperate members of the population—bomb victims, war veterans, war widows, orphans, the mentally ill—became Japan's new outcasts.[11] There was no social responsibility assumed toward these suffering people who haunted public places until the late 1950s; perhaps the humiliation of defeat, the scarcity of resources, and the relentless pursuit of economic development were all factors in their mistreatment. So culturally widespread was this stigmatization that it seems to have been internalized by the victims themselves. In a comic book series, "Hadashi no Gen" ("Barefooted Gen"), there is a pictorial representation of the chaos right after the A-bomb in which children are chased by mothers whose faces are completely burnt out and unrecognizable even to their own children. The author of the series, Keiji Nakazawa, had personally witnessed the Hiroshima bombing in which he lost his father, sister, and brother. In Shindo's earlier film, *Children of Hiroshima*, the teacher's former employee tries to shield his burned and blinded face in shame. The sentimentalization here is precisely a disavowal of the en masse isolation of the bomb victims, who are presented by Shindo as subjects of compassionate treatment by others.

In *Onibaba*, Shindo attaches different meanings to the distorted faces under the mask in terms of both class and gender. The samurai tells the woman that he wears the mask on the order of his father, both to look strong and to hide his exquisitely beautiful face so that it will not be marred by war. Wearing a mask on the order of an older samurai was

common during the Edo period (1600–1868, prior to Japan's modernization under the Meiji dynasty), an expression of a *shudo* relationship, that
is, an erotic relationship between a younger, pre-adult male and an older
man.[12] If lovers were to be separated it was common among samurai for
the older man to ask the younger one to cover his face with a mask so as to
not attract other lovers. *Onibaba*'s mise en scène is set in this period, and
in asking the audience to read the narrative as "an old legend of war and
tragedy, of the primitive that underlies the civilized veneer," Shindo
paints the relationship between the emperor and the samurai as incestuous. The emperor devours and binds the militaristic young men, who in
turn submit to this regime because of the power it confers on them. The
samurai's boast that the mask hides his beautiful visage and makes him
strong is ripped apart by the peasant woman to reveal the face of a
hibakusha—the defeated face of the Japanese military.

His boast also reveals the delusions of a militaristic class hiding its
humiliation under the veneer of a medieval institution—the emperor.
Upon seeing his disfigured face under the mask, the old woman exclaims
contemptuously, "so this is a samurai general's face. You made others die.
Now it is your turn." *Onibaba*'s plot actually refers to *two* emperors, possibly alluding to the U.S. Occupation and the Emperor's regime. The
Left, forced to go underground during the American occupation, saw little difference between the pre-war repression of left-wing criticism and
its continued censorship during the U.S. Occupation. Iwasaki Akira, who
had been involved in shooting footage of the destruction of Hiroshima
and Nagasaki that the Americans confiscated, and who became the producer of Kaimei Fumio's *A Japanese Tragedy* (1945)—a film banned by the
Occupation—referred to the United States as the *gunbatsu*, or military
clique. From the perspective of most ordinary citizens, the Occupation
forces and the emperor *both* reinforced authority, obedience, and militaristic regimes. As Hachi explains to the two women, the war between
the emperors has nothing to do with people like him. He had served one
emperor, then the other, and finally managed to escape after pretending
to be dead. The old woman sees the death she brings on the samurai as just
punishment for starting a war that killed many, including her son. "The
dead are the losers," she says, "they cannot come to life."

When the old woman puts on the mask, however, its meaning becomes more complex. At first the mask serves her well. Like the samurai,
she too uses it to frighten another into submission, namely her daughter-
in-law, who comes to believe that it is divine punishment for her affair

with Hachi. The film's rationalist and humanist logic is apparent here, as the old woman's stories of divine punishment are revealed for what they really are: folk superstitions used as a form of maintaining repression. Yet even these seemingly medieval tales, so familiar to the horror genre, are transformed by Shindo into metaphors for the A-bomb. The old woman speaks of a strange time when there was frost in the summer, rumors of a horse birthing a calf, a black sun that turned day into night as if the earth was being turned upside down.

The old women's power over the mask lasts only briefly. *Onibaba*'s climax is unrelenting in its visual and expressive allegory of the price paid by ordinary Japanese people for donning the demonistic, cursed mask—the militaristic ambitions of the ruling class. The mask sticks to the old women's face on a dark, stormy night when the daughter-in-law manages to evade the masked figure and run into her lover's arms. The rain echoes the black rain accompanying the bomb, and the lonely, forlorn, masked figure of the old woman the plight of the ordinary people who had internalized the emperor's holy war, a war that called on them to "endure the unendurable." Unlike the samurai, however, we are invited to have some sympathy for the old woman, who, as mentioned, chases her daughter-in-law and crosses over the black hole claiming, "I am not a demon, I am a human being." This is among the film's most outright statements by means of which the supernatural is humanized as being nothing but the repression of the dead, while the losers of history are shown jumping over history's dark hole instead of falling into it.

In representing history as a process of unmitigated horror from the perspective of its losers, Shindo not only makes a passionate allegorical statement about life amidst scarcity and class, and gender antagonism, he also reveals the political impulses underlying the horror genre itself. Marxist criticism and aesthetics is concerned with developing a vibrant political culture through the creation of revolutionary texts as well as through the ideological critique of existing ones. In making manifest the contradictions of the horror genre, *Onibaba* works at both levels. While he uses generic horror conventions—identified by Tania Modleski as "repetition in a plot that is minimalist, like a well-known fairy tale, with the emphasis on evoking horror through mise-en-scène"[13]—he does not repress the social antagonisms heightened by the horror film. Fredric Jameson has argued that the task of the Marxist critic is to uncover and bring to the surface the political unconscious, that is, the desire for the end of class struggle and a movement toward the realm of freedom lying

The terrifying mask (which hides something even more terrifying underneath) in *Onibaba* (1964)

buried and repressed in popular texts.[14] This adversarial position with respect to the contemporary world is, Robin Wood has claimed, implicit in the horror genre.[15] As an example, Wood cites *The Texas Chainsaw Massacre* (1974) as an indictment of capitalism, in that displaced slaughterhouse workers take to cannibalism in order to survive. While the contemporary horror film is often apocalyptic and nihilistic, however, *Onibaba* makes a biting and passionate criticism of the existing world.

Shindo's radicalism also lies in another formal break with the generic conventions of horror cinema, namely his astute recognition of gender as a fundamental source of social antagonism. While terror in the horror film is, according to Modleski, sustained at the expense of women both as victims and on the side of the monsters, Shindo constructs his vision of horror from the perspective of two female peasants. From their viewpoint, history is nothing but a black hole from which to try to escape. The women survive war by killing, but their killing does not make them demonic; rather, it makes evident their tenacious grip on life. Shindo is recognized as a *feminisuto* (feminist) filmmaker, and he trained under Mizoguchi Kenji, whose films often concerned the imprisonment of women in feudal society. As Richard Tucker has argued, however, the main thematic purpose of women in Mizoguchi's films lay in their relationship to men.[16] Moreover, like Ozu, Mizoguchi's view of history was actually *trans*historical, as he took suffering to be inevitable in human life.

Shindo, though, does not romanticize either the women's relationship with each other or their efforts to survive. In the midst of excruciating scarcity the women join forces in order to live, but they have little room for affection. They are often shot asleep or eating together, with minimal contact or laughter. In several shots, a wooden bar splits the frame right between them. Furthermore, the old woman's dehumanizing jealousy is portrayed not as a demonic act of irrational possessiveness but as the outcome of sheer economic dependence. She fears that her daughter-in-law, were she to get involved with Hachi, would abandon her, and so she pleads with Hachi to wait until the war's end when she could return to farming again. As she tells Hachi, "I cannot even kill without her." However, sheer economic scarcity is not all that dehumanizes the old woman. The film also dwells on her intense longing and loneliness in one shot whose eloquence is underscored by its non-repetition. Coming on the couple in a passionate embrace, the old woman clutches her breasts as if in excruciating pain and wraps herself around a lone tree in the open field. The camera tilts to reveal the tree to be deadly white with a vulture sitting on its scorched branches. In *Onibaba*, Shindo takes what could have been a cautionary tale condemning an old woman (a role played with immense power by his wife, Nobuko Otowa) and transforms her into the true protagonist, not only of his film but of history; for it is from her position, one in which there is no investment in war or private property, that human society can escape its previous era of barbarism. In Shindo's view, it is the old woman peasant who becomes, like Marx's proletariat, history's protagonist.

Conclusion

Depicting nuclear disaster without addressing it realistically or even as the main subject dominates Japanese film post–World War II. For instance, all of Ozu's life-cycle films that insist on the transitory nature of human existence and the accommodation of technology in everyday life can be seen as a resistant response to the bomb's destructiveness. And Desser has suggested that Akira Kurosawa's films between 1947 and 1952 can, in one way or another, be seen as a reflection on war. He reads the themes of physical ruin and metaphysical doubt that predominate *Rashomon* (1951), for example, as a rumination on the present state, in which nothing is certain. The idea of *oni* (demons) can also be seen in two sections of Kurosawa's *Dreams* (1990) that deal with nuclear disaster and post-nuclear horrors.

Of course, the most popular monster associated with the A-bomb is Godzilla, who first appeared onscreen in 1954. Godzilla, born in the sea as a result of nuclear testing, is a mix of the horror film monster and the science-fiction film.[17] In the 1957 sci-fi film *The Mysterians,* fears of a post-nuclear wasteland are displaced onto aliens when, at the conclusion, the hero discovers that the masked aliens have radiation burns on their faces. In both of these genres, science fiction and horror (as well as in Japanese animation), anxieties about nuclear war are typically expressed in terms of the future and technology. *Onibaba,* by contrast, looks back in time to make a statement about the contemporary world by invoking the past as horror from which the present can make a break. Moreover, Shindo turns his historical allegory into a passionate appeal to the audience to take on the real world through the use of certain rhetorical strategies. These strategies include repetition, direct addresses to the spectator through intertitles, and the construction of the woman peasant as the center from whose perspective the horror of history is revealed.

The immensity of the tragedy unleashed by the bomb naturally evokes a response of horror, and subsequently the move to horror and science fiction in Japanese cinema to represent war is understandable. In fact, such representations can help express anxieties and anger about nuclear warfare and suggest resolutions to them within the diegetic world. In *Onibaba,* however, Shindo consciously politicizes the horror genre and subverts its accommodating impulses, making explicit the historical roots of the genre in a world marked by scarcity and antagonism.

Notes

Thanks to Yuki Tanaka and Ippei Watanabe for research assistance, comments, criticism, and acquisition of Shindo's films. Thanks are also due to the astute critiques of the editors, Steven Jay Schneider and Tony Williams, and the discussions with my students, particularly Faustina Robinson in the Spring 2000 graduate seminar on the Japanese New Wave.

   1. *Capital, Volume One,* in *The Marx-Engels Reader,* 2nd ed., ed. Robert C. Tucker (New York: Norton, 1978), 430, 435.
   2. David Desser, *Eros Plus Massacre* (New Brunswick, NJ: Rutgers University Press, 1988).
   3. For an incisive social history of Japan following World War II, see John W. Dower, *Embracing Defeat: Japan in the Wake of World War II* (New York: Norton, 1999).
   4. Desser, *Eros Plus Massacre,* 31.
   5. Oshima Nagisa, *Cinema, Censorship and the State: The Writings of Nagisa Oshima,* trans. Dawn Lawson (Cambridge: MIT Press, 1992), 137.

6. In an interview with Ehime Shinbun (*Ehime Newspaper*), Shindo talks about his filmmaking and Ehime prefecture, online at http://www.ehime-np.co.jp/kikaku/shindou, accessed September 3, 2003.

7. Kyoko Hirano, "Depiction of the Atomic Bombings in Japanese Cinema during the U.S. Occupation Period," in *Hibakusha Cinema: Hiroshima, Nagasaki, and the Nuclear Image in Japanese Film,* ed. Mick Broderick (London: Kegan Paul, 1996), 103–19.

8. Donald Richie, "*Mono No Aware:* Hiroshima on Film," in *Hibakusha Cinema,* 23.

9. In fact, this dance form would not premiere in Tokyo until 1959, in a performance by Tatsumi Hijikata and Yoshito Ono.

10. The Japanese New Wave rejected *mono no aware* as an aesthetic principle because of its insistence on the transitory nature of human life as opposed to the natural world, and its acceptance of (rather than resistance to) the external world. History in this transcendental view becomes, as Desser argues, cyclical and mythical, an endless cycle of birth and death rather than a product of economic, political, and social forces.

11. See Dower, *Embracing Defeat.*

12. Gregory M. Pflugfelder, *Cartographies of Desire: Male-Male Sexuality in Japanese Discourse, 1600–1950* (Berkeley: University of California Press, 1999).

13. Tania Modleski, "The Terror of Pleasure: The Contemporary Horror Film and Postmodern Theory," in *Film Theory and Criticism,* ed. Leo Braudy and Marshall Cohen (New York: Oxford University Press, 1999), 694.

14. Fredric Jameson, *The Political Unconscious: Narrative as a Symbolic Act* (Ithaca: Cornell University Press, 1981).

15. Robin Wood, "An Introduction to the American Horror Film." In *Movies and Methods: An Anthology,* vol. 2, ed. Bill Nichols (Berkeley: University of California Press, 1985), 195–219.

16. Richard Tucker, *Japan: Film Image* (London: Studio Vista, 1973).

17. For an excellent sociohistorical reading of the Godzilla films, see Chon A. Noreiga, "Godzilla and the Japanese Nightmare: When Them! Is US," *Cinema Journal* 27, no. 1 (1987): 63–77.

5

"Terror Australis":

AREAS OF HORROR IN THE AUSTRALIAN CINEMA

Jonathan Rayner

Within the reemergent Australian cinema, critics have often identified a tension between areas of film production (and criticism) concerned with the commercial potential of the industry, and those aiming and aspiring toward an artistic cinema of cultural relevance.[1] In such a conceptualization of the national film industry, the horror films that have been made since 1970 would seem destined for a derogatory classification in the former category, along with other generic products, such as road movies, which are indebted to American cinematic traditions. In these terms, an overtly commercial strand of Australian horror filmmaking is identifiable in the output of producer Antony I. Ginnane, including *Thirst* (Rod Hardy, 1979), *Harlequin* (Simon Wincer, 1980), and *The Survivor* (David Hemmings, 1980). These films are aimed at an international market and as a consequence avoid specific reference to or representation of Australia and Australianness.

However, all branches of contemporary film production in Australia have been characterized by strong generic profiles. The cycle of period film production that held sway in the 1970s and 1980s reflected the influence of art cinema models, and adopted the mise en scène of European literary adaptation. This supposed high point in cultural relevance and aesthetic refinement for the new national cinema has been described (and derided) as the "AFC genre"[2] because of the Australian Film Commission's alleged support and encouragement for such formulaic filmmaking. If in this case an officially sanctioned cultural cinema is indebted and reduced to a "genre," then it should be noted how the characteristics of popular American film genres have been deployed in Australian films to a culturally relevant end. The musical, in the examples of *Starstruck* (Gillian Armstrong, 1982), *Strictly Ballroom* (Baz Luhrmann, 1992), and *The Adventures of Priscilla, Queen of the Desert* (Stephan Elliott, 1994), has served to articulate issues of gender, multiculturalism, and identity within an Australian context. Similarly, the war film and the western have been amalgamated, naturalized, and nationalized in embodying celebratory images of Australian masculinity in *Gallipoli* (Peter Weir, 1981) and *The Man from Snowy River* (George Miller, 1982). In this national cinematic ethos, in which conventional film genres are adopted, adapted, and hybridized and from which new indigenous genres evolve in self-reflexive ways, the horror film's role, as a commercial genre imbued with a specific cultural significance, requires an acknowledgment on equal terms with more "official" forms of filmmaking. In this way, the relevance of Australian films of the 1970s can be compared with that of American horror films from the same, and earlier, decades.

A Peculiar Kind of Horror: Australian Gothic

The earliest and most distinctive brand of horror film to be recognized in Australian cinema of the 1970s was the gothic. In the gothic the hybridization and subversion of film genres imported from America is clearly discernible, and this approach serves as a template for the ironic and self-conscious Australian films of the 1980s and 1990s. The best examples of Australian Gothic exhibit a diversity of allusion, referring to the conventions and iconography of varied popular cultural texts, including multiple film genres such as westerns and road movies as well as horror and science-fiction films. Among the most successful gothic films are the components of the *Mad Max* trilogy (George Miller/George Ogilvie, 1979/1981/1985). The distillation of the gothic from its sources can be seen in these examples, since the violence is at once visceral and comedic, and the iconography is that of the road movie and post-apocalyptic science fiction. However, it is the reliance on the characterization and narrative themes of the western that connects the *Mad Max* films with the Australian Gothic's depiction of horror in the rural landscape.

The investment of the Australian landscape as a site of the uncanny is a key feature of the gothic, but in the earliest instances it is the human habitations in the landscape that represent the true locus of horror. An antecedent of the Australian revival and of the gothic in this respect is *Wake in Fright* (Ted Kotcheff, 1970). In detailing the moral disintegration of an educated Englishman absorbed into an outback community, *Wake in Fright* emphasizes the fragility of civilization in the face of isolation. The teacher (Gary Bond) who arrives in the secluded town of Bundunyabba is at first superior to and dismissive of the simple, hospitable locals. He seeks to escape from the exploitation he experiences in his post at Tiboonda (a place name given to a school, a bar, and a train stop) by exploiting the local manifestation of the national obsession with gambling. He bets and loses all his earnings in an illegal two-up game, and is forced to live on the unthinking charity of the locals. In accepting their offers of drinks and beds for the night, he is gradually divested of his intellectual superiority. His downward spiral is completed in a bloodthirsty and drunken kangaroo hunt, and a nightmarish sexual assault. When his loathing of "The Yabba" and himself reaches a peak, he tries desperately to escape the town, then to murder the Mephistophelian doctor (Donald Pleasence) he holds responsible for his downfall, and finally to commit suicide. He is saved, and returns to Tiboonda a sadder and wiser man.

The horror and moral challenge of the town's isolation are depicted as insuperable in Kotcheff's film, but the guilt for human degradation lies in the community itself rather than in the natural landscape. The seclusion precipitates the tragedy rather than causing it: the failings of all the inhabitants are shown to be innate and are merely exposed and exaggerated by the situation of the town. This degradation of human life is accompanied by a devaluation of all life existing in this landscape. Along with this leveling judgment of human behavior and society, the town's representativeness of the country at large is also emphasized. The town's quietly corrupt police chief (played by the icon of outback masculinity and dependability, Chips Rafferty), ignores the gambling and the high suicide rate but observes Anzac Day religiously. His assertion that "The Yabba" is the best town in Australia perhaps acknowledges that this is the best and only town possible, with these or any people in this location. As the film's conclusion shows, the teacher knows and accepts more about the town, the country, and himself because of his sojourn than he could otherwise have learned.

This characterization of the corrupt and corrupting rural community, perceived from the perspective of the outsider, becomes a staple of the Australian Gothic. The nihilistic horror of immorality, isolation, and idiosyncrasy recurs in the pseudo-western narratives of *The Cars That Ate Paris* (Peter Weir, 1974) and *Shame* (Steve Jodrell, 1987). Weir's film previews the *Mad Max* trilogy in foregrounding another national obsession, the fetishization of the car, and also mirrors or anticipates contemporary American examples. The arrival of an innocent (Arthur Waldo [Terry Camilleri], traumatized by a car accident in which his brother was killed) in the remote town of Paris is the catalytic event that results in the mushrooming of violence and the eventual destruction of the town. Whereas in the traditional western the heroic outsider acts to purge and correct the iniquities of the frontier town, in Australian Gothic (from *Wake in Fright* onward, and even in the case of the *Mad Max* trilogy) the putative hero figure is either unable to save the community and defeat the law- and taboo-breaking behavior he encounters, or is seduced by and absorbed into it.

Parallel streams of activity mark Arthur's stay in the town: his integration into the town's way of life (including his "adoption" by the mayor of Paris, played by John Meillon), and his tentative investigation into the circumstances of his car accident. He discovers that the decaying town survives on a twilight economy of automotive and human wreckage harvested from car accidents, which the inhabitants cause deliberately on the surrounding country roads. Clothes, spare tires, and the vehicles themselves are recirculated in a barter system. Any crash survivors are recycled, being adopted into the mayor's family like Arthur or subjected to the local doctor's surgical experimentation. In the midst of a national economic crisis, the townspeople have turned to this opportunistic cannibalism in order to survive. The elders dream of a new Paris of the future, but their ruthlessness breeds rebellion in the younger generation. Having been raised with cars and car crashes, they customize and idolize their vehicles and resist the hypocritical efforts of the town's council and police to rein in the escalating violence. Ironically, their immersion in the town's culture of automotive violence is total. When one youth's vehicle is burned in public as a punishment, the mayor's henchman warns him that the other "cars are unhappy." This equation of car and vehicle (and anthropomorphism of the vehicles, suggested by the film's title), is completed by the animal roars that accompany the cars' climactic attack on the town.

The iniquity of the town (and its first family) soon envelops Arthur. Because of the crash (and an earlier accident in which he ran down a pensioner) he has a driving phobia that prevents him from leaving the town. At the same time the mayor's offer of a home presupposes an end to his attempts to leave Paris, and to alert the outside world to the town's secret. In collaborating with the mayor, Arthur places himself between the rival factions when he assumes the farcical but dangerous job of traffic warden. When the youths of Paris revolt and attack the commemorative Paris Pioneers Ball (an ironic celebration of the pragmatism and perseverance of the first settlers), Arthur fights back with a car under the mayor's command.

He kills another driver in self-defense and, thus cured of his phobia, he drives away gleefully into the night while the town implodes behind him.

As an influential forebear, *The Cars That Ate Paris* functions as a definitive gothic text. In mimicking and quoting many antecedents, it establishes the generic hybridity and self-consciousness of this brand of Australian horror. The town is characterized through the conventions of science fiction (the soulless conformist population move like the dehumanized suburban population of *Invasion of the Body Snatchers* [Don Siegel, 1956]), horror (the doctor's brain-damaged patients recall the zombies of *Night of the Living Dead* [George A. Romero, 1968]), and the western (the youths' dust coats, and the camera angles used for stand-offs in the street evoke the spaghetti westerns of the previous decade). The vivid coloration and cartoonish violence are reminiscent of Roger Corman's American exploitational films of the 1960s, and ironically *Cars* served as a direct inspiration for the Corman-produced *Death Race 2000* (Paul Bartel, 1975). The fetishistic treatment of vehicles, their status as weapons, and their anthropomorphic association with their drivers, are also transplanted, admittedly with greater success, into the western revenge narrative of *Mad Max*. While in this instance it may be said to have inspired the most commercially successful Australian films in the gothic mode, *Cars* can be compared with equal justification with *Weekend* (Jean-Luc Godard, 1967), in its comic but unflinching critique of capitalism and consumerism as cannibalism and murder. At a further remove, both these films parallel and anticipate the critique of consumerism, modern society, and its moral vacuity found in the work of Canadian director David Cronenberg. His *Shivers* (1974) draws its characterization and social commentary from the examples of Romero and Godard, but the themes of these films and Weir's feature debut reach their fullest articulation in *Crash* (1996). In return, the influence of Cronenberg on Australian Gothic horror is discernible in *Body Melt* (Philip Brophy, 1993).

Brophy's film features a prologue in the form of a television advertisement, comparable to that which opens *Shivers*, for a health farm offering vitamin supplements and treatments promising "nourishment, energy, and sensational pleasure." In fact, the chemical company behind the operation is conducting covert human experiments, through the supply of its "Vimuville" (Visceral/Muscular Vitalization of Latent Libidinal Energy) products to an emblematic suburban community. The societal cross-section that inhabits Pebbles Court in "Homesville" satirizes the representation of Australian television, especially soap opera. While the avowed

One of the customized, anthropomorphized vehicles in *The Cars That Ate Paris* (1974)

target of this horror lesson (contemporary middle-class obsessions with bodily perfection and corporeal pleasure) equates with that of Cronenberg's films, the specificity of the gothic is apparent in the catalogue of psychological, sexual, and criminal disruption and bodily abjection (in sexual fantasy, infidelity, nightmarish miscarriage, and murder) inflicted on the sanitized and stereotyped version of Australian culture.

Cars' depiction of seductive, pragmatic evil, and iniquitous control foreshadows numerous bathetic and menacing portraits of authority in later Australian films. The gothic father figure (the police chief of Bundunyabba, the mayor of Paris) reappears as the secretive and manipulative patriarchal leaders in *Strictly Ballroom, Muriel's Wedding* (P. J. Hogan, 1994), and *Shine* (Scott Hicks, 1996). Corrupt rural police pursue personal vendettas (in *Incident at Raven's Gate* [Rolf de Heer, 1988]), commit their own serious crimes (in *Deadly* [Esben Storm, 1991]), and, in siding with the lawbreakers, pervert the course of justice (*Shame*). In *Deadly,* a disgraced city detective (Jerome Ehlers) travels to an outback town to investigate the suspicious death in custody of an Aboriginal prisoner. The prisoner has been murdered, not because of an unfocused, instinctual racism but because of specific sexual jealousy. However, as in *Bad Day at Black Rock* (John Sturges, 1954), the entire community seems culpable in its silence, and its intolerance toward miscegenation. The multiplication of such prejudices (the detective's hatred of drug addicts in the city is matched by the rural policeman's contempt for Aborigines) culminates in the recognition of repeated, institutionalized wrongdoing, when an earlier, identical murder perpetrated by the city cop's boss also comes to light.

Where *Deadly* portrays the connection between the violent prejudices of individuals in the rural setting and the persistence of institutional racism in the country at large, *Shame* links the conservatism of traditional Australian masculinity with a pervasive and inherent misogyny. The outsider from the city confronts a gang of young rapists, whose repeated attacks are condoned and left unpunished by the town's elder male authorities, including the local police. In this case the outsider is not only a lawyer but also a woman, Asta Cadell (Deborra-Lee Furness), whose proximity to the victims is increased by her own narrow escape from the gang. The submission of the town's women in the face of this ritualistic humiliation is answered by the heroine's defiance. She succeeds in bringing the gang to justice, despite the climactic murder of a victim she has encouraged to testify. As *Deadly* revises the format of the noir thriller within the context of nationally specific race politics, *Shame* subverts the image of rural Australian masculinity with its exposure of an innate and complacent barbarism. The amalgamation of horror, thriller, and western motifs in both films, in the service of their overt social critiques, illustrates the diversity of reference and relevance in the Australian Gothic.

While this mode in Australian cinema does not necessarily equate with the conventional model of the horror film (in not foregrounding fantastic or supernatural horror, or the lethal, personal violence of the slasher film), it does establish its own continuities and consistencies: the rural landscape represents an anti-Eden in which communities and individuals appear as fallen or compromised, and act as the focus and the magnification of societal and cultural flaws. In this respect, Australian Gothic coheres with the portrayals of monstrous rurality in contemporary American horror films, such as *Deliverance* (John Boorman, 1972), *The Texas Chainsaw Massacre* (Tobe Hooper, 1974), and *The Hills Have Eyes* (Wes Craven, 1977). Philip Brophy identifies the 1970s as a key moment in the development of the horror film, as developments in the genre mark a break from the products of American studios in the classical period, extend the explicitness and exploitation value of representation seen in British and American films of the 1960s, and anticipate the horror franchises of the 1980s and 1990s in their self-conscious and black comedic address to the generically informed audience.[3] The popular cultural and intertextual reference, contemporary social commentary, and dark humor of Australian Gothic epitomizes these trends: "It is not so much that the modern Horror film refutes or ignores the conventions of genre, but it is involved in a violent awareness of itself as a saturated genre. Its rebirth as such is qualified by *how* it states itself as genre. The historical blueprints have faded, and the new (post-1975) films recklessly copy and re-draw their generic sketching."[4]

Abhorring the Vacuum

The depictions of the rural community in these examples of Australian Gothic offer a shocking and subversive revision of a natural landscape otherwise presumed to be tamed. It is notable that the narratives discussed so far turn on the arrival and intervention of an outsider bearing connotations (albeit spurious in some cases) of urban sophistication. This ambiguity of approach toward both the rural idyll and the urban environment is redolent of the contradictions underlying conceptions of national character. The representative image of a predominantly city-dwelling multicultural population remains the self-reliant white male in the outback. This icon persisted through the filmmaking revival in parodic and reverential forms. Arguably the most successful film of the revival, *Crocodile Dundee* (Peter Faiman, 1986), negotiates this contradiction in a simultaneously self-reflexive, iconoclastic, and celebratory fashion. The catalytic contact between representatives of city and country communities in the gothic does not work exclusively to discredit the insular, perverse, or prejudiced rural groups: urban life and the inhabitants of cities are subject to exposure and criticism, as the narratives *Wake in Fright* and *Deadly* suggest. Later gothic films, such as *The Last Wave* (Peter Weir, 1977) and *Long Weekend* (Colin Eggleston, 1979), foreground the city dweller's experience and again point to broader but still culturally specific readings of film horror.

   The Last Wave extends the "low-keyed, realistic focus on the monstrousness of the commonplace"[5] found in *Wake in Fright* and *Cars,* and details a supernatural menace that threatens the entirety of modern, urban existence. David Burton (Richard Chamberlain), a middle-class white Sydney lawyer, has his personal and professional life thrown into chaos when he agrees to defend four Aborigines charged with murder. Before the trial he is beset by series of troubling dreams and hallucinations, at the same time as the country is besieged by violent and increasingly bizarre weather. The film's prologue shows a destructive and unprecedented hail-storm hitting an outback school. Later a plague of frogs seems to herald a divine judgment, and a rain of black oil provides a fittingly apocalyptic vision for the energy-conscious 1970s consumer society. These occur-rences are rationalized meteorologically by the impotent authorities, but the portentousness of the weather finds its focus in the lawyer's night-mares and visions concerning the natural element of water. Water enters his consciousness and his home simultaneously, cascading down the stairs from an overflowing bath. The farcical nature of this event is undercut by the discovery of a minimal but apparently fatal quantity of water in the lungs of the murder victim. The intrusion of water into living space increases, until the lawyer experiences nightmarish visions of the city underwater, destroyed by a tidal wave foretold in his premonitory dreams.

The gradual invasion of the family home by the weather and water coincides with the disruption of the previously held certainties of com-fortable suburban life. When he abandons his usual work in corporate taxation, the lawyer's colleagues become more hostile to his liberal defense of the Aborigines through legal aid. Inviting the defendants into his home to discuss the case ostracizes his wife, and eventually he is left alone in the house as a climactic storm bursts in at the windows and doors. The incursion of these natural elements (weather, water, and the Aborig-ines characterized as Other—a traditional, spiritual community) repre-sents the irruption of materials repressed in terms of domestic, spiritual, and cultural existence. In interpreting his dreams and defending the case he is forced to recall, admit, or discover disconcerting facts about his fam-ily history, his descent from an ancient mythical race of seers, and the dis-possession of Australia's indigenous peoples. The revelation of the existence of an intact Aboriginal tribe within the modern city, and of their sacred site underground containing prophesies of the imminent natural catastrophe, make palpable the history of repression in personal (textual) and historical (extratextual) terms.

The offenses of modern urban civilization and materialistic exis-tence against the natural world (incarnated by the continent's weather and its indigenous peoples) suggested by *The Last Wave* are rendered in a more explicit and conventional form in *Long Weekend*. Weir's film amal-gamates an "imagination of disaster"[6] evocative of science-fiction film with a judgmental, supernatural characterization of nature reminiscent of *The Birds* (Alfred Hitchcock, 1963). *Long Weekend* details the crimes committed against the flora and fauna by an emblematic and unsympa-

The home of lawyer David Burton (Richard Chamberlain) is flooded in *The Last Wave* (1977)

thetic suburban couple, Peter (John Hargreaves) and Marcia (Briony Behets), in the course of a futile camping trip. Rather than simply incarnating a heedlessly destructive Western civilization, Scott Murray identifies the couple as "ugly caricatures of known Australian types—trendy, inconsiderate and cruel, and unhindered by any sense of value or purpose in life."[7] The weekend excursion is conceived as an attempt at reconciliation between the bickering couple, after the wife's affair has ended with the abortion of an unwanted pregnancy. Newly acquired equipment includes a rifle and pesticides, both of which are used indiscriminately. The couple's casual destruction of wildlife (dropping burning cigarettes, running over a kangaroo in their jeep, chopping down a tree for no reason, shooting a sea cow in the surf) is answered by implacable and vengeful (super)natural forces. Peter finds the remains of other camps and vehicles apparently overwhelmed by the forest and sea. At night, he panics and kills Marcia by accident with his spear gun, before being run over by a truck forced to swerve due to a Hitchcockian cockatoo.

The menace of the natural environment in *Long Weekend* resides in its reinstatement of its otherness, overturning as a result the callousness and complacency of both contemporary consumerism and colonial history. A fenced and supposedly owned plot within easy reach of the city can become an inescapable wilderness. Nature's passive resistance causes prepackaged food to rot, and forest paths to disappear, but this is extended to include physical attacks from eagles and possums. However, the tribulations and deaths of the husband and wife are essentially self-inflicted. Their destructiveness vented on the landscape rebounds on themselves when one kills the other and then the survivor is crushed by a truck—the personification of heedless commercial and technological progress—carrying livestock to a slaughterhouse. The return of the dead, in the inexplicable and terrifying movements of the sea cow's corpse toward their camp, suggests the unspoken source of the guilt and retribution in the wife's abortion. This compromising of human reproduction, in a termination bearing the stigma of social rather than spiritual disapproval, seems to be a greater motivation for the couple's revulsion at the teeming land, and a fuller vindication of the land's reprisals.

The mysterious fecundity of the Australian landscape, which is depicted in miraculous terms in *Walkabout* (Nicolas Roeg, 1970), becomes in *Long Weekend* a source of repulsion. The emptiness of the continent's interior, largely untouched by white incursions, is (ir)rationalized as an unacculturated and abhorred vacuum. Both *The Last Wave* and *Long Weekend* embody the "settler culture's 'original sin,'"[8] acquisition of *terra nullius* and dispossession of its indigenous peoples, and connect it with the soullessness of contemporary suburban life. Despite the liberal sensibilities discernible in the films (in consideration of contemporary racial and environmental issues), the representations of the landscape in Eggleston's film and of Aboriginal culture in Weir's are interpretable as manifestations of the archaic mother.[9] Reproductiveness is characterized as a source of horror, repression, and abjection, in the smashed eagle's egg and orphaned young in *Long Weekend,* and the uterine and excremental connotations of the sacred Aboriginal cave, located under a modern sewage plant, in *The Last Wave.* In return, the revenge that the natural world wreaks on the empty and immoral suburbanites articulates an abhorrence of the spiritual vacuum within Western civilization. These films again illustrate the hybridity of the gothic in combining horror and science fiction with the angst-ridden self-interrogation of the European art film.

A Family of Horrors

The location of horror within the married couple in *Long Weekend* and the family home in *The Last Wave* underlines the trend in contemporary horror for the association of this most conservative of social structures with cruelty, deviance, and repression. This placement within American horror, in films such as *It's Alive!* (Larry Cohen, 1973) and *Poltergeist* (Tobe Hooper, 1982) is replicated in gothic portrayals of the Australian family as a domain of malign influences and forbidden practices. The "triadic adherence of horror, science fiction, and family melodrama,"[10] discernible in American family horror, is expressed in Australian Gothic through a morbid investigation of taboo-breaking family relationships and defamiliarized social environments. The analysis of destructive behavior in sexual and violent terms is accompanied by and reflects on the alienation and emptiness experienced in contemporary existence.

Rolf de Heer's films *Incident at Raven's Gate* and *Bad Boy Bubby* (1993) epitomize the rural and urban manifestations of the gothic respectively, but both also foreground the danger in proximity caused by the enforced or deliberate isolation of the family group from a stabilizing social context. In *Incident at Raven's Gate*, a family composed of a farmer, his wife, and younger brother are beset by adulterous urges and alien visitations, which result in the destruction of both the couple and their homestead. The film accords with many other gothic narratives in portraying a corrupt and shadowy governmental authority, which in this case tracks, records, and covers up the evidence of extraterrestrial activity in the outback. The forces of the establishment choose not to intervene to prevent the "incident," but are shown to be prepared to murder to maintain its secrecy. However, this conspiracy-theory narrative exists only as a subplot, outlined in a predictable fashion in a story frame preceding and succeeding the main narrative. In strong contrast, the central, melodramatic narrative of the adulterous and incestuous family and their encounter with aliens epitomizes Vivian Sobchack's definition of the hybridized generic triad. In the paradoxical and black comedic manner typical of the gothic, the science-fiction elements are at once illustrative of and incorporated into the family conflict, but barely register in the consciousness of the human protagonists until the film's violent climax.

Although the farm is associated with another remote township, the family's isolation is exaggerated by the married brother Richard's (Ritchie Singer) obsessive and unconventional farming techniques (hydroponics) and the younger brother Eddie's (Steven Vigler) stigma of a criminal record. The tension generated in the home by the younger sibling's undisciplined farm work, in addition to the sexual tension between him and his brother's wife Rachel (Celine O'Leary), is paralleled and exacerbated by Eddie's relationship with the local barmaid, which provokes the local policeman into a jealous and vindictive rage. This murderous jealousy, either influenced by or simply coincident with the aliens' presence, results in the deaths of Richard and the barmaid, leaving the venial couple of Eddie and Rachel alive to witness the establishment cover-up. *Incident at Raven's Gate*'s disconcerting shifts between soap operatic, science-fictional, and horror materials are typical of the gothic's repeated generic and tonal wrong-footing. It is not simply that the film "finds its chosen path constantly leading it away from its main concern,"[11] but rather that the main concern is the narrative of a self-destructive family (and community) to whom the supernatural events appear coterminous and allusive, but strangely irrelevant. The violent and arbitrary intervention of unseen extraterrestrials and unaccountable government agents exist as vague and providential interruptions to an otherwise self-sustaining series of sadomasochistic relationships.

De Heer's representation of the family declines further into decay and immorality in *Bad Boy Bubby*. The titular character (played by Nicholas Hope) is a mature man kept as a child by his complete removal from human society. He is imprisoned in a windowless urban slum by his ageing mother who maintains her control over him through an incestuous relationship and fear of the "poisons" in the air outside their cell. The unexpected return of his father, a corrupt priest, forces Bubby to kill his parents and finally venture outside. He trades abuse at the hands of his family for the manipulative and punitive ministrations of the religious and judicial authorities of the outside world, before meeting a redeeming woman who also needs to be rescued from a judgmental and sadistic family. (A similar dystopianism marks the portrayal of the fallen, adulterous, and incestuous family in Raw Lawrence's *Bliss* [1985]). Bubby's impressionable state allows for the defamiliarization of all aspects of contemporary society, which is portrayed as either indifferent or antagonistic toward the needs of individuals. Bubby and Angel (Carmel Johnson) do surmount the institutional obstacles to personal happiness, but the world's atmosphere remains "poisoned" by malevolent external authorities.

The motif of incest, suggested in *Raven's Gate* and explicit in *Bad Boy Bubby*, recurs alarmingly in the gothic as the defining flaw of the Australian family. In the putative thriller *Summerfield* (Ken Hannam, 1977) and the slasher/supernatural horror film *Cassandra* (Colin Eggleston, 1986), incestuous relationships become synonymous with the inheritance of an isolated and introspective colonial culture. As in *Raven's Gate,* the isolation of the incestuous group of brother-father, sister-mother, and daughter-niece in *Summerfield* is increased by the separation of the family farm from the nearest town. The Summerfield estate is an island inhabited by five successive generations of the Abbott family, before the intrusion of the local schoolteacher, investigating a different and non-existent mystery, precipitates a tragic revelation. In *Cassandra,* incestuous relationships across two generations culminate in numerous deaths. The twin siblings of an incestuous couple exhibit supernatural powers, and the male child Warren (Dylan O'Neill) forces the sister-mother to commit suicide. After years of institutionalization, he tracks down his father who now lives in a family composed of another sister in the role of adoptive mother, and Warren's sister Cassandra (Tessa Humphries). The hesitant relationship that develops between Warren and Cassandra (who is ignorant of her past and his identity) runs parallel to Warren's murderous punishment of his father's sin. The climactic killings take place at the site of the mother's suicide, the family's iconic but now-derelict white weatherboard house in the country.

The interrogation of a tainted but commemorated past (in the revealing photographs kept by Cassandra's father, and in the nineteenth-century interior of the Abbott's home) illustrates the gothic perspective on colonial history. In contrast to the nostalgic and normative picture of cultural history in contemporary AFC genre films, gothic narratives portray the past as the origin of the degradation and invalidation of colonial habitation. In common with the gothic's subversive depictions of the archetypal rural Australia, and its abjection of the natural landscape, the potential reassurance of cultural heritage is denied by the exposure of a secret and depraved past, in familial and national terms.

Conclusion

Australian Gothic may be taken to encapsulate many of the characteristics and functions of the horror film in terms of its historical development and of its post-1970 diversification into self-conscious, reflexive, and hybridized forms (as seen, e.g., in *Angel Heart* [Alan Parker, 1987], *Halloween H20* [Steve Miner, 1998], and *The Blair Witch Project* [Daniel Myrick and Eduardo Sánchez, 1999]). The gothic also bears comparison with contemporary and clearly influential horror filmmaking in America, in the relocation of the judgmental aspects of horror's meaning in the environment and composition of the superficially mundane middle-class family. However, the inverted characterization of the family as institution, as not redemptive or rehabilitative, is extended to the level of cultural critique in Australian Gothic. The "horror of personality"[12] contained in the portrayal of the secretive and fallen family also encompasses a horror of nationality, based in a simultaneous abjection of the land and guilt in its acquisition. As noted by Richard Dyer,[13] the connection between whiteness, blondness, and horror goes beyond stereotyped notions of victimhood to suggest corruption, death, and the perpetration of evil. The ubiquity of blond (predominantly female) children in Australian Gothic (the vengeful spirits of *The Survivor*, and the incestuous issue in *Summerfield* and *Cassandra*) as the incarnation of corruption is suggestive of the incongruity and invalidity of the colonial presence on the continent. Far from embodying a virginal vulnerability, the stigma of blondness and whiteness within this landscape is doomed importation, redolent of impurity and insularity.

Australian Gothic envelops and recruits a panoply of generic forms in its elucidation of a culturally specific horror. The recurrence of familial conflict vindicates Sobchack's amalgamation of horror and melodrama, while the loathing and menace of the landscape as a judgment on Australian society connects the gothic with the "natural attack" form of the disaster movie.[14] In its hybridized and self-conscious (in both filmic and cultural terms) approach, the Australian Gothic encapsulates a specific deployment of horror, in application and interpretation, attuned to post-colonial experience.

Notes

1. Susan Dermody and Elizabeth Jacka, *The Screening of Australia*, vol. 1, *The Anatomy of a Film Industry* (Sydney: Currency Press, 1987), 35.
2. Dermody and Jacka, *Screening of Australia*, 132. See also Susan Dermody and Elizabeth Jacka, *The Screening of Australia*, vol. 2: *Anatomy of a National Cinema* (Sydney: Currency Press, 1988), 31; and Scott Murray, "Australian Cinema in the 1970s and 1980s," in *Australian Cinema*, ed. Scott Murray (St. Leonards, Australia: Allen and Unwin, 1994), 92.
3. Philip Brophy, "Horrality—The Textuality of Contemporary Horror Films," *Screen* 27, no. 1 (1986): 4.
4. Brophy, "Horrality," 5.
5. T. J. Ross, Introduction, in *Focus on the Horror Film*, ed. Roy Huss and T. J. Ross (Englewood Cliffs, NJ: Prentice Hall, 1972), 9.
6. Susan Sontag uses this phrase to describe the destruction of society, and personal and communal identity, seen in American science-fiction films. See Susan Sontag, "The Imagination of Disaster," in *Film Theory and Criticism*, 3rd ed., ed. Gerald Mast and Marshall Cohen (Oxford: Oxford University Press, 1985), 451–65.
7. Scott Murray, "*Long Weekend*," *Cinema Papers* 20 (March–April 1979): 303.

8. Tom O'Regan, *Australian National Cinema* (London: Routledge, 1996), 276.

9. Barbara Creed, *The Monstrous Feminine: Film, Feminism, and Psychoanalysis* (London: Routledge, 1993), 17. See also Julia Kristeva, *Powers of Horror: An Essay on Abjection* (New York: Columbia University Press, 1982), 54.

10. Vivian Sobchack, "Bringing It All Back Home: Family Economy and Generic Exchange," in *American Horrors: Essays on the Modern American Horror Film,* ed. Gregory A. Waller (Urbana: University of Illinois Press, 1987), 178.

11. Philip Strick, *"Encounter at Raven's Gate," Monthly Film Bulletin* 57, no. 675 (1990): 103.

12. Charles Derry, "More Dark Dreams: Some Notes on the Recent Horror Film," in Waller, *American Horrors,* 163–64.

13. Richard Dyer, *White* (London: Routledge, 1997), 210.

14. Maurice Yacowar, "The Bug in the Rug: Notes on the Disaster Genre," in *Film Genre Reader,* ed. Barry Keith Grant (Austin: University of Texas Press, 1986), 217–18.

6
Kiwi Gothic:
NEW ZEALAND'S CINEMA OF A PERILOUS PARADISE

Ian Conrich

New Zealand is a pastoral paradise, a country of harmony, tranquility, and great natural beauty. Yet if New Zealand can be regarded as an Eden, a principal and primordial landscape, then excess and disorder can also be observed to exist within this overgrown garden. New Zealand's rich natural resources form a sustained part of a national myth in which the land is viewed as offering freedom and, in retreat, protection. Images of hysteria, horror, despair, and murder are rarely discussed.[1] In places of isolation, in communities geographically and psychologically "on the edge," individuals appear trapped in a landscape that is both enchanting and seemingly "alive."

Many New Zealand films have depicted this conflict and crisis—a reviewer for *The Times* (London) wrote in 1994, "[j]udging by its recent films, New Zealand is a great place to grow mad, twisted and bitter"[2]—and in this essay I will consider the characteristics of this cinema, for which I suggest the term Kiwi Gothic. The idea of the gothic has appeared in discussions concerning a small number of New Zealand films, most commonly Jane Campion's *The Piano* (1993) and Peter Jackson's *Heavenly Creatures* (1994).[3] However, the idea of a nationally specific form of the gothic has yet to be located, and the extent of this aspect of New Zealand cinema remains unexplored.

On the perimeters of the gothic there is a distinct New Zealand cinema of violence and collision, most visible in the seminal *Sleeping Dogs* (Roger Donaldson, 1977), the internationally successful *Once Were Warriors* (Lee Tamahori, 1994), and the less celebrated *The Grasscutter* (Iane Mune, 1989) and *Broken English* (Gregor Nicholas, 1996). All are films with a strong political content that address issues of nation and identity, particularly in relation to post-settler communities. Such issues are also explored in the body of New Zealand films that question authority and notions of law and order, what I have termed "A State of Mild Anarchy" and considered elsewhere in a discussion on hegemony and resistance.[4] Here, accounts of true crime are presented in films such as *Beyond Reasonable Doubt* (John Laing, 1980), *Bad Blood* (Mike Newell, 1981), and *Heavenly Creatures;* and drug trafficking in *Dangerous Orphans* (John Laing, 1987), *Scarfies* (Robert Sarkies, 1999), *The Shirt* (John Laing, 2000), and *Crooked Earth* (Sam Pillsbury, 2001). These films may offer gothic moments, yet they are not the essence of a Kiwi cinema of the gothic. Rather, they are part of what Sam Neill, commenting on a century of New Zealand film, has called a "Cinema of Unease," and they are necessary for understanding patterns of cultural production.[5]

Lying just beyond these texts is New Zealand's production of gothic horror, a most striking cluster of films and an aspect of Kiwi Gothic that will be considered here through a discussion of two key areas: landscape, and family and the home. (Another aspect of Kiwi Gothic cinema not discussed here is gothic fantasy, marked by a dark imagination and exaggeration and located outside the generic boundaries of horror. This tradition can be observed in such films as *The Navigator: A Medieval Odyssey* [Vincent Ward, 1988], and the melodramatic *Desperate Remedies* [Stewart Main and Peter Wells, 1993].) First, though, I will provide some background on the development of New Zealand's tradition of cinematic horror in its various forms.

Formation

New Zealand, to date, has made around 190 feature films, with approximately 88 percent of the productions coming after 1976. A significant cinematic New Wave, filmmaking in this country has been largely supported by a 1978 act of Parliament, in which the New Zealand Film Commission was established "to participate and assist in the making, distribution and exhibition of films."[6] The early productions of this New Wave were predominantly testosterone-fueled: the result of a male-dominated industry in which films offered stories of aggression, stunts, pranks, and subversion.

The first New Zealand feature fiction film to be made solely by a woman was in 1984, Melanie Read's *Trial Run,* followed a year later by Gaylene Preston's *Mr. Wrong* (1985). Interestingly, both films are examples of gothic horror, and specifically of a style of narrative—the Radcliffian mode—that emerged with the gothic literature of Ann Radcliffe and her late-eighteenth-century novels *The Mysteries of Udolpho* (1794) and *The Italian* (1797).[7] Radcliffe's stories, which are a cornerstone of the female gothic, present a persecuted heroine threatened by a secret from the past. In these tales of the phantasmal, the heroine is caught within her immediate environment, and is likely to suffer a repeating moment that challenges her autonomy.[8] In Read's film *Trial Run*, Rosemary Edmonds (Annie Whittle), a mother with an assignment to photograph a group of rare penguins, relocates to a remote coastal cottage to gain proximity to the bird's breeding ground. The cottage soon becomes a threatening habitat, however, one that appears to be haunted by the spirit of its previous occupant, a divorcée, Mrs. West. Writer-director Melanie Read said that the concept was "to make a film that challenged the idea of woman as victim in thriller or horror films. So I decided on the classic situation of a woman on her own in the country, in a deserted area, and just took it from there."[9]

Similarly, *Mr. Wrong* seeks to subvert the sexual politics of the traditional horror movie. In this film, Meg (Heather Bolton) proudly purchases a Mark II Jaguar, but soon finds that the car is haunted by its previous owner, Mary Carmichael (Perry Piercy), who was murdered in the vehicle by a mysterious man (David Letch). But while this film shares similar narrative and stylistic concerns with *Trial Run*, there are also notable differences. Radcliffe incorporated the power of the landscape into the fabric of her gothic stories, and this is a feature of *Trial Run*. It is not, however, a feature of *Mr. Wrong*. And although *Mr. Wrong* is Radcliffian in style, it does not conclude in the Radcliffian mode; instead it avoids the use of the explained supernatural, whereby the previously unknown and the mysterious is rationalized into the accepted laws of nature. At the end of *Mr. Wrong*, the ghostly Mary remains firmly outside the natural world, an avenging spirit who manages to destroy her killer after locking him in the car. In contrast, and with a particular ghostly apparition of Mrs. West aside, the phantasmal disturbances in *Trial Run* are resolved as the orchestrations of Rosemary's son James (Christopher Broun), who was attempting to scare his mother, a long-distance runner in training, into increasing her fastest time.

Clearly there are different forms of the gothic, and it would be inexact to leave all New Zealand horror films unidentified and lumped together under one Kiwi Gothic umbrella. Besides which, many of the films that are relevant here were, at the time of their release, considered and marketed as thrillers or as psychological dramas, this despite their horror content. Certainly the female gothic continued in films such as

Sally Smith's 1991 short *Timetrap* and Alison Maclean's 1992 feature *Crush*. Moreover, prior to the incipience of the female gothic in *Trial Run* and *Mr. Wrong*, there were a few other examples of a developing horror genre in New Zealand cinema.[10] Even in these formative years, however, there was a notable diversity in content.

The earliest New Zealand–produced horror film is arguably Michael Laughlin's *Dead Kids* (a.k.a. *Strange Behavior*, 1981), an Australian co-production that utilizes recognizable elements of the American form of the genre. Set in a small town of Illinois—though shot in the Auckland suburbs of Remuera, Epsom, and Avondale—the film concerns the experiments of a Dr. Le Sangel (Arthur Dignam), an employee in the psychology department of the town's college, who with the aid of drugs has programmed the local youth to commit horrific murders. *Dead Kids* is an example of the slasher cycle that dominated U.S. horror film production at the time, and which was clearly imitated by other international filmmakers. Other slasher-style horrors, films in which a group of teenagers are murdered in turn by a malevolent force, have been scarce in New Zealand, and include *Bridge to Nowhere* (Ian Mune, 1986), *No One Can Hear You* (John Laing, 2000), and *The Locals* (Greg Page, 2003). *Dead Kids* is a hybrid film—part slasher, part medico-horror tale (of which New Zealand's only other example is *Death Warmed Up* [a.k.a. *Brain Damage*, David Blyth, 1984]), and part splatter movie. Of the latter subgenre, Peter Jackson's grotesque style of "splatstick" comedy-gore as seen in *Bad Taste* (1988) and *Braindead* (a.k.a. *Dead Alive*, 1992) has had the strongest audience following.

Despite the disguising of its native origins, the locations used for *Dead Kids* are of relevance to a consideration of the New Zealand small town on film. Such consideration extends to Jackson's *The Frighteners* (1996), a horror-comedy ghost story supposedly set in the American town of "Fairwater," yet filmed in the New Zealand South Island community of Lyttleton. It also extends to *No One Can Hear You* and *Exposure* (David Blyth, 2000), both filmed around Auckland city districts but made to look as if they were made in America.

The archetypal small town New Zealand horror film is Sam Pillsbury's *The Scarecrow* (a.k.a. *Klynham Summer*, 1982), based on the bleak novel by well-known local author Ronald Hugh Morrieson. For this tale of sexual deviance, an ageing John Carradine was hired to play the cadaverous illusionist Herbert Salter, a serial killer, necrophiliac, and a recently arrived stranger in the quaint town of Klynham, who bewitches and terrorizes its inhabitants.[11] In an interview with William Dart, Pillsbury labeled the film an example of Rural Gothic, though this is a term needing further definition.[12] Small town New Zealand Gothic, in which is depicted a community filled with gossip and rumor, locals with responsibilities, and perhaps civic buildings, is different to such Kiwi horror-thrillers as *Heart of the Stag* (Michael Firth, 1984), *Jack Be Nimble* (Garth Maxwell, 1993), and the short *Home Kill* (Andrew Bancroft, 2001)—what could be termed Agricultural Gothic—all of which focus on remote farmsteads, the terrifying tensions between a small group of family members/farm workers, and their particular relationship to the surrounding land.[13] Additionally, there are the gothic shorts *The Singing Trophy* (Grant Lahood, 1993) and *Possum* (Brad McGann, 1997), which present dark or deadly animal narratives in which a hunter or trapper's woodland space of domesticity is threatened.

Location is of prime importance to a consideration of Kiwi Gothic. Beyond the spaces of the small town and the farmstead there is the domestic gothic of the short films *Kitchen Sink* (Alison Maclean, 1989) and *The French Windows* (Steve Bayson, 2001), and the feature *The Returning* (John Day, 1991); the coastal spaces of *Moonrise* (a.k.a. *Grampire* and *My Grandad's a Vampire*, David Blyth, 1991); the urban gothic of *The Irrefutable Truth about Demons* (Glenn Standring, 2000) and *Kung Fu Vampire Killers* (Phil Davison, 2002); the institution-horror and asylum confines of *The Ugly* (Scott Reynolds, 1996); and the vast open spaces, mountains, and lakes of Fiordland in *The Lost Tribe* (John Laing, 1985).

Landscape

The varied sites employed by Kiwi Gothic films is not surprising considering the diversity of location possibilities that New Zealand has to offer. A 1999 Production Guide, published by Film New Zealand to attract and assist locally based filmmaking projects from overseas, has the title "The World in One Country"; "we're not exaggerating," write the Guide's authors. On evidence, New Zealand can be a convincing substitute for the suburban and small-town spaces of America. For the land in this country is sufficiently fertile to assist the realization of the most imaginative of fictitious settings. As the home of the gothic struggles of Middle Earth, for example, New Zealand was the ideal location for Peter Jackson's *The Lord of the Rings* trilogy (2001–2003), its swathes of untouched and uninhabited lands appearing primordial or even removed from history altogether.

Of course, there has been a human presence in New Zealand for around 1,000 years, with the Maori, the indigenous population, holding immense physical and spiritual importance in the region. The struggles over land ownership that followed the initial arrival of the *Pakeha* (Europeans) intensified issues of possession. As Priscilla Pitts writes, New Zealand "is, in truth, an occupied zone whose constantly reread and rewritten histories do not lie in quiescent layers but jostle, shift, and thrust, as changing and unstable as the land itself."[14] Pitts also writes that "[t]he land is without doubt, *the* great New Zealand subject," and this is perhaps most striking in its representation in art, literature, and popular culture.[15] The land dominates New Zealand culture and is within it a towering image.

In New Zealand film, as in much of the local art, figures are either absent, small, or alone within images of the landscape. Films such as *Trial Run, The Lost Tribe,* and *Vigil* separate their protagonists from civilization into spaces where the land appears formidable, uncontrollable, and "alive." As New Zealand filmmaker Gaylene Preston puts it, "[t]here's something that comes out of the land here which is bloody spooky. I don't feel it anywhere else I've been in the Western world. I feel it when I'm here."[16] In *Trial Run,* for example, Rosemary takes a walk on a deserted beach and hears the screaming of the gulls. Suddenly, a few loose stones scuttle from a rock face, and this is followed by an audible crack. Rosemary looks up at the cliff top, from where a tremendous branch hurtles toward her and, spearlike, lands and pierces the sand inches from her feet. There is no implication that the branch was thrown by anybody; in such an active landscape it could simply "fall" from an overhanging tree. In these New Zealand screen landscapes of the gothic, human figures are vulnerable to the forces of nature, psychologically weakened by an overwhelming sense of isolation and incapacitation, threatened by realms of the unknown, and in awe of the primordial, in which there is often an uneasy space of belonging.

The Maori people have a strong sense of belonging, a belief in *mauri* (life force), *wairua* (spirituality), and a relationship to *whenua* (the land). Many geographical features such as *awa* (rivers), *ngahere* (forests), *ana* (caves), *rere* (waterfalls), *roto* (lakes), and *maunga* (mountains) were named by the Maori, and these were crucial genealogical indicators. Maori culture also has many myths and legends that establish particular histories for the significance of the land and *moana* (the sea). Yet, remarkably, Maori society and culture has been almost totally absent from the screen versions of the Kiwi Gothic. In 2002, a series of dramatized Maori short horror stories, *Mataku* (which translates as fear or fright), was broadcast on New Zealand television on TV3. Until then, however, a Maori form of the gothic had only appeared in Laing's *The Lost Tribe*. In this film, Max Scarry (John Bach), an anthropologist working from a coastal hut suffocated by dense bush and on the edge of remote Fiordland waters, has been searching, in an area covered in superstition, for the *tapu* (sacred) graves of a lost Maori tribe. The bones of the Maori are found positioned in a "monster's cave," described as such by Max's daughter who sees the image in her dreams. She has the gift of ESP, not unlike Danny Torrance (Danny Lloyd) in Stanley Kubrick's *The Shining* (1980), and senses a dark force, one that has seemingly affected her father's psychological state and leads him to murder his twin brother.

The "monster's cave" is one of the few instances in New Zealand horror cinema in which caves or holes are used for gothic effect.[17] The children's film *Moonrise* also uses a shoreline cave, though, in this instance, as a hiding place for a vampiric grandfather. For a country in which the landscape is so dominant, and the location possibilities so vast, it seems strange that many of the perhaps predictable geographical features—the sea, forests, lakes, rivers, caves, and mountains—have barely been touched by film productions of the gothic. Of further interest are New Zealand's various ghost towns, abandoned settlements such as Bendigo on the South Island's East Coast, and Waiuta on the West Coast, remnants from the nineteenth-century gold rushes. Again, such location possibilities have been largely ignored by New Zealand film, though in 2002, *Kung Fu Vampire Killers*, a low-budget, shot-on-video comedy-horror movie, was made in the city of Dunedin. It incorporated aspects of local history that relate to the gold rush and the many Chinese prospectors it had attracted. In this hybrid horror tale a student extracts DNA from the corpse of a Chinese prospector and, unaware that it is the body of a vampire, unwittingly unleashes an epidemic of bloodsuckers.

A part of history is also borrowed in the film *Bridge to Nowhere*, shot on location around the region of a particular curiosity, in another abandoned area, near Pipiriki and Raetihi, and on the North Island's Whanganui River. This was once planned farmland; however, the settlers struggled and many had left by 1940. A bridge had been built in 1936 to encourage development but, with the desertion of the area, the track became overgrown, leaving the famous bridge that goes nowhere. The structure was employed as a striking image in a film that addresses isolation and abandonment, a slasher story involving a group of hedonistic city kids who venture into the remote bush only to be met by a manic stockman, Mac (played by the iconic Bruno Lawrence, the archetypal "Kiwi bloke"), who is violently protective of his property and his younger wife. *Bridge to Nowhere* is of interest for the collision of urban and rural cultures, and for its depiction of the horrors contained within the bush. The film also addresses the image of the rugged frontiersman and the instability of domestic life.[18]

The Family and the Domestic

The early settler history of New Zealand by the Europeans appears as a crucial factor in the definition of the Kiwi bloke. This particular cultural image of *Pakeha* masculinity is, as Andrew Spicer writes, "forged in relation to a landscape," and it presents a male who "has a basically republican temper, a refusal to kow-tow to authority and a belief in freedom."[19] New Zealand was long viewed as a man's country, one where "men could prove themselves through hard physical activity, away from the feminizing influences of polite society," but this changed later as the pioneer married, settled, and embraced the domestic space and family life.[20] The attraction of the rugged pioneer life has never been lost, however, and the *Pakeha* male appears torn between the refinement and security of family life on the one hand, and on the other, the tests of virility, the physicality, and the self-dependency of being the "man alone," existing on the edges of society. The man alone, who is capable of extreme violence, is present in both *Bridge to Nowhere* and *The Lost Tribe*, in the figures of Mac and Max respectively. Max is distant from his family during his archaeological search, while Mac, with his wife dead (she was shot by one of the teenagers), destroys his dogs and burns all of his possessions by setting fire to his home. Here, a much darker side of the unsettled loner is revealed as both men appear crazed.

By way of contrast, in the shorts *The Singing Trophy* and *Possum*, the frontiersman maintains a domestic space, though he must struggle to free it from an invasive animal that threatens the stability of the home. Kiwi Gothic appears to function through the conflict between certain binary oppositions, of which those of primary importance are domestic/wild and master/slave. The home of the settler is a shelter from the wilderness—from the rugged and unpredictable land for which there has been a desire to master and regulate. However, the wild is not always so easy to

control, and the settler can be faced with constant challenges that may
lead to entrapment, loss, or retreat.

Shot in sepia and with an eerie soundtrack, *Possum* is a good example here. The possum is an animal regarded as a pest, a creature of the wild
that can invade the home, and one that appears harmless from a distance,
though is actually quite ferocious. In the nineteen-minute film, possum
can be read as the autistic child "Kid" (Eve-Marie Brandish), who because
of her feral behavior and biting of family members has to be chained to a
bedstead at night. Her father, a trapper of possum, works in the surrounding woods maintaining his mastery of the land, yet within his home
his own daughter is an animal that cannot be controlled. Kid, who is discussed in conjunction with the devil, is eventually discovered dead outside
the house, accidentally caught in one of her father's traps.[21]

Kiwi Gothic cinema has a tendency to present the instability of the
domestic space, and the family as well, as dysfunctional.[22] Images of horror, fear, and the abnormal appear to thrive in screen versions of the New
Zealand home. Reynolds' film *The Ugly* explores the mind of an incarcerated serial killer, Simon Cartwright (Paolo Rotondo), and reveals that in
his childhood he was humiliated and tormented by a monstrous mother.
Jack Be Nimble is especially disturbing along these lines, concerning as it
does the separation in childhood of a psychic brother and sister as their
parents' marriage fails and their mother has a nervous breakdown. The
brother, Jack (Alexis Arquette), is adopted by a frightening, farming family who, with four witchlike daughters, now desire a strong son to work on
their land. But Jack is too weak in their view, and in his teenage years he
is persecuted, tortured, and brutalized, including being whipped across
his back with barbed wire. He finally achieves revenge through typical
Kiwi ingenuity: the construction in metalwork class of a bizarre, steam-
powered hypnotizing machine that enables him to master his stepfather
and successfully instruct him to lie down in the road and be killed by a
passing truck. A film concerned with repression and revenge, it ends with
Jack hanging upside down from a tree, his eyes, ears, and mouth sewn shut
by his stepsisters.

Garth Maxwell, the director of *Jack Be Nimble*, has said that inspiration for the film came from a story he read of a New Zealand child who
was whipped with barbed wire by his parents.[23] Disturbingly, this is in a
country that in the 1950s was viewed as offering "a great place to bring up
kids," and with providing a "great way of life."[24] Perhaps here, then, can
be seen a first fissure in the idyllic myth. New Zealand life, for many, has

The monstrous mother (Jennifer Ward-Lealand) of a serial killer in *The Ugly* (1992)

appeared so normal, ordered, and consummate that it became mundane and predictable. Referencing the work of horror theorist Robin Wood, Philip Matthews observes this condition and writes of the filmic images of horror in New Zealand as addressing a desire to destroy the oppressive normality. Jim Sharman's cult classic horror-comedy-musical *The Rocky Horror Picture Show* (1975) is definitely an example in defense of this argument. The film was derived from the stage production *The Rocky Horror Show* (first performed in 1973), which was the brainchild of Richard O'Brien, a New Zealander who grew up in Hamilton, a city with a particular reputation for being uneventful.

Socially and culturally, the home (with the all-important well-maintained garden), carries an immense value in New Zealand and is central to the virtues of local and national citizenry.[25] In Jackson's *Braindead* it becomes the main location for an orgy of zombies, consisting of the assembled family members and neighbors who infect each other. This middle-class home, set in parochial Wellington in 1957—during the peak of New Zealand's "good way of life"—is simultaneously an honorable property and a site of family repression. Lionel (Timothy Balme) is suffocated by his domineering Mum (Elizabeth Moody), a monstrous mother who then becomes quite literally an abject threat when she is bitten by a Sumatran rat-monkey that transforms her into a putrefied and pustulous body. The various stuffy figures who are rapidly infected and zombiefied eventually fill every room of the large colonial home—an apocalyptic secret of mass local social disintegration that Lionel struggles to contain. In what appeared to be a previously spotless home, the wildly inhuman are an invasive and rabid mess that Lionel finally "cleans up"

Jack's (Alexis Arquette)
horrifying demise in *Jack
Be Nimble* (1993)

with the help of that trusty icon of Kiwi domesticity, the hovermower, which he uses to slice and splatter through the socially monstrous creatures. A now gargantuan Mum is the last to be destroyed, ripped open by Lionel from the inside as he fights his way out of her all-enveloping body to be reborn.[26]

Further examples of the invaded New Zealand home occur in the effectively disturbing shorts *Kitchen Sink* and *The French Windows.* Lionel's home is shared with an unwelcome horde and is at the heart of a perverse new social order; however, the monstrous in these short films intrudes into a domestic space where the owner resides in isolation. Generally, isolation from the local community in New Zealand takes place within the rural landscape, and not the domestic. Here, though, we find home-alone horrors erupting precisely from the domestic and the mundane: In the award-winning *Kitchen Sink,* a hairy creature that grows into a strange man is yanked by a woman from the plughole of a sink[27]; in *The French Windows,* a man who has just completed glazing his living room, and who discovers that there is now perpetual darkness outside his glass doors, is dragged out of his home by a shadowy figure and exiled into this terminal realm.

Such experiences of the unfamiliar and unhomely, or, to use Freud's term, the "uncanny," tap into feelings of vulnerability in reaction to a sense of place. "Especially a new place," writes William J. Schafer,[28] who views the mobilization of the uncanny as part of the development process of cultural identity: "[t]he transition from *unheimlich* [unhomely] to *heimlich* [homely] is the process of nation building, of acculturation. We move from a sense of alienation and rootlessness—being separated and detached from the landscape around us—to a sense of being rooted in it, sprung from it, possessed and haunted by it."[29] In furthering his argument, Schafer refers to the American poet Robert Lee Frost, who asserted that "to possess a place is to be possessed by it."[30] Interestingly, New Zealanders stress that this is their experience, yet they are also quick to reject, deny, or condemn the many accounts and fictional Kiwi Gothic stories of the horrific and the unknown. Sam Neill's 1995 documentary, *Cinema of Unease*, was widely criticized by New Zealanders for its dark portrayal of local culture. In the country's main weekly publication, the *Listener*, Neill was accused of making a documentary that seemed to be "primarily for a British audience. It expounds a view of New Zealand that is rather tired and condescending."[31] The local satirical critic Raybon Kan, who does recognize New Zealand's cinema of the gothic, nevertheless proclaims that "[w]e owe it to ourselves to project as attractive and non-disastrous an image as we can in our movies."[32] But to hide the issue is not the way forward. As I co-wrote in the introduction to a 2000 book titled *New Zealand—A Pastoral Paradise?* "the increasing recognition and representation of the country's imperfections can be taken as an indication of a growing self-confidence in New Zealand's identity."[33]

Notes

1. Of interest here is the artwork of photographer Ann Shelton. Her "environmental documentation" includes a series of landscape images associated with New Zealand true crime. For instance, her diptych *Doublet (After Heavenly Creatures) Parker/Hulme Crime Scene, Port Hills, Christchurch, New Zealand* (2001), captures the scene now of where there had been a 1954 matricide: a secluded pathway that is pregnant with the past. See the catalogue *Slow Release: Recent Photography from New Zealand* (Victoria, Australia: Heide Museum of Modern Art, 2002).

2. Quoted in Clare Barry, "Reviewers Hold Candle Stick to *Jack Be Nimble*," *New Zealand News UK,* February 16, 1994, 24.

3. See, for example, Cyndy Hendershot, "(Re)Visioning the Gothic: Jane Campion's *The Piano*," *Literature Film Quarterly* 26, no. 2 (1998): 97–108; Estella Tincknell, "New Zealand Gothic?: Jane Campion's *The Piano*," in *New Zealand—A Pastoral Paradise?*, ed. Ian Conrich and David Woods (Nottingham, UK: Kakapo, 2000), 107–19; Maureen Molloy, "Death and the Maiden: The Feminine and the Nation in Recent New Zealand Films," *Signs: Journal of Women in Culture and Society* 25, no. 1 (1999): 153–70.

4. Ian Conrich, "A State of Mild Anarchy: Lawlessness and New Zealand Film," unpublished paper presented at the *Focus on Australian and New Zealand Cinema* conference, Institute of Commonwealth Studies, University of London (October 4, 1997); Ian Conrich, "In God's Own Country: Open Spaces and the New Zealand Road Movie," in Conrich and Woods, *New Zealand—A Pastoral Paradise?*, 31–38.

5. *A Cinema of Unease: A Personal Journey by Sam Neill* (1995). Documentary commissioned by the British Film Institute for the "Century of Cinema" series.

6. See Ian Conrich and Sarah Davy, *Views from the Edge of the World: New Zealand Film* (London: Kakapo, 1997), 2. See also Gregory A. Waller, "The New Zealand Film Commission: Promoting an Industry, Forging a National Identity," *Historical Journal of Film, Radio, and Television* 16, no. 2 (1996): 243–62.

7. For a discussion of Ann Radcliffe, see Robert Miles, *Ann Radcliffe: The Great Enchantress* (Manchester, UK: Manchester University Press, 1995).

8. See Michelle A. Massé, *In the Name of Love: Masochism, and the Gothic* (Ithaca: Cornell University Press, 1992), esp. 10–39.

9. Alison Maclean interview with Melanie Read, "Trial Run," *Alternative Cinema* 11, no. 4 (1983/1984): 14.

10. Predating these examples of New Zealand female gothic is the Australian film *Next of Kin* (Tony Williams, 1982), a haunted house horror financed with assistance from the New Zealand Film Commission. This was for the development of the script, then titled *Sticky Ends*, written by New Zealanders Michael Heath and Tony Williams.

11. For further discussion of Pillsbury's film, see Jo Seton, "Subjects of the Gaze: Controlling and Containing Women in *The Scarecrow*," *Illusions* 1 (Summer 1986): 18–20.

12. William Dart, "Kiwi Rural Gothic: An Interview with Sam Pillsbury," *Art New Zealand* 24 (Winter 1982): 36–39.

13. Another farming film that, though not horror, is of relevance to Kiwi Gothic, is *Vigil* (Vincent Ward, 1984).

14. Priscilla Pitts, "The Unquiet Earth: Reading Landscape and the Land in New Zealand Art," in *Headlands: Thinking through New Zealand Art*, ed. Mary Barr (Sydney: Museum of Contemporary Art, 1992), 87.

15. Pitts, "Unquiet Earth," 87.

16. Jonathan Dennis, "Reflecting Reality: Gaylene Preston, An Interview," in *Film in Aotearoa New Zealand*, 2nd ed., ed. Jonathan Dennis and Jan Bieringa (Wellington, New Zealand: Victoria University Press, 1996), 171.

17. There is, of course, the vast tunnel that is dug from fourteenth-century Cumbria, England, to twentieth-century Auckland, New Zealand, in Ward's gothic fantasy *The Navigator: A Medieval Odyssey*.

18. For further discussion, see Andrew Spicer, *An Ambivalent Archetype: Masculinity, Performance and the New Zealand Films of Bruno Lawrence* (Nottingham, UK: Kakapo, 2000). On masculinity, see also Jock Phillips, *A Man's Country? The Image of the Pakeha Male—A History* (Auckland, New Zealand: Penguin, 1996).

19. Spicer, *Ambivalent Archetype*, 2.

20. Ibid.

21. For a series of discussions on *Possum*, and an interview with the director, see *p.o.v.* 7 (March 1999).

22. David Callahan views the dysfunctional family as a constant in New Zealand cinema; see "The Functional Family in New Zealand Film," in Conrich and Woods, *New Zealand—A Pastoral Paradise?*, 97–106.

23. See Barry, "Reviewers Hold Candle Stick to *Jack Be Nimble*," 24; Philip Matthews, "Local Infections: New Zealand Horror," *Landfall* 201 (August 2001): 183.

24. See Introduction, in Conrich and Woods, *New Zealand—A Pastoral Paradise?* 8; Claudia Bell, *Inventing New Zealand: Everyday Myths of Pakeha Identity* (Auckland, New Zealand: Penguin, 1996), 30.

25. See Harvey Perkins and David Thorns, "Houses, Homes and New Zealanders' Everyday Lives," in *Sociology of Everyday Life in New Zealand*, ed. Claudia Bell (Palmerston North, New Zealand: Dunmore Press, 2001), 30–51; Barbara Brookes, ed., *At Home in New Zealand: Houses, History, People* (Wellington, New Zealand: Bridget Williams, 2000).

26. For further discussion, see Barry Keith Grant, *A Cultural Assault: The New Zealand Films of Peter Jackson* (Nottingham, UK: Kakapo, 1999); Barbara Creed, "*Bad Taste* and Antipodal Inversion: Peter Jackson's Colonial Suburbs," *Postcolonial Studies* 3, no. 1 (2000): 61–68; Lawrence McDonald, "A Critique of the Judgement of *Bad Taste* or Beyond *Braindead* Criticism," *Illusions* 21/22 (Winter 1993): 10–15.

27. For further discussion of *Kitchen Sink*, see Miro Bilbrough, "*Kitchen Sink:* An Unchastening Tale," in *NowSeeHear!: Art, Language and Translation*, ed. Ian Wedde and Gregory Burke (Wellington, New Zealand: Victoria University Press, 1990), 45–47; Richard Raskin, "An Interview with Alison Maclean on *Kitchen Sink*," *p.o.v.* 13 (March 2002): 100–110; and the collection of essays in *Pleasures and Dangers: Artists of the '90s*, ed. Trish Clark and Wystan Curnow (Auckland, New Zealand: Longman Paul, 1991), 50–67.

28. William J. Schafer, *Mapping the Godzone: A Primer on New Zealand Literature and Culture* (Honolulu: University of Hawai'i Press, 1998), 141.

29. Schafer, *Mapping the Godzone*, 144.

30. Ibid., 142.

31. Philip Matthews, "Art of Darkness," *Listener* (October 14, 1995): 30.

32. Raybon Kan, *Five Days in Las Vegas* (Wellington, New Zealand: Daphne Brasell, 1992), 202.

33. Introduction, in Conrich and Woods, *New Zealand—A Pastoral Paradise?*, 9.

Irish Horror:

NEIL JORDAN AND THE ANGLO-IRISH GOTHIC

Brian McIlroy

> I thought of Bram Stoker, whose derelict house I used to pass on my
> way to school, at the Crescent, in Marino. But perhaps the most aus-
> tere, the most complete ghost behind this script, was that of a con-
> temporary of Stoker's, Oscar Wilde. A film which becomes in the
> end a necrophiliac romance, in which a living couple fall madly and
> blissfully in love with a couple who have been dead for centuries can
> only aspire to his sublime sense of fantasy and cynicism.
>
> Neil Jordan on the sources for the film *High Spirits*

> The classic Irish Gothic novel . . . is characterized by a combination
> of narrative complexity, emotional hysteria and the incursion of
> supernatural systems on a hopelessly flawed and corrupt "real" world.
> In the Gothic vision, any hope of social change in the present is belied
> by the persistence of the sins of the past. The message is that we are
> all victims of history, only most have not recognized it yet.
>
> Gerry Smyth

Apocalyptic visions, madness, extreme obsessions, psychosis, and the
metaphorical (and sometimes real) disinterring of the dead are inextricably linked to Irish literature and culture as well as to Irish history. The burden of the past in Ireland still haunts—from the disagreements over how
many died in the famine in the 1840s and whether or not the local and
national authorities could have saved hundreds of thousands of poor,
starving people, to the heart-wrenching and painful efforts of families to
find and unearth the remains of their loved ones who were murdered,
dumped, and buried unceremoniously during the conflict in Northern
Ireland in the last thirty-five years. Other recessive traumas are too easy to
mention—the many battles between the British Crown and the Irish
nationalist and republican forces over 800 years of colonial experience,

added to vicious and chronic local sectarianism, have kept the profession of Irish historian alive and well.

It is no surprise then that Irish artists seek ways to address these events, even if what they finally produce might appear lame and inadequate to the demanding historian. The tendency among Irish filmmakers has been to adopt a "kitchen-sink" realist style to approach these issues, leaving the imaginative field fairly open to Ireland's most known cineaste. Why has this been the tendency? It is as if Irish people, mostly represented visually as working class, are always looking back in anger (à la John Osborne and other Northern English books, films, and plays of the 1950s and early 1960s). This aesthetic also extends to Scottish cinema, except for Peter Mullan's remarkable film *Orphans* (1999), which is influenced by magic realism.[1] Generally, Celtic narrative cinema (Ireland, Scotland, and Wales) has not taken up a new aesthetic to accompany new content, nor been particularly interested in the horror genre; the small corpus of Irish-related horror/thrillers include Hilton Edwards's *Return to Glennascaul* (1951) and Robin Hardy's *The Fantasist* (1986), both of which are minor works. In what follows, I argue that Neil Jordan's oeuvre is important as an aesthetic and political bridge between the literary forms of the Irish Gothic and the more immediate pleasures of cinematic horror.

Political and Literary History

Many writers, filmmakers, and critics are fixated on a dichotomy between the English imperial apparently "rational" order and the Irish "sublime sense of fantasy and cynicism" Neil Jordan mentions above. And here, to understand the latter—for we have only to conjure up Cromwell and the Roundheads to understand the former—we must have some understanding of the nuances of Ireland's political history. One of the truisms of English imperial power—and one that is often misunderstood—is that it successfully ruled and colonized Ireland just as much by manufacturing consent and negotiation as by the threat of force and Protestant settlement. It was this fact that drove Irish nationalists and republicans in the late nineteenth and early twentieth centuries to look for a Gaelic Revival to differentiate the Irish from the English and to force the "West Brits" (Irish people steeped and comfortable in British culture—represented, for example, by Gabriel Conroy in James Joyce's short story "The Dead") to make a stark choice.

Part of this political program purposely put a lot of value on the Irish peasant experience and folklore, for it was these people who had suffered the most during the famine and British rule generally. In the imaginings of W. B. Yeats and Patrick Pearse, Celtic mythology became a source of strength and mystery, a counterbalance to the conservative Roman Catholic Church. This pagan power suggested a necessary founding myth of the putative Irish nation. In this context, the recourse to the supernatural—including leprechauns, faeries, banshees, faith healing, somnambulism, and plain old miracles—is more readily appreciated. The ignorant Irish peasant lout of English caricature is reframed as an idiot savant with a magical channel to a natural and supernatural reservoir of knowledge and spirituality.

But this is only one camera position from which to "treat" Ireland, and through which Robert Stevenson's *Darby O'Gill and the Little People* (1959), for example, is informed. Neil Jordan refers more favorably to the influences of Bram Stoker and Oscar Wilde, which present a camera position from a minority urban sensibility forced to consider a majority rural perspective. We are now in the world of the much written about Anglo-Irish Gothic, a mode summarized succinctly in terms of the novel by Gerry Smyth. The Irish Gothic is inextricably tied to the Anglo-Irish settler culture and the colonial experience generally. In this paradigm, with theoretical help from Frantz Fanon and Homi Bhabha, it is assumed the Protestant populace's awareness of its insecurity produces a monstrous tension that reveals itself in supernatural and highly emotional writing. Indeed, Alison Milbank argues that Bram Stoker's *Dracula* (1897) was perceived by his peers as an attempted "mediating between Catholic and Protestant conceptions of Christianity."[2] Others, though, simply argue that the vampire in his castle stands in for the rapacious British and Protestant colonizer and settler emanating out from Dublin Castle and other de facto garrisons with the express purpose of feasting on the native Irish. Seamus Deane—perhaps too cleverly—sees a direct (yet perversely inverted) link between Stoker's 1890s Dracula who travels by sea in a coffin during the day and the so-called coffin ships that poor Irish famine immigrants had to endure to reach North America.[3] Both were living dead, and both would come back to haunt.

What Milbank and other writers on the gothic, such as W. J. McCormack, have ventured is that the Act of Union in 1801 that dissolved the Dublin Parliament left the Irish Protestant elite directionless.[4] Specifically, it created a duality—apparent supporters of the colonial system but also victims of it, since the center of local power had shifted from Dublin to London. Julian Moynahan also points out that Charles Maturin and Joseph Sheridan Le Fanu, two of the great Irish Gothic writers, emerged from Dublin-based Huguenot heritage, not the landed gentry of the (Protestant and Anglican) Big House.[5] They had, in other words, in their family history faint echoes of Catholic persecution in France. This history goes some way toward explaining why many of their novels take place in medieval, Mediterranean Catholic Europe, a place where barbarians and monsters thrive! So, one can see the Irish Gothic as Protestant unease within Ireland, penned by almost reluctant and guilty intellectuals speaking for and about a native Irish who were still struggling in the 1800s to articulate a sense of self-worth in political terms. One can also see the various mechanisms of literary gothic as an acceptance of the irrational not just in religious terms but also in the areas of personal activity and feeling. Vampirism, for example, attracts and repels in equal measure, whether it be read or viewed in Stoker's *Dracula*, Murnau's *Nosferatu* (1922), or Jordan's *Interview with the Vampire* (1993).

Jordan and the Gothic

Yet the interesting question here is why should Neil Jordan, an Irish Catholic-educated writer, find the so-called Protestant Gothic of particular force? Arguably, the Dublin-centered Jordan shares with the urbane sophisticates of Maturin and Le Fanu an equal sense of fear and wonder about the wild Irish countryside and its inhabitants. More directly, he prefers the exploration and release of the supernatural because it allows ready discussion of race, gender, and nationality issues. Of course, it further allows the sensational treatment and examination of sexuality, matters most difficult to address in a culture that has often tried to deny the reality of such desires. This restrictive atmosphere is best revealed by the continual (though mostly narrow) debates over abortion, effectively still illegal in Ireland. In March 2002, a referendum was held in the Republic of Ireland to decide whether a 1992 Supreme Court ruling that a woman could have an abortion if she were deemed suicidal, should be struck down. The decision was 51 percent to 49 percent in favor of the ruling, with the urban vote largely liberal and the rural vote largely conservative. Every year it is estimated that 7,000 young women travel from Ireland to England for abortion services. In Northern Ireland, abortions can occur for "medical reasons," but by refusing to transfer the 1967 "Liberalization

Act" of England and Wales to Northern Ireland (which effectively decriminalized homosexuality and abortion), the current Northern Ireland Assembly aligns itself with the policy of the Republic of Ireland.

Beyond the political and social climate, Jordan is clearly influenced by many artistic strains—the linking of violence and Catholicism in Martin Scorsese's gangster films, such as his *Mean Streets* (1973); the whimsical nature of many European art films of the 1960s, such as Michelangelo Antonioni's *Blowup* (1966)—but mostly he seems comfortable in Hollywood's general melodramatic tendencies, where sentiment and emotion are encouraged to live. Witness the passions in *The End of the Affair* (1998), which depends on the supernatural—a religious miracle—to play a major part in how the main characters experience the meaning of their existences. Look at the exotic titles of Jordan's fictional works—*Night in Tunisia* (1979), *The Dream of the Beast* (1983), *Sunrise with Sea Monster* (1994).[6] He uses the term "Miracle" for his 1991 film to describe a boy discovering his long-lost mother for the first time, not to mention the ambiguous term "Angel," the title of his first feature film (a.k.a. *Danny Boy*, 1982). His work with writer Angela Carter on *The Company of Wolves* (1984), and with Anne Rice on *Interview with the Vampire,* opens his gothicism out in plain view.

Even when Jordan turns to a rather unsuccessful attempt at Hollywood comedy in *High Spirits* (1988), we see his recycling of all these themes that I have been discussing: the monstrous, incestuous familial bonds; the presence of the past as a determining power in the present; and the outbreak of general madness and mayhem. In this film, Castle Plunkett is in dire straights and Peter Plunkett (Peter O'Toole) chances on the idea of marketing his Irish castle as one full of ghosts and ghouls. While his American tourists are unimpressed with the staff's best ghostly efforts to scare them, the guests do suffer and enjoy the awakening of the dead Plunketts. Much of the humor rests on the conceit of living people loving most of all those who are dead.

This raising of the dead forces a revaluation of contemporary relationships and sexuality. Sharon (Beverly D'Angelo) has been sent over by her father, Jem Brogan, the Irish American who will retain the rights to the Castle if the Plunketts cannot make their loan payments. He wishes to transfer the Castle to California, brick by brick, to create a kind of theme park. Peter Plunkett delivers a vicious assault on Brogan's family by suggesting that one of his ancestors hoarded food during the famine. Ironically, Peter's decision to market Irish heritage (a haunted castle) as a tourist destination is not qualitatively different from Jem Brogan's own intentions. One of the niceties of Jordan's script is that Sharon ultimately falls in love with a male ancestor, Martin Brogan (Liam Neeson), thereby suggesting not just a necrophiliac romance but also an incestuous one. With Jack's (Steve Guttenberg) marriage to the once-dead Mary Plunkett (Daryl Hannah), who magically lives as Sharon dies, the productive link between Ireland and America is solidly made. Of course, this strategic move in the scripting taps into the fantasy of many Irish Americans fascinated with their heritage, and the romantic notion of returning to claim a special touchstone to the past.

Additionally, Jordan's interest in turning *High Spirits* into a sex comedy reveals itself in his fervent satire of the Catholic priesthood and its strictures against fornication and sexual thoughts generally. The American Brother Tony (Peter Gallagher) sees this trip as a retreat to finally decide his path in the Church. He is fully tempted by Miranda (Jennifer Tilly) and succumbs to his general happiness. A most compelling image is this white-collared novitiate surrounded by ghostly nun habits while steam rises from his groin, almost as punishment for desiring Miranda. Along with jokes about Martin Brogan's body odor and natural functions, Irish hang-ups about sex and the body could hardly be made more obvious and critiqued more clearly.

Despite the general attempt at humor—and *High Spirits* did not succeed well critically or commercially—there is a difficulty with the reliance on the past as a form of modernization for the castle. At one level, in what is probably the best scene in the film, the real family ghosts appear, appalled at the failure of the Plunketts and the staff to create believable ghosts and save the castle. At another level, Jordan seems to be suggesting—much in keeping with notions of the gothic—that harmony is restored when past and present are reunited. This explains the rather touching scene between father (Ray McAnally) and son, a conversation about feelings that probably only could occur because one of the participants is dead. So, in this film, the strange happenings in the middle of the night, so common to gothic and melodramatic works, turns out to be restorative and life-affirming. The gothic horror here serves to free the characters to be themselves.

Ten years later, Jordan would take on a more troubling gothic-influenced investigation of small-town Ireland in the early 1960s. While *High Spirits* attempts to begin a dialogue about American perceptions of Ireland (and Irish perceptions of American perceptions of Ireland),

Steam rises from the groin of Brother Tony (Peter Gallagher) in *High Spirits* (1988)

Jordan's 1997 film *The Butcher Boy* is a more sophisticated, self-assured, and edgy piece of work. Based on the Pat McCabe novel, Jordan's co-scripted work with the novelist delves much deeper into the Irish neurosis and the recent past of 1962 Ireland, a time similar to his own upbringing. As the filmmaker reveals: "[I]t gave me an opportunity to reinvent that extraordinary mixture of paranoia and paralysis, madness and mysticism that was the Ireland I grew up in, in the '50s."[7] As a youth, Jordan was fed a staple of religious films, and one can certainly argue that *The Butcher Boy* is a keenly religious but anti-Catholic film.[8]

The fragmented town life of Francie Brady (Eamonn Owens) is beset with internal and external pressures. We are not so much watching an extended metaphor of Francie as an abused child of Irish history, as one critic has suggested,[9] but rather an exploration of the inadequacy of traditional Ireland and its institutions—particularly the Roman Catholic Church—and its failure to nurture its young, to confess to its own sickness, to acknowledge that its various forms of denial have created and perpetuated mental illness. It is now commonplace to observe that from the late 1950s onward Ireland began a slow and painful process of internationalization, of opening out to the world, inviting foreign investment and industries. Initially, however, this modernization was tied to the urban centers, particularly Dublin. It is no accident that on Francie's trip to Dublin from his small Monaghan town he attends a science-fiction horror movie about alien invasion (a typical American displaced manifestation of the fear of Russian invasion during the cold war).

He also purchases here a model of an Irish country family, depicting a happy colleen sewing outside her cottage; it is ironic that he must travel to modern Dublin to find a distillation of an idealized rural Ireland. He buys this gift for his mother Annie (Aisling O'Sullivan), unaware that she has killed herself, possibly pushed over the edge by the fact that Francie had temporarily run away from home. To arrive at his mother's funeral cortege with this imaginary happy family tucked under his arm reveals the lie of Eamon De Valera's desire for an Ireland of "comely maidens,"[10] whereas the reality of many is mental illness, domestic violence, depression, and suicide. Jordan complicates this apparent urban/rural division by analyzing the small town, a place neither completely rural nor completely urban; it is always a place of becoming, beckoning sometimes to the urbane future and sometimes to the unsophisticated natural past. It is also a border country, close to that other "British" Ireland of Northern Ireland.

The urbane future is full of shocks and horrors of a different kind than the rural stagnant past. At first, it seems to be liberating. The arrival of television, on which Francie and Joe (Alan Boyle) can sneak peeks of their favorite *Lone Ranger* series as well as the series titled *The Fugitive* (actually broadcast 1963–67), ushers in a fantasy world as much as the comic books they steal from Phillip Nugent (Andrew Fullerton). One of the facts of early 1960s comics in Ireland and the United Kingdom is that the Americans produced many of them in color, whereas the homegrown product was invariably in black-and-white. No doubt this helps to explain why Jordan accompanies the film's opening credits with drawings of these attractive American comic book heroes. The myth of the American West as frontier is not so far removed from the small town in rural Ireland, though it is interesting that the boys can identify with Sitting Bull and Geronimo as much as with the Lone Ranger. Are they noble savages or delusional Robin Hood figures?

But this American influence intrudes in a very real way via radio reports of the Cuban missile crisis and the possibility of nuclear annihilation. This news feeds into Francie's imaginings, as well as his depressing reality. He moves into the world of "what if?" projecting a nuclear strike in his hometown that would create devastation and the emergence of mutants with pig and bug heads; in some respects, to Francie, this would explain perfectly the reality of his current existence, his family laid waste by the metaphorical bomb of small town and Church expectations. Doctors and priests logically, therefore, take on alien heads, and he senses he is living in a world of grotesquery, assisted by the fact that he acquires a job in a slaughterhouse. It is as if he is one of the few human survivors in the world of that classic 1950s sci-fi horror movie, *Invasion of the Body Snatchers* (1956).

If America connotes agency, freedom, and risk, Ireland is replete with feelings of repression, failure, limitation, and dullness. Its horrors are too visceral. Francie must seek the miraculous for his active mind to survive, and he achieves this by having visions of the Virgin Mary, played in a coy manner by singer Sinead O'Connor (a controversial casting decision in itself, given her famous ripping up of the Pope's picture on television, and her allegations of child abuse when she was a young girl, the authenticity of which has been challenged by her own family). The cycle of illness—Francie's father (Stephen Rea) also seems to have been through a reform school run by a Catholic order—appears to be tied to Francie's self-loathing and desire to see himself above what he calls the "Bogmen" with their "bony arses" with whom he has to consort. These people are the peasants synonymous with the rural Ireland that De Valera embraced, and which Francie (and Neil Jordan) seem to think of as an unimaginative and limited form of Irish identity.

However, though we understand that Francie experiences rural Ireland as a nightmare—which is perhaps why he sees the Virgin Mary in the middle of a peat bog, a substance fully representative of Ireland's traditional economy—it is odd on the surface that all his hatred should focus on the Nugents, who have returned from England with "airs." This jealousy revolves around wealth: Phillip Nugent can afford American comics and has a television at home, good clothes, and so on. This wealth and middle-class aspiration steals away Francie's friend Joe, despite the pair's blood-brother partnership. England also figures largely in the failure of his musician father, for Francie's Uncle Alo (Ian Hart)—like many Irish—traveled, worked, and eventually settled in London to make his way in the world. To go to England for work was not exactly an Irish dream, but a practical necessity, often undermining the self-esteem of those who stayed behind (and, it should be said, the emigrants often received a frosty reception in England). In this way, Francie's father sees himself as a failure, a feeling picked up by his son all too clearly. The latter's gross murder of Mrs. Nugent (Fiona Shaw), his daubing of the walls in her blood, and his attempt at a fiery suicide, are his response to an Irish society that is sick beyond redemption, and which has made him sick. In an odd and disturbing way, a boy influenced by American action heroes murders a woman influenced by British culture, who is effectively a "West Brit." The triple colonization of Britain, America, and De Valera's rural and small town imaginary—a nation of small shopkeepers, as some commentators opined—literally explodes the Irish family depicted in the film.

Jordan and Ireland

What is it then that would make Jordan so uncomfortable in Ireland that he would turn to the gothic? Certainly, his unease with the Roman Catholic Church must take pride of place. In his first film, *Angel*, he seems to idolize the freelancing faith healer who works out of a tacky caravan compared to conventional Catholic institutions; also in this film, Jordan's fear of the provincial and its attendant isolation, sometimes determined by a powerful Catholic Church, is reflected by a minor character's decision to kill herself. In *The Butcher Boy*, Francie is molested by a deranged priest (Milo O'Shea), and this would be blackly comic if not for the current joint Irish Government and Roman Catholic Church payout of over 800 million Euros to settle the claims of 3,500 Irish adults who were abused as children in Catholic state-supported schools.[11] In *Michael Collins* (1996), Jordan seems to work his way through to a hybrid Irish nationalism that accepts the existence of fiery emotions—murder and mayhem—but also the necessity to keep them in check. The gothic license, as defined by transgression of norms, is expressed further with the addressing of lesbianism in *Mona Lisa* (1986), homosexuality and bisexuality in *The Crying Game* (1992), and the feminized male in many of his works, although some observers may regard this interest as an unfortunate form of erotic and sexual tourism. As Jordan admitted in updating the story "Guests of the Nation" by Frank O'Connor for the script of *The Crying Game*, he felt what was missing was the erotic thread, one sure to be controversial and destabilizing.

The generic horror film is another, more accepted way to explore these boundaries, and it has often allowed for the articulation of deep fears and anxieties—fear of technology runs riot in James Whale's *Frankenstein* (1931) and Fritz Lang's *Metropolis* (1926), for example, and fear of the female body runs throughout Brian De Palma's *Carrie* (1976), normally considered a displaced discourse on the taboo of menstruation. To steal a title from Barry Keith Grant's recent collection, it is the "Dread

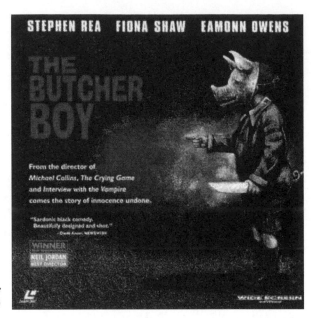

Cover art for *The
Butcher Boy* (1997)

of Difference" that frequently drives the narrative and compels us to watch.[12] But Jordan's films are not horrific in the cheap, sensational way that many horror movies work; his characters are too well-formed to allow the plot to rattle along at a tremendous, unthinking speed. If there is a problem with Jordan's *In Dreams* (1999)—a picture that fared quite poorly at the box office[13]—it is because the director takes all the necessary plot points of a horror-thriller and then refuses to up the tempo, attracting the criticism that his timing and talent do not fit the conventional melodramatic horror film or thriller format. A typical popular review response is that of Peter Rainer for *New York* magazine, who called *In Dreams* "a dollop of supernatural claptrap" and Jordan "the wrong director for a supernatural horror thriller." Rainer does make the point, however, that Jordan's "genius is for conveying the visionary in the everyday."[14] In response to his critics, Jordan argued that with this film he was attempting to make a serious horror movie with a psychological exploration rooted in childhood fairytales, in particular *Snow White.* This is in line with earlier efforts such as *The Company of Wolves,* a film that explored werewolf mythology and offered a variation on *Little Red Riding Hood.*

One might say that Jordan's success with *The Crying Game* was fortuitous, coming at a point in North American cultural discourse when debate was centered on the very issues of gender identity addressed in the film. Judith Butler's *Gender Trouble* was published two years before *The Crying Game* appeared, for example.[15] His success with *Interview with the Vampire* relied to a great extent on the star billing of Tom Cruise and Brad Pitt, as well as on the pre-sold property of Anne Rice, but it allowed him to delve once more into *The Company of Wolves* territory. The point about these latter two films, somewhat similar to *High Spirits*, is their confidence in alternative realities, and yet equally, the confidence that these realities are neither utopias nor fully dystopias. The vampires of *Interview with the Vampire* live forever, liminal characters that haunt our imaginations. They are appealing hybrids.

Despite the personal, commercial, and cultural imperatives to seek out the gothic, Jordan's work is a kind of Wildean sublime, an exalted state that induces awe and terror, a negative pleasure.[16] It attracts Jordan's interest for it is a literary (and filmic) form that appeals to the visual, to excess, to fragmentation, to the refusal to serve a particular ideology. It is an artist's weapon against conformity. In the surplus value provoked by the gothic, one can see the impossibility of certitude for a bourgeois subject and an aspiring bourgeois society. In sum, the horror that Jordan's gothic brings to Irish eyes is predicated on an inner knowledge that the healthy imagination cannot express itself in a suffocating and institutionalized culture. More politically and controversially, Jordan would seem to agree with Northern Ireland's main Unionist politician, David Trimble, at least in relation to the past, that the barely repressed horror of the Republic of Ireland is the recognition of a "pathetic, sectarian, mono-ethnic, mono-cultural state."[17]

Notes

1. See Duncan Petrie, "Devolving British Cinema: The New Scottish Cinema and the European Art Cinema," *Cineaste* 26 (2001): 55–57, 4.
2. Alison Milbank, in *Bram Stoker: History, Psychoanalysis and the Gothic*, ed. William Hughes and Andrew Smith (New York: St. Martin's, 1998), 12.
3. See Stephen de Vere's report of one such "coffin-ship" journey in Noel Kissane, *The Irish Famine: A Documentary History* (Dublin: National Library of Ireland, 1995), 162–63. See also Seamus Deane's take on the import of *Dracula* in his *Strange Country: Modernity and Nationhood in Irish Writing since 1790* (Oxford: Clarendon Press, 1997), 89–94.

4. See W. J. McCormack, *Dissolute Characters: Irish Literary History through Balzac, Sheridan Le Fanu, Yeats, and Bowen* (Manchester, UK: Manchester University Press, 1993).

5. See Julian Moynahan, *Anglo-Irish: The Literary Imagination in a Hyphenated Culture* (Princeton: Princeton University Press, 1995), 109–35.

6. Lori Rogers provides an excellent reading of *The Dream of the Beast*. See her "'In Dreams Uncover'd': Neil Jordan, *The Dream of the Beast*, and the Body-Secret," *Critique* 39, no. 1 (1997): 48–54.

7. Neil Jordan, "Production Notes," online at http://www.butcherboy.warnerbros .com, 3, accessed December 5, 2002.

8. In "Neil Jordan's Guilty Pleasures," *Film Comment* 28, no. 6 (1992), Jordan mentions the forced feeding of religious films such as Henry Koster's *The Robe* (1953) and Henry King's *The Song of Bernadette* (1943).

9. See Martin McLoone, *Irish Film: The Emergence of a Contemporary Cinema* (London: BFI Publishing, 2000), 213–23.

10. Eamon De Valera is very much the father figure of the Irish Republic, having been involved in the Easter Rising of 1916, surviving to be the dominant political figure in the Irish Republic from the 1930s to the late 1950s. He ended his career as president of Ireland from 1959–73. See Roy Foster, *Modern Ireland, 1600–1972* (London: Penguin, 1988), 485.

11. The Roman Catholic Church in Ireland has agreed to pay only 25 percent of this figure, so that the Irish taxpayers, including the victims, are effectively paying to settle their own abuse claims. See Shawn Pogatchnik, "Irish Taxpayers to Bear Brunt of Abuse Claims," *National Post* (Canada), February 1, 2002, A14.

12. Barry Keith Grant, ed. *The Dread of Difference: Gender and the Horror Film* (Austin: University of Texas Press, 1996).

13. On a $30 million budget, *In Dreams* recouped only $11.3 million in North America. Contrast this with *Interview with the Vampire*, which made over $100 million in the United States alone and $221 million worldwide (on a budget of $50 million). Figures drawn from the Internet Movie Database, online at http://www. imdb.com, accessed September 5, 2003.

14. Peter Rainer, quoted from his review found online at http://www.nymag.com/ critics/view.asp?id=20, accessed September 5, 2003.

15. Judith Butler, *Gender Trouble: Feminism and the Subversion of Identity* (New York: Routledge, 1990).

16. On the gothic sublime, see Vijay Mishra, *The Gothic Sublime* (Albany: State University of New York Press, 1994). Mishra sees the gothic sublime as perfectly in keeping with post-modernism and post-structuralism.

17. David Trimble, Keynote address to the Ulster Unionist Party Annual Conference, Belfast, March 9, 2002.

8

Thailand Haunted:

THE POWER OF THE PAST IN THE CONTEMPORARY THAI HORROR FILM

Adam Knee

One of the latest generic trends in the recent resurgence of Thai cinema (at least on Asian screens and at international festivals, if not yet on Western screens) has been the reemergence of the Thai horror film. Over the course of several months from late 2001 into early 2002, no fewer than four Thai horror films were released in Thai theaters—a substantial enough phenomenon (given the dozen or so Thai films being produced annually in recent years) to elicit a two-page feature article in the Weekend section of one of Bangkok's English-language dailies.[1] Subsequently, the mid-year Thai release of two pan-Asian horror films made with some Thai personnel and financing, along with the planned release of a number of additional Thai horror films later in the year, elicited still another newspaper feature on the phenomenon.[2] This rediscovery of the horror film may be attributable in part to the singular success of Nonzee Nimibutr's *Nang Nak* (1999), a ghost film that broke box office records in Thailand and notably increased the international profile of Thai cinema. But the trend speaks also to the ongoing cultural relevance of the horror film in Thailand, especially given that these latest Thai horror films appear, by and large, aimed primarily at a local Thai audience. These films mark a retrieval of the past, a return to a genre quite popular in the heyday of Thai cinema. They do, to some extent, engage modern global (read Hollywood) conventions of the horror genre, but also very specifically refer back to the local genre tradition, itself deeply rooted in local folklore, with such featured spirits as the *pii bporp* (a malevolent, liver-consuming spirit), *pii kraseu* (a rotten meat-eating female ghost, usually represented as a head with dangling entrails), and *pii dtai tang krom* (the ghost of a woman who has died during childbirth, Nang Nak being the best known of these).[3] Thai traditions and history are thus multiply engaged in many

141

of these texts, which make a return to past tradition as a source for narratives explicitly dealing with the return of the past in supernatural form. As preoccupied as these texts are with the past on several levels, they appear almost equally preoccupied, this essay shall contend, with issues of gender—and, more specifically, with the embattled status of women in Thai society. These preoccupations, moreover, are intimately linked: the hidden pasts by which these texts are haunted are primarily those pertaining to women's oppression. The past and the feminine are figured as sources of anxiety through their linkage to the supernatural, an anxiety that these texts choose variously to exorcize or come to terms with.

Nak Revived

The cultural resonance of the story of Nang Nak, a nineteenth-century woman who dies in childbirth while her husband is away in battle, then attempts to reclaim him from beyond the grave on his return home, is immediately evident merely from its singular popularity as a basis for films (reportedly more than twenty versions have been made), television shows, theatrical productions, comic books, prose fiction, and even poetry.[4] Like the character herself, the story of Nak simply refuses to stay dead; indeed, popular industry lore has it that when a director's career is lagging, directing a new version of *Nang Nak* will revive it. In point of fact, director Nonzee's career was hardly lagging, his successful debut feature *Daeng Bireley's and Young Gangsters* (a.k.a. *2499: Antapahn Krong Meuang,* literally "1956: Gangsters Rule the City," 1997) having already given him some international recognition.[5] An awareness that *Nang Nak* would likewise have international circulation partly shapes the film's approach to the classic horror story—an approach that evokes nostalgia for both a past era in Thai filmmaking history and a still earlier past era in Thai history more broadly. This foregrounding of the past is initially suggested by way of a title at the film's opening, which sets the start of the action in 1868, as well as through the intercutting of historical mural paintings of some of the film's events into the credit sequence, and through a pre-credit voiceover narration, immediately following the husband Mak's departure for battle, which informs us that "Nak's ghostly spirit is said to be a true story, long-told over generations. The legend has it that Nang Nak, local to the Prakanong District [of Bangkok], was a true and perfect wife, highly loyal to her husband. Even death could not make mortal her love and loyalty. Her loving soul wandered, awaiting for her husband to return."

This narration speaks to the film's two primary audiences—its local audience and its international film festival audience—at once, though in slightly differing ways. The general outline of the story is not necessary for the local audience, all of whom are fully familiar with it; in this regard, the viewing of a Nang Nak film by the Thai audience does not involve the same level of mystery and suspense that might ordinarily accompany the viewing of a horror film. Such a film for a Thai audience is rather more a ritual reenactment of a familiar (if also horrific) tale. Indeed, it is precisely this sense of ritual, this sense of a connection to tradition, that the opening narration—"long-told over generations"—invokes for Thai viewers, while also anticipating through its choice of descriptive terms one possible judgment toward Nak and her actions. This sense of tradition is certainly invoked for international viewers as well, but since the nature of that tradition is likely to be unfamiliar to such viewers, the outlining of the tale functions to bring them up to speed on the local legend.

The ritualistic function and the connection to past texts comes to the fore with the film's inclusion of certain de rigueur sequences, certain anticipated narrative moments that appear in most every version of the tale. These are, most importantly, the scene where Nak's (Intira Jaroenpura) arm unnaturally extends to retrieve an item that has fallen to the ground beneath her house while she prepares a meal (in this version as in many others also the moment of Mak's [Winai Kraibutr] realization that his wife is a ghost), and the scene where a local clergyman attempts to protect Mak from Nak's influence by setting up a border around him with string and chanting. What marks these scenes as different from earlier versions is perhaps most centrally their greater technical proficiency, their increased concern with rendering their fantastic occurrences with a degree of plausibility. The potential unconvincingness of images of the extended arm, for example, is circumvented through swift editing and a distant camera position that allow the event to register but prevent any dwelling on details. The threat from Nak during the chanting scene at a local *wat* (Buddhist temple) is inventively and startlingly represented with Nak's appearance upside down on the ceiling in a number of cleanly executed special effects shots. This increased emphasis on plausibility and technical proficiency—in contrast to the flimsy effects and often facetious tone of many horror films of earlier decades (including earlier versions of the Nak narrative)—is in keeping with this *Nang Nak*'s positioning itself as a "world-class" film, one that can succeed with international audiences.

The concern with plausibility is also suggested by the unusually extensive historical research that went into the production, which, according to one local commentator, resulted in "a stunning horror movie that sparked also a tremendous amount of interest among Thai audiences, not only about ghostly matters, but about their own history as well."[6] The film's nostalgia for this Thai history is perhaps most evident in its lovingly rendered images of an idealized agrarian past; the film is infused with images of sun-drenched rice paddies, lotus leaves dripping with rain, Thai-style houses on stilts giving out onto quiet waterways, and—an integral part of this idealized mosaic—Mak and Nak sitting on the branch of a tree out in a field as a water buffalo lounges peacefully nearby. These images serve the dual function of elegizing the past and broadcasting the film's national origins; they loudly and clearly tell us, "Made in Thailand," thus paradoxically working to position the film for international festival consumption (articulating "Thainess" as a means of product differentiation) in a global industry at the same time as they imply regret over the loss of a distinctly local past.

But while the film is characterized by a certain nationalistic nostalgia, not all is right in its idyllic past; it is, after all, a horror film, and its central emblem of times past, its title character, instills terror in most of those with whom she comes into contact, as spirits of the dead are wont to do. One apparent paradox here is that Nak, while fear-inspiring, is also set up as a paragon of certain feminine virtues; again, as the opening narration notes, her return from the dead is understood as a function of her unflagging love and loyalty. It is precisely this tenacity, however, that ends up making her such a horror—a tenacity arguably emblematized in the grotesque iconographic image of her long-reaching arm. Such is Nak's single-mindedness in keeping her marriage alive that she does not hesitate to kill those who would reveal her ghostly secret to Mak. While what is scary about Nak then is in part the ardent nature of her love, it is instructive to keep in mind that Mak is haunted not only by her but also by the spirit of his dead child; the haunting thus seems to embody a male fear over a powerful female desire and over domesticity more broadly. It is the family from which he cannot escape.

The particular narrative form that the struggle with Nak takes is also significant in attempting to "read" this haunting. One dimension of the legend that Nonzee takes care to underscore is Nak's defiance in the face of various levels of patriarchal power. Her spirit repeatedly shows an indifference to the apparatus of the patriarchal Buddhist state; indeed, her very existence is an affront to Buddhist epistemology, as she is a *pii*—

a ghost or spirit—and thus a holdover from earlier belief systems that have tenaciously continued to coexist with Buddhism in Thailand.[7] Nak repeatedly ignores the injunctions of the local head monk, whose rituals seem utterly irrelevant to her. "Scaring the monks is a sin," he reminds her when she appears on the ceiling of the *wat*. However, when he goes on to insist she stop bothering Mak, she responds, "I listen to no one." Shortly afterward, a local exorcist brought in by villagers has still less success in driving away Nak's spirit. It is only when a high Buddhist dignitary from neighboring Thonburi journeys to Prakanong to confront her that she finally accedes to the patriarchal-Buddhist order. In the light of these details it would seem that, beyond signaling anxiety over overweening love or the obligations of power, Nak's apparition also points to a fear of feminine recalcitrance and willfulness, of female agency as a threat to patriarchal systems of power, and of realms of knowledge and belief that run counter to those of the state-adopted religion—the "official version" of reality.

In one sense, the striking image of Nak upside down on the ceiling of the *wat* nicely sums up the opposition she poses to male order. She literally inverts the male frame of reference—a notion previously suggested in the monk's instruction to Mak to bend over and look between his legs if he wants to apprehend Nak's true nature. She is upside down to the men's right-side up, one to their many, feminine (indeed, she again appears here holding her baby) to their masculinity, spectral to their earthliness. But while this is an overdetermined image of oppositionality, it is also one of complementarity; Nak completes the picture, dwells in the space where the men do not, and wields a power of fertility (the presence of the baby reminds us) that the men on their own are lacking. For Mak this sense of complementarity is immediately felt, which is why he remains far more drawn to her than repelled by her and cannot be persuaded to turn against her. Indeed, the film, from the opening narration, is decidedly mixed in its attitude toward Nak, suggesting that she is not to be seen as purely a horrific figure; she is, after all, a model of devotion, and in effect suffers because of it—suffers through her husband's absence at war and suffers through a painful and finally deadly pregnancy. Her existence beyond death too is shown to be profoundly sorrowful to her (despite moments when her brutality gets the better of her), as suggested when she examines her hair coming out in the mirror, or when she gets up in the middle of the night to prepare rice for her husband for fear that she might not be able to stay with him much longer. "Don't you pity me?" she tearfully asks of her husband after defying the elder monk in the scene at the *wat*—and indeed we as viewers do.

It is in keeping with an understanding of Nak as something other than the embodiment of evil (despite her opposition to the established pillars of law, order, and morality) that the narrative does not conclude with her utter destruction; rather, the resolution of the film seems predicated on an understanding that Nak—and what she stands for—is something to be contained rather than erased, an integral (if also occluded and repressed) part of culture. Her spirit eventually dwells in a piece of her skull bone, the narration informs us, worn by the dignitary until his dying day, then "handed down to many others, nondetected, till now nobody knows where the item is." Thus, while feminine forces become partially hidden within patriarchal history—female suffering secreted within the institutions of marriage and motherhood—these forces, like Nak, cannot be fully buried and must be eternally acknowledged, for example, through narrative rituals such as this film and through respect paid at the real-life shrine that still exists for Nak in twenty-first-century Bangkok.

Bliss Cua Lim's recent theoretical consideration of the phenomenon of haunting in the cinema (for which she, not incidentally, utilizes two Asian films centered on female ghosts as her prime examples) provides a useful frame of reference here for the kind of feminine disruption of the present and reassertion of the past I am positing for *Nang Nak*—and will attribute to other recent Thai horror films as well. As Lim argues, "the ghost narrative opens the possibility of a radicalized concept of non-contemporaneity; haunting as ghostly return precisely refuses the idea that things are just 'left behind,' that the past is inert and the present uniform."[8] Nak's presence does indeed "[trouble] the boundaries of past, present, and future," insisting on its own simultaneous frame of reference and thus pointing to the possibility of the kind of "radicalized historical consciousness" Lim describes, even if another ideological effect of the film is to contain the feminine threat Nak represents by providing a safely circumscribed space in which to articulate and thus partially assuage oppositional concerns, to give ritualized expression to that which is ordinarily kept securely underground, behind the housefront, or in a linearly conceived past.[9]

Fearful Females

Such a sense of the disruption and problematizing of the present—and, more specifically, the modern—is likewise strongly articulated throughout the omnibus film *Bangkok Haunted* (*Pii Sam Baht*, literally "Three-

Baht Ghost," 2001, the first two segments directed by Pisuth Praesaeng-iam and the third by Oxide Pang); it is even suggested through the film's English-language title, Bangkok in some senses being practically syn-onymous with Thailand's modernity. The decentering of time and the deauthorizing of any single conceptualization of history arguably increases exponentially here, in that each of the film's three stories has multiple interwoven time frames that are never clearly related across one another nor back to a fourth framing narrative of the stories being told. This tension between temporal regimes explodes into the film's visual field in the kind of spatio-temporal overlay that Lim finds also character-izes the two films she discusses: the jarring physical juxtaposition of dif-fering temporal realms is inherent in the post-modern setting of Bangkok, a city that, in an architectural sense, is haunted indeed—with the old and the new, the disused and the thriving often crammed into the same spaces.[10]

One example of such an overlay is in the setting of the framing nar-rative: the film's three stories are told among friends in a trendy, modern café that has been constructed in the shell of an old building in Bangkok's historic Chinatown. But the film's most striking architectural palimpsest occurs in the first of the three narratives during which a woman under the influence of a ghost has a vision of past events at her historic wooden house on Bangkok's Chao Phraya River; although the witnessed events are presumably taking place in the past, the seemingly spectral presences of two modern apartment towers on the other side of the river dominate the background of several shots, as though the past were being haunted by the present. The overlay of past and present naturally continues when we return to the setting after the vision has apparently ended; even in the "real" version of things, the old Thai-style house and the modern high-rises coincide, both time frames remaining coexistent and coextensive.

As in *Nang Nak*, this haunting is again related to female will and agency and is in some instances precipitated by the unresolved state of historical injustices against women; female agency is most literally sug-gested in the fact that the three tales are each narrated by a woman, while the link between the feminine and the spectral is driven home when these three narrators are revealed at the film's close to be ghosts (or the product of another female ghost's imagination). The sense of female agency is perhaps strongest in the third tale, which focuses on a police detective investigating an apparently suicidal death he suspects may have been a murder. While the detective appears largely in control of events for the better part of the narrative (save for where the ghost of the victim seems to appear), the tale's denouement reveals that the course of events had been carefully orchestrated by the ghost in order to exact revenge against a number of men for having spurned her love or—in the case of her husband—for having forced her to miscarry. In each case, the woman's past oppression—and, more specifically, the attempt to thwart her desire and reproductive power—is an occluded fact coexistent with the historically "present" reality of a given man, but the man is eventually forced to face the past misdeed and to pay for it with his life. A brutal attempt to thwart a young woman's desire is what precipitates the haunting in the first tale as well; there the ghost is a young woman murdered by a man some decades in the past whom she relates to as a brother but who is jealous of her newfound attraction to another man. It is the spirit of this past victim that possesses the body of the segment's present-day protagonist, in the sequence described earlier, after a drum containing the woman's severed arm mysteriously shows up at the protagonist's antique shop.

Anxiety and fear related to woman's desire is a more distinctive focus of the second of the tales, which concerns a lonely young Bangkok woman who turns to a recommended love potion in her pursuit of male companionship—unaware that the potion is made from fluid drained from a woman's corpse (significantly, by a man who also seems interested in ravishing the corpse) in the city morgue. With the benefit of the potion the young woman successfully pursues first one, then another man who strikes her fancy. As might be expected in such a horror narrative there is a price to be paid for this newfound sexual freedom; we can see that the ghost of the woman from whose body the potion was made hovers around the man on whom the potion is placed, indeed joining him and the protagonist as they sleep together (although apparently unbeknownst to them). The result is the mysterious illness and death of the men the protagonist sleeps with, one of whom returns from the grave to murder her. Thus, while this particular tale seems to force a certain retribution on men for the past suffering of women it also posits a woman's free expression of sexual desire as something that calls for containment and punishment. The sense of sexual panic suggested here can be seen as a part of the film's confrontation between modernity and the past: the protagonist's sexual aggression (as seen, for example, in her rubbing up against a man she is interested in on a crowded commuter boat) is something entirely out of keeping with traditionally "proper" Thai female behavior, something immediately associated with Bangkok and the modern age. That the first negative result of her sexual activity is her lover's deathly illness, in a city hard-hit by the AIDS crisis, is also immediately suggestive of the historically and nationally specific dimensions of such a sexual panic. One could further note that the female protagonists of *Bangkok Haunted* consistently express interest in men of higher class status than they—a detail that associates the city's unregulated sexual desire with social and economic ambition as intertwined symptoms of modernity.

The sexual dimensions of the clash between differing historical frames of reference are still more pronounced in the contemporary supernatural film *Body Jumper* (*Bporp Wheed Sayong*, literally "Bporp Scream Horror," 2001), directed by Heamarn Cheatamee. This film's engagement with the past is, like *Nang Nak*'s, based partly on its allusion to earlier narrative models—both a tradition of popular tales of *pii bporp* and an earlier series of successful *bporp* films. In its recurrent slapstick humor and generally farcical approach, *Body Jumper* indeed appears much closer in tone to the often comic Thai horror films of earlier decades than does the relatively sober 1999 *Nang Nak*, which arguably dispenses with a local sense of humor in making itself a "world-class" horror film. The sense of collision between past and present (and, in conjunction with this, between rural and urban) is narrativized in a plot about a *bporp* that has been contained in a clay pot (a usual method) in an upcountry village in 1932, then is accidentally unleashed by some visiting college students from Bangkok in the modern day. The freed *bporp* immediately possesses the most seemingly innocent of the female college students, commenting that "kids nowadays sure grow up quick" when it looks down at the budding breasts on its newly acquired body. When the possessed girl, Ger (Chompunoot Piyapane), then returns to Bangkok, her new nature expresses itself in a now sexually provocative style of dress and behavior.

While what is fearful about a *bporp* is its insatiable appetite for human livers, it does not take much of an interpretive step to see that such an appetite here metaphorizes a modern teen sexual appetite: Ger acquires livers not by chasing after victims (in traditional ghostly fashion) but by seducing them. The casting of a diminutive actress in the role of the possessed co-ed emphasizes an unsavory sense of underage sexuality, while her modus operandi of having sex with strangers in strange bedrooms and parking lots invokes concerns over modern female teen promiscuity, as well as concerns over teen prostitution. Also relevant is the fact that one of her anonymous "pick-ups" occurs at Bangkok's Royal City Avenue nightclub strip—an area notorious for catering to college-age (and sometimes younger) patrons and sometimes targeted by various guardians of law and public morality for this reason. The sense of the *bporp* as representing a distinctively sexual danger is also clearly suggested in the fact that one of the weapons eventually used in the fight against the spirit is an "anti-*bporp* condom," which comes in a three-pack and, when inflated, can temporarily halt the entity's onslaught—this, it should be noted, in a locality where condom usage became popularized by the government specifically as a weapon against the spread of AIDS. Although Ger's victims die immediately, there is also a clear suggestion of infection present here; the *bporp* can (and eventually does) jump from one host to another. There is additionally a sense of a deadly "queerness" linked to the possessed girl's (hetero)sexualized activities in that she retrieves livers from a number of her willing and sexually aroused back-alley victims by "fisting" them, reaching up through their rectums to gain hold of the desired organs.

While the film's sexual anxiety is related to, among other things, modern teen sexual mores in an age of AIDS, and more particularly to female sexual desire, this anxiety is also linked to a concern over foreign sociocultural influences—not surprising, given that foreign forces are often held to blame for various modern problems in Thailand in a range of popular and governmental discourses. For example, in the eyes of many, foreign media influences are key to the loss of tradition among youth, and foreign money is what has reshaped Bangkok into a modern metropolis, one teeming with tourists who may bring negative moral influences, not to mention sexually transmittable diseases. One linkage the film establishes between its sexual panic and the influence of things non-Thai rests in the fact that one of the first of Ger's promiscuous conquests is evidently Afro-Thai. In one of the film's many crude, throwaway gags, Ger pulls out a magnifying glass to disappointedly examine the man's genitals once he disrobes—a gesture that engages racist stereotypes to simultaneously indicate the lascivious nature of the young woman's appetites and link such appetites with foreignness.

The film's reference to foreignness continues with another Afro-Thai character, Kong, whose face, in its physical difference, initially scares one of the male protagonists when he unexpectedly encounters him in a library. The fact that Kong ends up a hero, working with the college students and using his special skills to thwart the *bporp*, does somewhat counter the film's implicit racism and xenophobia. But it is also suggested that Kong has his ghost-fighting skills because of his link to the fearful supernatural; in him foreignness and nonhumanness become ciphers for each other. This is most explicitly articulated in the scene where the college students go to get Kong at the traditional Thai house where he resides. Upon meeting Kong's Thai mother, one of the students somewhat indecorously inquires as to what his non-Thai half is. The Thai audience would have already assumed the father was likely an African American serviceman. The mother's response, however, is that Kong is "half-ghost, half-human," a formulation that clearly aligns Thainess with humanness, foreignness with the ghostly forces that need to be battled. Paradoxically, however, Kong's foreignness is also linked to modernity through the high technology he employs in battling the supernatural: he utilizes a laptop computer to direct the battle (though it is never made clear quite how) and offers up an arsenal of high-tech weapons to aid the college students in confronting the ancient *bporp*, including a "Ghost Gun Millennium Edition." The whole notion of pursuing ghosts in a systematic, professional fashion with high-tech weaponry is a foreign influence in this rendition of a traditional Thai tale—a knowing allusion to Hollywood's *Ghostbusters* (1984). (One can argue a similar Western cinematic influence in the film's preponderance of gags concerning teen tumescence, the legacy of Hollywood teen sex comedies in the mold of *Porky's* [1981].)

What these Thai "ghostbusters" end up doing battle with, however, is an emblem not of modern or foreign influences but, quite clearly, of a fear-inspiring, hungry, desirous, monstrous femininity. After jumping among a number of bodies, the *bporp* ends up possessing Fah (Angie Grant), a character who, significantly, has earlier expressed her own (initially unreturned) amorous desire for one of the male protagonists. Fah's newly monstrous form is one of grotesquely amplified corporeal femininity, a grayish, fleshy body with large breasts and a distended—indeed, almost pregnant-looking—belly. The image is thus akin to other images of fearful fertility and grotesque motherhood in the modern Thai horror film, such as Nang Nak's ghostly mothering of her ghostly baby, or the gory shot of a miscarriage being induced with a wire hanger in the third segment of *Bangkok Haunted*. (Indeed, *Body Jumper* opens with another image of monstrous motherhood, a flashback in which a young boy, unaware or unbelieving of his mother's possession by the *bporp*, runs to her for comfort and is strangled.) The attack on the monstrous-feminine is now executed by driving a computer-guided electric current through the *bporp*'s pendulous breasts, markers of fertility and revulsion. Thus, modern technology exorcizes the ancient feminine curse, with the end result being a docile Fah, once again fitting the mold of a safe femininity.

Unsettled Histories

In a number of other supernatural films the clash between past and present arises when the fallout of certain historical secrets, certain unresolved events, pushes its way into the here-and-now. For example in Anukul Jarotok's *The Hotel!!* (*Rong Raem Pii*, literally "Ghost Hotel," 2002), the owner-residents of the titular establishment find themselves under attack by a supernatural force they cannot recognize—until clues finally reveal that a ghost (played by a heavily made-up Winai Kraibutr) is trying to wreak vengeance against the family because its patriarch had, some decades earlier, eloped with the fiancée of the previous hotel owner. Resolution only comes when the ghost confronts a daughter who looks strikingly like the woman he lost and accedes to her pleas for forgiveness and her explanation that "Revenge doesn't undo what was done; it just adds to your sin."

This theme of needing to discover and resolve historical secrets arguably has very strong resonance in Thai culture, particularly in relation to a number of key events in late-twentieth-century Thai history. Thailand has a long history of corruption, hidden deals, and favoritism in business and politics, a tradition that came under sustained critical scrutiny in the time period of the film productions described in this essay—as voters became increasingly tired of corrupt politics and, after the economic crash of 1997, as Thailand was forced to begin to implement reforms in business and politics in order to regain credibility in the global marketplace and in international politics.[11] Nowhere among these films is the connection between national history and the need to deal with a hidden past more evident than in Somching Srisupap's *303: Fear/Faith/Revenge* (*303: Kloor/Klah/Ahkaht*, 1998). Unlike the other films discussed here, this film's generic lineage lies more in the Hollywood teen slasher subgenre—though it, too, retains a link to Thai supernatural traditions, as ghostly possession proves to be central to murders taking place at an exclusive boys' prep school in 1960. These murders begin shortly after a group of new students tries to investigate why a young royal had reportedly killed himself at the school eight years earlier, despite their being warned by the school's head priest not to do so. They make use of a Ouija board to initi-

The spirit of Prince Daovadueng (Jesdaporn Pholdee) helps save the day in *303: Fear/Faith/Revenge* (1998)

ate their investigation, and it is this, the head priest explains when he later learns of it, that "opens the door for evil" to enter their school.

This sense that old problems—past historical traumas and secrets—are better left undisturbed is driven resoundingly home as the film reaches its conclusion. It is eventually revealed that the prince did not take his own life, but rather was a bystander killed in a shooting rampage in 1952, along with several other students, by a student who was upset at being bullied and ostracized. Now, in 1960, the awakened spirit of the murderer has possessed one of the friends initially involved in the investigation, and he proceeds to murder several more students, taking particular aim at bullies. Order is restored only when the spirit of the prince also springs into action, helping to destroy the murderer's evil spirit. The surviving friends now willingly participate in the redisguising of the earlier murders, as well as the finessing of the facts around the new ones, with the main protagonist's voiceover narration informing us, "We can only hope this terror will never be repeated and hope everything that happened here will remain a secret with us forever."

This desire to keep past wounds from opening up, to quietly resolve rather than amplify past difficulties, is echoed in the resolutions of some other Thai horror films, which have a way of ending in compromise rather than with the utter vanquishing of an opposing force—witness the final negotiation with the ghost in *The Hotel!!*, and the containment (rather than destruction) of the eponymous spirit in *Nang Nak*. This tendency agrees with the high value Thais have traditionally assigned to the quality of self-control or *jai yen* (literally, "cool heart").[12] A number of distinctive factors in *303*, moreover, lend themselves to a reading of this kind of resolution as having particular resonance for Thai culture. For one thing, the death of the prince by a gunshot under mysterious circumstances in the film echoes the actual mysterious death of a young Thai royal—a king, in fact—by a gunshot wound just a few years previously, in 1946. This potentially explosive death too was the object of considerable speculation and confusion and contributed directly to a level of political instability, just as the prince's death, when suddenly the focus of the students' curiosity, threatens to bring disorder in the school.[13]

Two other historical referents that would have more direct bearing for the late 1990s Thai audience, however, are the violent university unrest of the mid-1970s and a bloody crackdown on anti-military protest in 1992 in which many civilians were shot; *303*'s vague black-and-white flashback images of student corpses in uniform might indeed directly recall circulating imagery of the former of these referents.[14] These events are highly resonant with the occurrences in the film as historical traumas that are still cloaked in mystery and controversy, which still, to the present day, threaten social disaffection and disruption; central events in modern Thai historical consciousness, they both remain bitter sites of contestation—of attempts to clearly determine facts, assign guilt, and dole out punishment—as well as of battles over the representation of the past in classroom textbooks and popular media alike. Although the troublesome status of these modern traumas is certainly not the only determining factor in the uneasy attitude toward the past in *303* and other Thai horror films, the events' continuing cultural predominance does readily lend to their cinematic purchase.

Bestial Doings

Another Thai supernatural tradition (both in folktales and in film) that has reappeared in recent productions has to do not with ghosts but with entities that are part human and part animal—or with humans who have otherworldly connections to animals. In these animal-related supernatural films, however, the same preoccupations with the past and with the feminine have a marked presence. A woman is at the center of the themes of supernatural horror in Somching's follow-up, *Mae Bia* (literally, "The Cobra's Hood," 2001), for example—although the woman does not have any supernatural properties, she is watched over by a jealous snake, which causes peril for the various men in her life. Themes of relationships between women and snakes have a long-standing tradition in Thai cinema—in an earlier version of *Mae Bia* and in a number of films about women who are part snake (such as *Ngu Pii* [literally, "Ghost Snake," 1966]).[15] The new *Mae Bia,* like many of the other films discussed here, foregrounds the fact of the modern remaking of a traditional tale, while also forging links between the feminine, the supernatural, and the historical. The film's modern-day story develops as an urban, yuppified, Western-educated Thai businessman, Chanachol (Puthichai Amatayakul), falls for the rural-dwelling Mekhala (Nakapapapa Nekaprasit)—as well as her traditional lifestyle—after taking a journey into the Thai countryside. Mekhala's link to the past resides not only in her old-style homestead but also, once more, in past secrets and past suffering: while growing up in a polygamous household in which she and her mother were not in favor, she learned to accept the comfort and protection of a snake that chose to watch over her and still continues this task, striking out at would-be attackers and would-be lovers alike. A passionate affair develops between Mekhala and the businessman but with tragic consequences, both because of Mekhala's supernatural connection to a difficult past and the man's connection to the present—the wife and child he has in Bangkok.

The coincidence of supernatural animal themes and polygamy occurs as well in Suthud Intaranupakorn's *Krai Thong* (2001), also a remake of an earlier film based on an old Thai legend. While on its most surface terms this narrative concerns the exploits of the brave and skillful title warrior who manages to save a small village from attacks by a voracious and enormous crocodile, its contours also suggest a primal struggle for patriarchal dominance by gaining control over wealth and also over all the most desirable women in a given community. Krai Thong (Winai Kraibutr once more) makes his way to the village when the news has spread that the village chief will give half his riches to whatever warrior can kill the animal that has been terrorizing them and soon after arriving makes clear his amorous interest in one of the chief's daughters (Tong, played by Wannasa Thongwiset). However, the crocodile, Chalawan, who has the ability to change into human form and who lives in a nearby underwater cave, has similar designs on the daughter. During a ceremony intended to bring blessings to the village in their battle against the crocodile, Chalawan shows up and takes hold of Tong, bringing her down to his underwater cave in his jaws, and then (in human form) making love to her, much to the consternation of the two wives he already has—wives who are also crocodiles able to assume human form. Krai Thong, in pursuit of the kidnapped daughter, eventually reaches the cave and successfully does battle with Chalawan, wounding him and taking off with Tong, though not before pausing to admire the beauty of the crocodile wives. Once back at the surface, the overjoyed chief offers Krai Thong the promised half of his fortune and the hands of both his daughters in marriage.

The reciprocity of ostensible hero and ostensible villain, as mirror reflections of each other on either side of the water's surface, is quite striking; each is a powerful warrior with two wives, and each has a cross-species attraction to one or more of the other's women. Now, however, as Chalawan recovers from his injury, he vows never to kill again. Krai Thong, on the other hand, becomes determined to kill the crocodile to bring peace to the villagers and to lift an affliction facing Tong: she lost her voice following her encounter with Chalawan and only his death will cure her. Krai Thong eventually succeeds at this (in part through the advice of his late warrior father, whose spirit is able to communicate with him), and, like the model of an alpha male, he also takes both of the crocodile wives as his own, living half the time in one world, half in the other.

As fables often do, this one certainly lends itself to many kinds of interpretation. It can, for example, be understood as concerning Thai civilization's prehistoric relationship to the animal world or to water and aquatic life more specifically—relationships central in Thai culture as in many others. It can likewise be understood as pertaining to the Thai people's relationship to neighboring peoples, Thailand having historically seen many kinds of migration and intermixing with peoples from adjoining regions. The tale also concerns the nature of social order and hierarchy and the nature of social succession in a patriarchal society, clearly detailing male violence and sexual aggression (both figured as literally animalistic) as a historical part of this order and succession. An interesting particular is that all of the film's scenes of lovemaking are interspecies and technically underwater, in the crocodiles' caves. While on the one hand this echoes a universal association between water and fertility (one hinted at as well in the heavy presence of the river in *Nang Nak*), on the other hand it links both fertility and desire with otherness. At the same time it places passion—and more particularly an aggressive, violent, male-dominated passion for the other—literally out of view of the socially ordered land-dwelling world. Such desire and aggression, it seems, are yet another troublesome historical secret, which must be kept hidden below the surface despite their formative significance.

Examined in a broader view, then, contemporary Thai horror films consistently appear as a cultural means of grappling with the past, with

The monstrous-
feminine makes an
appearance in *Body
Jumper* (2001)

secrets and traumas still haunting the country. These films look to the past
by (variously or in combination) reengaging with earlier folk and cinematic narrative and generic traditions, by representing earlier historical
periods, and by dramatizing tensions between (and confusions among)
differing historical frameworks and perspectives. Bangkok, as an emblem
or instantiation of modernity, is a key reference point for the historical
contradictions in a number of the films (especially *Bangkok Haunted, Body
Jumper,* and *Mae Bia*) and often appears to engender an anxiety over foreign influence and the loss of traditional mores, especially in relation to
sexuality. More broadly, these films consistently return to anxieties over
gender-related issues, often coincident with irresolution regarding past
trauma—concerns over the violence of male sexual aggression (particularly *Krai Thong, The Hotel!!, Bangkok Haunted, Mae Bia,* and, arguably,
303: Fear/Faith/Revenge), the suffering and oppression of women in
patriarchal society (*Nang Nak, Bangkok Haunted, Mae Bia*), and the disruptive potential of female agency and desire (*Nang Nak, Bangkok
Haunted, Body Jumper*). The relish with which the horror genre has now
been taken up suggests just how provocative these issues remain.

Notes

I would like to express my gratitude to director Nonzee Nimibutr and to Noparroot
Vicharnpootorn and Panu Aree (of the foreign sales departments of RS Film and Saha-
mongkol Film, respectively) for discussing the Thai film industry with me during the
preparation of this essay; to Chalida Uabumrungjit of the Thai Film Archive for sharing
her expertise and providing access to some unavailable Thai horror films; to Duangkamol

Limcharoen and Pornpisuth Osathanond for helping coordinate research and helping with translations; and to Mansfield University and its Faculty Professional Development Committee for funding a research trip to Thailand.

1. Hanuman, "A Dying Breed," *The Nation* (Bangkok), March 8, 2002, Weekend section, 8–9. Given current trends, the annual number of Thai feature films is expected to rise dramatically, to thirty-five or forty by 2003.

2. Kong Rithdee, "The Sum of All Fears," *Bangkok Post,* August 9, 2002, Realtime section, 1. The mid-year releases were the Thai co-produced omnibus film *Three* (*Ahrom/Ahthun/Ahkhat,* literally "Emotion/Curse/Vengeance"), the first segment of which is directed by Nonzee Nimibutr and features a Thai period setting; and the Hong Kong–produced feature *The Eye,* directed by Oxide and Danny Pang (Hong Kong–based brothers who often work in Thailand) and including a lengthy sequence set in Thailand. Among the horror releases announced for later in 2002 were *999–9999,* a supernatural thriller about an evidently dangerous phone number, and *Krasue,* based on a traditional Thai ghost legend.

3. A brief overview of some of these spirit beliefs can be found in William P. Tuchrello, "The Society and Its Environment," in *Thailand: A Country Study,* 6th ed., ed. Barbara Leitch LePoer (Washington, DC: U.S. Government, 1989), 101–2. See also Niels Mulder, *Inside Thai Society: Interpretations of Everyday Life,* 5th ed. (Amsterdam: Pepin, 1996), chap. 5.

4. For an overview of the Nak phenomenon and some key interpretations of it, see Ka F. Wong, "Nang Nak: The Cult and Myth of a Popular Ghost in Thailand," in *Thai Folklore: Insights into Thai Folk Culture,* ed. Siraporn Nathalang (Bangkok: Chulalongkorn University Press, 2000), 123–42. Various documents pertaining to the phenomenon are reproduced in Anake Nawigamune, *Mae Nak: Classical Ghost of Siam* (Bangkok: Nora, 2000) (in Thai), while more than twenty posters from various Nang Nak films are reproduced in Dome Sukwong and Sawasdi Suwannapak, *A Century of Thai Cinema,* trans. and ed. David Smyth (London: Thames and Hudson, 2001), 52–55.

5. For a brief overview of the director's career, see Mitch Davis, "The Rain Beneath the Earth: An Interview with Nonzee Nimibutr," in *Fear Without Frontiers: Horror Cinema across the Globe,* ed. Steven Jay Schneider (Surrey, UK: FAB Press, 2003).

6. Hanuman, "A Dying Breed," 9.

7. For an interpretation of the myth that accords with this one, see Wong, "Nang Nak," 135. On the relationship between Buddhism and other forms of belief, see Charles F. Keyes, *Thailand: Buddhist Kingdom as Modern Nation-State* (Boulder, CO: Westview Press, 1987), 178–81, and Siraporn Nathalang, "Conflict and Compromise between the Indigenous Beliefs and Buddhism as Reflected in Thai Rice Myths," in Nathalang, *Thai Folklore,* 99–113.

8. Bliss Cua Lim, "Spectral Times: The Ghost Film as Historical Allegory," *Positions: East Asia Cultures Critique* 9, no. 2 (2001): 288. The films Lim discusses are *Rouge* (*Yanzhi Kou,* 1987, directed by Stanley Kwan) and *Haplos* (*Caress,* 1982, directed by José Luis Pérez).

9. Lim, "Spectral Times," 287.

10. Ibid., 289–92.

11. On corruption and its political consequences in modern Thailand, see Pasuk Phongpaichit and Sungsidh Piriyarangsan, *Corruption and Democracy in Thailand* (Chiang Mai, Thailand: Silkworm Books, 1994); and Pasuk Phongpaichit and Chris Baker, *Thailand's Crisis* (Chiang Mai, Thailand: Silkworm Books, 2000), chaps. 5–6.

12. See Mulder, *Inside Thai Society,* 85–86.

13. Keyes, *Thailand: Buddhist Kingdom as Modern Nation-State,* 71–72; Alec Waugh, *Bangkok: The Story of a City* (Boston: Little, Brown, 1971), chaps. 12–13; and David K. Wyatt, *Thailand: A Short History* (New Haven: Yale University Press, 1984), 263–66.

14. The key 1970s events were a student uprising in October 1973, which led to the overthrow of two military leaders and the appointment of a new prime minister, and a bloody coup in October 1976, which allowed for the return of certain right-wing military elements to power. See John L. S. Girling, *Thailand: Society and Politics* (Ithaca: Cornell University Press, 1981), chap. 5; and Wyatt, *Thailand: A Short History,* 297–303. On the violent crackdown on anti-military protest in May 1992, see Duncan McCargo, *Chamlong Srimuang and the New Thai Politics* (New York: St. Martin's, 1997), chap. 8. One commentator interestingly likens the May 1992 events and their aftermath to a horror-film narrative—and suggests this may help explain the popularity of horror films in that time period; William A. Callahan, *Imagining Democracy: Reading "The Events of May" in Thailand* (Singapore: Institute of Southeast Asian Studies, 1998), 156–58.

15. Some of these popular films about snake women were in fact produced in neighboring Cambodia. For an interesting special issue of an online journal about the Asian snake woman phenomenon, see *The Illuminated Lantern* 10 (2001), online at http://www.illuminatedlantern.com/snakes/index.html, accessed June 18, 2002.

III

HORROR IN THE SOCIAL REALM

9

The Spanish Horror Film as Subversive Text:

Eloy de la Iglesia's *La semana del asesino*

Andrew Willis

In his 1993 book *Hammer and Beyond: The British Horror Film*, Peter Hutchings argues that the products of Hammer Films and other British horror film producers need to be regarded as part of a national film culture, that is, one that addresses specifically national issues and concerns. He goes on to argue that, while there may be generic codes and conventions that are reproduced across national boundaries, horror cinema produced within particular national contexts will differ in significant ways. For Hutchings, much critical work on the genre abstracts it from these various contexts in its search for the essential elements of the horror film. Regarding such criticism, he argues that, "Attempts that have been made, particularly in their insistence on the genre having either a fixed function or a central core of meaning . . . have necessarily lifted films out of the national contexts within which they were produced, thereby evacuating them of much of their socio-historical significance."[1]

Whatever the wider generic codes and conventions are, their actual manifestation at a particular historical moment and within particular national, political, and social contexts must inform any interpretation and understanding of the potential meanings of the texts at hand.

With this in mind, I wish to discuss Eloy de la Iglesia's *La semana del asesino* (*Week of the Killer*, a.k.a. *Cannibal Man*), a film produced in the Spanish cinema of the early 1970s. Following on from Hutchings's observations, I intend to anchor my reading of this film in the historical moment of its production and consider how far it might be considered a radical critique of Spanish society at this time. In particular, I wish to discuss gender and the representation of violence in the horror cinema of the period. My argument is that the horror genre's manifestation in Spanish cinema must be understood as part of a particular set of national circumstances, circumstances that impacted greatly on the use of the generic codes and conventions of the horror film by Spanish filmmakers of the period. I will also discuss the way in which horror offered directors the opportunity to challenge and critique the dominant values of the Franco regime.

Horror and Spanish Cinema

The boom in horror film production in Spain began with the success in 1967 of *La marca del hombre lobo* (*Mark of the Werewolf*), starring Paul Naschy as Daninsky the Werewolf, and was consolidated by the popularity of Narcisco (Chicho) Ibáñez-Serrador's 1969 film *La residencia* (*The House That Screamed*).[2] However, it is possible to see the origins of Spanish horror in earlier, internationally financed films that utilized a perceived mystery in Spanish locations and settings. One such example is *Pyro,* which was made by American International Pictures on location in Galicia in 1963. This film was shot with a Spanish crew and, apart from the lead performers such as Barry Sullivan, a Spanish cast. Directed by Spaniard Julio Coll, the film tells the story of a British architect who is seduced by what he sees as the exoticism of Spain. The mystery of Spain is represented early in the film by the passion of Flamenco, shown in a nightclub sequence just after the characters first arrive in the country. The main drive of the narrative involves Sullivan's character, Vance, seeking revenge after he is disfigured in a deliberately set fire. While on the surface a psychological thriller, the burned hero prefigures some of the disfigured characters who would later appear in films more clearly of the "horror" variety.

Pyro also looks forward to the co-productions that would become a mainstay of the Spanish horror boom. With *Pyro* the co-production was with American International Pictures, a company that specialized in low-budget genre films that were easily marketed to a youth audience. The centrality of marketing to the successful distribution of these types of films explains the rather over-the-top alternative titles that many of them were sold under. *Pyro,* for example, also existed as *Pyro, the Thing without a Face* and *So a Cold Wind from Hell.* Indeed, Joan Hawkins argues that the Spanish horror films of this period were very much the product of economic necessity. She states that,

> When the government tightened restrictions on cheap co-productions, the Spanish film industry needed to find films they could make cheaply and expertly. . . . Horror seemed the perfect choice. These

films were popular and they sold well. Drawing on the formulae already established by England, Italy and the U.S., the Spanish film industry churned out a large number of Hammer take-offs, psycho killer flicks and gothic supernatural thrillers. Most of the films were European and Euro-American co-productions. Some were filmed outside Spain.[3]

However, it would be wrong to simply dismiss these low-budget Spanish horror films en masse. Like many low-budget exploitation films produced in other national cinemas it would be short-sighted to see them as uniformly uninteresting as there are films made during this period that offer significant reflections on the society in which they were produced. In this essay I argue that some of the films that appeared during the Spanish horror boom offered a complex meditation on the genre and may be seen as enormously subversive when placed within the context of Spanish cinema under Franco. I will now turn to the radical potential of exploitation filmmaking generally, before moving on to the specifics of Spanish horror.

Exploitation cinema has been widely written about in relation to the Hollywood film industry, and some of those observations can assist in an understanding of the Spanish horror film. Talking about the U.S. film industry, Jim Hillier argues that, "the term 'exploitation' differentiates a certain kind of overly exploitative product from the supposedly nonexploitative product of the majors, and implies that movies thus labelled take advantage of their audiences."[4] Within European cinema, the distinction may be made between serious "art" films and the more popular and exploitative genres that exist in and across particular national boundaries. One of the most obvious differences is the level of marketing that operates around popular forms. Indeed, marketing is central to exploitation cinema, as it is through this medium that generic classification can take place and the target audience be reached. The marketing of exploitation movies therefore demands a certain level of mutual knowledge on behalf of the filmmakers and their audience. The promotional materials produced for Spanish horror films in and outside of Spain had to acknowledge the age of the audience and their generic expectations, many of which were based on familiar imagery and characters drawn from Universal 1930s horror, British Hammer, and Italian gothic and *giallo* films. Spanish horror can therefore be understood as attempting to exploit the international success of those products. Promotional posters of the period were adorned with images of scantily clad women, torture, mutilation, shadows, vampire cloaks and teeth, werewolves, caves, castles, and old dark houses.

It is the relatively low critical esteem in which the horror genre is held as compared to more serious European art cinema that goes some way to explaining its gross neglect. Indeed, exploitation cinema is often viewed as simply delivering material that contains "the bizarre, the licentious, and the sensational"[5] and little of critical worth. This explains why so many of the recent works on Spanish cinema ignore it so completely.[6] However, some of the works' perspectives offer useful ways of considering Spanish horror films of the period. For example, Marsha Kinder in her important 1993 study *Blood Cinema,* devotes a chapter to violence in Spanish cinema of the 1960s, although her analysis concentrates on "serious" rather than genre pictures. For this reason, she chooses not to address the violence that appeared in the horror genre during this time. Her arguments do, however, shed some light on the violence in horror and its potentially subversive nature. Kinder argues that

> within the Spanish context, the graphic depiction of violence is primarily associated with the anti-Francoist perspective, which may surprise foreign spectators. . . . During the Francoist era, the depiction of violence was repressed, as was the depiction of sex, sacrilege and politics; this repression helps explain why eroticized violence could be used so effectively by the anti-Francoist opposition to speak a political discourse, that is, to expose the legacy of brutality and torture that lay hidden behind the surface beauty of the Fascist and neo-catholic aesthetics.[7]

Violence therefore brings with it the potential to operate subversively, flying, as it did, in the face of the Francoist censors who wanted wholesome representations of Spanish life to be the norm. Kinder goes on to suggest that this was not a new thing, that Spanish culture has a strong model for politically motivated images of violence, most significantly the paintings of Goya. Kinder makes much of works such as *Satan Devouring His Son,* arguing that they offer a radical and direct critique of society. But she goes on to indicate that Goya also offered more subtle versions of social criticism and critique within such established genres in painting as the court portrait and his rustic scenes of Spanish folklore.

It is Kinder's acknowledgment of Goya's work in already-established forms that is of interest to me here. Indeed, it is this tradition of using established genres as a vessel for politicized ideas and social critiques that offered a model for some of the Spanish filmmakers who consciously turned to the horror genre in the early 1970s on the heels of its newfound popularity. The violence that Kinder identifies as having a radical and subversive potential in earlier forms became central to the established codes and conventions of the horror genre. In particular, the horror genre conveys the "eroticized violence" that Kinder specifically discusses; without a doubt, the appeal of the horror film depended on this being part of the marketing strategy. However, the genre also offered space for directors to find a way of articulating challenges to the dominant ideas and beliefs of Francoist cinema and its celebration of catholic family values.

Kinder goes on to argue that the question of violence is a key to understanding the cultural specificity of Spanish cinema in the late 1960s and 1970s. She suggests that the Franco regime sought to repress images of violence because they operated counter to their vision of Spain's heroic past. When it did occur, she claims that, "usually depicted as the consequence of a repressive society beset by poverty, violence was included . . . in genres that justified its presence."[8] Strangely, given the period she is discussing, Kinder does not mention any films that would fit broadly in the horror genre and might constructively contribute to her discussion. This becomes even more of an oversight when one considers that she mentions Vicente Aranda's *Fata Morgana* (1966) and *Las crueles* (1969) but fails to discuss his violent and blood-drenched 1972 film, *La novia ensangrentada* (*The Blood Spattered Bride*). Kinder also spends time analyzing the violence in *Los desafíos* (*The Challenges*, 1969), but does not extend her discussion to include one of the contributors to that film, Claudio Guerín Hill, who in 1973 directed the highly regarded horror film *La campana del infierno* (*The Bell of Hell*). Both *La novia ensangrentada* and *La campana del infierno* use violence in the ways outlined by Kinder, offering within the codes and conventions of the horror genre clear critiques of aspects of Spanish society at the time. An acknowledgment of the potential of horror to critique social structures is central to understanding de la Iglesia's 1972 film, *La semana del asesino*. I now focus on this film in more detail.

La semana del asesino

Before moving into television and then cinema in the late 1960s, Eloy de la Iglesia worked in the children's theater, Teatro Popular Infantil. He has been a controversial figure in Spanish cinema, in particular his post-Franco melodramas that mixed politics and sexuality, such as *El diputado* (1978), eventually adding drugs and youth culture to the mix with *El pico* (1983). Paul Julian Smith offers one of the few detailed studies of de la Iglesia's films in his 1992 book, *Laws of Desire*. Smith argues that "the cinema of Eloy de la Iglesia is by no means academically respectable,"[9] later stating that, "in Spain to speak of de la Iglesia is to risk ridicule or worse."[10] However, his work has slowly begun to be reassessed. John Hopewell, who calls de la Iglesia's films "refreshing," and labels *La semana del asesino* "outstanding,"[11] was one of the first writers to offer a positive view of his work. Alongside Smith, Stephen Tropiano has offered a detailed analysis that focuses on the images of homosexuality in de la Iglesia's films.[12]

Tropiano also argues that de la Iglesia has received little critical attention due to the sensationalist subject matter of his films and his use of the commercial codes and conventions of popular genres, especially the melodrama. He argues that critics looking at post-Franco Spanish cinema have tended to focus on more clearly "artistic" directors, such as Carlos Saura. Significantly, Smith too sees de la Iglesia's films as raising issues of "taste and value," arguing that "in order to address such a body of work at all we must confront problems of genre (exploitation) and historicity ('shelf life')."[13] As I have outlined, and bearing in mind Smith's point, *La semana del asesino* must therefore be placed in the context of popular Spanish filmmaking of the 1970s, in particular the horror films produced during this period.

In his chapter of the book, Smith chooses to focus on the films that de la Iglesia directed from the mid-1970s to the early 1980s, a period whose start coincided with the end of the Franco regime. Apart from mentioning the fact that at the 1972 Berlin Film Festival the distribution company handed out sick bags as a promotional gimmick, his study does not include any detailed consideration of *La semana del asesino*. Nevertheless, some of his points about de la Iglesia's films more generally are useful. Smith writes that de la Iglesia's films have been critically attacked, and that "critical abuse of de la Iglesia ... has been motivated by an inability to 'read' his use of genre."[14] This is certainly the case with *La semana del asesino*, which, on occasion (as the Berlin anecdote shows), has been marketed as a gore-drenched horror film. However, in many ways the actual text resists this straightforward generic description. In the United Kingdom the film was certainly perceived in this manner, leading to its being placed on the list of prohibited films following the passing of the

Bright bill, and labeled a "video nasty" in the early 1980s.[15] In a similar vein, the British rerelease of *La semana del asesino* on video by Redemption featured a meat hook on the cover, suggesting to potential purchasers that the film has obvious similarities to other horror movies of the period such as *The Texas Chainsaw Massacre* (1974) and *Three on a Meat Hook* (1973), which were marketed in a similar fashion.

La semana del asesino is certainly violent, and features a number of progressively brutal killings, but the film is better understood in terms of generic fluidity. The popularity of horror within the context of Spanish film production may explain the graphic images that would enable the picture to be marketed in this way to a fan and mainstream audience. However, unlike *La novia ensangrentada* for example, *La semana del asesino* uses the conventions of social realism as well as horror. The horrific events that unfold in the film are always situated firmly in a contemporary setting and are clearly socially motivated, particularly through de la Iglesia's use of mise en scène, which carefully constructs a believable social milieu. Indeed, the creation of a believable social reality through mise en scène suggests that however extreme the events depicted are they can always be understood as having direct social and economic causes.

Although he focuses on a number of American horror films of the 1970s, Tony Williams's 1980 essay "Family Horror" is of some assistance when considering the subversive potential of the horror genre in general. Williams suggests a way of thinking about cinematic horror that informs my reading of *La semana del asesino*. He argues that

> reaction to personal oppression can take several forms. When the conflict between personal identity and socially allotted role becomes unbearable, the victim usually has feelings of guilt and inadequacy. . . . Unless the decision is taken to acquiesce and vegetate another alternative path is found, a long road begins that can lead to torment and even insanity. . . . In the horror film, the alternative to the norms of society is usually monstrous, a psychotic reaction against the conventions of everyday life, but also an attempt at beginning to articulate another way which has yet to be defined. At this stage, the alternative is usually destructive: its monstrous nature reflects that of the society which produced it.[16]

Marcos (Vicente Parra), the central character of *La semana del asesino*, is constrained and tormented by society, and his frustration takes a particularly

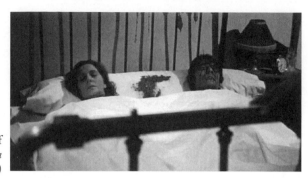

A mise en scène of
horror in *La semana
del asesino* (1974)

monstrous form. The only potential alternative hinted at in the film,
homosexuality, was enormously problematic for an uneducated man in
Spain in the early 1970s. The horror of this film arises from Marcos's brutal reaction to the demands of the society in which he is forced to live.

Skillfully played by Parra,[17] Marcos is a working-class man who
lives on the fringes of Madrid society. The film's credit sequence neatly
establishes his outsider status by moving through a series of shots of the
city that end with Marcos's home, isolated on a piece of wasteland, part of
the city but also removed and on its edge. This follows a sequence showing Marcos at work in a slaughterhouse. After some graphic images of
slaughter we cut to a shot of him eating a meat sandwich, oblivious to the
brutality going on behind him and essential for the creation of his meal.
Marcos's inability to make these obvious connections suggests that he is
also unable to make wider links concerning his position and exploitation
in Spanish society. It is therefore possible to read Marcos as representative
of the more lumpen elements of the industrial working class. This also,
from the outset, begins to explain why Marcos reacts to the extreme and
violent situations that follow in the confused manner in which he does.
These opening sequences are essential to the film's potentially subversive
approach to its subject matter and characters.

The plot outline of *La semana del asesino* certainly sounds like that
of a horror film: a man living on the outskirts of a large city murders several visitors to his home, slowly disposing of their bodies in the slaughterhouse where he works. However, the film also has a rather downbeat
feel, one that comes very much from its anchorage of the horrific events
that unfold within a contemporary social reality, namely Madrid in the

early 1970s. Marcos is not presented as a conventionally "evil" character but instead is shown fitting into his world and being liked by those around him. This is certainly reflected in the scenes taking place at his local bar where he is always shown to be welcome. However, his life experiences and social position as a member of the working class have disenfranchised him, and the film explores how a seemingly "normal" person such as Marcos can find himself in such a murderous position. The society in which he lives is not excused for its involvement in his actions. Indeed, de la Iglesia reinforces Marcos's social position through the way he sets up the first murder and its aftermath.

This murder occurs after Marcos goes on a date with his young girlfriend. Fearing that her father would disapprove, the pair are careful to keep their relationship discreet. On the surface it is suggested that this is due to their age difference; however, Marcos makes clear his feeling that it might be due to his lower-class status. At the end of their evening out, the couple gets a taxi home. As they kiss in the back seat the driver becomes very agitated and annoyed. He is clearly someone who does not approve of public displays of sexuality. It is possible to read the taxi driver as representative of the social etiquette closely associated with Spain's older generation, a generation marked by their support for the Franco regime and its ideas, beliefs, and values. Indeed, the violent nature of this society and the way it kept people in line is reflected in the driver's comment that he will give Marcos's girlfriend the beating that her father should have given her. In the process of stepping in to defend her from the driver's assault Marcos pushes him to the ground and hits him in the head with a rock. The next day, when reading the newspaper, they discover that the driver died from his injuries.

This marks the beginning of Marcos's descent into violence, as he cannot think of a way out of his situation. Significantly, he knows that his place in society ensures that the authorities will not deal with him sympathetically. His girlfriend wants him to go to the police and confess his role in the driver's death. Marcos, though, attempts to articulate (to the best of his limited ability) why he cannot go. He begins by noting that the police "will never listen to someone as poor as I am. A nobody." His girlfriend argues that he is being ridiculous. For her the judicial system seems fair and just. Her more middle-class background has prevented her seeing the miscarriages of justice a person of Marcos's social status would be only too familiar with. He retorts by arguing that "the police will listen to the rich only," and that he cannot even get a lawyer to represent him because "a good lawyer costs money, too much money." One challenge that de la Iglesia has to work around is the fact that the character of Marcos is inarticulate. The sequence with his girlfriend is as close as he can come to expressing his position in society verbally. At one level this limits the film's subversive potential; however, de la Iglesia attempts to overcome this limitation by using mise en scène to reveal Marcos's oppression, instead of relying on plot and dialogue.

For example, the impact of social forces on Marcos is clearly indicated through mise en scène in the sequence that follows the opening credits, showing Marcos resting in his home. In particular, heterosexuality and the desire for sex with women are shown as restrictions that entrap him. We are shown successive shots of Marcos's apartment walls, which are decorated with pictures of bikini-clad, semi-naked women taken from magazines. The acknowledgment of the social pressures placed on men in a macho society such as that of early 1970s Spain is a key to grasping some of the critical and potentially subversive aspects of *La semana del asesino*. Marcos literally lives with these pressures "in his face," and the sequence displaying the photos of women is intercut with shots of Marcos restless and unable to get comfortable in his own apartment. Even his own environment no longer allows for peace of mind, as societal forces impact on his personal life and space.

In this and similar sequences, Marcos is presented as an unhappy person. The cause of his discomfort is not made explicit through dialogue but is revealed through a combination of mise en scène and Parra's controlled, unsmiling performance—one that perfectly communicates Marcos's state of mental unease. The scenes that follow show Marcos at his local bar, at work, and again at home in his apartment, all emphasizing his increasing isolation. He does not engage people in conversation even when, as in the bar, they attempt to talk to him. Continually, as in the opening slaughterhouse shots, he is framed alone, even when in potentially social situations. His conversations with the barmaid Rosa (Emma Cohen) are uncomfortable as she flirts and makes very clear that she is available to him for sex. Marcos is once again depicted as uneasy in such situations, often excusing himself and leaving the bar and her company. Later in the film, when Rosa unexpectedly turns up at Marcos's home and they do have sex, he ends up murdering her.

Marcos responds in the expected heterosexual manner to Rosa's advances, but is shown as being far from pleased with the situation. Sex with women does not make him happy. Indeed, the only time we see

Marcos smile is when he goes swimming with a man, Nestor (Eusebio Poncela), who lives in an apartment complex nearby and who for some time has been watching Marcos and attempting to befriend him. The potentially homosexual nature of their relationship, while not made explicit, is certainly clear. Nestor's pursuit of Marcos often takes place after dark in secluded settings as the former walks his dog. Marcos, however, represses this side of their interaction, often appearing uncomfortable and again excusing himself to be alone. It is possible to argue that this is because Marcos does not understand why his relationship with Nestor is the only one that makes him even remotely happy. Having been subjected to the socializing process of Spanish machismo, as implied by the photos of bikini-clad women on his wall, Marcos is not able to escape its ideological structure, his frustration and confusion worked through symbolically via the murders he commits. He is alienated from the mainstream of society by his class, his apartment is run down, but he knows nothing else and has no political consciousness, even though middle-class housing developments are being put up all around him. Throughout *La semana del asesino*, de la Iglesia suggests that the middle classes were much better cared for than the working class in Spain under Franco's rule.

Similarly, Marcos cannot articulate his feelings of contentment, much less the reasons for it, when spending leisure time with another man. Although class and sexuality are not conflated in *La semana del asesino*, the inability of characters to do what makes them happy is revealed as having the same source: the repression of working in the interests of a heterosexual, bourgeois elite. Certainly, heterosexuality was the only official option available in Francoist Spain. As Alberto Mira has noted, "From the 1940s onwards an all-pervading censorship and keen mistrust for any kind of marginality (particularly where sexual dissidence was concerned) made the construction of homosexual identities virtually impossible."[18] Marcos's lumpen position in the working class makes him unable to analyze his social position or act to change it. He is therefore as much a victim as the animals he kills and disposes of in the slaughterhouse.

The pressure placed on Marcos by the society in which he lives is most critically and explicitly depicted as he tries to rid his home of the stench of his decaying victims' bodies. After he has killed five people, four of whom lay decomposing in his bedroom, Marcos futilely attempts to use air freshener and cologne to remove the smell. The structure of the film during this scene is very precise. The shots of Marcos spraying his house are intercut with a series of images representative of the social forces and influences that are working on him to mold his identity and world. Not surprisingly from a filmmaker who was associated with the Spanish Communist Party,[19] these are, first and foremost, the media, as indicated by a shot of a television set. (On TV is the same type of family-based advertising shown earlier in a "Flory soup" commercial; ironically, Marcos works at the Flory factory and so after his disposal of body parts in the slaughterhouse the company's soup is likely to contain parts of his victims.) Second, the church, represented by the shot of a statue of Our Lady. Third, the family, represented via a photograph of Marcos and his brother standing with their mother. And finally, heterosexuality, indicated by a shot that further fragments the pinup images on Marcos's wall, presenting women as mere sexualized bodies available for men to look at and desire.

Clearly then, through the juxtaposition of these shots, de la Iglesia seeks to remind his audience that Marcos is the product of a particular society, and that significant social forces have impacted on him to create the "man" he is—and by logical extension the person capable of the outrageous actions we have watched him commit. In Althusserian terms, the ideological factors listed here have served to "position" Marcos in society. As Mark Jancovich argues in relation to Althusser's notion of "interpellation," "subjects are addressed by society. One takes up positions in society which are defined by the social structure. These positions are not natural and inherent to individuals, but individuals 'misrecognize' or mistake these positions as being natural and inherent to themselves."[20] Marcos wants to be a particular kind of (heterosexual) man. The kind that he continually sees represented by the ideological powers of the media, the church, the family, and heterosexual machismo, but ultimately cannot be. Marcos's adornment of his home with girlie pinups, and his sexual encounter with Rosa, reveal his struggle to behave in a manner he thinks society expects. Of course, the film suggests that this brings him nothing but frustration, pain, and confusion.

The Madrid setting is another vital element in de la Iglesia's critique of Spanish society. The location is made clear through the shots of the underground and the locales characters inhabit at the beginning of the film. This distinguishes *La semana del asesino* from many other Spanish horror films produced during the same period. A large number of the horror films made between 1967 and 1975 were set outside Spain, for fear of upsetting the Francoist censors and authorities. For example, Paul Naschy's famous werewolf character, Waldemar Daninsky, was Eastern

European rather than Spanish. Naschy, one of the most prolific figures of the Spanish horror boom, made a number of pictures set in medieval France rather than Spain, including his own directorial debut, *Inquisición* (*Inquisition*, 1976). Other significant horror directors also chose to utilize foreign settings, including Amando de Ossario, whose *Las garras de Lorelei* (*Grasp of the Lorelei*, 1973) was set in Germany.

One reason for the pan-European settings of these films was a desire to appeal to markets across Europe and beyond. As Cathal Tohill and Pete Tombs argue,

> Spanish horror was born out of commercial necessity. The govern-ment had been clamping down on cheap co-productions. To recoup the costs of their bigger budgets, Spanish film-makers were being forced to find formula that appealed to overseas markets. Leon Klimovsky . . . recalls that foreign distributors were not interested in Spanish films—but they were interested in horror films, no matter where they came from. So, initially, the films were a combination of elements drawn from the successful markets at which they were aimed—the *Psycho*-style mad killer films from the US, for example, Hammer films, and the Italian Gothics of Bava and Margheriti.[21]

Whatever the reason, by setting the films outside Spain their potential subversiveness would be diminished for domestic audiences. Unlike some other commercial horror filmmakers, de la Iglesia chose to make his pic-ture specific to contemporary Spain. Unable to be overtly critical of the Franco regime in his films of this period, one of the ways he suggested his views was by setting *La semana del asesino* in a contemporary reality, one that would easily be recognized by Spanish audiences. Of course that did not mean the film could not be sold outside Spain, as is testified to by the English-dubbed version currently available.

De la Iglesia also presents a critique of the mores and values of Span-ish society at the time through his depiction of the relationship between Marcos and Nestor. The latter, as mentioned, is a young bourgeoisie man who lives in the recently constructed apartment complex that overlooks Marcos's home, and who walks his dog on the land surrounding it. In many ways he is a pivotal character in the film as he offers a point of contact for Marcos but is also removed from him in terms of class. The relationship between the two men is certainly difficult to read. On one level this is because it seems to be potentially homosexual in nature during a time when to explicitly depict such a relationship would cause problems with the censor. On another level it is because Marcos is unable to fully accept the possibilities that seem to be open to him. Looking at *La semana del asesino* in hindsight, and especially in light of de la Iglesia's gay-themed melodramas (such as *El pico*, 1983), it is possible to see the strong suggestion of a potentially gay relationship between Marcos and Nestor, one that offers Marcos a release from the pressures he feels. On one of the occasions when they meet, Nestor makes the point that "we are both strange birds," and says that Marcos should have a home and a family and perhaps be putting a down payment on a car. Marcos's response is telling, as he says that "marriage is just not for me right now." On hearing this, Nestor makes a link between the two men, noting that a friend of his would call them outcasts. On some levels the film certainly seems to agree, visually linking the two men in a number of sequences.

The most significant of these sequences occurs after a meeting in the local bar. Marcos calls in for something to eat, and Rosa, the owner's wife, clearly makes a pass at him as she cleans up some spilt milk from his jeans. This seems to make him uncomfortable and he rejects her advances. As he leaves, Nestor picks him up in his car and offers to take him for a late night swim at his club. Marcos agrees and they leave. One might see this sequence as rather superfluous to the narrative drive of the film, but its significance lies in the fact that only here, away from his barrio and the factory, Marcos allows himself to relax and smile as he unselfconsciously splashes in the pool with Nestor. Released from the drudgery of his everyday life and in the company of another man, Marcos is finally at peace. This is emphasized when, on the pair's return home later that evening, Marcos wakes up after sleeping in the car, saying that "I just can't recall when I slept so well."

Later that morning Rosa appears at his house and offers to make him breakfast. As if to symbolically deny the happiness of the night before and to remove any confusion he may have about his feelings, Marcos makes love to her. Afterward, she wants to clean the room containing the bodies and Marcos is forced to kill her to prevent her from discovering them. Following this, de la Iglesia once again frames Marcos with the pinups, thereby linking his actions with the ideological forces that emphasize heterosexuality and that cause him so much anxiety, especially after his evening with Nestor. He has had the opportunity to gain a new perspective on his life, but the power of the ideas and beliefs of the dominant ideology proves too much to overcome.

Homosexual subtext in
La semana del asesino
(1974)

De la Iglesia does not ignore the class differences between Marcos and Nestor. One of the most striking aspects of the film's commitment to exploring the issue of class is the fact that, although Nestor offers Marcos some potential to escape his background, he is also exploiting him. The immediate post-credit sequence has Nestor looking into Marcos's house with binoculars; he is clearly wealthy as his apartment and car show, and is therefore different, with different social needs, from Marcos. This is shown most clearly when the pair sit talking outside a bar. The local police walk past and ask them for identification, but when they see Nestor's address they leave them alone. The suggestion here is that if Marcos had been on his own their reaction would not have been the same.

It is certainly possible to read Nestor as a middle-class "tourist" excited by his brush with the working-class Marcos, and indeed sexually thrilled by him. His ability to watch and observe, as he is repeatedly shown doing, highlights his relative social power. Like Marcos's young girl-friend, Nestor feels that he has nothing to fear in this society. This in turn means that even if he has seen Marcos's murderous actions from his upper-story apartment vantage point, he does not view himself as a future victim. It is here that the futility of Marcos's actions is most obvious. He kills those closest to him—including Rosa and his own brother—rather than those responsible for his oppression. The brief moments of relief and happiness he gains when he is closest to accepting his repressed sexuality must therefore be set against the social and economic restrictions that the mere act of sex would never relieve. It is this crucial fact that one might argue lies at the center of de la Iglesia's later, more sexually explicit (in terms of content) melodramas.

It is often small moments such as these that reveal the ways in which de la Iglesia consciously utilizes the generic conventions of the horror film, alongside those of social realism, to create a work that stands as a direct challenge to the values and beliefs of mainstream Spanish society of that period. Made during a time when many working-class cinemagoers in Spain were choosing to go to see, or due to censorship were only able to see, horror rather than the more elitist, art-house fare produced by directors such as Carlos Saura, de la Iglesia's use of the genre for political means becomes all the more important. Its intervention into a particular social, historical, and cultural moment—that of the Franco regime and popular resistance to it—is especially significant because it was accessible to the very people it was concerned about and who populate its images. For this reason, *La semana del asesino* is a striking example of radical, popular filmmaking in Spain in the early 1970s, and one that deserves more critical attention that it has received thus far.

Notes

1. Peter Hutchings, *Hammer and Beyond: The British Horror Film* (Manchester, UK: Manchester University Press, 1993), 17.

2. See, for example, Cathal Tohill and Pete Tombs, *Immoral Tales: Sex and Horror Cinema in Europe, 1956–1984* (London: Titan, 1995); and Joan Hawkins, *Cutting Edge: Art-Horror and the Horrific Avant-Garde* (Minneapolis: University of Minnesota Press, 2000).

3. Hawkins, *Cutting Edge*, 93.

4. Jim Hillier, *The New Hollywood* (London: Studio Vista, 1992), 40.

5. Thomas Patrick Doherty, *Teenagers and Teenpics: The Juvenilizing of American Movies in the 1950s* (London: Unwin Hyman, 1988), 3.

6. For example, Peter Evans, ed., *Spanish Cinema: The Auteurist Tradition* (Oxford: Oxford University Press, 1999) contains no chapters on horror auteurs, or on the horror work of established art-house auteurs such as Bigas Luna, or on maverick popular filmmakers such as Alex de la Iglesia.

7. Marsha Kinder, *Blood Cinema: The Reconstruction of National Identity in Spain* (Berkeley: University of California Press, 1993), 138.

8. Kinder, *Blood Cinema*, 155.

9. Paul Julian Smith, *Laws of Desire: Questions of Homosexuality in Spanish Writing and Film* (Oxford: Oxford University Press, 1992), 129.

10. Smith, *Laws of Desire*, 159.

11. John Hopewell, *Out of the Past: Spanish Cinema after Franco* (London: BFI Publishing, 1986), 221.

12. See Stephen Tropiano, "Out of the Cinematic Closet: Homosexuality in the Films of Eloy de la Iglesia," in *Refiguring Spain: Cinema, Media, Representation*, ed. Marsha Kinder (Durham, NC: Duke University Press, 1997), 157–77.

13. Smith, *Laws of Desire,* 130.
14. Ibid.
15. A concerted campaign was waged in Britain against the so-called video nasties, which for the most part were low-budget horror films. This was led by a number of newspapers who fueled a moral panic about the content of these pictures and the effects they were having on young viewers. For a more detailed study of the movement, see Martin Barker, *The Video Nasties: Freedom and Censorship in the Media* (London: Pluto, 1985).
16. Tony Williams, "Family Horror," *Movie* 27/28 (1980): 117.
17. Parra had been a popular actor in films and on stage throughout the 1960s; indeed, he was something of a matinee idol. His commitment to *La semana del asesino* is reflected in his producing credit. He went on to work with Eloy de la Iglesia again on the 1973 film, *Nadie oyó gritar (No One Heard the Scream).*
18. Alberto Mira, "Laws of Silence: Homosexual Identity and Visibility in Contemporary Spanish Culture," in *Contemporary Spanish Cultural Studies,* ed. Barry Jordan and Rikki Morgan-Tamosunas (London: Edward Arnold, 2000), 244.
19. See Hopewell, *Out of the Past,* 277.
20. Mark Jancovich, "Screen Theory," in *Approaches to Popular Film,* ed. Joanne Hollows and Mark Jancovich (Manchester, UK: Manchester University Press, 1995), 129.
21. Tohill and Tombs, *Immoral Tales,* 66.

10

Genre Bending and Gender Bonding:

Masculinity and Repression in Dutch "Thriller" Cinema

Steven Jay Schneider and Kevin W. Sweeney

In a discussion of recent Dutch TV crime shows, Joke Hermes points out that prior to the late 1980s, "virtually all television fiction and feature film production [in the Netherlands] . . . resisted the idea that to follow a generic formula could lead to a quality product."[1] Hermes explains this resistance primarily in terms of "the enduring sensitivity of the Dutch to the high-low culture divide": "Genre is associated with cheap American mass produced fiction. Not something that one would want to make or could make for that matter with money funded by the Dutch government."[2] Because the Dutch film academy showed a marked preference for auteurist product, with its emphasis on traditional, romantic notions of artistic originality and innovation, it did not "therefore teach much genre rules and conventions at all."[3] As a result of eschewing generic conventions for their low-culture connotations, Dutch filmmakers were ill equipped to make successful genre pictures at home, much less abroad. Following the blockbuster successes of Dutch directors such as Paul Verhoeven (*Total Recall* [1990], *Basic Instinct* [1992], *Starship Troopers* [1997) and Jan de Bont (*Speed* [1994], *Twister* [1996]) in America, however, Dutch producers have begun to realize that "genre rules are not to be looked down on but to be used inventively"[4] in order to ensure larger and more reliable audiences. Nevertheless, Dutch directors, on the whole, still evince less interest in using generic conventions than their Hollywood counterparts.

These observations concerning the distinctly nongeneric quality of Dutch cinema—partly a matter of choice and sensibility, partly a result of inadequate training—are supported by a look at the difficulties in coherently situating two prominent Dutch "thrillers" of the mid-1980s according to established genre codes and conventions. Although Paul Verhoeven's

De vierde man (*The Fourth Man,* 1983) and George Sluizer's *Spoorloos* (*The Vanishing,* 1988) share certain affective aims (the manufacturing of suspense, tension, and anxiety in viewers) as well as some basic narrative and plot points (strained relationships, mysterious backstories, and the threat or likelihood of murder), it seems futile, if not completely beside the point, to group these films together in generic terms, to speak of their being members of a Dutch horror/thriller "tradition." This is because, despite their similarities at the level of emotional cueing and plot, the differences between these films when it comes to specific genre quotation and hybridization are obvious: *The Fourth Man* self-consciously combines elements from the film noir, the gothic, and the erotic thriller traditions; while *The Vanishing,* to the limited extent that it engages with generic convention at all, seems to be part psychological thriller, part love story with horrific overtones.

It looks like our reading choices here are limited. Either we force these two films into a preexisting and loosely defined genre (the "thriller," the "suspense film," etc.), implicitly downplaying if not simply ignoring their numerous points of divergence. Or else we give up on the idea of comparative analysis altogether, choosing instead (in the best European art cinema tradition) to read these films as idiosyncratic and wholly "unique" auteurist texts, ones whose stylistic signatures and narrative or thematic particularities are far more interesting and important than any common features they might be thought or observed to share.

Neither of these options is particularly appealing, and the implicit dichotomy they represent is misleading at best. The former presupposes that classification by genre is the only or else the best way scholars have of grouping films together so as to identify and investigate shared features. In fact, as Gary Needham argues with particular reference to the 1970s–80s series of Italian *giallo* horror-thrillers, there is a strong need in academic film studies for "redefinition concerning how other popular film-producing nations understand and relate to their products.... [T]he *giallo* challenges our assumptions about how non-Hollywood films should be classified, going beyond the sort of Anglo-American taxonomic imaginary that 'fixes' genre both in film criticism and the film industry in order to designate something specific."[5] The latter option, meanwhile, promises to elide key questions and issues concerning the national character of Dutch cinema, naïvely relying on auteur theory when it is precisely a contextualization and qualification of traditional (hermeneutical) auteurism that is called for here.

By way of constructing a third option, one that allows us to break free of this critical dichotomy and sidestep its inherent weaknesses, we propose to investigate *The Fourth Man* and *The Vanishing* as members of a family or tradition of Dutch "thrillers" with an essentially national (and socioculturally specific) dimension.[6] As with the Italian *giallo,* we might say that Dutch thriller cinema is "not so much a genre . . . as a body of films that resists generic definition." Yet at the same time, this body of films "can be understood as an object to be promoted, criticised, studied, etc."[7] Despite their incorporation of conventions from different genres, and despite the undeniable presence of auteurist elements in each of them, it is possible to identify an underlying thematic preoccupation across both *The Fourth Man* and *The Vanishing,* namely the male protagonist's severe anxiety about his relationship with a female partner, anxiety that generates an imaginative and obsessive desire for control that winds up being repressed at the conclusion of the narrative. Furthermore, as the story proceeds, these intense feelings get displaced onto a clash between a socially acceptable and a socially challenging (i.e., nonnormative) form of relationship. The protagonist's anxiety is manifested at different levels of the film in question, levels that correspond roughly to David Bordwell's division of types of filmic meaning into the "literal" (in the case of *The Fourth Man*) and the "implicit" (in the case of *The Vanishing*); but it is Bordwell's notion of "symptomatic" or "repressed" meanings—meanings that are "assumed to be at odds with [literal] or implicit ones"[8]—that is our ultimate lens for examining the Dutch thriller tradition as a whole. For we claim that these films present a thematic opposition or conflict faced by the protagonist in a struggle for control; instead of resolving this conflict at film's end, however, it ends up being repressed.

Homosexuality and the Femme Fatale in *The Fourth Man*

Based on a popular Dutch novel with the same name, Verhoeven's 1983 film—the last one he made in Holland before heading off to Hollywood—*The Fourth Man* chronicles the trip of Gerard Reve (Jeroen Krabbé), a highly regarded albeit alcoholic Dutch writer and a mystical Catholic, to give a reading to the Flushing literary society. (The author of the novel from which the film is adapted is also named Gerard Reve and is a Dutch writer of some literary repute, a convert to Catholicism whom one suspects has a history of imbibing.) While awaiting his train at the Amsterdam train station, Reve becomes romantically captivated by a handsome young man whom he gazes at but is unable to meet. After his lecture, Gerard is invited by the treasurer of the literary society and local hairdresser, Christine Halsslag (Renée Soutendijk), to spend the night at her seaside home. That evening he seduces her, although she excites his sexual interest mainly because of her boyish figure.

Charmed by the luxurious attentions he receives the next day and the generous cash payment for his lecture, Gerard accepts Christine's invitation to stay on at the house. However, what clinches his decision to accept her hospitality is that, in snooping around her office, Gerard discovers a picture of the very same young man he saw at the train station. (Christine seems to have deliberately left the photo where Gerard will be sure to find it.) Gerard learns that this young man he lusts after is Christine's lover, Herman (Thom Hoffman). Scheming to meet Herman, Gerard decides to accept Christine's generous new proposal to be her writer-in-residence at the seashore. Christine's conniving to get Gerard to stay on is now matched by Gerard's subterfuge to seduce Herman. He vows, "I've got to have you even if it kills me." Yet, just as Gerard succeeds in seducing Herman in Christine's family crypt, he discovers what he takes to be a final piece of evidence convincing him that Christine is a witch who has killed her three previous husbands. What's more, he is now fearful that she intends to kill again, to kill *the fourth man*. Somewhat surprisingly, however, the fourth man turns out not to be Gerard, through whose skewed subjectivity we are given our primary means of interpreting the events taking place within the diegesis. Instead it picks out Herman, whose "accidental" death occurs shortly thereafter in an automobile crash that Gerard survives but in a severely traumatized state. Gerard believes that Herman's death occurs because of the latter's romantic/sexual relationship with the beautiful but inevitably unlucky-in-love Christine.

Two points are worth mentioning here. First, the "fourth man" label does not designate any particular male, but is instead an open position waiting to be filled by whichever male willingly accepts the role of Christine's fourth partner. It is precisely Gerard's refusal to take on this role—a refusal prompted in great measure by the fact that he is a practicing homosexual who only seems capable of achieving erotic satisfaction with young men[9]—which prevents (more accurately, protects) him from filling the shoes of the eponymous male character. As he informs Christine at one point, "I'm not the right man for you." Second, the very appellation "fourth man" (just like the first "three men," Christine's previous spouses, who likewise suffered apparently accidental deaths) signifies two positions in the narrative simultaneously—husband and victim—thereby implying that the two are effectively equivalent. This last point is supported by the film's closing scene, in which we observe Christine allowing herself to be picked up by a young man at the hospital where Herman's corpse has been deposited following his fatal car crash.

Delivered in a heightened state of anxiety, Gerard's extraordinary claim that Christine is a witch has been anticipated in the film almost from the very first scene. *The Fourth Man* builds a series of Gerard's visionary experiences, flights of fantasy, and dreams that while seemingly subjective often have some counterpart in the objective mise en scène (e.g., the cemetery and Christine's crypt match elements of Gerard's earlier dream). The film begins with an imaginary episode, a fantasy insert of Gerard strangling and killing his roommate lover with a black brassiere and breaking the violin the roommate was playing. Yet in the very next scene we see the same young man still playing his a violin. The lack of cues to introduce such a fantasy sequence and the abrupt transition that follows almost render the short insert a sight gag.[10] The connotation expressed here is that Gerard desires to exercise a controlling influence, to silence his often critical roommate. While recognizing the imaginary nature of later such episodes Gerard still affirms his power to see some truth in them. "I lie the truth," he tells the Flushing literary society, conflating his role as author with his personal perspective on the world. After several of these imaginary episodes, especially those focusing on Christine and Herman, the viewer begins to see them as reflective of Gerard's position as an author within the diegesis. Gerard wants to write the story of Christine's men and in this role brings to bear several generic contexts for the film.

The Fourth Man plays with the traditions of the gothic thriller as classically stated in films like Hitchcock's *Rebecca* (1940) and in more generically disruptive texts such as *Psycho* (1960).[11] Common elements of the genre include a large house visited by a guest who acts as the diegetic and exegetic stand-in for the viewer. The guest comes to believe that the house's owner has a secret and that the house (the cellar, attic, or surrounding buildings) itself contains clues or evidence relating to that secret. Gothic elements of this sort abound in Verhoeven's film. Gerard finds himself alone in Christine's house and gradually discovers what he thinks are its secrets—secrets about Christine's past. Gerard's wild sensibility, alcohol enhanced, leads him to propose what would ordinarily be considered an outrageous hypothesis: that she is diabolical, in human form a black widow spider like the one shown during the film's opening credits.

Gerard's seeming discovery of Christine's crypt and the urns containing the ashes of her three former husbands corresponds to the gothic narrative's revelation of the hidden secret within the house. What would ordinarily seem to be the coincidental deaths of three men provoke Gerard's suspicious imagination to extraordinary heights. Objective and subjective imagery is interwoven in the fabric of the narrative: realistic mise en scène is transformed in Gerard's eyes into religious vision, and dream settings later appear as actual locations outside the dream. A tension and clash between objective and subjective imagery, as well as between natural and supernatural explanations, continually reverberates throughout the text, provoking the viewer to ask whether the coincidence between the seemingly visionary aspects of Gerard's dreams and later objective occurrences in the narrative is due to chance, to Gerard's alcohol-inspired delirium, or else to some supernatural explanation.

Gerard's increasing conviction that Christine is a witch is given some plausibility in an otherwise naturalistic context because the film's narration favors Gerard's role as an author. The figure of authorship appears at different levels of cinematic discourse in *The Fourth Man*. It frames the film because of the nominal resemblance between the author of the original novel and the protagonist of the adapted narrative. The effect of this resemblance is to privilege the protagonist and credit him with a certain sanity. For, if one grants that the author in question is rational, one is inclined (without evidence to the contrary) to make a similar assessment about a character who is the author's stand-in. Moreover, as the stand-in for the author, the protagonist assumes a position of narratorial privilege, able to influence how the tale is told. As an author, the protagonist assumes the active power of a narrator able to manipulate the direction of the plot, to favor his point of view, and to tell the story the way he wants it told.

Although much of *The Fourth Man* focuses on Gerard's ambiguous status as author and narrator, he is not the only character in the film with authorial powers. At times, Christine too assumes such a position within the narrative. Gerard seems to acknowledge her prescience and agency when he recognizes that Herman's fatal car accident occurred on the same route that Christine had taken, thereby identifying her as in some sense responsible for Herman's death. The viewer also credits her with manipulating Gerard into staying on in Flushing and so having an effect on the course of narrative events. Her repeated interest in shooting home movies, both of her past husbands and their demise as well as of Gerard and Herman, suggests a competing authorial role of diegetic filmmaker to Gerard's status as diegetic writer. The first images the viewer sees of Christine, in fact, are of her filming Gerard at his lecture.

Sensing that Christine is manipulating the course of events Gerard begins to fear that he is living out a sequence of actions that has already been scripted. Finding Christine's home movies, Gerard stumbles around her study in an inebriated stupor. While playing with the films, he finds that when he stands directly in front of the projector the films are projected onto the screen of his own body. The image of Gerard as movie screen suggests that Christine can project her desired course of events onto Gerard, and that he is powerless to control this unfolding process. The home movies and Christine's being a filmmaker introduce another reflexive aspect to the film, in addition to the one produced by the similarity between the film protagonist and the original novelist. Moreover, these two reflexive authorial interests clash: Gerard has sought to learn Christine's secrets and schemed to get her to introduce him to Herman; Christine has manipulated Gerard into staying on in Flushing and seems (at least to Gerard) to have further nefarious plans. Under the surface contest between these two characters is a clash of authorial forces, a striving for control of the narrative. Both have scripts that they are trying to privilege in order to control the story's outcome.

This clash over authorial control is a source of great anxiety for Gerard. At his talk to the Flushing literary society Gerard's imaginative approach to reality is challenged both aesthetically and ideologically. A member of the audience, a doctor—a man of science rather than fantasy—who is also an amateur author, challenges Gerard and advocates instead a naturalistic aesthetic that directs attention to life and death. Gerard is questioned about how he can maintain his mystic Catholicism while living in a scientifically materialist world. He replies that religion and science both depend on the imagination and smugly proclaims that science is religion. Nevertheless, while Gerard advocates a similar reliance on imagination with respect to both institutions, *The Fourth Man* ultimately contrasts their differing attitudes toward private experience. This difference emerges in the film's final scenes, during which the doctor's empirically based beliefs are pitted against Gerard's mystical experiences.

In shock after Herman's fatal accident, the hospitalized Gerard reveals to the doctor what he holds to be Christine's true nature, along

Gerard Reve (Jeroen
Krabbé) as movie screen
in *The Fourth Man*
(1983)

with her evil intentions. He charges that she is diabolical, citing as evidence his dreams, visionary experiences, and the warnings he believes are contained in uncanny coincidences. The doctor, who has known Christine for several years, counters that Gerard's charges are fabrication based purely on chance, supporting his view with reference to the effects of Gerard's alcoholism and aesthetic creed. Besides, poses the doctor, if Christine is in fact a ghoulish creature, how has Gerard managed to elude her clutches? "By Grace," is Gerard's reply as he gazes up, looking for reassurance into the eyes of a nurse; surprisingly, this appears to be none other than the mysterious lady in blue, the young mother who has turned up unexpectedly throughout the film to warn Gerard of the dangers posed by Christine. On his train ride to Flushing, Gerard had a vision of this woman as the Virgin Mary, fitting her little boy with what looks like a halo but is really just an apple peel. Yet the nurse remains silent here, neither protesting nor confirming Gerard's anxious, mystically inspired charges. The clash of explanatory forces, between fantasy and knowledge, myth and science, private projection and public empiricism, thus remains unresolved. *The Fourth Man* ends with the repression of Gerard's authorial perspective and his anxiety. Nevertheless, the final scene shows Christine actively seeking another partner. We see her meeting and flirting with a handsome young stranger as she leaves the hospital, her agency suggesting a different generic context for the film.

It is largely due to the construction of Christine's character that *The Fourth Man* warrants consideration in film noir terms. An immediately recognizable, even over-the-top version of the noir's traditional femme fatale (whose supernatural powers of seduction are attributed to her further depiction as a "witchy woman" and a devil in disguise), Christine is repeatedly associated with the female black widow spider. This connection is made manifest from the opening scene, which shows a black widow in close-up spinning its web somewhere up above Gerard's head. And midway through the film, when Gerard first arrives at Christine's luxurious country home-cum-beauty salon, some of the neon letters spelling out the name of her business are not lit up with the others; the sign thus reads "SPIN" ("spider" in Dutch) instead of "SPHINX" (a word with its own enigmatic connotations). But whereas the American noir tends to divide up its principal female characters pretty "neatly into two basic types: alluring—and dangerous—femme fatales on the one hand, and dependable, respectable, safe and undemanding partners, wives and girlfriends on the other,"[12] *The Fourth Man* breaks with convention by collapsing these two types into one: the female who is both deadly *and* domestic; or rather, deadly *because* domesticating.

In a 1993 essay, Deborah Thomas argues that the domesticating female can be just as threatening to the male film noir protagonist as the femme fatale, and that more than one femme fatale turns out to be a would-be wife.[13] Lest it be claimed that our analysis of *The Fourth Man* assumes too rigid a dichotomy between the two types of women in traditional noir cinema, and sees the domesticating woman as rather more "safe" than she sometimes appears, it should be noted that the radical manner in which Verhoeven's film collapses the two types of noir females extends beyond Thomas's important considerations. Besides the literal as opposed to merely metaphorical danger Christine poses as wife and girlfriend, Verhoeven makes her the only plausible candidate for both female roles in the traditional noir love triangle of male protagonist, femme fatale, and domesticating woman; the collapse in question is therefore not merely character-driven but structural. Contrast this with one of *The Fourth Man*'s closest American counterparts, Bob Rafelson's *Black Widow* (1987). In the latter film, the Theresa Russell character marries and then murders a string of wealthy men. Unlike Christine in *The Fourth Man*, however, Russell's vixen is opposed by a federal investigator (played by Debra Winger) who represents in looks and actions the narrative's safe, reliable, "good" (albeit single) woman. Thus, despite offering up the figure of a domesticating woman who literally kills her unsuspecting mates, Rafelson sticks with noir convention by maintaining—even while reconceiving—the dichotomy between his central female characters. Crucially, the same can be said of Verhoeven himself in his 1992 Hollywood blockbuster, *Basic Instinct,* a film the director has called a "less esoteric, more . . . mainstream" version of *The Fourth Man.* "[14] Following a screenplay by Joe Eszterhas, Verhoeven introduces into this "version" of his film a stereo-typically (at first) domesticating woman (Jeanne Tripplehorn) to coun-terbalance Sharon Stone's femme fatale, only to play around with this dichotomy by temporarily making Tripplehorn's character the apparent killer. As much as anything else, it is this bifurcation of the female lead into two different parts that makes *Basic Instinct* more conventional than *The Fourth Man.*

Like the noir's younger and trashier cousin, the so-called erotic thriller (a category in which *Basic Instinct* also fits quite comfortably), *The Fourth Man* is intentionally—and quite literally, in Bordwell's sense of the term—constructed so as to keep the viewer guessing as to whether or not the sexy female lead is in fact a ruthless killer.[15] The ambiguities and con-tradictory evidence presented by the narrative make it impossible to ascertain for sure whether Christine is in some way directly responsible for the tragic deaths of her various male partners or whether she is herself the victim of shockingly bad fortune, destined to be a widow no matter how many men she marries. The cause of this interpretive dilemma is twofold. First, as an alcoholic and overimaginative novelist whom we know from the opening scenes is subject to hallucinatory visions, Gerard is not the most reliable of narrators. We have to wonder whether every-thing he thinks he sees is not just a dream, a nightmare, even a fantasy, or perhaps just a paranoid reading of some abnormal but by no means malevolent occurrences.[16] And second, there are a number of scenes in which Christine responds to Gerard with passionate and seemingly gen-uine emotion, though it is of course possible that she is simply putting on an act in order to make herself look innocent in his (and our) eyes. Even if one decides to grant Christine the benefit of the doubt, however, her history with husbands makes her a no less dangerous spouse.

It is important to note that the anxiety simultaneously triggered and exploited by *The Fourth Man* is not about female sexuality per se. After all, premarital sex with Christine seems to pose no special danger to the men in her life, despite Gerard's difficulties getting sufficiently stimulated for intercourse (see note 9). Thus, the film is not particularly susceptible to the charges of misogyny that have often been levied against Verhoeven, especially for those U.S. productions (*Basic Instinct* and *Showgirls* [1995]) in which Eszterhas served as screenwriter. Rather, it is Gerard's suspicion that commitment to an exclusively heterosexual relationship with Christine will lead to his untimely death that primarily provokes the fear and terror. This explains why it is Herman and not Gerard who becomes the "Fourth Man" of the film's title: whereas the former potential husband/victim chooses to disavow his homosexual inclinations (inclinations that are revealed in the crypt seduction scene initiated by Gerard) in order to pursue his engagement with Christine, the latter vehemently, even hysterically, elects to reject Christine after having a vision that suggests her previous husbands' accidental deaths might (as well) have been murder.

If this were a North American horror film, we might expect active female sexuality itself to be figured as monstrous here;[17] either that or the male homosexual impulse, representing as it does "the most obvious threat to the 'norm' of sexuality as reproductive and restricted by the 'ideal' of family."[18] As Robin Wood argues, following Herbert Marcuse, both of these deviations from the institutionalized norm of monogamous heterosexuality are the targets of particularly severe psychosocial repression in U.S. society. Instead, and in keeping with our ideas concerning Dutch thriller cinema, what proves truly horrifying in *The Fourth Man* is the repression of Gerard's sexual character and authorial voice. Despite the occasional indication to the contrary—notably his passionate but unconsummated make-out session with Herman—Gerard's deviations from the established patterns of bourgeois society are ultimately subject to *re*-repression: there is no way of permanently escaping the spider's web of marriage and its associated fetters unscathed. His sense of agency remains frustrated, his attempt to "lie the truth" when confronted by established medical practice and a scientific worldview finally overwhelmed.

Gerard may have been spared an early death by rejecting the affection and security, financial as well as emotional, offered by Christine, but as the film's ambivalent ending in the country hospital makes clear, the price he must pay for such "freedom" is virtual lobotomization and an accompanying loss of sexual as well as creative energy (the latter representing the former's sublimated, non-erotic manifestation). From all appearances, it looks as if Gerard will never write, much less have sex (of any kind), again. And for a country like Holland, famous for its long-standing tradition of advocating liberal policies toward social issues such as homosexuality, prostitution, abortion, and birth control, the existence of such a state of affairs—one in which "alternative" (e.g., non-reproductive, non-monogamous, non-hetero) sexualities are ultimately overpowered or else rendered impotent by the pressure to conform and enter into an exclusive, lifelong relationship with a member of the opposite sex—would indeed be a cause for alarm among a large segment of the population.[19]

This symptomatic (Bordwellian) reading of *The Fourth Man* situates the film within the Dutch "thriller" tradition understood as a group of national and culturally specific texts, yet it still seeks to do justice to Verhoeven's status as another in a long line of European auteurs lured to Hollywood by the promise of big budgets and even bigger audiences. As critics and scholars never tire of pointing out, despite the vastly different production circumstances and creative obstacles to contend with, Verhoeven in both geographic phases of his career has evinced a fascination, even a preoccupation, with "the darker sides of sexuality."[20] This can be seen, for example, in his depiction of acts of sodomy, gang rape, S&M, promiscuity, and graphic sex, as well as in his predilection for showcasing bodily mutation, male nudity, vulgarity, and scatological humor. Although *The Fourth Man* may be somewhat tame, even prudish, in comparison with the director's earlier Dutch classic, *Turks fruit* (*Turkish Delight*, 1973) and his later American bomb, *Showgirls*, the film nonetheless fits comfortably in his cross-continental oeuvre with its scenes of Gerard masturbating and going down on Herman in the crypt, as well as its images of violent bodily penetration (Herman is killed while driving at high speed when a swinging construction pole impales him through the eye) and gore effects (most infamously, the shot of Gerard's lopped-off penis seen in his castration nightmare).

The highly publicized furor that took place in the American gay community over *Basic Instinct*'s bisexual killer notwithstanding,[21] it can be plausibly maintained that Verhoeven's exploration of non-traditional sexualities rarely constitutes exploitation, particularly when it comes to the portrayal of homosexuals. As the director has commented:

> It was always there in my Dutch movies, such as *The Fourth Man*. So from my earliest work you can see that I have always discussed homosexuality. Even if you look at *Basic Instinct*, you will see that I portray homosexuality as a central part of society. What I did in that film was not to treat it as an issue, which would have been wrong, but rather I used it as a plot mechanism. I felt this was the best thing to do in order to make a pro-gay statement. I have always felt from growing up in Holland, with its tolerance of the gay community and then later working with so many cast and crew that were homosexual gave me a

good perspective on this issue. Anyway, I actually think that we are all born bisexually and it is only really in adolescence that our sexual futures are decided.[22]

Verhoeven's longstanding concern with depicting homosexuality as a "central part of society" made him the ideal filmmaker to direct a picture in which the main source of anxiety is the male protagonist's subconscious recognition that normative heterosexuality, embodied in the institution of marriage, cannot be successfully resisted.

Out of Sight, Not Out of Mind: Homosociality in *The Vanishing*

The difficulties alluded to so far, of "coherently situating . . . Dutch 'thrillers' of the mid-80s according to established genre codes and conventions," are most vividly seen in critical discussion of *The Vanishing*.[23] Sluizer's film centers on the obsessive and ultimately fatal search engaged in by Rex Hofman (Gene Bervoets) for his missing girlfriend Saskia (Johanna ter Steege), who was randomly abducted from a service station three years earlier by a distinctly normal-looking sociopath-cum-family man (Bernard-Pierre Donnadieu) while the young Dutch couple was vacationing in central France. Lauded both at home and abroad on its initial release, reviewers and scholars from the United States and the United Kingdom have consistently, even insistently, analyzed *The Vanishing* in generic terms, if only to highlight Sluizer's innovative "take" on mainstream/Hollywood horror, thriller, or suspense conventions.

So, for example, Marion Pilowsky gushes that *The Vanishing* "represents one of the most extraordinary realisations of the psychological thriller captured on film,"[24] the superlative "extraordinary realisation" a near-oxymoron that serves to simultaneously mark the film's distinctiveness from and conformity with an established tradition of psychological thrillers. Similarly, Roger Ebert writes that *The Vanishing* "is a thriller, but in a different way than most thrillers. It is a thriller about knowledge—about what the characters know about the disappearance, and what they know about themselves. [Its] plot . . . makes you realize how simplistic many suspense films really are."[25] And in a recent essay, Kevin Sweeney proposes to "discuss the film's nature as a horror film, paying attention to why it should be considered as such even though several respected theories of cinematic horror would exclude it from such a classification."[26]

Ultimately, Sweeney's argument focuses on how *The Vanishing* encourages a particular affective response in viewers in virtue of its ethics and themes—a horrifying reaction. Yet the most this line of argument can conclusively establish is that *The Vanishing* is horrifying, not that it is a horror film as conventionally/generically understood. To argue for the film's generic character one needs to grasp its relation to other films warranting that label, to show that a body of works or a cinematic tradition exists that merits being grouped together as a genre. The present essay takes up precisely this problematic concerning *The Vanishing*'s generic identity.[27]

A number of critics have seen fit to draw comparisons between Sluizer's film and the work of Alfred Hitchcock. Regarding the dramatic shift in hermeneutic code effected by Sluizer via his early disclosure of the abductor's identity, Steve Murray writes: "remember [Hitchcock's] decision to reveal Kim Novak's true identity midway through *Vertigo*? *Spoorloos* is less interested in giving you a quick jolt than in planting seeds of unease that continue to sprout long after you leave the theatre."[28] While for Hal Hinson, "there's a clinicism . . . in Sluizer's methods; he lays out the story . . . dispassionately, as if he were dissecting a frog. And yet his style seems supple, and not the least bit mechanical. His work is like that of a slightly more laconic, slightly more intellectualized Hitchcock—Hitchcock in a beret."[29] For the most part, however, such comparisons constitute less a shift to auteurist analysis than a group effort at sidestepping difficult questions about *The Vanishing*'s generic status by making "Hitchcock" (with its overused adjective, "Hitchcockian") a genre in its own right.

At the other extreme, and not that surprisingly, the Dutch film community elected not to read *The Vanishing* as a genre picture at all, stressing instead its distinctive "artistic" and "intellectual" merits. In The Hague's 1988 survey of Dutch releases, Sluizer's film is held to "succeed without star actors, sex, horror or sensational speedboat stunts in the canals of Amsterdam. Instead it offers a chilling plot, . . . well-timed doses of humour and some memorable observations on an age in which romanticism has given way to cold cynicism. The film does not provide mindless entertainment and Sluizer demands some intellectual effort from his audiences."[30] And according to Tim Krabbé, co-writer with Sluizer of *The Vanishing*'s screenplay and author of the 1984 Dutch novel, *Het Gouden Ei* (*The Golden Egg*), from which the film was adapted, "I've never thought of . . . *Spoorloos* as belonging to any genre, and I certainly didn't mean it to belong to any. I know nothing about the horror genre.[31] Interestingly, however, Krabbé argues (though not without a hint of qualification) for *The Vanishing*'s status as an archetypal love story:

> If this story belongs to any genre, then obviously it is a love story: two
> lovers are separated by God and reunited by him when the man is
> ready to pay the highest price, and drinks the magic potion. . . . The
> lovers are reunited in eternity—the ultimate happy ending. The film
> stresses this even more than the book. Critics in Holland, both of
> book and of film, generally saw this. Very few thought they had read
> or seen a thriller.[32]

Without wishing to deny the viability of an interpretation of *The Vanishing* in such terms, we would argue that the film's "love story" dimension is less indicative of its allegiance to cross-national (much less mythic or archetypal) generic convention than of its place in Holland's distinctive and nationally specific thriller tradition.

Whereas Gerard's manifest ambivalence and anxiety about binding himself to a female partner in a normative heterosexual relationship clearly forms part of *The Fourth Man*'s literal meaning, Rex's apprehension about committing to a lifelong partnership with his girlfriend, as well as his own repressed/unconscious homosexual inclinations, are only revealed by the text indirectly. These aspects of Rex's personality thus form part of *The Vanishing*'s implicit meaning, what George Wilson, elaborating on Bordwell, defines as a "content that the filmmaker . . . intended to convey, suggest, or otherwise invoke by constructing the segment, where the segment is already freighted with its particular referential and explicit meanings."[33] At the surface level of referential and explicit (i.e., literal) meaning,[34] *The Vanishing* tells the story of Rex's obsessive, life-consuming quest to unravel the mystery behind his girlfriend's disappearance, his psychological refusal to break the vow he made Saskia never to abandon her, no matter what. A closer look at some of the film's dialogue, characterization, and mise en scène, however, indicates that, at a deeper level this is actually a story about Rex's inability to obtain release from his commitment to Saskia, and to normative heterosexuality more generally.

The underlying tension in Rex and Saskia's relationship is evident from the very beginning of the film, as the couple bickers about seemingly trivial matters while driving toward their holiday destination. Throughout the opening scenes Rex's insecurity with his masculinity is revealed by the harsh, clumsy manner in which he seeks to impose it on Saskia, while simultaneously (and for the same reason) attempting to force her into the role of member of the "weaker" sex. So, for example, when Saskia states that "I'm just looking at the gas meter," Rex snaps, "You just look in your mirror," implying that Saskia should be more like what he takes other women to be: vain, unconcerned with practical matters, focused on their own image rather than the external world. After teaching her some words in French—the master-pupil dynamic evidently feeding his ego and sense of control over the relationship—he orders Saskia to "peel me an orange." And when they run out of gas in the middle of a dark tunnel Rex yells at Saskia not to be hysterical, assuming a stereotypically feminine irrational response on her part even though she makes the perfectly reasonable point that "I'm not hysterical—I'm scared." Knowing full well how frightened she is, Rex proceeds to leave her all alone in the tunnel in order to locate the nearest gas station. It is here that the first real cracks in Rex's psyche begin to show, as his temporary abandonment of Saskia can be interpreted as much as an unacknowledged (and ultimately unsatisfiable) desire to run away from his relationship as an effort to do the "manly" thing and solve the problem at hand.

Shortly thereafter, during the couple's reconciliation at a busy rest stop, Saskia pressures Rex into swearing that he will never abandon her again. It is crucial to note that Saskia has to effectively put the words in Rex's mouth here, straddling him on the ground and commanding him to "repeat after me"; she then proceeds to force-feed him the lines as he playfully (or so it seems) squirms beneath her. One might compare Saskia with Christine Halsslag here, insofar as both women are depicted as capable of binding the men in their life under virtual spells from which there is no means of healthy escape. *The Vanishing* is a more "realistic" text than *The Fourth Man*, however, and so the vow of "till death do us part" is rendered by Sluizer in psychological and emotional rather than paranormal or supernatural terms: instead of dying under mysterious circumstances or suffering from threatening hallucinatory visions (like Gerard in Verhoeven's film), Rex lets his new girlfriend Lieneke (Gwen Eckhaus) walk out on him because he is constitutionally incapable of breaking his prior commitment to Saskia.

If we take Rex's various separations from the women in his life (Saskia physically, Lieneke emotionally) as forming a pattern, one that indicates a desire on his part to break free from long-term heterosexual relationships, then Rex's meetings with Raymond later in the film begin to take on the aspect of a homosocial, perhaps even homosexual, courtship. While waiting for Raymond to show up for their prearranged rendezvous at a Nîmes café, Rex confides to Lieneke, "Do you know what I'm afraid of? That he stops sending postcards." Abstracted from the literal narrative context, in which Rex pursues Raymond solely in order to find out what happened to Saskia, the above confession makes Rex sound very much like a man in love and frightened of being abandoned by his beloved; he thus adopts a traditional "feminine" position relative to Raymond, one that is analogous to Saskia's position relative to Rex earlier in the film.

As for Raymond, whose obsessive efforts at control match Rex's anxiety and angst, he seems to relish playing the role of masculine initiator. Despite being even more firmly entrenched in a committed, long-term heterosexual relationship than his pursuer (he is married with two daughters, and is every bit the faithful family man), there is an important sense in which Raymond is more "out" than Rex, insofar as he carefully orchestrates the entire sequence of events that will result in the development of a powerful homosocial bond between the two men. During their first face-to-face encounter approximately two-thirds of the way through the film, Raymond tells Rex that "I thought a lot about our meeting. . . . Right from the start I felt the need to see you. When you left the café at Nîmes, I realized I couldn't wait any longer." And when revealing the means by which he came to abduct Saskia at the rest stop three years earlier, Raymond interprets his seemingly random choice of victims as a clear indication that he and Rex were fated to meet: "Destiny, Mr. Hofman." Raymond thereby reduces Saskia's significance in the narrative to her function as a bridge between him and Rex; this is in line with observations concerning the gender asymmetry of erotic love triangles in European fiction by René Girard and, more recently, Eve Kosofsky Sedgwick. Discussing Girard's work, Sedgwick notes that "What is most interesting . . . is [his] insistence that, in any erotic rivalry, the bond that links the two rivals is as intense and potent as the bond that links either of the rivals to the beloved; that the bonds of 'rivalry' and 'love,' differently as they are experienced, are equally powerful and in many ways equivalent."[35]

By far the most loaded conversation between Raymond and Rex takes place during their lengthy ride to Raymond's cottage, where he has admitted to taking Saskia after kidnapping her. At one point the pair stop by a park to stretch their legs—a seemingly innocuous activity that is strange in and of itself, considering how long Rex has been waiting to find

Raymond and how desperate he is to find out what happened to Saskia. Their awkward exchange in the park, filled as it is with coded references, bilingual word play, and flirtatious banter, actually sounds more like a first date between potential lovers than a civil conversation between long-time adversaries. Aware that Rex was once an amateur cyclist, Raymond—a Frenchman—attempts to show off his knowledge of the sport by mentioning a popular Dutch biker named "Zoltemeque," saying that "it sounds like a Mexican god, not Dutch." Rex, however, is unmoved, noting that Raymond pronounced the name wrong: "Zoltemeque" is really "Zoetemelk," a word that, as Rex explains, means "sweet milk." Raymond replies, "Mr. Sweetmilk. Some weird names you have there." Although he doesn't elaborate, he seems to be alluding to the fact that this male Dutch name possesses distinctly feminine connotations. Instead of taking offense or reacting homophobically, Rex offers up what he takes to be a similarly "weird" Dutch name: "Naahtgeboren. Born naked." In a clear echo of the film's opening, in which Rex playfully taught Saskia some words in French, Rex now begins teaching Raymond some words in Dutch, a lesson that culminates in "Dodeman: Mrs. Deadman. Marriage produces some strange combinations." At a level that is not merely linguistic, Rex here calls attention to the fact that, at least where he comes from, being married can also mean being dead.

Not to be outdone, Raymond recalls that "In the Nîmes phonebook, there's someone called Mr. Poof." Following the logic of the conversation, and French marital law notwithstanding, it would seem that the man in the phonebook took his wife's last name and became a "poof" (slang for an effeminate homosexual) on getting married. Despite the manifest animosity Rex has been expressing toward Raymond up until now, he clearly finds this amusing, and a small smile breaks out across his face—perhaps the first time he has smiled since Saskia's disappearance. The mise en scène here is quite telling: in the background, Raymond is standing on the bars of a jungle gym, arms spread wide apart to stay balanced, his body vulnerable and receptive; while in the foreground, Rex is standing with his back to Raymond, hands in pockets. Unlike his relationship with Saskia, in which he was the dominating partner, here Rex plays a passive role, allowing himself to be "seduced" by the more open and aggressive Raymond. Before heading off, Rex responds to Raymond's latest comment with the words, "Yes . . . Poof."

Back in the car, Rex asks Raymond if he raped Saskia. Raymond replies, "Come on, Mr. Hofman," as if even the mere suggestion of such

A coded conversation in
Spoorloos (1988)

a crime is an insult to his character. Although Rex drops the issue here, it is not clear why he does so; after all, Raymond is a self-described sociopath, and his answer above is not exactly unambiguous. The possibility of rape arises again when Raymond tells Rex what will have to take place if he ever wants to find out what happened to Saskia: "I'm going to drug you, and after that you'll experience exactly what she experienced." When Rex rejects this plan as ridiculous, Raymond tries to tempt him by asking, "What about the uncertainty? The eternal not knowing? That's the worst thing, Mr. Hofman." On the surface level of the text this is all in reference to Saskia's fate, yet at the level of implicit meaning, the "uncertainty" and "eternal not knowing" can be taken as referring to Rex's repressed homoerotic impulses; in keeping with the underlying thematic of Dutch thriller cinema it is the prospect of these impulses remaining repressed (or else being re-repressed), rather than their emergence in the form of a monster, that is held to be "the worst thing."

      This is reinforced by *The Vanishing*'s ending. After a lengthy internal debate Rex finally musters up the nerve to put himself completely at Raymond's mercy, drinking the spiked coffee and allowing himself to be manhandled the same way Saskia was (though crucially, she had no choice in the matter). The scene in which Rex makes his decision shows him exhibiting intense anxiety, literally running around in circles outside in the pouring rain: his desire for control is in conflict with his desire to place himself in Raymond's hands, to be "initiated" into the latter's secret world. In the penultimate scene Rex awakens to find himself buried alive inside a pitch-black wooden coffin. It would be too easy to attribute the power of this disturbing and memorable climax to Rex's realization that he is doomed, left for dead with no hope of survival. Metaphorically and implicitly speaking, Rex ends up trapped not so much in a coffin as in the closet, while the true nature and depth of Raymond's monstrousness is revealed: despite the freedom he initially grants Rex from normative (monogamous and lifelong) heterosexual commitment, he ultimately binds the young man to his girlfriend for all eternity, burying the couple side-by-side in his garden.

Elsewhere Steven Jay Schneider has compared and contrasted the original Dutch version of *The Vanishing* with Sluizer's own big-budget Hollywood remake, released under the English-language title in 1993 to lousy (at best) international reviews and disappointing (also at best) box-office receipts.[36] The remake lacks the keen sense of black humor manifest in the original; it privileges spectacle and action over character development and subtlety of plot; and it exhibits a more conventional (and therefore more predictable) generic sensibility, lacking the subtle psychological characterizations and elaboration of philosophical themes present in Sluizer's first version. Ultimately, the remake fails to reassert the repression that contributes to the original ending's overall horrifying effect. The repeated offering of the drug-spiked coffee to various characters in particular gives the remake's finale a shallow, unintentionally comic quality.

Conclusion

By arguing for a symptomatic or repressed overall meaning to these two pictures, and by extension to the tradition of Dutch thriller cinema more generally, we have appealed to what is in effect an inversion of Wood's influential "formula" for the American horror film. According to Wood, "the true subject of the horror genre is the struggle for recognition of all that our civilization represses or oppresses, its reemergence dramatized, as in our nightmares, as an object of horror, a matter for terror, and the happy ending (when it exists) typically signifying the restoration of repression." Thus his contention that, in the typical U.S. horror movie, "normality is threatened by the Monster."[37]

In contrast (though not in contradiction) to Wood, we have argued that the primary source of negative emotion in Dutch thriller cinema is not a hyperbolic return of the socioculturally repressed in the form of a monster. Rather, such emotion—be it horror, terror, dread, or what have you—is generated largely via the protagonist's subconscious recognition that such repression is impossible to overcome. We prefer the phrase "sub-conscious recognition" here because it is not at all certain that the films' protagonists are fully aware that "re-repression" has occurred. Gerard is chemically knocked-out at the end of *The Fourth Man,* and Rex upon awakening in his coffin lapses into a visionary reverie about Saskia. What the protagonists' respective anxiety shows is that psychologically they are confronting a conflict, and that they are being overwhelmed by it.

This explains why the final restoration of repression in both films does not result in anything like a "happy ending" as traditionally con-ceived, but something far more downbeat and chilling instead. Neither wholly uniform in their employment/deployment of plotlines, character types, and iconography, nor utterly idiosyncratic and "unique" auteurist works of art, Verhoeven's *The Fourth Man* and Sluizer's *The Vanishing* constitute two superb entries in a tradition of heretofore unexamined Dutch "thrillers"—a tradition that can be seen to bring nation-specific issues and anxieties to bear on long-established and geographically wide-spread generic codes and conventions.

NOTES

Our sincerest thanks to Richard Allen, David Gerstner, Steffen Hantke, Joke Hermes, Ernest Mathijs, and Deborah Thomas for their helpful comments and suggestions on ear-lier versions of this essay.

1. Joke Hermes, "Family Matters: Recent Dutch Television Crime Drama," unpub-lished draft (2002): 12.
2. Hermes, "Family Matters."
3. Ibid. See, by way of comparison, Anneke Smelik, "For Venus Smiles Not in a House of Tears: Interethnic Relations in European Cinema," *European Journal of Cultural Studies* (2003).
4. Smelik, "For Venus Smiles Not in a House of Tears."
5. Gary Needham, "Playing with Genre: An Introduction to the Italian *Giallo,*" *Kino-eye* 2, no. 11 (June 10, 2002), online at http://www.kinoeye.org/02/11/needham11. html, accessed September 6, 2003. Less radically, Hermes notes that "national con-text is enormously important in how global genres are reworked to fit local context" ("Family Matters," 12).
6. Three other Dutch serial killer films from the mid-1980s that, for reasons of space, could not be included for discussion here are Marleen Gorris's *Gebroken spiegels* (*Broken Mirrors,* 1984), Dick Maas's *De lift* (*The Lift,* 1983), and Maas's *Amster-damned* (1987).
7. Needham, "Playing with Genre."
8. David Bordwell, *Making Meaning: Inference and Rhetoric in the Interpretation of Cinema* (Cambridge: Harvard University Press, 1989), 8–9.
9. As Verhoeven explains, in Gerard's one sex scene with Christine, "he tries to trans-form her into a male" by covering and flattening her breasts with his hands, and by

focusing his attention on a mirror-reflected image of her back (which could be that of a young boy) during intercourse: "he needs to see a young boy in her to make love to her.... [We were] trying to do a heterosexual scene but hidden behind that is a homosexual scene," Director's Commentary, *The Fourth Man* DVD, Anchor Bay, 2001.

10. This technique is characteristic of Verhoeven's cinema. See, for example, the opening scene of *Turks fruit* (*Turkish Delight*, 1973).

11. For a discussion of the gothic's generic conventions, see Eve Kosofsky Sedgwick, *The Coherence of Gothic Conventions* (New York: Methuen, 1986); and Valdine Clemens, *The Return of the Repressed: Gothic Horror from* The Castle of Otranto *to* Alien (Albany: State University of New York Press, 1999).

12. Steve Neale, *Genre and Hollywood* (London: Routledge, 2000), 160.

13. Reprinted in Ian Cameron, ed., *The Movie Book of Film Noir* (New York: Cameron, 1993).

14. *The Fourth Man* DVD Director's Commentary.

15. See Steven Cohan, "Censorship and Narrative Indeterminacy in *Basic Instinct:* 'You Won't Learn Anything from Me I Don't Want You to Know!'" in *Contemporary Hollywood Cinema*, ed. Steve Neale and Murray Smith (London: Routledge, 1998), 263–79. According to Verhoeven, "Throughout [*The Fourth Man*] you will never know if the main character is schizophrenic, under the influence of alcohol, or if it's really true what's happening there" (DVD Director's Commentary).

16. At one point on the DVD Director's Commentary, Verhoeven claims that "She [Christine] is a projection of him [Gerard]."

17. See Barbara Creed, *The Monstrous-Feminine: Film, Feminism, Psychoanalysis* (London: Routledge, 1993). There is a nod to the woman-as-monster construct in *The Fourth Man*'s notorious castration scene where Gerard awakens from a nightmare to discover Christine crouched over his genitals with a pair of scissors. Just as she snips off his penis, however, Gerard wakes up a *second* time to find that everything is still in place.

18. Robin Wood, *Hollywood from Vietnam to Reagan* (New York: Columbia University Press, 1986), 167. See Harry M. Benshoff, *Monsters in the Closet: Homosexuality in the Horror Film* (Manchester, UK: Manchester University Press, 1997).

19. For further discussion of the history of homosexual policymaking in Holland, see Gert Hekma, "Same-Sex Relations among Men in Europe, 1700–1990," in *Sexual Cultures in Europe: Themes in Sexuality*, ed. Franz X. Elder, Lesley A. Hall, and Gert Hekma (Manchester, UK: Manchester University Press), 1999, 79–103. See also A. X. van Naerssen, "A Research into Homosexuality in the Netherlands," *Journal of Homosexuality* 13 (Winter 1986): 1–8; and Rob Tielman, "Dutch Gay Emancipation History (1911–1986)," *Journal of Homosexuality* 13 (Winter 1986): 9–17.

20. Angela Ndalianis, "Paul Verhoeven and His Hollow Men," *Screening the Past* 13 (December 2001), online at http://www.latrobe.edu.au/screeningthepast/firstrelease/fr1201/anfr13a.htm, accessed September 5, 2003.

21. See Cohan, "Censorship and Narrative Indeterminacy in *Basic Instinct*," 264–67.

22. "The (Un)Hollow Man: Paul Verhoeven Discusses the Politics of Pulp with Xavier Mendik," *kamera.co.uk,* January 22, 2002, online at http://www.kamera.co.uk/interviews/paul_verhoeven.html, accessed September 5, 2003. For a sympathetic auteurist reading of Verhoeven's most superficially exploitative film, see I. Q.

Hunter, "Beaver Las Vegas! A Fan-Boy's Defence of *Showgirls*," in *Unruly Pleasures: The Cult Film and Its Critics*, ed. Graeme Harper and Xavier Mendik (Guildford, UK: FAB Press, 2000), 187–201.

23. Some material from this section appears in Steven Jay Schneider, "Spoorloos (1998)," in *24 Frames: Cinema of the Low Countries*, ed. Ernest Mathijs (London: Wallflower, 2003).

24. Marion Pilowsky, "Spoorloos (The Vanishing)," in *The International Directory of Films and Filmmakers*, 4th ed., ed. Sara Pendergast and Tom Pendergast (Farmington Hills, MI: St.James Press, 2000), 1136.

25. Roger Ebert, "The Vanishing [Spoorloos]," *Chicago Sun Times*, January 25, 1991, online at http://www.suntimes.com/ebert/ebert_reviews/1991/01/631706.html, accessed September 6, 2003.

26. Kevin W. Sweeney, "The Horrific in Sluizer's *The Vanishing*," *Post Script* 21, no. 3 (2002): 99.

27. See Rick Altman, *Film/Genre* (London: BFI Publishing, 1999).

28. Steve Murray, "*Vanishing* Act Makes *Lambs* Look Tame," *Atlanta Journal and Constitution*, December 27, 1991, Section D, 1.

29. Hal Hinson, "The Vanishing [Spoorloos]," *Washington Post*, March 8, 1991, online at http://www.washingtonpost.com/wp-srv/style/longterm/movies/videos/thevanishingrhinson_a0a9db.htm, accessed September 5, 2003.

30. "The Vanishing," *Dutch Film 1987–88* (The Hague: Government Publishing Office, 1998), 170. The reference to "sensational speedboat stunts in the canals of Amsterdam" is a dig at Maas's serial killer film, *Amsterdamned*, released the previous year.

31. E-mail correspondence with the author, June 19, 2000.

32. Ibid., December 8, 2000.

33. George Wilson, "On Film Narrative and Narrative Meaning," in *Film Theory and Philosophy*, ed. Richard Allen and Murray Smith (Oxford: Clarendon Press, 1997), 224.

34. Bordwell analyzes "literal meaning" into two subcategories: "referential meaning" (when the viewer or critic "builds up some version of the *diegesis*, or spatio-temporal world, and creates an ongoing story (*fabula*) occurring within it" [*Making Meaning*, 8]) and "explicit meaning" ("when the viewer or critic takes the film to be, in one way or another, 'stating' abstract meanings," 8). This distinction is admittedly blurry, and Bordwell himself explains that "referential and explicit meaning make up what are usually considered 'literal' meanings," 8.

35. Eve Kosofsky Sedgwick, *Between Men: English Literature and Male Homosocial Desire* (New York: Columbia University Press, 1985), 21.

36. Steven Jay Schneider, "Repackaging Rage: *The Vanishing* and *Nightwatch*," *Kinema* 17 (Spring 2002): 47–66. It would also be well worth comparing and contrasting *The Vanishing* (both versions) with Sluizer's 1996 film, *Crimetime*, a British-American co-production that also centers on the complex and shifting relationship between a middle-aged, married male killer and an obsessive younger man who is clearly unsatisfied with his girlfriend.

37. Robin Wood, "An Introduction to the American Horror Film," in Wood, *Hollywood from Vietnam to Reagan*, 75, 78.

11

Hong Kong Social Horror:

TRAGEDY AND FARCE IN CATEGORY 3

Tony Williams

With the recent theatrical successes of *The Matrix* trilogy (1999–2003), Ang Lee's *Crouching Tiger Hidden Dragon* (2000), and the direct-to-video, reedited, rescored, and (drastically) altered releases in the Jet Li Collection, Hong Kong cinema is once again attracting international attention. It is a cinema often admired for its kinetic qualities of martial arts, blood-drenched gangster shootouts, and fantastic themes rather than one dependent on certain sociohistorical features also common to its Western neighbors. This is no less true of the Hong Kong horror film and its 1980s offshoot, "Category 3." Although frequently championed as escapist pictures, like all horror films they have some disturbing links to material aspects of their culture often ignored by viewers and promoters. This is particularly so of certain examples such as *The Untold Story* (1993), *Dr. Lamb* (1992), *The Underground Banker* (1994), *Ebola Syndrome* (1996), and *The Untold Story 2* (1998). These are not just exploitation movies, they are grim embodiments of a dark social reality affecting Hong Kong society in the last decade of the twentieth century.

   The titles mentioned here belong to the Category 3 label, a new rating system introduced in the industry during 1989 to define certain films with graphic representations of sex and violence.[1] However, for Julian Stringer they also reveal the "repressed underside of more respectable cultural forms,"[2] by embodying damning portraits of a ruthless Social Darwinist system that rarely appear in Hong Kong mainstream productions. One exception to this is Jacob Cheung's *Cageman* (1992), a rare example of a serious "social problem" film within a cinema more noted for style and special effects. *Cageman* deals with the housing shortage affecting impoverished Hong Kong citizens who literally lived in small cages within large buildings scheduled for re-development and gentrification.[3] *Cageman* significantly appeared in the same year as the infamous, yet more financially successful, Category 3 production *Dr. Lamb.* This latter film starred the accomplished Hong Kong screen actor Simon Yam Tat-wah, who for a time seemed to face confinement within that genre. As Hong Kong film critic Sek Kei pointed out, "few films from 1990–1996 portrayed Hong Kong society in all its reality."[4] But, as Lisa Stokes and Michael Hoover note, other directors "chose different means, using a metaphorical approach by developing subtexts which allowed their narratives to comment upon the real world."[5] This tactic was employed in several Category 3 films.

Category 3 films are important artifacts that use graphic techniques familiar to the horror genre in order to comment indirectly on a world of social exploitation common to both the colonial system of government and its post-1997 Special Administrative Region (SAR) status. Furthermore, although *The Underground Banker, Ebola Syndrome,* and *The Untold Story 2* represent loose sequels to *Dr. Lamb* and *The Untold Story* in a manner exemplifying the Hong Kong industry's desire to cash in on a successful formula, especially via the use of parody,[6] they too bear an intrinsic relationship to their social origins. As Karl Marx comments in "The Eighteenth Brumaire of Louis Napoleon," history often occurs "the first time as tragedy, the second as farce."[7] His statement may equally apply to the above examples of Category 3 horror films as long as we bear in mind their socioeconomic relevance. But as products of a late capitalist era where Western politicians applaud the non-welfare, low-income nature of these Eastern service economies, tragedy and farce now intermingle in a very ironic manner in several of these films. Although many Category 3 pictures were designed as sensational money-making exercises, certain examples contain revealing images of another side of Hong Kong society complementing the more critically conscious images in serious films by directors such as Evans Chan and Jacob Cheung.

Class Issues in Cat 3 Horror

As Li Cheuk-to points out, Hong Kong horror films have a long history. While 1950s and 1960s examples denied the presence of ghosts and spirits in a manner akin to Hollywood films such as *The Cat and The Canary* (1927/1939) and *Mark of the Vampire* (1935), a distinctive horror genre emerged following the Hong Kong release of *The Exorcist* in 1974. Although Hong Kong horror is as hybrid in nature as its other cinematic genres, Cheuk-to notes that "quite a few commentators have remarked on the Horror genre's resurgence with the territory's preoccupation with its future and the question of China taking over control in 1997."[8]

However, Category 3 films have less in common with more prestigious examples such as the *Chinese Ghost Story* series influenced by the work of Ching Dynasty storyteller Pu Songling (1640–1715),[9] and more to do with the type of U.S. socioeconomic horror film typified by *Race with the Devil* (1975) and later examples such as *Henry: Portrait of a Serial Killer* (1990) and *American Psycho* (2000).[10] These last two films have unmistakable naturalistic overtones that parallel the fiction of Émile Zola, whose Jacques Lantier in *La bete humaine* is very much a serial killer influenced by both family and environmental factors. Lantier is definitely a literary ancestor of both Henry (Michael Rooker) and Patrick Bateman (Christian Bale). Furthermore, *Dr. Lamb* and *The Untold Story* employ a distinctively neo-noirish visual style derived from a classical model that has many points of contact with naturalist literature.[11] As a complex literary phenomenon appearing in many areas of world literature and cinema, naturalism is not to be understood as a mere cataloguing of mundane descriptions but as an interrogative device often commenting on oppressive social conditions. Zola's *La bete humaine*, *L'argent*, and *Au bonheur des dames*, as well as Frank Norris's *The Octopus* and Theodore Dreiser's *An American Tragedy*, represent relevant examples of this particular critical practice.[12]

Dr. Lamb, *The Untold Story*, *The Underground Banker*, and *The Untold Story 2* are all set in a lower-depths environment representing the dark side of the Hong Kong economic miracle. As Stokes and Hoover point out, although the former colony is classified as a high-income economy, the wealth is not shared by the majority of the population who live on less than 5 percent of the land in crowded townships. While the rich live in lavish homes far removed from the urban metropolis, most of the less well-off inhabit "subsidized housing, much of it in dense, high-rise dwellings that sit alongside production sites and commercial facilities in the New Territories,"[13] in extremely cramped living conditions. Stokes and Hoover also note disturbing features such as the absence of a minimum wage, the lack of any official poverty line, no full employment policies, and minimal welfare provision. They quote an apt comment by Marx from *Capital*, Volume 1, namely that "Capital comes (into the world) dripping from hand to foot, from every pore with blood and dirt."[14] This description is certainly applicable to Category 3 psychotic serial killers, who subsist in an economic wasteland.

The imagery depicted in these films often represents an irrational bloodthirsty revenge by a low-income proletariat against forces they perceive as oppressive. It is unorganized, random, and chaotic, highly characteristic of a society well known for its political apathy. But the violent forces unleashed have intrinsic connections with the very nature of that society. Traditions of censorship and self-censorship ensure that the real causes of such cinematic violence remain unexplored; this is the result of a colonial system of government averse to any form of criticism and political opposition. Furthermore, as Stringer notes, "Category 3 films are a lower-class phenomenon. Films bearing this classification are exhibited in the theaters of the working-class, projected for spectators who cannot easily afford entry to the latest Hollywood blockbusters playing in the more expensive first-run venues."[15] They also appeal to audiences who will never fully achieve the financial rewards of Hong Kong society by depicting the stressful nature of surviving at the lower depths. By concentrating on non-affluent characters they operate in a similar manner to films such as *The Texas Chainsaw Massacre* (1974) and *Race with the Devil*, which feature communities who are losers in the American dream and avenge their social exclusion by acts of ritual violence.

Class features within these films are by no means accidental. The depicted violence functions as a "return of the repressed," which Robin Wood has described as one of the key features of the horror genre, particularly in terms of its socioeconomic manifestations.[16] Furthermore, the environments depicted in these pictures parallel those working-class communities common to the films of British director Ken Loach. But rather than articulating comments by characters concerning social exploitation, these Category 3 films eschew the type of didactic narrative common to Loach and instead concentrate on acts of graphic violence. Despite the gratuitous nature of these scenes, they do, however, bear an intrinsic connection to the society they reveal—no matter how much this link is concealed.

The Untold Story

Like *Dr. Lamb,* Herman Yau's *The Untold Story* contains several features of the "true crime" formula employed within the graphic parameters of Category 3. Based on a real-life murder case in Macao during the 1980s, *The Untold Story's* prologue begins in Hong Kong. As Stringer perceptively notes, the film opens with an overhead 360-degree panning shot exploring a group of tenement buildings before pausing at its chosen location. The device not only echoes those introductory shots characteristic of Hitchcock films such as *Shadow of a Doubt* (1943) and *Psycho* (1960), which explore the external environment before interrogating its dark underside, but also presents to the audience a social location relevant to the forthcoming violence. The tenement buildings represent the cramped living spaces that represent home for the majority of low-income Hong Kong citizens.

When the image cuts abruptly to the interior, the audience sees the volatile cook Wong Chi-hang (Anthony Wong Chau-sang) confronted with an accusation of cheating at mahjong by his boss. Faced with the impossible economic request of paying his debts, Wong overpowers his employer and burns him alive. Stringer points out that this scene represents a further take on the colony's obsession with gambling, often treated humorously in films such as the *God of Gamblers* series (1989–1996), Michael Hui's *Games Gamblers Play* (1974), *The Gambling Ghost* (1991), *Gambling Baron* (1994), *Drunken Master 2* (1995), and many, many others.[17] As Stephen Teo points out, "Gambling is a subject close to the hearts of Chinese all over the world."[18] It parallels the American obsession with winning the lottery and the recent worldwide popularity of game shows promoting millionaire lifestyles. Furthermore, in *The Untold Story,* Wong first uses a huge frying pan to assault his employer before battering his head against the wall. When he later decides to deal with a potential blackmailer in Macao, he uses a huge soup ladle in a similar manner. If *The Untold Story* subverts the gambling sequences of many Hong Kong films for subversive purposes, it also, in a macabre way, utilizes the cuisine motif common to many Hong Kong films (e.g., *God of Cookery,* 1996). If gambling and food appear as common signifiers in many Hong Kong films, *The Untold Story* suggests that these elements contain darker undertones in relation to a society based on economic exploitation.

Ironically, the cannibalist motifs that appear later on in the picture are not only inspired by 1970s Italian exploitation films dealing with cannibalism, but also have Hong Kong cinematic antecedents. For example, Tsui Hark's second film *We're Going to Eat You!* (1980) anticipated the main theme of *The Untold Story* and secondary narratives involving comedy, such as the latter's subplot dealing with androgynous female detective Bo's (Emily Kwan Bo-wai) unrequited love for her boss, Inspector Lee (Danny Lee Sau-yin). Such hybrid plot mixtures are characteristic of

Hong Kong cinema. Furthermore, as John Charles notes, the title of Tsui Hark's earlier film more appropriately functions as a metaphor for capitalism rather than communism, a fact that may have resulted in the type of censorship affecting his next film *Dangerous Encounter—1st Kind* (1980), which led to the director moving away from making explicit social commentary films.[19]

Credits begin as Wong moves to Macao to assume a new identity signified by both his changed appearance and a new identification card. The date of the prologue is 1978, four years after the appearance of Michael Hui's comedy box-office success *Games Gamblers Play*. This opening scene presents the dark side of a gambling obsession often treated humorously in Hong Kong films, but which regularly ends in tragedy and violence in real life. Eight years later a beachcombing Macao family discovers a Union Jack shopping bag containing severed limbs washed up on the beach. Emerging from a colony known for its strict censorship practices the film ironically chooses another location for this grisly discovery while indirectly pointing the finger at a British administration that bears direct responsibility for the social conditions of Hong Kong.

The Untold Story then follows the general formula of the Category 3 crime narrative involving the investigation of the case, arrest of the suspect, and confession mediated via flashback sequences. Its jarring use of comedy involving Inspector Lee's subordinates—who resemble graduates of the *Police Academy* series—may also be a critique of the Hong Kong police force. In several Danny Lee films (produced by his Magnum company), including *Organized Crime and Triad Bureau* (1994) and *Twist* (1995), the cops use third-degree methods on their helpless suspects. However, the Cantonese-speaking Macao police inspire little confidence on the part of the audience. Their boss appears like a playboy, walking into the police station regularly accompanied by a different "hooker of the week." It is not too farfetched to see in these images a satirical view of the Hong Kong police, and also one of Danny Lee himself, known for his various cop roles in that national cinema.[20]

Once the police arrest Wong they engage in ruthless third-degree tactics to make him confess his crimes. The tactics elicit a degree of sympathy for the brutal killer in the latter part of the film. At one point they incarcerate Wong in the same cell as Cheng Poon (Shing Fui-on), brother of the murdered owner of the Pat Sin Restaurant. Played by an actor well known for his portrayal of gangsters in the Hong Kong film industry, this literally subjects Wong to a "fate worse than death." After eliciting a confession the Macao police discover that Wong has not only murdered his employer, his family, and some suspicious co-workers, but also used their remains to make pork buns, which he has given to the police as "freebies"! This is but one of several ironies in the film. The Macao police refuse to allow Wong's deportation to Hong Kong where he would face the death penalty for murdering his boss in 1978. Instead, they decide to claim the prestige of arresting Wong themselves, despite the fact that he could gain parole after only fifteen years since the Portuguese territory does not allow capitol punishment. Politics, one-upmanship, and the Oriental quality of "face" are not the only factors involved but also economic greed. Wong had attempted to sell the Pat Sin Restaurant for $180,000, but lacked the necessary documents of ownership to satisfy legal requirements. However, when Wong hears that the Macao police intend to sue him for ownership of the restaurant this becomes literally the "straw that broke the camel's back." After undergoing interrogation, torture, prison brutality, urine drinking, and hospital injections preventing him from sleeping, he decides to commit suicide by protesting his outrage at these new economic police tactics. "They can't sue me! They can't!"

Despite its graphic violence, *The Untold Story* is not to be dismissed as a sleazy, gratuitous production. It also deals with real-life social issues involving violence and exploitation in Hong Kong society. As Stringer cogently notes, by situating violent real-life stories within working-class environments, certain Category 3 films such as *Run and Kill* (1993) and *The Untold Story* "do not provide their audiences with any means out of the spiral of poverty and vice; one breeds the other as cause and effect."[21] An explicit social message is irrelevant since the films implicitly depict the real causes generating such brutal events without the need of any further commentary.

Dr. Lamb

Co-directed and produced by Danny Lee, *Dr. Lamb* is a Category 3 depiction of the murders committed by real-life serial killer Lam Guowen. The film begins by depicting the childhood of its main character, who is clearly a victim of child abuse and also inhabits an impoverished environment that is a breeding ground for crime. The film switches to the present when Lam (played by Simon Yam Tat-wah, reprising his performance from a television miniseries) engages in a bout of serial killing.

His victims are young women whose naked bodies he photographs. Lam's undoing begins when the manager of a photo shop alerts the Hong Kong police about the suspicious nature of the images. He has taken the photographs to an establishment in the Mongkok district that is, presumably, not too far away from the cramped apartment he shares with his family. As Stokes and Hoover note, inadequate housing is a major problem in Hong Kong: "Overall, almost 450,000 Hong Kong households, comprising more than 1.2 million people, suffered from inadequate housing in 1994. Hong Kong's population density, one of the world's highest, is most graphically revealed in the 150,000 thousand per square kilometer living in the Mongkok district."[22] Although the film never gives any explanation for the title character's psychosis, the social environment clearly bears some degree of responsibility. However, since Hong Kong censorship would never allow any explicit commentary of that nature, suggestive elements function in an indirect and oblique manner throughout the narrative.

Dr. Lam's prologue opens with the young impressionable character being prompted by a friend to remove his sister's underpants. This provokes the anger of his stepmother who complains to her husband about her stepson's growing sexual curiosity. Since privacy is impossible in the family's cramped quarters, young Lam's voyeuristic fascination with his parent's sexual coupling leads to his removal outside. Clearly, he cannot avoid gazing at this "primal scene." Also, although his father dismisses Lam's activities as an adolescent phase, he does nothing to help his son, who misses the presence of his dead mother. Young Lam is a Norman Bates in the making as several shot parallels to *Psycho* reveal. But he is also a victim of bad peer group influence, uncaring parents, and an environment that clearly bears a high degree of responsibility for his future activities. When we next see Lam, now as an adult, he is significantly framed in close-up against a birdcage, depicting his psychic entrapment in an unmistakably symbolic manner. Succeeding shots showing Lam driving his taxi down the Kowloon district of Hong Kong's "mean streets" evoke unmistakable parallels to the dark spiritual odyssey of Travis Bickle's (Robert De Niro) "God's Lonely Man" in Martin Scorsese's neo-noir *Taxi Driver* (1976).

When the photography shop owner alerts Inspector Lee, the police begin a stakeout to arrest their suspect. Although they are not presented in as blatant a *Police Academy* manner as their equivalents in *The Untold Story*, their efficiency still leaves much to be desired. Led by gross Sergeant Bing (Kent Cheng Chuk-see), they begin gambling inside their

A brutal attack by the
eponymous serial killer
(Simon Yam Tat-wah) in
Dr. Lamb (1992)

police car and forget about their surveillance duties. It is only the shop
owner's alerting them to Lam's leaving that results in his arrest. The police
begin their third-degree interrogation of Lam led by the abrasive Buffalo
Hung (Parkman Wong Pak-man) who clearly relishes this aspect of his
police work. Finally, Emily Kwan Bo-wai appears in a similar performance to her role as policewoman Bo in *The Untold Story* as the victim of
countless sexual taunts inflicted on her by her male colleagues. As in the
later film the humiliations suffered by Kwan form an ironic counterpart
to the more graphic assaults by the serial killers on their helpless female
victims.

Boundaries between normal and abnormal worlds are more blurred
in this film than in *The Untold Story*. For example, during several scenes,
looks are exchanged between nominal hero Inspector Lee and Lam as if
linking them in some form of dark brotherhood. Lam has clearly relished
his eventual arrest by Inspector Lee, whose newspaper image is attached
to the inside of a cabinet containing incriminating specimens. In the concluding scene of the film Lee visits Lam in his prison cell for some undefined reason. Now facing life imprisonment after escaping the death
sentence, Lam demands the return of photos and videotapes depicting his
murdered victims. When Lee refuses his request Lam again gazes at him
in a dark manner and performs the same orgasmic dance of death before
his visitor that he earlier displayed during his confession. Apart from
drawing an ambiguous Joseph Conrad "Secret Sharer" connection
between the two characters, a direct analogy between them appears difficult to comprehend. However, like the rest of the film, this scene contains

dark paranoid visual overtones hinting at some undefined meaning (or "untold story") lurking within the shadows, suggesting that these two contrasting characters are really products of the same system.

Other parallels occur between certain scenes in *The Untold Story* and *Dr. Lam*. Whereas the former film shows the Macao cops enjoying their free pork buns until they learn about the nature of the contents, the latter film depicts the Hong Kong police voyeuristically gratifying their appetites on the nude photos of Lam's female victims until they discover what they actually represent. They initially share a dark necrophilic fascination with their suspect who enjoys revealing the truth to his unsuspecting victims in the same manner as Wong does in *The Untold Story* concerning the ingredients of his pork buns. While the Macao cops vomit in *The Untold Story* in response to the revelation, their Hong Kong counterparts in *Dr. Lam* view a home video of Lam's final successful necrophilic union with a third female victim. They initially enjoy the voyeuristic spectacle until its real nature becomes apparent as Lam inserts his grinning, orgasmic close-up into the camera, thereby leading to their revulsion as spectators. Although Stringer correctly asserts that little logical connection occurs between the individual and social roots for graphic representations of male sexual hatred for women in these films, he does recognize certain "familiar class markers of Category 3 political paranoia" that operate to blur ostensibly distinctive boundaries, such as those telling visual matching shots between "hero" Inspector Lee and "villain" Dr. Lam. "The protagonist and his family have to share a cramped apartment; Lam's job takes him on night work to the prostitute areas and sex cinemas of Kowloon; and the police are overworked and undermotivated."[23]

The Underground Banker

Bosco Lam Hing-yung's *The Underground Banker* (1994) represents an uneasy amalgamation between the realms of horror and satire. Although this Wong Jing Workshop production aimed at the ingenious premise of combining Category 3 actor Anthony Wong and Dr. Lam in the same movie, it fell far short of the similarly inspired dream-team casting of Anthony Wong and Simon Yam in *Awakening* (1994). Despite these problems, however, *The Underground Banker* has indelible connections to the social roots of horror characterizing so many Category 3 films. The title character is a Triad loan shark who forces the wife of truck driver

Tong Chi-ming (Anthony Wong) to pay back the huge interest accumulated by her gambling debts by working as a hooker. Tong and his family have recently gained public housing, moving away from their cramped quarters (resembling the family home of *Dr. Lamb*) into a high-rise apartment. Ironically, during one of Tong's bad days (when he has faced harassment by Triad gang members), a woman mysteriously falls from such a building, splattering both herself and Tong's lunch in the process. As Tom Weisser suggests, this may be the same apartment that Tong and his family move into shortly thereafter.[24] Similar to *The Untold Story,* dark connections between poverty, gambling, food, and violence are revealed to be present in a society where economic cannibalism is rampant. Although Tong sells his truck and property to redeem the loan, he loses the money, which results in the Triads setting fire to his apartment. His wife dies in the blaze and his young son becomes horribly disfigured. Tong cannot free them because the gang has used security chains (which most low-income apartments have) to trap the victims inside.

Earlier in the film, Tong discovers to his horror that the recently paroled Dr. Lam is his new neighbor. Played by Lawrence Ng Kai-wah in a sinister yet gentle manner, Lam allows Tong's son to play games on his computer and adopts the boy like a kindly uncle. The interactions between the paranoid Tong—who fears that his new neighbor will revert to his old habits—and Lam himself, represent the film's comic highlights. However, Tong finally decides to enlist his new neighbor to take revenge on the Triads. During one of the film's climactic scenes, Anthony Wong not only delivers an in-joke referring to his celebrated *Untold Story* role by muttering "Human Pork Buns! Human Pork Buns!" while pursuing his enemy, but also exhibits the same type of demented "class rage" exhibited by Fatty (Kent Cheng) in *Run and Kill,* who has lost his daughter at the hands of psychopath Ching Fong (Simon Yam).[25] The violent nature of Hong Kong economic life creates an interesting class revenge alliance between Tong and Dr. Lam.

Ebola Syndrome and *The Untold Story 2*

Ebola Syndrome represents a dark comedic sequel to *The Untold Story* by inverting its premises in several ways. While the earlier film's prologue begins with an act of violence presented in a serious manner, *Ebola Syndrome* opens with the nerdish Kai (Anthony Wong) taking revenge on an annoyed husband who discovers him screwing his wife. Since Shing Fui-on here plays the husband in a picture made by the same director of *The Untold Story* and featuring its now infamous star, *Ebola Syndrome* is clearly meant to be satirical. But it also shares the same social roots as other Category 3 horror films.

After avenging himself on Shing Fui-on's character (in effect) for his brutal prison beatings in *The Untold Story,* as well as committing two additional murders, Wong's character flees not to Macao but to South Africa. Although the owners of the Pat Sin Restaurant in *The Untold Story* appear not to know about their employee's criminal activities, the mercenary Taiwanese couple who own the South African restaurant clearly know about Kai. They deliberately exploit him as an illegal immigrant on slave wages. When Kai contracts Ebola, the couple decide to dump his body outside. Kai does not suffer the full effects of the virus, however, but instead becomes a carrier. He then avenges his victimization not only by killing the Taiwanese couple and using their bodies for African "pork buns" but also by infecting virtually the whole of South Africa and Hong Kong before he is killed. However, the film ends with not only the nominal hero and heroine infected by the virus but a little girl whose dog has licked Kai's infected blood on the street.

The final image is of Kai staring at the camera and muttering a line heard frequently throughout the film, "Bully me?" Throughout the film, Kai has suffered various forms of abuse, such as threatened castration by his Hong Kong boss and verbal assaults by South Africans and the wife of his Taiwanese employer. Despite Kai's violent nature, the film suggests that had he not suffered this treatment, events may have taken a different direction. Although in both films Anthony Wong plays characters who are literal time bombs the bumbling Kai is marginally less dangerous than his counterpart in *The Untold Story.* But like Wong's character in Herman Yau's *Taxi Hunter* (1993), who turns from meek insurance agent to avenging nemesis when a rapacious taxi driver refuses to drive his pregnant wife to hospital, Social Darwinist influences contained within the tiger economy eventually lead to a violent cataclysm.[26]

Ng Yiu Kuen's *The Untold Story 2* (1998), released a year after the Colony's return to the Mainland, is less a sequel to the original than a reworking of its premises. This time the killer is played by Pauline Suen Kai-kam in the role of Fung, a recently arrived Mainlander who is cousin to Kuen (Helena Law Lan), the greedy, adulterous wife of restaurant owner Cheung (Cheung Kam Ching). After Fung's arrival, Kuen takes her on a shopping expedition and teaches her the new Special Adminis-

Kai (Anthony Wong) at the end of his rope in *Ebola Syndrome* (1996)

tration Region's economic facts of life, which differ little from those of the former Colony. Fung's interests will be served "by attracting a rich boyfriend." If getting "something for nothing" is impossible, so is "working hard" in Hong Kong. Asserting her economic independence (based on raiding her hard-working husband's cash till), Kuen also informs Fung that money rules everything. While Kuen tries on a dress in a fashionable boutique, Fung touches with fascination an expensive imported garment. As she does so, a snobbish shop assistant, who recognizes her impoverished Mainland status, treats her in a demeaning manner. Fung angrily responds, "If you feel I have offended by not buying it, why do you *despise* me?" Hearing the commotion, Kuen rushes out of the changing room and blames her cousin rather than supporting her. "You lose my face, too." Ironically, Kuen is a former Mainlander who now rejects her former homeland for the Hong Kong economic dream.

Previously, when Cheung met the newly arrived Fung, a lavishly dressed middle-aged Hong Kong female taunted her as a "Mainlander!" This led to Fung following her into the restroom, throwing paint over her, and attempting to set her on fire. Although the film's narrative ascribes Fung's condition to her traumatic witnessing of a family massacre and her incarceration in a Mainland mental asylum, *The Untold Story 2* contains enough alternative evidence for the audience to regard this "explanation" as being on the same level as Simon Oakland's institutional discourse in *Psycho*. Director Ng Yiu Kuen uses deliberate references to Hitchcockian voyeurism in *Psycho* and elements of Clouzot's *Les diaboliques* (1955); he also employs the "rebirth" motif of *Vertigo* (1958) in an ingenious manner by relating it to Hong Kong everyday life. Like James Stewart's Scottie, Cheung becomes both impotent and helpless by becoming a victim of circumstances he cannot control. Unlike Hitchcock's "hero," however, he never gains any position of male assertion but instead remains impotent throughout the entire film.

The Untold Story 2 opens by showing Cheung's failure to satisfy his wife's sexual appetites. It also shows him witnessing the murder, dismemberment, and barbecuing of his wife's body, so that she ironically becomes a "tasty delicacy" in death as well as life by appealing to a different form of male appetite. Eventually, Cheung finds himself unable to fulfill Fung's sexual demands, and becomes a crucified victim of the Hong Kong economic dream when Fung nails his hands to the marital bed. Fung deliberately sets out to seduce Cheung, displace the greedy Kuen, and follow Hong Kong economic values to become a new version of her murdered cousin. The Untold Story 2 is another Category 3 social horror movie produced after 1997, with SAR censorship as restrictive as that operating in the former Colony. In depicting the Hong Kong economic dream as a cannibalistic nightmare the film cannot be as explicit as it may desire. Instead, it resorts to several relevant subtextual motifs that are more important than the "official" explanation.

The Untold Story 2 represents that curtailed tradition of social criticism seen in Tsui Hark's 1980 works such as Dangerous Encounter—1st Kind and We're Going to Eat You and also presents a particular fear on the part of Hong Kong audiences. If 1997 did not bring that apocalyptic bloodbath feared in so many Hong Kong films made prior to the handover, The Untold Story 2 represents another type of foreboding. What if Mainland interest in Hong Kong did not involve changing it into a Maoist realm but rather in copying its worst practices? The rapid nature of Fung's appropriation of her cousin's role, her seduction of Cheung, and her demands for his unquestioning fidelity uncannily depict deep-rooted fears concerning the former Colony's appropriation by the Motherland. Ironically, Fung moves from the traditional role of demure Mainland female to castrating mother during the course of the film. It is only the accidental involvement of "Officer Lazybones" (Anthony Wong), a crooked, incompetent cop, that ends her reign of terror. However, like Ebola Syndrome, the film ends on a disturbing image. Fung's dead body looks at the audience, eyes wide open, suggesting that this untold story has no real conclusion.

Despite their exploitative nature, these Category 3 productions echo motifs contained in dystopian fiction such as H. G. Wells's The Time Machine (1898), where the Morlock and Eloi imagery represents fears concerning the eventual consequences of economic Social Darwinism. The Morlocks not only provide food for the effete Eloi race but also eat them after dark. In a world rapidly retreating from Depression-era welfare philosophies into a dog-eat-dog consumerist mentality, it is hard not to see a certain social relevance in these Hong Kong productions, which are not as far removed from our world as we may think. If Wells used science fiction to depict a grim future, these Category 3 "tiger economy" productions reveal another dystopian cinematic future whereby capitalist exploitation and a supposedly primitive mode of cannibalism will logically coexist in a brave new social world.

The films discussed in this essay can thus be seen as key texts for understanding human dilemmas caused by recent post-capitalist global developments in Southeast Asia, developments that have resulted in social dislocation and dehumanization. They also grimly forecast a society relevant to post-1997 Hong Kong and also to the rest of the Western world—a world whose populace may soon experience a far different type of consumption than they expect.[27]

Notes

1. See Julian Stringer, "Category 3: Sex and Violence in Postmodern Hong Kong," in *Mythologies of Violence in Postmodern Media*, ed. Christopher Sharrett (Detroit: Wayne State University Press, 1999), 361–79.
2. Stringer, "Category 3," 362.
3. For an excellent review of this critically acclaimed film, which drew limited audience support, see Lisa Odham Stokes and Michael Hoover, *City on Fire: Hong Kong Cinema* (New York: Verso, 1999), 171–75. Evans Chan also refers to the plight of the cagemen in Hong Kong society in his brilliant interrogative documentary-fictional essay, *To Liv(e)*, which also significantly appeared in the same year as *Cageman* and *The Untold Story*. For various commentaries on the work of Evans Chan, see Gina Marchetti, "Transnational Cinemas, Hybrid Identities, and the Films of Evans Chan," *Postmodern Culture* 8, no. 2 (1998); and Tony Williams, "Hong Kong Cinema, The Boat People and *To Liv(e)*," *Asian Cinema* 11, no. 1 (2000): 131–42.
4. Sek Kei, "Hong Kong Cinema from June 4 to 1997," in *Fifty Years of Electric Shadows* (Hong Kong: Urban Council, 1997), 124.
5. Stokes and Hoover, *City on Fire*, 175.
6. See, for example, the various "sequels" of successful films such as *Aces Go Places* (1982), *A Better Tomorrow* (1986), *God of Gamblers* (1989), and *Royal Tramp* (1992) documented in John Charles, *Hong Kong Filmography, 1977–1997* (Jefferson, NC: McFarland, 2000). Hong Kong cinema has employed the device of parody from the very beginning of its history. As Stephen Teo has aptly noted, the colony's idea of post-modernist parody may be entirely different from the Western model. See

Teo, *Hong Kong Cinema: The Extra Dimensions* (London: BFI Publishing, 1997), 243–56. Parody is both a common and often extremely rich device in Hong Kong cinema.

7. See Karl Marx, "The Eighteenth Brumaire of Louis Napoleon," in *Marx-Engels Selected Works* (Moscow: Progress, 1968), 96.

8. Li Cheuk-to, Introduction, in *Phantoms of the Hong Kong Cinema: The 13th Hong Kong International Film Festival* (Hong Kong: Urban Council, 1989), 9.

9. For an informative treatment of the author of *Strange Tales from a Chinese Studio,* who has influenced directors such as King Hu and Tsui Hark, see Stephen Teo, "In the Realm of Pu Songling," in *Phantoms of the Hong Kong Cinema,* 63–67.

10. For the first two examples, see Tony Williams, *Hearths of Darkness: The Family in the American Horror Film* (Cranbury, NJ: Associated University Presses, 1996), 193–96, 254.

11. See Foster Hirsch, *The Dark Side of the Screen: Film Noir* (New York: A. S. Barnes, 1981), 49.

12. See, for example, Raymond Williams, *The Politics of Modernism: Against the New Conformists* (London: Verso, 1989), 83, 113–16. Note also the role of AIZEN, the Association International for Multidisciplinary Approaches and Comparative Studies related to Émile Zola and his Time, Naturalism, Naturalist Writers and Artists, Naturalism and the Cinema Around the World. It publishes an annual journal, *Excavatio.*

13. Stokes and Hoover, *City on Fire,* 11.

14. Ibid., 12.

15. Stringer, "Category 3," 366.

16. See Robin Wood, *Hollywood from Vietnam to Reagan* (New York: Columbia University Press, 1986), 70–94.

17. Stringer, "Category 3," 369. Stringer also notices the prologue's employment of the stop-motion techniques pioneered by Wong Kar-Wai in *As Tears Go By* (1988) and *Days of Being Wild* (1991). Cheng Yu sees gambling as a key secondary motif in Hong Kong Cinema: "The Chinese people have a fondness for gambling, they are practically addicts. Gambling occupies an important spot in the lives of Hong Kong people." See Yu, "The Gambling Streak as Seen in Hong Kong Movies," in *Changes in Hong Kong Society through Cinema: The 12th Hong Kong International Film Festival* (Hong Kong: Urban Council, 1988), 32.

18. Teo, *Hong Kong Cinema,* 141.

19. See Charles, *Hong Kong Filmography,* 338; and Tan See Kam, "Ban(g)! Ban(g)! *Dangerous Encounters of the 1st Kind," Asian Cinema* 8, no. 1 (1996): 83–108.

20. See Tony Williams, "Danny Lee: Hong Kong's Real Supercop," *Asian Cult Cinema* 26 (2000): 51–54. According to Ken Hall, "Lee has the distinction of having played more variations on the cop role than just about any other Asian or Western actor, and he has done so with intelligence, conviction, and a special magnetism." See Hall, "Danny Lee," in *Encyclopedia of Chinese Film,* ed. Yingjin Zhang and Zhiwei Xiao (New York: Routledge, 1998), 214. In *Cop Image* (1994), Anthony Wong's wannabe cop closes the film by dedicating it to Lee.

21. Stringer, "Category 3," 370.

22. Stokes and Hoover, *City on Fire,* 10.

23. Stringer, "Category 3," 376.

24. Thomas Weisser, *Asian Trash Cinema: The Book (Part Two)* (Miami: Florida Vital Sounds, 1995), 128.

25. See the excellent analysis by Stringer, who comments as follows: "As Fatty's family has been evacuated from the stinking detritus of Hong Kong's post-colonial society, he is left to rub shoulders with the criminal underclass in a Category 3 cinema" ("Category 3," 369).

26. *Taxi Hunter* is based on a real-life situation in Hong Kong. As John Charles points out, "HK taxi drivers are not known for their politeness, choosing their passengers based on their destinations, sometimes demanding extra money for late night trips, and refusing to perform basic services" (*Hong Kong Filmography*, 303). When the film was first released it drew applause from audiences in the same manner as *Death Wish* (1974) originally did on its New York release. Among the highlights of the film are Wong's recreations of De Niro's "You Talking to Me?" scene from *Taxi Driver*, and the slaying of cabbies who refuse to pick up an old lady or rape teenage passengers.

27. After completing this essay, I read Michael Hoover and Lisa Stokes's essay "Enfant Terrible: The Terrorful, Wonderful World of Anthony Wong," in *Fear Without Frontiers: Horror Cinema across the Globe*, ed. Steven Jay Schneider (Surrey, UK: FAB Press, 2003), 45–59. I highly recommend it to those interested in Hong Kong Category 3 horror.

12

Beyond Dracula and Ceausescu:

PHENOMENOLOGY OF HORROR
IN ROMANIAN CINEMA

Christina Stojanova

We are in Transylvania, and Transylvania is not England. Our ways
are not your ways, and there shall be to you many strange things.

Count Dracula to Jonathan Harper in Bram Stoker's *Dracula*

The study of Romanian cinematic horror must be based on instances
scattered over genres and years since horror films in the Western sense
have not been made in Romania until recently.[1] Following Freud's discussion of the uncanny, which attributes terror to the collapsing of the
psychic boundaries of self and other, life and death, reality and unreality,
the peculiarities of horror representation in Romanian cinema can be
explicated with reference to tensions between traditional Eastern awareness (predicated on irrational beliefs and collectivism) and the modern
Western one (promulgating rational individualism).

The first section of this essay analyzes the Dracula/Vlad Tepeş controversy—symbolic of the incongruity between the Eastern and Western
mindsets—locating it with respect to the historical idiosyncrasies of
Romanian culture. The horror motifs in interwar literature, discussed in
the second section, are linked to the mounting frictions between traditional Romanian ways of life and modernization. Interwar cinema is
referred to briefly here because it identified solely with the modernizing
role, ignoring the place of tradition. Communist-enforced modernity
confined supernatural beliefs to the margins of Romanian society, but horror resurfaced in the country's cinema, yielding both supernatural and psychological motifs, which are the focus of section three. Finally, the fourth
section of this essay reflects on the abundance of horror motifs in post-
communist Romanian cinema, seen as attempts at diffusing old as well as
emerging tensions between tradition and (post-)communist modernity.

Horror East and West

Bram Stoker's legendary monster put Transylvania and vampirism on the map of modern Western European imagination at the end of the nineteenth century. His Dracula is a gothic literary construct, born from a need to confront the horrors of death and the frustrations of sexuality. And while these are allowed to rage freely in Dracula's castle lost somewhere amidst the Carpathian Mountains, in civilized England they are sanitized by the good doctor Van Helsing, whose confrontation with Dracula epitomizes the critical clash between Western culture and Eastern nature.

In Romania, where Stoker's novel was translated only in the early 1970s,[2] Vlad Tepeş (1431–1476) is a historical personage: a nobleman and a national hero. Son of Vlad Dracul, known as Vlad the Impaler or Vlad the Brave, he has been mythologized for his tenacious fight against the Ottoman invaders.[3] Thanks to Prince Vlad, his native Transylvania— one of the three major Romanian provinces (the other two being Moldova and Wallachia)—gradually came to denote *all* of Romania, despite the long-lasting territorial and ethnic disputes over the province with neighboring Hungary.[4]

The squabble over whether Tepeş should be identified with Stoker's Dracula first emerged during the dawn of modernity,[5] exposing cultural discrepancies that were to plague both East and West perceptions of Eastern Europe for centuries to come. The negative image of Eastern Europe, especially the Balkans, can be understood in psychoanalytical (Jungian) terms as stemming from its representation as the West's "shadow," revealing the hidden or repressed contents of the Western collective unconscious, which becomes manifest in popular and official texts. In Eastern European popular discourse it is the West that is viewed as the significant "Other," and as a source of frustrating inferiority due to the ever-growing economic divide. Yet is the East only a victim of arrogant stereotyping and political intrigues, as Maria Todorova and Slavoj Žižek have forcefully argued?[6] Or are there peculiarities in the cultural tradition of Eastern Europe, which thwart any adequate assessment in such terms by the enlightened minds of the modern world?

As the renowned Romanian cultural anthropologist Mircea Eliade states, "the Balkan peninsula is both a crossroad and a zone of conservatism in which the arrival of a wave of higher culture does not necessarily dissolve and obliterate the earlier form of culture simply by its success."[7]

Romania is a land whose vampire tradition is as "prevalent both in city and market-town as in the villages . . . gather[ing] together . . . almost all the beliefs and superstitions that prevail throughout the whole of Eastern Europe."[8] Indeed, Romanian folklore teems with so many species of bloodsucking, flesh-eating, and sexually disturbing creatures of the night, disruptive of harvest, livestock, and family life, that "the generic term vampire is rarely used."[9] Besides the traditional garlic, stake, cross, and incantations, specialists discuss a rich array of other defense strategies. They attribute the "prevalence of the vampire and the 'bat god' beliefs in Transylvania" to invasions and the eventual settlement of Tibetan and Mongolian tribes in the ninth and thirteenth centuries AD.[10] Romanians share many of these beliefs with Hungarians and Slavs, their neighbors for centuries.

Other scholars have tracked the roots of Eastern European demonology to Mithraism and Manichaeism, both Persian (Zoroastrian) sects successfully competing with Christianity throughout the Roman Empire during the first to fourth centuries AD.[11] Although little is known about these cults today, the gist of their mysteries can be reduced to the "opposition of a good, creative god, associated with light and spirit, to an evil, destructive god, associated with darkness and human bodies."[12] After prolonged attacks on dualist mysticism, Christianity (both Orthodox and Uniat) finally succumbed to its influence, adapting many a pagan ritual to its canon, including the anathema on "criminals, bastards, magicians, and Christians who convert to Islam or Roman Catholicism." These accursed individuals would "remain incorrupt and entire in their graves, rambl[ing] at night and spend[ing] only daytime in their tombs until excommunication is lifted." In more stubborn cases priests even sanctioned impaling.[13] It is precisely this dualistic dynamic of the good Christian god and the demonic forces of Nature that accounts for the enduring vigor of Romanian tradition.

Modernity between the Marvelous and the Uncanny

With the belated advent of modernity in the late nineteenth century, such a resilient tradition was bound to create tensions between the rapidly developing cities and the "ignorant" countryside. As Eliade wrote in 1957, the "active classes" of southeastern Europe undoubtedly "belonged to the 'modern' world," while the majority of the population "still maintains its attachment to a traditional and half-Christian spiritual universe."[14] In Eliade's view, the peculiarities of Balkan modernization allowed for the coexistence of two layers of culture, and modern culture never really attempted an obliteration of its archaic core—at least not until the violent onset of communism—but was instead constantly challenged by it. The friction between the two layers generated a crisis of conscience prompted not so much by the existential horrors of death and frustrated sexuality, as in Western Draculiana, but by the heavy toll taken by modernization on the traditional way of life.

The chaotic and scarce history of film production in interwar Romania reflects this endemic tension between traditional culture and modernity. Tales of the sinister and the demonic failed to attract the attention of Romanian filmmakers, despite their popularity abroad, for example, in films and serials like *Der golem* (1917), *Les vampires* (1915), and *Nosferatu* (1922). And even though Romanian audiences welcomed the few homemade melodramas with mystic motifs, their success remained isolated.[15] The authoritarian state was primarily concerned with sponsoring patriotic shorts and nationalist epics; its attitude toward tradition could be defined as conservationist and ethnographic: a compromise between the enlightenment fervor of the Leftist intelligentsia[16] and the elitism of the conservative literati, resulting in the so-called art documentaries. The most famous pre–World War II Romanian film, Paul Calinescu's *Tara Molitor* (*The Land of the Motzi*, 1938)—winner of the Best Documentary award at the 1939 Venice Film Biennale—was replete with not-so-subtle chauvinism and propagated the "mystique" of the countryside. Although most of the films produced before World War II[17] featured trendy melodramatic plots, Romanian cinema trailed far behind literature in both talent and popularity. Literature was in fact the uncontested leader of Romanian culture; its prerogatives of "high" art and custodianship of tradition were closely guarded against the advances of film, which was perceived by many as a vehicle of modern profanity and "low" genres.

In the light of Tzvetan Todorov's discussion of the fantastic, representations of the supernatural in traditional/folkloric discourse could be defined as marvelous in its medieval sense, "signalling a rupture in the natural order, one, unlike the miraculous, not necessarily divine in origin and a challenge to rational causality."[18] In other words, the "supernatural remains unexplained"[19] by definition. Romanian interwar literature sees traditional ways of life—predominantly rural, but also urban—as marvelous. The threats to tradition, in contrast, are presented as uncanny or as "the supernatural explained."[20] The Freudian uncanny, we are told, "derives its terror from something strangely familiar, which defeats our efforts to separate ourselves from it."[21] In that, the nostalgic mysticism of Romanian interwar literature bears an "uncanny" similarity to the anti-modernist pathos of fin-de-siècle symbolism and surrealism. Or, in Eliade's terms, tradition is seen as marvelous in its divine sense. His "traditional man" (or "homo religious") experiences the world as sacred, while modern man can only experience the world as profane.[22]

In Mihail Sadoveanu's classic 1930 novel *The Hatchet,* for example, the mysterious disappearance of a wealthy shepherd and his strong-willed wife's quest for revenge are depicted, and perceived, as marvelous. The powers that rule death and life remain beyond the grasp of the "laws of reality," that is, of modern rationalism.[23] Eliade's own "mystic" stories are themselves examples of the marvelous as sacred. They offer no explanation for the supernatural (or "spiritual") experiences of his characters. When Eliade allows for an explanation, it is to expose the uncanny horrors of modernity, which threatens tradition with its profanity. In "Miss Christina," the hero is stuck in a gloomy estate, haunted by the ghost of its beautiful but corrupt former mistress. However, it is the hungry and overworked peasants, who brutally murdered the woman during an uprising, who provoke his actual fear.[24] For Liviu Rebreanu, the Great War is that uncanny, apocalyptic force shattering traditional life and its spiritual universe, encouraging traitors and condemning nobles to the gallows. Death in battle therefore is perceived as a sublime reprieve from the horrors of modern life.[25]

The Politics of Horror under Communism

After the film industry's nationalization in 1948, the communist state was exceptionally generous to Romanian cinema for obvious propaganda reasons, and by the late 1950s the craftsmanship and technological sophistication of Buftea Studios reached world standards. Cinema, that "most important art" according to Lenin, usurped the leading place of literature and, to a large extent, its social prestige. Yet it also adopted its didactic pathos and elitist attitude toward popular genres, rejected this time around not as "low," but as "capitalist" and decadent.

The enforcement of socialist realism as normative aesthetics effectively reversed the dynamics of filmic representation. According to socialist realism, cinema depicts life not as it is but as it should be. The traditional way of life was therefore to be portrayed as uncanny, leaving no doubt that superstition and backwardness were the only explanations for the persistence of demonic and "semi-Christian" beliefs. The enemy classes and the West were also promptly demonized as enemies of the people.

The marvelous "new life," meanwhile, was featured as the sacred domain of perfect new men and women, very much in the spirit of avant-garde futurism. The officially endorsed film productions were a unique attempt at constructing an artificial mythology, disclosing in the process a superb form of political *enantiodromia*. A Jungian term, borrowed from Heraclitus, *enantiodromia* is "an essential characteristic of all homeostatic systems," pertaining to "the inherent compensatory tendency of all entities, pushed to the extreme, to go over to their opposites."[26] In other words, the transformation of the communist system, a miraculous hybrid of Western rationalism and Eastern collectivism, into its opposite—irrational and exploitative tyranny—was manifested in a fossilized iconography of representation remindful of the Orthodox Church canon.

Yet even within such a master framework there are moments when the canon becomes negotiable. For Romanian cinema this was the period from the early 1960s to the mid-1970s when it experienced a true golden age, profiting immensely from adaptations of bestselling interwar novels. True, traditional rural life, still thriving and vibrant, was here presented in a somewhat abstract and stylized fashion. Thanks to the mystical motifs, however, these films could be read as a coded defiance of the new eschatological myth of a radiant communist future, and a preview of the very real horrors yet in store for the Romanian people, especially in the countryside.[27] Among the notable adaptations relevant to this discussion are *Codine* (1962), directed by Henri Colpi, and *Baltagul* (*The Hatchet*, 1969), directed by Mircea Muresan, a leading director at the time.

The French-Romanian co-production *Codine* was a sign of thaw, one linked to the political interregnum that spanned the last years in office of Gheorghe Gheorghiu-Dej (1952–65) and the ascension to total power of Nicolae Ceausescu (1965–89). Based on a short story by émigré writer Panait Istrati,[28] it is about a mystical, blood-sealed friendship between a young boy and a former convicted killer with a heart of gold, a sturdy mountain of a man called Codine (Alexandru Virgil Platon). Strongly reminiscent of the trademark encounter between the Monster and the little girl from the 1931 *Frankenstein* movie classic, the boy's devotion fails to deliver Codine from his demons. And yet Codine is not seen as a victim of uncanny social forces or uncontrollable laws of nature, as socialist realism or metaphysical naturalism would have it. His accursed passion for a beautiful gypsy girl belongs to the realm of the marvelous; his bouts of gambling and jealousy are "ruptures in the natural order"—sacred, but not divine. The looming tragedy unravels when, after a row over money, Codine's old mother Anastasia (Germaine Kerjean), in an act of ultimate betrayal, pours a bucket of boiling oil on him, killing him in a most horrific way.

Codine is constructed as a benign monster, childishly ignorant concerning the intricacies of love and money. The demonic image of Anastasia, though, originates in what Julia Kristeva calls "the archaic mother": the "mother-as-primordial abyss . . . the cannibalizing black hole from which life comes and to which all life returns."[29] The archaic mother is a source of deepest terror in the Eastern European vampire tradition, abounding with children-devouring female monsters like the *strigoaica*. The archaic mother is closely associated with death since "both signify a monstrous obliteration of the self, and both are linked to the demonic."[30]

"The total dedication of the archaic mother to the generative, procreative principle,"[31] has nurtured the formidable archetype of the Eastern European matriarch, essential for the survival of the region. Usually widowed and totally committed to her family, she readily ignores morality and law in the name of her children and even kills without qualms or repentance. Such an overwhelming mother figure is more than just "castrating" or "abject": she is sublime.[32] In this light, Anastasia's murder of her tormented son acquires the mythical dimensions of sacrificial redemption.

The Hatchet offers another compelling evocation of this image. Following the shepherd's widow Vitoria (Margarita Lozano) in her quest through the Moldovan countryside, the stunning camerawork indulges in the raw beauty of life as ordained by God and Nature. Vitoria wins our sympathy through the power of her love and her readiness to follow the mystical lead of her visions. Yet when she finds the bones of her husband at the bottom of a gorge she turns into a cunning monster, enticing her young son to kill the already terrorized murderer just before his arrest, for she believes only in her own justice.

Duminica la ora 6 (*Sunday at 6 O'Clock*, 1965), the first film of Lucian Pintilie, is one of the few Romanian modernist auteur films. It is a pessimistic rejection of the sacred and the marvelous in the traditional as well as ideologically constructed senses of the terms. The story, about a couple of young, anti-Fascist fighters who are persecuted and killed by the Iron Guard[33] after being betrayed by one of their own, meets socialist realism requirements to a point. The film's style, however, takes on a life of its own, and the poetic parable about the Angels of Light confronting the Demons of Darkness is transformed into a disturbing psychological thriller, replete with sadistic torture scenes. From a close-up on the perspiring face of the hiding boy, the camera rapidly zooms down the elevator shaft to reveal the girl's body far below in the dungeons, and then cuts to a sun-bleached courtyard where young people are happily chatting, thus escalating the foreboding anticipation to the limit. The recurring audio-visual leitmotifs (the dark stairwell, the sounds of elevator machinery, the overexposed courtyard) trigger a series of flashbacks, introducing bit by bit the poignant story of two people destroyed by the uncanny forces of history. Thus, Pintilie's film yields a transparent existential metaphor for the despondency of young people in his country, trapped in the shaft of communist dictatorship. Small wonder that his second film, *Reconstituirea* (*Reconstruction*, 1968), focusing on the existential horrors of contemporary Romania, was promptly banned and the director banished.

At the height of Ceausescu's rule, indignation with Western Draculiana acquired epic dimensions thanks to state-induced chauvinistic fervor, anti-Western sentiment, and general fear and compliance. The hysteria came to a head when American actor George Hamilton was refused a Romanian visa for his portrayal of Dracula in Stan Dragoti's 1979 Hollywood comedy, *Love at First Bite*.[34] In an effort to set the record straight, Romania Film produced Doru Nastase's *The True Life of Dracula* (a.k.a. *Vlad Tepeş*, 1979), an expensive nationalist epic shot "in a spectacular manner, full of force and manhood, [and] imbued with a strong dramatic conflict," according to the official press kit.

This removal of Dracula from the nocturnal domains of horror and death to the brightly lit terrain of the heroic nationalist epic constituted a significant political and psychological event. Traditionally, the occurrence of Eastern European nationalist epics are symptomatic of national crises—real or anticipated—and are used as a rallying weapon by the powers that be.[35] The emergence of a number of nationalist epics in the 1960s and 1970s[36] could be explained primarily with reference to Ceausescu's need to consolidate his position vis-à-vis powerful Party rivals, but also with respect to his megalomaniac ambitions to see himself as part of the indigenous monarchic succession. As Karen Jaehne has wittingly put it, "the major history lesson . . . is that Vlad Tepeş was faced with betrayal and rancor in the ranks no less complex than that of a modern Romanian ruler, for example Ceausescu!"[37]

The representation of Dracula (played by Stefan Sileanu) as a Romanian national hero, struggling to unite his country in the face of both internal and foreign foes, resulted in a bland, pseudo-historical rendition of "facts" culled from the life of the infamous ruler. Despite its questionable aesthetic values, Nastase's film admittedly does a good job justifying Ceausescu's atrocities, evoking the myth of the "historical necessity" of present suffering in the name of the nation's bright future. Indeed, the loyal filmmakers seem to have stumbled on the method in Vlad's madness. As history teaches us, the Draculian type of seemingly irrational terror, practiced "as a means of social integration and political control,"[38] has been around since the dawn of time. Thus, one can hardly help appreciating the macabre irony in Ceausescu's attempts to rehabilitate his comrade in arms, the Impaler!

This and other attempts at "historicizing" Dracula, however, deprived the myth of what Jung calls "numinosity," or a sense of awe and exultation, and rendered it inefficient for the deeper life of the psyche. Fossilized and externalized, the ultimate demonic myth of modernity could not provide the rapidly modernizing Romanian people a much-needed palliative for their growing fears. Ceausescu was only partially successful in filling the void and becoming a symbol of modern Romanian demonology as his bureaucratized tyranny and petty personality were no match for Prince Vlad's sublime wickedness.

The Supernatural Revisited

The communist project was promptly dismantled after the collapse of Ceausescu's reign of terror in 1989 and replaced by "true" Western modernization, complete with market economy and democratic institutions. In tune with the times, Vlad Tepeş has turned into a promotional gig for "trips to the country of Dracula." Meanwhile, Lucian Pintilie has become Romania's most awarded director of the 1990s. He is also the director most engaged in attempts to purge the demons of Romania's tragic past from the collective psyche. *Balanta* (*The Oak*, 1992), possibly Pintilie's most programmatic work of the decade, borrows the structure of the Renaissance picaresque—a quest with a moral message—and gives it a feminist twist: the *picaro* or rascal is Nela (Maia Morgenstern), an eccentric and intellectual young woman.

After the death of her father, a former high-ranking *Securitate* (Secret Police) officer, Nela sets off on her picaresque to bury his ashes. Her trip through the uncanny absurdities of provincial Romania on the eve of Ceausescu's downfall is paralleled by an internal one through her own privileged past, in search of her family's responsibility for these horrors. Nela's desire to have her dear father absolved humanizes the formidable *Securitate,* whose very mention used to petrify Romanians, while her hatred for her cunning sister, a *Securitate* agent, restores the emotional balance. The post-modern interplay between these two levels of representation—grotesquely alienating and beguilingly intimate—has the cathartic effect of discharging powerful emotions linked to fear and betrayal on a personal and a collective level.

Nela's sexual assault by local miners targets another, more recent agency of horror, associated with traumatic betrayal. After their sinister role in the suppression of the nascent democracy in June 1990, the image of Romanian miners, once hallowed as the epitome of the communist future, degenerated in popular demonology into that of Marx's lumpen-proletariat and infernal symbols of ferocity.

The representation of physical and psychological horror as a form of social criticism escalates in Pintilie's latest films. *Terminus paradis* (*Next Stop: Paradise*, 1998) concerns a love triangle that ends in a sadistic bloodbath, while *Dupa-amiaza unui tortionar* (*The Afternoon of a Torturer*, 2001) is based on a novel by Doina Jela, inspired in turn by an interview with an ancient torturer.[39] The film cleverly leaves the horror of the torturer's confessions mostly to the viewer's imagination, but the psychological impact is as disturbing as that of the graphic scenes of torture and humiliation in Serban Marinescu's *Cel mai iubit dintre pamînteni* (*Earth's Most Beloved Son*, 1993) and Radu Mihaileanu's *A trada* (*Betrayal*, 1993)—two films also obsessed with fear and betrayal under communism.

The characteristic display in *Earth's Most Beloved Son* of naked male bodies in prison shower rooms is a visual metaphor for the victims' emasculation since it positions them as passive objects of the gaze—homo-erotic, sadistic, or vulgar—of men in power, thus yielding the ultimate form of psychological horror in any machismo culture. The representation of male victimization in Romanian cinema is typical of the general post-communist crisis of masculinity. The place of the hero—tragic or existential, or a flamboyant "new man"—is arrogated by the Jungian ambivalent trickster, "subhuman and superhuman, bestial and divine,"[40] born in the no-man's-land between communism and post-communism. Razvan Vasilescu, Pintilie's favorite actor, owes much of his popularity to the trickster role of the rowdy provincial doctor in *The Oak*, Nela's savior and consort.

Dumitru (Dan Condurache), the male protagonist of Sinisa Dragin's *În fiecare zi Dumnezeu ne saruta pe gura* (*Every Day God Kisses Us on the Mouth*, 2002), is another trickster figure dominated by the inhuman and the bestial, as well as a victim of perennial betrayal. After his final supervised shower, Dumitru, a convicted killer and butcher by profession, is released from prison, but on the train home he meets a gypsy gambler, wins his money, his goose—an ancient symbol of potency—has a brief lovemaking bout with his beautiful wife, and kills him. She curses him and from that moment on Dumitru's life takes a macabre downward turn, plagued by supernatural coincidences and omens. Once at home he finds his timid wife pregnant with his brother's child. Devastated by this double betrayal, he kills him. On that very same night the gypsy woman torches his house, burning his wife and mother alive. Strongly reminiscent of *Codine*, the film remains ambiguous as to whether this chain of misfortunes is explainable by uncanny social laws, or should be seen instead as divine retribution, brought about by the curse. The ubiquitous presence of weird birds, and of gypsies—one of the few archaic symbols whose numinosity has remained intact—further blurs the boundaries between reality and unreality.

Once settled in the big city, Dumitru kills again, first his mistress for having cooked his pet goose for dinner, then his new friend, a policeman, for having confronted him about her murder. The story so far would have made a good "slasher" horror movie, and Dumitru a perfect serial killer in the tradition of butcher-killers (Claude Chabrol's classic *Le boucher* [*The Butcher*, 1969] and Gaspar Noé's *Seul contre tous* [*I Stand Alone*, 1998] come to mind), if the murders were graphic and central to the narrative. But they occur predominantly offscreen and in an offhand manner, rendered almost unreal by the expressionist black-and-white visuals that underscore the effects of the apocalyptic demise of the boundaries between tradition and modernity. Once more, social and psychological motifs take over the representation of "pure" horror for horror's sake. Against the backdrop of the post-communist "idiocy of village life" and its moral stupor Dumitru's wickedness looks like a perfectly normal survival skill. On a symbolic level, however, Dumitru's inhuman torment is a path to divine revelation. Haunted by surreal visions of his beloved wife, he marries a deaf-mute girl, but when she turns into a white goose

The convicted killer Dumitru (Dan Condurache) returns home in *Every Day God Kisses Us on the Mouth* (2001

Dumitru sees it as the beginning of yet another vicious cycle and summons death. In an act of diabolical reversal, God "kisses him on the mouth" once again by keeping him alive as evil incarnate, and Dumitru comes to believe that he is now a part of His plans. Thus Dumitru the trickster becomes a spiritual werewolf, both bestial and superhuman, stuck between life and death, the demonic and the sacred.

With this last, brief look at some of the most powerful instances of horror representation in Romanian cinema to date, this study has come full circle, unearthing in *Every Day God Kisses Us on the Mouth* the archaic core of Romanian culture, intact under the layers of rubble, left over after several painful attempts at its dissolution and obliteration. When the Old is no more and the New is uncanny, tradition always emerges as a marvelous sanctuary. In addition, this study has demonstrated that, following the ethical impetus of interwar literature and auteurist cinema, Romanian

Dumitru (Dan Condurache) goes on the attack in *Every Day God Kisses Us on the Mouth* (2001)

cinematic horror is invariably associated with obsessive fear of betrayal—an ancient, numinous motif, haunting Romania's collective unconscious since the times of the Impaler.

Notes

1. In November 2002, came the release of Adrian Popovici's *Vlad nemuritorul* (*Dracula the Impaler*). According to Romanian film critic and academic Dana Duma, this poorly received film is "the first Romanian production to accept the idea that Vlad Tepeş . . . was a vampire." Pretending to restore the voivode's "true image," *Vlad nemuritorul* imagines a story located in present-day New York, where Tepeş is looking for his ancient enemy, Vambery, who turned him into a vampire. He accepted this curse in the past, in order to become more powerful for his fight against the Turks. The cast of *Vlad nemuritorul* is dominated by some good theater actors, like Adrian Pintea (Vambery) and Marius Bodochi (Tepeş). For Duma, however, the best thing in this English-spoken movie is "the voice lent to Bodochi by Marcel Iures, the bright Romanian actor who has appeared in such Hollywood productions as *The Peacemaker* (1997) and *Hart's War* (2002)." E-mail correspondence with the author, December 23, 2002.

2. In the academic journal *România literara* (July 1971). See Radu Florescu and Raymond T. McNally, *Dracula: A Biography of Vlad the Impaler, 1431–1476* (London: Robert Hale, 1973), 210n35.

3. Florescu and McNally note that "The Impaler has been exploited by [Romanian] authors with various *arriere pensées* . . . but [he never] corresponded to the Western Dracula . . . [and] when vampires are mentioned, they are Dracula's opponents, not friends" (*Dracula*, 145).

4. Transylvania was part of the Austro-Hungarian Empire (1688–1919), and currently has a sizeable Hungarian minority.

5. *Historie von Dracole* (Leipzig, 1493).

6. See Maria Todorova, "The Balkans: From Discovery to Invention," *Slavic Review* 53, no. 2 (1994): 453–82; and Slavoj Žižek, "Giving Up the Balkan Ghost," in Žižek, *The Fragile Absolute, Or, Why Is the Christian Legacy Worth Fighting For?* (London: Verso, 2000), 5–11.

7. Mircea Eliade, *Zalmoxis, the Vanishing God: Comparative Studies in the Religions and Folklore of Dacia and Eastern Europe* (Chicago: University of Chicago Press, 1972), 160.

8. Montague Summers, *The Vampire: His Kith and Kin* (New Hyde Park, NY: University Books, 1960), 125.

9. According to Florescu and McNally, the worst of these creatures are the "*strigoi* and his wicked partner, the female *strigoaica; vircolac,* the Eastern European werewolf; *iele,* the seductive female vampire; *sburator,* the handsome male vampire-sexual predator; [and] *zmeu,* a huge flying dragon" (*Dracula*, 167–72).

10. Ibid., 167.

11. See Jan L. Perkowski, *Vampires of the Slavs* (Cambridge, MA: Slavica, 1976); and Jan L. Perkowski, *The Darkling: A Treatise on Slavic Vampirism* (Columbus, OH: Slavica, 1989), 23–26.

12. Perkowski, *Darkling*, 29.

13. Florescu and McNally, *Dracula*, 166, 171.

14. Eliade, *Zalmoxis, the Vanishing God*, 160.

15. Alfred Halm's *Tigancusa de la iatac* (*The Gypsy Girl in the Alcove*, 1923), about "the forbidden love of a spell-casting gypsy slave for the son of a nobleman and their mysterious and violent death," was the first Romanian film to break post–World War I box office records. Manuela Cernat, *A Concise History of Romanian Film* (Bucharest: Editura stiintifica si enciclopedica, 1982), 24.

16. The pressure to "regulate cinema and put it to public use began mounting in the 1910s. CIPETO (Cinema for All) society aimed at educating the public through cinema" (Cernat, *Concise History*, 19).

17. According to Cernat, fifty fiction films, thirty silent, and twenty talkies (*Concise History*, 30).

18. Hal Foster, *Compulsive Beauty* (Cambridge: MIT Press, 1995), 19.

19. Tzvetan Todorov, *The Fantastic* (Ithaca: Cornell University Press, 1973), 41.

20. Todorov, *The Fantastic*, 41.

21. David Morris, "Gothic Sublimity," *New Literary History* 16, no. 1 (1985): 299–319.

22. Mircea Eliade, *The Sacred and the Profane: The Nature of Religion* (New York: Harvest, 2001).

23. Mihail Sadoveanu, *Baltagul* (*The Hatchet,* 1930), in *The Hatchet: The Life of Stephen the Great,* vol. 3, *Classics of Romanian Literature* (New York: Columbia University Press, 1991).

24. Mircea Eliade. "Domnisoara Christina" ("Miss Christina," 1936), in *Mystic Stories: The Sacred and the Profane,* vol. 2, *Classics of Romanian Literature* (New York: Columbia University Press, 1991).

25. Liviu Rebreanu, "The Death Dance" (1919), in *Romanian Short Stories* (Oxford: Oxford University Press, 1971).

26. Anthony Stevens, *On Jung* (London: Routledge, 1990), 140.

27. In an attempt to uproot rural tradition, in 1974 Nicolae Ceausescu launched the "systematization" project to double the number of cities by 1990 and forced people into industrial-agricultural complexes, a monstrosity far exceeding the imagination of any mythological or literary demon.

28. Winner of the Best Script Award at Cannes in 1963.

29. Barbara Creed, *The Monstrous Feminine: Film, Feminism, Psychoanalysis* (London: Routledge, 1993), 25. See Julia Kristeva, *Powers of Horror* (New York: Columbia University Press, 1982), 64.

30. Creed, *Monstrous Feminine,* 30.

31. Ibid., 27.

32. It is not coincidental that the Bulgarian-born and raised Julia Kristeva was the first Western feminist to theorize the complex love/hate relations of the child with her "abject" or "archaic" mother.

33. Fascist organization (1933–44).

34. See Karen Jaehne, "The True Life of Dracula," *Cineaste* 10, no. 3 (1980): 38.

35. The first Eastern European big-budget nationalist epic was arguably the Romanian *Independence* (1912), directed by Grigore Brezeanu.

36. *The Rebel Tudor* (L. Bratu, 1963), *The Dacians* (S. Nicolaescu, 1966), *The Seven Haidouk Riders* (D. Cocea, 1970), *Michael the Brave* (S. Nicolaescu, 1971).

37. Jaehne, "True Life of Dracula," 39.

38. Florescu and McNally, *Dracula,* 180.

39. My thanks to Dana Duma for this source information.

40. Carl Jung, "On the Psychology of the Trickster Figure," in *The Archetypes and the Collective Unconscious: The Collected Works,* vol. 9a, trans. R. F. C. Hull (Princeton: Princeton University Press, 1990), 158–59.

13

Snapping Up Schoolgirls:

LEGITIMATION CRISIS
IN RECENT CANADIAN HORROR

Suzie Young

In his theory of culture and the study of history, Raymond Williams suggests that there is a "structure of feeling" in any historical period that is "a particular sense of life, a particular community of experience . . . as firm and definite as 'structure' suggests [but also] . . . the most delicate and least tangible." Thinking sociologically as well as aesthetically, Williams points to the arts of a period as the site where that lived experience can be given collective expression.[1]

This essay posits the multiple figurations of the schoolgirl as the *mise-en-abyme* in Canadian cinema that expresses the "structure of feeling" in contemporary Canada. Certainly the frequency of her appearance in recent Canadian films demands attention, but a survey of our cinema history also reveals that she is a new phenomenon—we have never had our Shirley Temple, Hayley Mills, or equivalents of American cinema's sex-child (Brooke Shields in *Pretty Baby* [1978]), woman-girl (Pia Zadora), prepubescent with a "soft center and sharp tongue" (Jane Withers), adolescent star (Patty Duke) or nymphet (Sandra Dee); even Canada's own Mary Pickford went south where her "suffering, simpering and sunshining" made her America's first sweetheart.[2]

A preliminary analysis of our schoolgirl in Canada's recent cinema suggests that her configuration in horror achieves an "expressionistic allegory of the real"[3] to expound a Canadian ethos that remains mostly subterranean in normal life, except perhaps when we bemoan that we "can't win 'em all."[4] In David Cronenberg's *Shivers* (1975), for example, fifteen-year-old Annabelle (Cathy Graham) is deliberately infected with a parasite by a university professor and so begins an epidemic of orgy and mayhem; in Cronenberg's *The Dead Zone* (1983), Alma (Roberta Weiss) is lured and killed on her way to school by the town's friendly deputy sheriff; in Pen Densham's *The Kiss* (1988), Amy (Meredith Salenger) is abducted by a demon-worshipping aunt who has seduced and subdued her gullible father. An equally naïve schoolgirl is betrayed and brutally victimized by a trusted adult in both Atom Egoyan's *Felicia's Journey* (1999) and Vincenzo Natali's *Cube* (1997); she is less innocent and more complicit in films like *Exotica* (1994), *The Five Senses* (1999), *The Life before This* (1999), *Poison* (1999), and *The Stalking of Laurie Show* (2000), but the familial incoherence that surrounds her exposes a world of patriarchal hysteria, treachery, and legitimation crisis. In fact, the quotidian has become thoroughly obnoxious in John Fawcett's *Ginger Snaps* (2000), provoking the schoolgirl's transgressions as well as inviting the audience's sympathies.

The figure of the schoolgirl persuades not by strict logic but by appealing to our sense of free play beyond its literal expression. Like the babies in *Rosemary's Baby* (1968) and *2001: A Space Odyssey* (1968) who reorient the "pressing cultural drama"[5] of crisis in contemporary patriarchy by contradicting both the literal and the semiotic traditions of childhood innocence and vulnerability, our schoolgirls crystallize a narrative concern into visible evidence but also transform it by departing from previous visual expressions. In two recent Canadian horror films, *Ginger Snaps* and *Cube*,[6] the troubled schoolgirl so effectively disfigures the cultural treasures of the suburban home and school that she configures a "seismic shift"[7] in the semantic fields of the gender gap and civic melancholy. Embodying malaise, personifying it, she is both "scene" and "obscene" (against the established scene); she simultaneously compels and repels our gaze.

Canada in the 1990s: A Structure of Feeling

Canada is commonly assumed to be a vast emptiness, an "area" sparsely populated where native peoples still hunt and fish over harsh, endless tracts of tundra while a few million transplanted Europeans cling as closely as possible to the American (a.k.a. "civilized") border. Although there is a grain of truth in any misconception, this one does nothing to address the inner world of Canada's 25 million urbanites, an inner truth that I suggest is richly evoked in the horror genre.

Almost everyone in Canada is an immigrant or the son, daughter, or grandchild of an immigrant. Indeed, the majority is three-or-fewer-generations Canadian, our multiethnic identities (English Canadian, French Canadian, Irish Canadian, Chinese Canadian ...) constituted by strong memories of being strangers and of trying to fit/pitch in. Although Canada by and large strives for inclusivity (Canadians have never elected a Fascist government), its prime minister with the longest service (William Lyon MacKenzie King, twenty-two years) was an anti-Semite;[8] a "head tax" was imposed on Chinese immigrants in 1885 (the only ethnic group ever assessed a tax for entering Canada[9]); and Japanese Canadians were interned, their families broken up, and their properties confiscated in World War II.[10]

Now consider the political and social world of the 1990s not as outsiders saw Canada but as Canadians lived it. At the start of the decade the country's major newsmagazine carried the headline, "A Dark Horizon";[11] it was a reference to the destruction—largely attributable to European and American overfishing—of the stocks at the Grand Banks, once the major source of income for three of Canada's ten provinces. By mid-year, the misnamed Meech Lake Accord (so labeled because it aimed at constitutional reform to make Canada politically acceptable to Québec separatists) began its ill-fated journey that ended five years later in a referendum the separatists lost by less than one percent.[12] Amidst periodic announcements throughout the decade that job security was "a thing of the past," news broke that our Red Cross had been distributing tainted blood that resulted in at least 300 cases of AIDS; that despite our incredible wealth we have the second highest rate of child poverty (after the United States) in the industrialized nations; that Eaton's (our great national retailer of almost 130 years) was bankrupt; that Bre-X (the Alberta company that claimed the world's "largest gold find") defrauded investors of billions of dollars; that twenty-somethings Paul Bernardo and Karla Homolka (handsome University of Toronto graduate and pretty accountant-trainee/veterinary-clerk) tortured, raped, and murdered teenage girls including Homolka's own fifteen-year-old sister; and that Canada's fresh water—the one resource thought absolutely sovereign—was suddenly for sale to the United States (even as hundreds grew sick and many died from contaminated municipal water in Walkerton, Ontario).

As the new millennium gets underway, all but a very little bit of Canada's mineral and oil reserves are controlled by Americans, "free trade" apparently working nicely for the United States even as it puts duties on Canadian softwood lumber exports[13] and as the last vestiges of Canadian retail get "Wal-Marted." Last year Canada joined its best friend in the "war on terrorism," from which the only Canadian casualties in Afghanistan were caused by American "friendly fire."[14] There is unfortunate symmetry when the Canadian anthem is booed in Detroit at hockey and basketball games since both sports, by the bye, were invented by Canadians.[15] Earlier this year a focus group in California complained that Canadians who wear the maple leaf overseas are "anti-American."[16] This is a portrait of expectations upset at every turn—something is not just horribly wrong but constantly and always horribly wrong. Amidst the wonder and beauty and abundance, all hell is loose and demons dance; uncertainty is the only sure thing.

Thus when Jürgen Habermas compares advanced capitalism's "free-market democracy" with traditional cultures' religion and myth and observes that today's elected governments are legitimized by representing themselves as an effective speaker of the will of the people and a benevolent guarantor of equal opportunity for all, I think of Canada's curiously different "legitimation crisis." In Habermas's discussion, since guaranteeing equal opportunity is in fact beyond the capacity of government in advanced capitalism (the market is neither free nor open but is predicated on competition that necessitates that many lose so that a few can win), what governments really do is intervene as crisis managers so that the populace is appeased and remains motivated; when the government's work is seen as merely tactics and antics rather than coherent strategy and philosophy, legitimation is withdrawn.[17] Canada, it seems to me, does not fit exactly with Habermas's model because of our continuing legitimation crisis (even if it double peaked in 1969 when the Front de Libération du Québec conducted a bombing campaign in Montreal and in 1995 when Canada came within 50,000 votes of national disintegration).

Ninety percent of Canadians live within a hundred miles of the United States border,[18] so from the view of the population Canada is shaped very much like Chile, only on its side. It is almost deceptive to say we share a border with America—we *are* the border with America. The two countries are each other's largest trading partner ($1.4 billion in daily commerce), but Canadian political institutions, intrusive as they are, do not ensure sovereignty; economically (85 percent of Canada's exports go to the United States) and culturally (Canadians accused of various crimes have tried to take the Fifth), it all really happens "down there."[19] Instead of a focal point that shapes a collective Canadian identity, increasing regionalism and lockstepped decentralization of federal power render more elusive the concept of "nationhood" north of the 49th Parallel; even our capital is situated geographically between the economically dominant provinces of Ontario and Québec, and the government of Canada insists that all who work there be equally conversant in English and French, the country's two official languages, inadvertently fashioning an entire social class unable and unwilling to identify with either the Francophone separatists or the Anglophone federalists.

Add to that the harsh conditions that prevail for most of the country (the thin northern soil, the long and relentless winters) and it can be understood why Canadians have a tentative view of all of life, including its political aspects: the crops and livestock might make it this year if the rain/sun comes early enough, is enough, but not too much; commerce that depends on crops, timber, and fishing suffers and all but invariably fails when the climate fails. Ennui and anxiety are as persistent as the northern blackfly in the summer woods. Furthermore, while Canada is in no way immune to the ill effects of patriarchy, its form of the disease is more insidious than blatant. Despite considerable battlefield accomplishments Canadians tend to celebrate the fallen, regarding fathers first as sons and brothers who can lay claim to heroism only in acts of death or other sacrifice. Lucien Bouchard, Québec premier (1996–2001) and founding chairman of the separatist Bloc Québecois, is famously reported for saying that "Canada isn't even a real country"; he was thereafter denounced for cutting too near the bone. On the other hand, Jean Chrétien, Québec native, federalist, Bouchard's political rival, and Canada's prime minister from 1993 to 2003, is purported to speak neither official language . . . or so the popular joke goes.

My point is that Canadian fathers do not resemble the cinematic patriarchs who incited Feminist Film Theory some decades ago. In a contemporary Canada of legitimation crisis in paternalism and nationhood, new theory is needed to illuminate our filmic representations of gender and social malaise. As a recurrent figure in our recent cinematic landscape, the schoolgirl embodies cultural as well as civic dis-ease, placed as she is at the emotional center of the feminine social where patriarchy is seen (for what it is) but not heard (not listened to). What kind of "snapping" is required for her to "progress through the ranks" from Girl to Woman?

Cube

A man is diced—as in sliced and diced—by a wire trap. Another is sprayed by acid that dissolves his face. Five more people are trapped inside a gigantic cube composed of thousands of fourteen-foot cubes stacked twenty-six high, deep, and wide—to a total of 17,576 rooms, to be exact—out of which they must find an exit before they starve, dehydrate, die of exhaustion, or are stabbed, sliced, disintegrated, or pulverized by one of the thousands of traps laced liberally throughout. And, needless to say, these five people, each with unique talents, do not get along.

Such is the world of *Cube* and, although the film did very little business during its theatrical release in its native Canada, there is something hauntingly familiar about this unreal world.[20] The plot is straightforward—this happens, this happens, then that; but there is also much discussion (paranoid, self-blaming, speculative, and otherwise) about what the cube actually is and what it means. The story ultimately distills to a survival theme but since the fight is to survive a situation that cannot be survived, it is both existential in its concern and romantic in its action.[21]

The characters are shocked to wake up in the Cube, somehow deposited there in the night; they don't know one another or why they are there or how to get out. Leaven (Nicole deBoer), the schoolgirl, cries out for help and thereby inaugurates the elements of relationships in *Cube*. Quentin (Maurice Dean Wint) hugs and quiets her ("It's okay; calm down") and tries to establish order—it turns out he is a policeman and, as such, he assumes the powers of leadership and makes claims to an ability to read people, to know their special and hidden abilities, to require their attention, and to expect compliance with his decisions. We gradually see that they each have some aspect of personality that brings them collectively closer to escape. Most obviously placed is Rennes (Wayne Robson), a famous French criminal who has escaped seven penitentiaries. He quickly becomes the de facto leader, and his presence leads us to two assumptions that shape the remainder of the film: that the Cube is a prison, and that it can be escaped. But Rennes is killed almost at once, his face eaten by acid sprayed by the monster machine, his capabilities in no way measuring up to the Byzantine complexities that underpin the Cube.

Leaven suggests they stay put, but she is ignored. She may be scared ("I just want to wake up!") and she may be naïve ("They have to feed us, don't they?"), but when her ability to identify prime numbers means she can tell if a room is booby trapped, she steps forward to lead the prisoners. Although she characterizes herself as someone who does "nothing"— "I just go to school; I hang out with my friends; my parents are these people I live with; I'm boring"—she gives the others their first mental image of the monstrous belly they are in as well as a safe way to move through it toward redemption. Later, she comes to recognize the Cartesian coordinates in the room numbers and thereby calculate the inner dimensions of the Cube; she determines that they are seven rooms "from the edge." As her name suggests, Leaven is the one who makes all the other parts work together. All this, of course, is the stuff of fantasy and blatant wish fulfillment: every self-absorbed teenage life out there is the hero of her own drama and Leaven is just another expression of that; but, significantly, she exceeds and therein disrupts the exhaustively standard Hollywood version in which a female matters as a body on display—as a "Pretty Baby" or "Pretty Woman"—instead of as a thinking person. In fact, Leaven rejects Quentin's proposed flattery when she corrects him about her mathematical aptitude: "It's not a gift; it's just a brain." In this way she refuses the manipulative relationship that gives power to the flattering man at the same time that she rebuffs the sexist stereotype that "girls can't do maths" (unless they're especially gifted).

Helen Holloway (Nicky Guadagni) is a middle-aged, educated, socially conscientious, free-clinic doctor and anti-government conspiracy theorist, lonely mother-figure liberal who is apparently mostly useless in this situation. She both decries that "only the government can build something this ugly" and pleads "I want to know who is responsible for this!" The scientist in her informs the others that they can last for three days without food and water; the sinner in her agonizes, "Are we being punished?" She longs for a cigarette though she "quit years ago." But however contradictory, however ambivalent, pessimistic, or paranoid, Holloway is sure about one thing: she never writes off but instead, repeatedly and compassionately protects the autistic Kazan (Andrew Miller) from the coldhearted calculations of Quentin and the indifference of the others.

Kazan, as it turns out, is the savant capable of solving the most important riddles of the Cube: when Leaven discovers that it is not a prime room number but the primes in that room number's factors that indicate the safe status of a room, Kazan is the only one who can factor to such high powers. In this way he proves—even more than does Leaven— the value of what is not obvious.

We find out that one of the men actually had a hand in designing the Cube but without knowledge of its owner or location or the slightest comprehension of its overall plan or purpose. Because of his "who cares" and "why bother" attitude, David Worth (David Hewlett) is at first considered pretty much worthless and is an early target of the soon-to-be crazed and murderous Quentin. Eventually, this seemingly cynical man proves worthy as he does his best to protect Leaven and Kazan from

Quentin, who is rapidly going mad and out of control. This too is a fantasy fulfillment of all the cynical twenty- and early-thirty-somethings out there: in the end they are really all right—that is, given the circumstances or opportunities, they would come through.

Steven Jay Schneider has shown that "the overwhelming majority of horror film monsters turn out to be . . . metaphorical embodiments of paradigmatic uncanny narratives."[22] In *Cube*, Quentin is the personification of authority-as-evil. Functionally, he works very much like just another of the Cube's booby traps, but he is human and so in the end many times deadlier than any of the macabre inventions that kill mechanically. Ultimately, Quentin's betrayal of the others is much worse than that of the Cube people who entrap them because, whoever they are, they are the faceless, ruthless powers that oversee the world without seeing its people, whereas Quentin owes an infinite responsibility to his companions. By acting as the Cube does, he identifies not with the human faces around him but with the irresponsible authority that made the Cube and put them in it—he identifies with barbarism. He is actively murderous (as opposed to the Cube's passive capabilities) and he racks up a much higher body count. Quentin is emblematic of patriarchy, rape, domestic abuse, the law, and, most poignantly, the Freudian maxim that the judge is only a sublimated executioner. In the end, he represents also the human capacity to destroy itself.

Together they make a useful and effective society—if they work and stay with one another and show compassion for the slow and the weak, as exemplified by Holloway's treatment of Kazan. But respectful cooperation is not forthcoming and all but one of them die in the Cube. It seems that experience (Rennes), insight (Holloway), practical (Worth) and academic (Leaven) knowledge, physical dominance and authority (Quentin) can never be complete or enough on their own. Rennes, though an "escape artist," is caught and exterminated by a trap. Despite her critical savvy about "the government," "the military-industrial complex," "the police," and society at large, despite being right most of the time and always fighting the good fight, despite her courage and compassion, Holloway ends up dead too because she trusted her companion inmates, even her murderer, Quentin, whom she had already surmised is a "Nazi," a wife beater, and child abuser. Worth, though knowing of the Cube because he built part of it, is nevertheless also its victim because he doesn't know about people (in particular, Quentin). Leaven, though having learned enough to understand and navigate the Cube because she is both educated and talented, also never gets out because her compassion for Worth allows Quentin to catch up to and kill both of them. Even Quentin, who is the law personified, becomes so feared and hated that he, too, is killed in the Cube. Nobody escapes, nobody wins . . . except Kazan. In the end, when Kazan runs out of the Cube alone into the light, he takes on the poetic value of the blind fool walking the edge of the cliff top at the end of Akira Kurosawa's *Ran* (1985). He is saved for nothing—because he knows and is nothing, and because nothing is out there, for all we can see. Kazan gets out, but it is by no means clear what "out" means. There is a sense that it makes little difference: given his autism, his escape from the Cube is simply the removal of a redundancy—he is still imprisoned, which is perhaps why he can escape.

Near the end, Leaven realizes that because the rooms themselves travel through the Cube, she and the others should have simply stayed right where they initially awoke, until that "entrance room" returned to its original position that connected to the outside world. Of course she did suggest this from the very beginning but the grownups—the cop, the doctor, the technician, and the ex-con—paid no attention to the schoolgirl. The temptation to which they all succumbed against Leaven's appeal is to do something, anything. The axiom for them, as for all Canadians, is this: once danger is kept at bay, once safety is ensured (in the film: once they can use the clue of the prime numbers to determine the trap-free rooms), they must act, take a step (go into the next safe room); and this pattern must be repeated if life is to go on. They cannot simply do nothing; they must do something, take small steps, even if, in the end, the strife will most likely lead to nothing and make no difference.

The inhospitable environment, the persistent effort, the eternal anxiety—these are familiar experiences in a nation populated by immigrants and the children of immigrants. The feeling is always there—of not quite fitting in, and everyone knowing something but not enough. Disaster lurks, or is expected, around the corner, but small careful efforts must nevertheless be made because the alternative—albeit perhaps only a collective anxiety, a waking nightmare—is that the land will take back everything, the landscape will swallow us up.[23] As we have seen in *Cube* and will see even more intensely in *Ginger Snaps*, this perpetual insecurity is made acute by the schoolgirl, whose presence is charged with strong desires and fraught with hidden dangers; we want to watch out for her but

Into the light at the end
of *Cube* (1997)

we will always be too late to save her from unexpected perils hidden in the terrains that remain stubbornly indifferent to human occupation.

Ginger Snaps

Ginger Snaps tells the story of two sisters, fifteen-year-old Brigitte (Emily Perkins) and sixteen-year-old Ginger (Katharine Isabelle), whose emotional and philosophical intimacy equips them, however precariously, to deal with the cheerleading, obsessive fashion-showing, and compulsive heterosexing high school culture that only leaves them feeling isolated and alienated. Brigitte's evaluation of high school is that she'd "rather wait it out in [their] room." At home, they are so acutely aware of the seams of suburbia that they are bored rather than embarrassed (a more typical adolescent reaction) by an idiotic mother and an irrelevant "henpecked" father; in Freudian terms, the sisters consider both parents castrated, and they desire neither for identification or as love object. Brigitte to Ginger: "I hate our gene pool."

Scorned by the other girls at school and mistaken by their mother as restless "tweens" awaiting womanhood, the Fitzgerald sisters are misfits and misanthropes whose only defense is a suicide pact ("out by sixteen or dead in the scene") and whose singular hobby is staging and photographing grotesque and even slightly ridiculous suicide scenes (which they endlessly discuss with deadly seriousness); imagining violent death is their best access to life. We will remember that Hamlet contemplated ending his life and, arguably, from just such contemplation found the will to act and to live fiercely; Harry Haller in Hermann Hesse's *Steppenwolf* strikes a pact with himself to find life worth living by his fiftieth birthday or to end it; one of the protagonists in Jean Paul Sartre's first volume of *The Roads to Freedom* strikes on the same idea: to know why to live by twenty-five or not to live at all. Their pacts with death—their contemplation of and negotiation with self-slaughter—give them psychical space and time in which to act fully and to live. So it is with Ginger and Brigitte who, against the normative scene, create an ob-scene, a world that flagrantly contains death; in this way, they begin a private world in which they too can live.

Roaming the neighborhood, meanwhile, is an unseen beast who butchers family pets, causing terror in one household after another. One night at the edge of the woods, the sisters find the dismembered remains of a dog; almost at the same moment Ginger sees (menstrual) blood run down the inside of her thigh and seconds later she is attacked by the beast. As Ginger gradually turns into a werewolf, her appetite for killing (which she initially mistakes as hunger for sex) becomes insatiable. Brigitte studies up on lycanthropy in the hope of finding a cure, but Ginger has turned too fast (*snapped!*) and cannot be saved.

Ginger Snaps is about the problem of time (Brigitte: "You said you'd die with me, because you have nothing better to do") or, more precisely, of timing (Ginger: "Poor B, I'm growing up and obviously you're not, huh?"). As the film begins, the sisters are "late" in getting their periods . . . but for the "wrong reason"—they are not pregnant out of wedlock (that indiscretion would at least make them "normal"); they have simply remained "girls" for too long. The result is that they have grown too closely bound to each other in a feminine social that they have created and that they constitute by themselves to the exclusion of everyone and especially of that "third term" so much privileged elsewhere—boys. However, once Ginger starts menses, the sisters lose their synchronicity and Brigitte fails to safekeep her older sister from the technologies of gender; Ginger is snapped up by the socio-sexual imperatives that take over with a vengeance.

The allegory is obvious, as menstruation, pubescent hormones, and adolescent ambivalences take shape in the beast that overcomes Ginger, who is both excited and confused by her transformations. In fact the metaphorical intentions of *Ginger Snaps'* authors are clear in a number of interviews in which director John Fawcett and screenwriter Karen Walton discuss the "new appetites" and "atrocities" of adolescence and explain that they wanted to make a "smart horror film" that had "purpose" and "meaning."[24] But I want to suggest more, to pay attention not only to the consciously intended but also to the film's unconscious: first, in its invitation to cheer as well as to fear the newly powerful Ginger, the film stages and encapsulates a structure of feeling that we might recognize as a familiar "Canadian ambivalence" toward power and success, and second, a different—strategic—allegorical reading can illuminate another set of realistic apprehensions chronicled in the film (this time through the trials of Brigitte): the pain of being left behind.

Daughters

Mothers lose their daughters to school—to logocentric patriarchy and scientific misogyny; fathers lose them there too—to patristic teachers and feminine secrets. The stakes are different, but high in both cases.

Confronting too suddenly her unspeakable strangeness—*Je est un autre!*—Ginger fares no better than Gregor Samsa in Kafka's *The Metamorphosis* (1915) or Rose in David Cronenberg's *Rabid* (1976): like Samsa, Ginger is cut off from humanity while still surrounded by family, and like Rose, she can only obey the absolute laws of hunger (for human blood) even though it means she infects and destroys others.[25] But whereas Samsa can only struggle through impotent self-awareness toward dusty death and Rose is horrified by the monstrosity of her new appetite, our schoolgirl is released; she tells her sister: "I'm a goddamn force of nature and I feel like I can do anything!" Ginger is Agave, the Bacchant who returns from the hills bouncing her son's head in her hands and seeing only the glory, the life fulfilled, freed in her bloody deeds.[26] For Ginger, to be herself—her new self—is to be apart, separate, but the glory of the transformation is too complete: her new self is too much better for her to want it otherwise. That death is the price makes death a bargain because life before was not life at all. In fact, the blood that transforms Ginger is not only that of menses, which is discarded dead blood and, as such, is not enough. Ginger needs to spill living blood as well; she must give herself to murder and mayhem and the absolute berserking release that rends limbs from bodies and at once blots out the life that denies living—destruction so absolute and furious that it is almost an act of creation, the making of a brave new world.

This is the condition to which Ginger ascends when she enacts her orgiastic killings: "It feels so good, Brigitte; it's like touching yourself—you know every move, right on the fucking dot, and after, you see fucking fireworks, supernovas!" Against Western culture's stereotypes of woman as whore, waif, or wife[27]—or in the old Ginger's words, "a girl can only be a slut, bitch, tease, or the virgin next door"—the new Ginger refuses the high school misogynist logic that "he got laid; I'm just a lay." Instead, she chooses to be what Helen Haste in *The Sexual Metaphor* calls a witch: "The witch has autonomous sexuality and makes demands on men. They do not have power over her. . . . The witch does not have only sexual power; she has social power, and she also has magical power."[28] Ginger is the daughter of our dreams turned to nightmare: we celebrate her and want her to win, to be all that she can be, all that our docile selves are not; but when this happens, when she becomes the power that cannot be stopped, we fear her even as we fear for her. We imagine a new Ginger but we are more comfortable with the old. As much as we want her to catch flame and burn so brightly that she consumes the wax of a thousand lives, we want her to go back to just smoldering. This unmatched power that is joined to pleasure by Ginger's exact metaphor of masturbation suggests too strongly the Canadian ambivalence toward pleasure and power: we want it but we're embarrassed by it; we want to get ahead but not be noticed too much for doing so; we want change but not a revolution.[29] Thus, we obsessively frame her within horror, where she is the emotional center—our thrill, our schoolgirl, and our monster. She is double edged and twice lost. What is there for her to do once Sleeping Beauty awakens from a sleep outside of which dragons and monsters have raged in fiery excess all around her, if not to go back to sleep if she is to "live happily ever after?" The Canadian dream is to go—unremarkably—on.

Sisters

Ginger Snaps uses cinematic conventions of horror even before the opening credits and film title: four still shots of a suburb and its roadside sign (Bailey Downs) lead to a low (knee-height) tracking shot that suggests something is moving urgently toward the suburb; in a backyard, similar low tracking shots approach from behind a woman raking leaves and a toddler playing in a sandbox. Then, in front of and in close-up, facing the toddler whose back is to his mother, we see he is puzzled by something that has smeared his hand; he looks at it, brings it to his nose to smell, then (to our further dismay) smears it on his face; we see that it is blood. From the background the mother begins to approach with a smile for her child—she doesn't see what we see. This "looking triangle" repeats the scene in Rupert Julian's *The Phantom of the Opera* (1925) in which we see the Phantom's unmasked face before Christine (Mary Philbin) does (she is the young opera singer seduced by his voice, heard through the walls of her dressing room). Linda Williams has famously suggested that our "belated adoption" of Christine's point of view undermines the typical audience identification and sympathy with her, permitting instead our sympathy for the Phantom as well as an identification between "the two objects of the cinematic spectacle who encounter one another in the look—the woman and the monster."[30] A similar relational triangle is established in *Ginger Snaps*, beginning with the backyard scene in which we are permitted to see and sympathize with the bloody child before his mother gets her view. Later and throughout the film, we understand the monstrous troubles of Ginger and Brigitte while Pam Fitzgerald (Mimi Rogers) remains their all-*un*knowing mother . . . until she is ready—quite late in the game—to really look. In this way, the opening scene is a concise visual metaphor for the maternal ignorance that will underpin the schoolgirl-sisters' intimate bond and ultimate conviction that they have only each other and no one else.

The film is titled *Ginger Snaps* but Ginger is only half the story. This is also the story of Brigitte, the only protagonist—Ginger included—who sees everything that goes on and fights all comers. Brigitte alone never gives in or up; she is on the side of her big sister, even when she is against her to be with her. Following Lucy Fischer's suggestion that there is "realism in the bizarre" when she examines *Rosemary's Baby* as a "'skewed documentary' of the societal and personal turmoil that has regularly attended female reproduction"[31] rather than just a fantastical story without reference to or relevance for pregnant women in real life, I propose that the psychological veracity in *Ginger Snaps* is the film's "expressionistic allegory" of the little sister's inevitable and yet private experience of losing her big sister when the latter's interests expand to a social circle beyond the home.

In fact, the emotional center of *Ginger Snaps* is not Ginger but, rather, her sister Brigitte, whose point of view we share and whose experience is chronicled in the film and explained in the title: it is to Brigitte and in Brigitte's view that Ginger has snapped. Before Ginger became an other, the sisters were one—not "connected at the waist" as their mother had complained, but very much "together forever" as we hear them declare over and over to each other. When a classmate deliberately knocks Brigitte down in a soccer game at school one afternoon, Ginger threatens, "Don't *ever* touch my sister again!" and she immediately comforts Brigitte, asking, "Want me to kill her? I'll kill her for you, B; anything you want!" Moments later, after a boy makes a pass at a minimally interested but mostly unfriendly Ginger, Brigitte makes her promise: "Say you won't go average on me; I'd rather *die* than be here without you." Later, as Brigitte realizes the problem and researches ways to reverse Ginger's beastly transformation, she pleads with her sister not to give up: "You give up now and you leave me here alone; I would *never* do that to you."

It is this union that puberty tears asunder, a separation that parallels that "immemorial violence" that Julia Kristeva calls the birthing of the child from the mother's womb.[32] We get the first clue when B asks, "Are you sure it's just cramps?" and Ginger snaps back, "Just so you know, the words 'just' and 'cramps'—they don't go together." Later, Brigitte insists and insists again: "Something's wrong; like, *more* than you just being female!" "This isn't you." "Something is definitely wrong with you."

That the separation is sickening and bloody is only extended metaphor. Each the other's only friend, together in a world apart, Ginger and Brigitte speak a private language. When Ginger's hunger becomes the only voice that she can hear, Brigitte loses everything—the past and the future—for out of situations and lives that were broken from the beginning, the girls made a life, fashioned an art form, and made meaning all their own. Together, their world had been one of perfect movement, of synchronicity and togetherness, of shared delight and simultaneous creation. Thus, when Sam (Kris Lemche), B's new boyfriend, urges her to take the werewolf antidote and flee with him, the choice is between entering alone a world that she does not know and has always found suspect, or staying with her sister in the room they always shared, in the world they imagined and imaged together. Brigitte's decision might lie in biology (in her changing body at the cusp of pubescence) or in sociology (in the call of compulsory heterosexual privilege), but she steps aside from both and chooses instead the familiar embrace of the sisters' childhood world, the only feelings of life that she has ever known. She flatly rejects Sam (now another irrelevant male) and rushes after Ginger with the vial.

There is much struggle at the house and Sam (who went along to help) is killed by Ginger whose beastly transformation is complete. In

Ginger's wolf side on
full display in *Ginger
Snaps* (2000)

their bedroom, with knife in one hand and the syringe of antidote in the other, Brigitte pleads: "Ginger, please! It's me!" In a final confrontation, she tells her older sister: "I'm not dying in this room with you! I'm not dying!" Ginger lunges at Brigitte on the bed and overpowers her, but then, suddenly, stops; Brigitte realizes her knife has stabbed the beast— whether instinctually on her part or suicidally on Ginger's is anyone's guess. Brigitte quickly backs away; she sees that the syringe in her other hand is still full. The beast doesn't move, lying on the ground breathing laboriously. The camera offers a close-up of B, who turns her eyes up to look at the photos taped on the wall—photos of their "suicide project," family snapshots of the sisters, a portrait of them smiling. Tears fill her eyes. She looks over at Ginger and makes a last—an everlasting?—choice: with the vial of antidote still unused at her side, she blankets her sister in an embrace; in a few moments, Ginger takes her last breath. We hear Brigitte's quiet sobs; a piano and a solo cello begin on the soundtrack.

As daughters become schoolgirls and big sisters become young women, mothers and little sisters are cast off and left behind. Ginger becomes a monster who reeks of human blood and torn flesh—kind of hyperbole of what every younger sister who loves and has been succored by her older sister knows or sadly must come to know.

What is also being suggested here is that an exact symbol has been found: not for the expressed concerns alone but also for the carefully repressed and pathologically unnamable that trip and bother the psyches of a nation that is "not a real nation," that can be secure in no fact—from ownership of the land, to sovereignty over the people, to control over the fish and the water and the healthcare that had once been there free and forever. Canada lives on the cusp, always on the verge of frightening and externally instigated change that occurs in spite of everything we do (or don't do). Canadians have no control over such things as the flag waving and war waging that are flaunted and taken for granted just over the border; we may do useful and necessary work in the world but, mostly, we "dispatch" to wherever our neighbor asks—as if Canada were the mobile auxiliary unit. This is why the schoolgirl—the Big Sister who cannot control the changes of her own flesh or her movement through time toward an adult world she at once fears, despairs of, and desires; and the Little Sister who must constantly watch what she most loves move away while she has no strength to stop it—has become our unconscious representative. We cheer/fear her as we mourn ourselves.

Notes

1. Raymond Williams, *The Sociology of Culture* (New York: Schocken, 1981), 48.
2. Julie Burchill, *Girls on Film* (London: Virgin, 1986), 13, 126. Burchill provides an acerbic, witty retrospective of female stars in American cinema.
3. Lucy Fischer offers an original and compelling reading of *Rosemary's Baby* as "an expressionistic allegory of the real" in which the societal and personal turmoil of pregnancy and birthing is no longer silenced or disavowed ("Birth Traumas: Parturition and Horror in *Rosemary's Baby*," in *The Dread of Difference: Gender and the Horror Film*, ed. Barry Keith Grant [Austin: University of Texas Press, 1996], 413).
4. "You can't win 'em all" and the shorter version "You can't win" are common catch-phrases in Canada; I have heard them all the way from the backwoods to the ivory tower. *A Dictionary of Catch Phrases* characterizes "you can't win" as a sense of futility about hoping to succeed or even to get something done. *American Heritage Dictionary of Idioms* explains that "you can't win" means "whatever one does is wrong or not enough," and "you can't win 'em all" means "success is not inevitable." Eric Partridge, *A Dictionary of Catch Phrases (British and American), From the Sixteenth Century to the Present Day* (London: Routledge and Kegan Paul, 1977; revised and augmented Second Edition, ed. Paul Beale, 1985). Christine Ammer, *American Heritage Dictionary of Idioms* (Boston: Houghton Mifflin, 1997).
5. Vivian Sobchack, "Bringing It All Back Home: Family Economy and Generic Exchange," in Grant, ed., *Dread of Difference*, 144.
6. The genres share plot elements and cross-fertilize and are by no means mutually exclusive, but I do treat *Cube* as horror rather than science fiction, primarily because of the film's critical attitudes toward the unknown (it threatens), curiosity (it endangers), science (it is inadequate), and "uncivilized desires" (they must be repressed/suppressed/expelled). *Cube* idolizes (even as it does not idealize) human community, and longs for a balanced professionalism (equal partnership between

the head and the heart); the film's eventual return to magic (the doctor, the technician, the mathematician, and the cop all die, while the prelinguistic idiot savant survives and walks into the light) ensures the survival of "paganism." Bruce Kawin convincingly illustrates in "The Mummy's Pool" that these are the familiar postures of the horror text rather than science fiction (*Dreamworks* 1, no. 4 [1981]). In the titular cube—which is a giant stomach, a gastrointestinal tract that breaks down life to blood, meat, and bone—curiosity only leads to more and faster deaths rather than to new knowledge; the deaths add up to nothing, solve nothing, prove nothing. *Cube* is the horror film that can be likened, following Kawin, to a nightmare or an anxiety dream; the monster is the inhumanity of science, technology, and the faceless corporation.

7. Dudley Andrew on the potential of figures, in *Concepts in Film Theory* (1984), quoted by Sobchack, "Bringing It All Back Home," 148.

8. King was Canada's tenth prime minister, serving three nonconsecutive periods between 1921 and 1948; he was also leader of the Liberal Party of Canada from 1919 to his retirement in 1948. In 1939, as prime minister, King turned away the *St. Louis,* a ship carrying more than 900 Jewish refugees from Europe; his response to urgent pleas for refuge was that it was not a Canadian problem. This is his diary entry from the previous year (March 29, 1938): "We must seek to keep this part of the continent free from unrest and from too great an admixture of foreign strains of bloods. I fear we would have riots if we agreed to a policy that admitted numbers of Jew." On display in Vancouver's Holocaust Education Centre as part of the exhibition (February to June, 2001) titled *Too Close to Home: Anti-Semitism and Nazism in Canada.*

9. In 1885—that is, at the completion of the Trans-Canada railway on which thousands of Chinese workers had labored (and died) along the most treacherous terrains (for wages substantially lower than their Caucasian counterparts, thereby saving the Canadian government an estimated $3 million dollars)—Canada imposed a $50 "head tax" on Chinese immigrants; the tax was increased to $100 in 1900 and to $500 in 1904 (*The Chinese Immigration Act*). Those who were unable to pay the taxes to bring their family members lived and died as "married bachelors." In contrast, during the same period European immigrants were given subsidies for their travel across the Atlantic as well as a quarter section of free land (160 acres) on their arrival (*Dominion Lands Act,* 1872).

10. Within days of Japan's attack on Pearl Harbor, over 1,000 Japanese Canadian fishing vessels were seized in Canada. By early 1942, both the Canadian and American governments removed all persons of Japanese ancestry living along the West Coast to inland isolated towns and camps. In Canada, about 22,000 were relocated under the *War Measures Act;* in the United States approximately 110,000 were relocated under the *War Relocation Authority.* Canada initially sent the men to road camps in the British Columbia interior, to sugar beet plantations in the Prairies, and to internment in POW camps in Ontario, while Japanese Canadian women and children were moved to six inland British Columbia towns created or revived to house them. The living conditions were so horrendous that the citizens in wartime Japan sent them supplemental food shipments through the Red Cross!

11. "A Dark Horizon," *MacLean's,* January 1990. Unless otherwise noted, subsequent news citations are from *MacLean's,* 1990–2000.

12. On October 30, 1995, about six in ten francophone Québecois voted to secede from Canada, but they represented ("only") 49.4 percent of the total number of votes cast and so lost the sovereignty referendum.

13. Dispute between the United States and Canada over the softwood lumber trade dates back several decades, but since the 1980s an American "Coalition for Fair Lumber Imports" petitioned the U.S. Department of Commerce to accuse Canada of injuring its neighbor's softwood industry by charging inappropriately low stumpage fees. The U.S. Department of Commerce investigated and concluded in 1983 that no countervailing duty was justified, but, pressured by senators from lumber-producing states, it imposed a series of import tariffs in 1986 (15 percent), 1992 (an additional 6.5 percent), 2001 (19.31 percent later reduced to 18.79 percent, then another 8.4 percent added that fall), and 2002 (27.4 percent). In response to Canada's petitions for an objective ruling guided by the Free Trade Agreement (FTA), the North American Free Trade Agreement (NAFTA), and the Generation Agreement on Tariffs and Trade (GATT), the binational FTA panels (in 1994), the U.S. International Trade Commission (in 2001 though not the following year), the trinational NAFTA panels (in 2003) and the World Trade Organization (in 2001 and again in 2003) all ruled that the tariffs were unjustified and must be refunded. In December 2003, an agreement was proposed by the Americans that would eliminate the current 27.4 percent tariff if Canada withdraws (i.e., not just suspends) its complaints to the trade tribunals, if a quota is observed by Canadian exporters, and if almost half of the USD $1.6 billion collected in tariffs is retained by American lumber companies and remains exempt from refund. Unchanged is the age-old demand by the United States that full access to the American softwood market requires Canada to abandon its forest management practice of leasing Crown land for stumpage fees and adopt, instead, the American system of market auctions for timber rights. This "surrender of forest-management control to the U.S. Dept. of Commerce" (Don Whiteley, "Fate of Proposed Softwood Pact Murkier Than Ever," *Vancouver Sun*, December 17, 2003, D3) "will mean the triumph of private bullying by the U.S. lumber lobby, deploying the full weight of U.S. trade law" (Mary Janigan, "Bullies in the Woods," *Maclean's*, December 24, 2001, 58). Even within the United States, opinions are divided. For example, consumer groups such as the U.S. National Association of Home Builders and the U.S. Real Estate Association oppose the high tariffs that they calculate would cost them tens of thousands of jobs. For a sampling of Canadian reactions, see news coverage by the Canadian Broadcasting Corporation archived online at http://archives.cbc.ca, accessed September 5, 2003.

14. Eight Canadians soldiers were wounded and four were killed when two U.S. fighter pilots hopped up on amphetamines dropped a 500-pound bomb on the Canadian troops conducting combat exercises near Kandahar on April 17, 2002. If convicted in a court-martial on four counts of manslaughter, eight counts of assault, and dereliction of duty (failure to exercise appropriate flight discipline and to comply with the rules of engagement), the pilots faced up to sixty-four years in prison. But the hearing officer investigating the charges concluded that although there is sufficient evidence for court-martial, administrative discipline would "adequately address . . . the interests of good order and discipline." Thus, sanctions were recommended to the court-martial convening authority who subsequently imposed

on the two pilots a forfeiture of one month's pay, confinement to quarters for one month, and restriction on travel for two months ("Friendly Fire Hearing Officer Recommends against Courts-Martial," *Air Force Link News*, March 20, 2003). But all's well that ends well: on December 15, 2003, the four deceased were awarded the American Bronze Star medals posthumously, presented to their widows by Paul Cellucci, U.S. Ambassador to Canada ("Bronze Stars Presented to Friendly Fire Victims' Kin," *Vancouver Sun*, December 10, 2003).

15. Canadian James Naismith invented and named basketball in 1891. Hockey as we know it today was first played in 1875 in Montreal, Québec, according to rules devised by J. G. A. Creighton, a student at McGill University.

16. This was briefly but multiply reported in Canadian media from coast to coast. See, for example, "Best Friend of the US, but Still an Independent Country," *Vancouver Sun*, December 16, 2003, A14.

17. Jürgen Habermas, *Legitimation Crisis*, trans. Thomas McCarthy (London: Heinemann, 1973), 68–92.

18. This is a well-known fact in Canada, but readers unfamiliar with it can obtain additional statistics and view a population distribution map online at http://www.canadainfolink.ca/popareas.gif, accessed September 6, 2003. The remaining 10 percent of the population, or 3 million Canadians, live somewhere north of that 100-mile border zone, in the 3.5 million square miles of prairie, forest, Arctic tundra, and islands that comprise the remaining 99 percent of Canada's landmass. In contrast to Canadians' proximity to the border (the largest border in the world between two countries, with roughly 4,000 miles horizontally bisecting North America and another 1,500 miles separating Alaska from British Columbia and the Yukon), only 10 percent of Americans live within 100 miles of it (although that 10 percent already equals 29 million in headcount, equivalent to 90 percent of Canada's total population).

19. *Maclean's* reported in December 2001, that Canada's then finance minister (now prime minister) Paul Martin was "still aiming to keep the books balanced, but only if a United States recovery begins by the middle of 2002 . . . pulling Canada's export-based economy up along with it" (John Geddes and Julian Beltrame, "Uncertain Times," *Maclean's*, December 24, 2001, 52).

20. Story and direction by Vincenzo Natali (who grew up in Toronto and refers to himself as a Torontonian); screenplay by Andre Bijelec, Graeme Manson, and Natali. Produced on a budget of only CAD $300,000, its impressive critical acclaim includes the City TV Award for Best Canadian First Feature Film at the 1997 Toronto International Film Festival, the Audience Prize, Critics Prize, as well as the Grand Prize at the 1999 Gerardmer International Fantasy Film Festival in France (the first time all three prizes have been won by one film), an invitation screening at the 1998 Sundance Film Festival followed by the Berlin International Film Festival and the Edinburgh International Film Festival. In Europe—especially in France where the box-office intake was $10.3 million—*Cube* achieved commercial as well as critical success. A sequel (*Cube 2: Hypercube*) was released in 2002, directed by Andrzej Sekula (famed cinematographer of *Reservoir Dogs* [1992], *Pulp Fiction* [1994], and *American Psycho* [2000]).

21. *Cube* did best in France, which is of course the most fertile soil in which existentialism ever grew and which gave the world absurdist theater, especially those plays of the 1950s and 1960s by Jean Paul Sartre, Samuel Beckett, and Eugène Ionesco. *Cube* is a direct descendant. Alex Comfort (*Art and Social Responsibility: Lectures on the Ideology of Romanticism* [London: Falcon Press, 1946]) defined romanticism as the fight against Death and all those who align themselves with Death and Barbarism; he was a conscientious objector in World War II.

22. Steven Jay Schneider, "Monsters as (Uncanny) Metaphors: Freud, Lakoff, and the Representation of Monstrosity in Cinematic Horror," in *Horror Film Reader,* ed. Alain Silver and James Ursini (New York: Limelight Editions, 2000), 174.

23. Margaret Atwood, whose writings are translated into more than twenty languages and read in many parts of the world, is Canada's prolific novelist, poet, cultural critic, literary theorist, and doyenne of Canadian literature. In "Death by Landscape," she told a story in which a girl who went behind a tree to relieve her bladder forever disappeared into the Canadian bush. The short story was first published in 1989 in *Saturday Night* (July 1989) and then the following year in *Harper's* (August 1990), and is reprinted in several collections, including Atwood's own *Wilderness Tips* (New York: Doubleday, 1991).

24. Interview conducted by *Rue Morgue Magazine* at the completion of shooting in late 2000, reprinted online at http://www.ginger-snaps.com/interview.htm, accessed September 5, 2003. The success of the metaphor can be seen in reviews that characterize the film as a "post-*Buffy* riff on the horrors of adolescence" (Nicole Armour, *Film Comment* [November 2000]: 18) or call attention to the pairing of "entry to womanhood" with "bloodlust and violence" (Linda Ruth Williams, *Sight and Sound* [June 2001]: 36). There are strong similarities to teenage horror movies such as *Carrie* (1976), *I Was a Teenage Werewolf* (1957), and *Teen Wolf* (1985), but *Ginger Snaps* is more than a "puberty horror," as I will show.

25. I borrow *Je est un autre* (trans. "I is an other") from Arthur Rimbaud's letter to Georges Izambard, as it describes perfectly how Ginger initially experiences and apprehends her changed self. Arthur Rimbaud, *Lettres du voyant*, May 1871.

26. Agave, "frenzied, blood-stained, with [her son] Pentheus' head on her thyrsus," calls to the Bacchants: "I bring to our halls from the mountains a tendril newly cut. Happy was the hunting. . . . Without a noose I snared it—the young whelp of a savage lion. . . . Do you praise me?" Euripides, "The Bacchants," in *Euripides: Ten Plays* (New York: Bantam, 1960), 307.

27. Helen Haste discusses four Western images of women and sexual power: woman as *whore* is seductive and available to men's pleasures and powers, woman as *waif* is sexually responsive but vulnerable and dependent on men, woman as *wife* is sexless and a "faithful helpmate" to men, and woman as *witch* is "mystifying and incomprehensible to men" (*The Sexual Metaphor* [Cambridge: Harvard University Press, 1994], 172–73).

28. Ibid., 173.

29. Canadian rising star Sarah Polley (*The Sweet Hereafter* [1997], *Guinevere* [1999], etc.) turned down the role of Ginger, and casting directors in Toronto refused to work for the film because the material was "too graphic"; casting eventually took

place in Vancouver. Furthermore, the Toronto Board of Education uncharacteristically withheld permission to film in its schools, leaving Fawcett to shoot outside of Toronto in Brampton, Markham, and Mississauga (Louis B. Hobson, "Director Sinks Fangs into 'Chick Werewolf Flick,'" *Calgary Sun,* May 8, 2001). However, since the film's successful run in Canada, enthusiastic responses in Britain, Hong Kong (where it ranked third for box-office intake), and other overseas markets, and following astonishing DVD sales, plans for two sequels were confirmed (Louis B. Hobson, "Snappy Sequels Soon," *Calgary Sun,* April 1, 2002). Fawcett is unavailable to direct but he executive-produces while Brett Sullivan who edited *Ginger Snaps* directs; shooting began in the winter of 2003; the films—*Ginger Snaps II: Unleashed,* the sequel, and *Ginger Snaps 3,* the prequel—will be released successively in the winter and the spring of 2004.

30. Linda Williams, "When the Woman Looks," in Grant, ed., *Dread of Difference,* 20–21.

31. Fischer, "Birth Traumas," 413.

32. Julia Kristeva, *Powers of Horror: An Essay on Abjection,* trans. Leon S. Roudiez (New York: Columbia University Press, 1982), 15.

IV

CONTESTED HORROR TRADITIONS

14

Beyond the Genre Formula:

IMPLICIT HORROR IN THE FILMS
OF JAN ŠVANKMAJER

Jan Uhde

The Czech animator and visual artist Jan Švankmajer (b. 1934) is without exaggeration one of the most accomplished film artists working today. The influential French film journal *Positif* considers him, together with the distinguished Russian animator Yuri Norstein (*Tale of Tales,* 1979), "a giant of contemporary film."[1] Czech film historian Jan Poš sees his work as "revolutionary."[2] And British film critic Julian Petley calls him, along with the Polish-born directors Jan Lenica and Walerian Borowczyk, "one of the key animators to have emerged in Eastern Europe since the war."[3] His work has influenced other filmmakers, such as the British-based American expatriates, the Quay Brothers,[4] and Tim Burton. In 1997, the Czech animator, a recipient of over forty international prizes and awards, was honored with the Persistence of Vision Award for his lifetime work at the San Francisco Festival. On receiving the prize, Švankmajer remarked: "Artists should receive awards at least 100 years after their deaths, but in such a state of decomposition how could they hold them?"

Under the Totalitarian Regime

Yet Švankmajer is little known internationally, although this is slowly changing. There are a number of reasons for his relative obscurity. The director has mainly worked in animated short film production, an area that has been marginalized by the existing international distribution system. In addition, Švankmajer has always been an independent filmmaker reluctant to compromise his unique and complex artistic vision—either for the totalitarian regime of the former Czechoslovakia or for the market economy of the present-day Czech Republic.

The artist's penchant for the dark, the bizarre, and the grotesque, his veiled political comments, and his formalistic style linked to the officially denounced surrealism were undesirable in an era that required filmmakers to conform to an artistic style known as socialist realism, which was really nothing more than an old Hollywood formula with a socialist label. Although Švankmajer was never prohibited from filmmaking in his country, his opportunities to shoot in Czech studios (the entire Czechoslovak film industry was state-run and state-controlled until the late 1980s) were severely restricted and he worked with considerable difficulties.[5] Several of his films were shelved and banned immediately after completion,[6] and a number of his scripts were not approved (some of these found their way into Švankmajer's post-1989 production).[7] This professional limbo in which he lived, together with the irrationality of repression and the mundane terror of bureaucratic caprice, have no doubt contributed to the artist's horror-laced irony and pessimism.

Paradoxically, the fact that Švankmajer was working in the relatively obscure and inexpensive domain of short film production may have saved him from the severe persecution that struck his more exposed colleagues in the feature film studios, especially during the post-invasion political crackdown of the 1970s.[8] His remarkable tenacity and creative thinking enabled him to occasionally outwit the regime's ideological watchdogs; these external pressures very likely helped him to sharpen his artistic tools—a familiar phenomenon replayed recently in Iranian cinema. Ironically, the traditional communist inefficiency that paralyzed the country's economy also weakened the regime's repressive system. Thus the director was able to work quietly on his animated shorts—but any publicity was out of the question.

The desire of the communist authorities to suppress Švankmajer's work was strangely mirrored in the West, which appeared to be quite oblivious to his existence. Although politically on the opposite side of the cold war fence, the "free world" was not interested in Švankmajer, as there was little financial gain for the big commercial players to be had from his type of cinema.

The Real and the Unreal

Aside from the bizarre, grotesque, monstrous, fantastic, surreal, and absurd, virtually all of Švankmajer's films involve horror. Not the explicit, direct, "physical" mainstream horror intended to produce terror and fear in the audience, so typical for the genre. Švankmajer's horror is sublime, implicit, sometimes even satirical, and its effects on the viewer are typically delayed.

Yet the films of the Czech animator are not targeted to the mainstream "general family" or children audience. This does not imply that children could not, or should not, watch them. But most of them would understand little of the philosophical aspect of these films, find a coherent plot and action missing, and in all likelihood be turned off by the more macabre elements.

To date, Švankmajer has worked mostly with 3-D animation and live action. Looking at production techniques, especially their technological aspect, the artist is stubbornly conservative. Švankmajer has always rejected advanced "state of the art" animation technologies—including computer animation that is, in most quarters, a very hot area today. He prefers to use ordinary household materials such as paper, wood, metal, glass, stone, clay, along with articles of everyday use, including fabric, puppets, dolls, figurines, and found objects. The Czech animator is fond of products from the early industrial age: crude mechanisms, primitive devices, and simple automatons manufactured from basic materials such as wood and fabric. The terms "crude" and "primitive," however, apply only when comparing their mechanical qualities with contemporary advanced technologies; in most other aspects these devices are examples of originality, ingenuity, and solid craftsmanship—some would even call them objects of art. The historical detachment, the curious oddity of these objects is well suited to strengthen the atmosphere of subtle horror Švankmajer likes to conjure.

The turning point in Švankmajer's professional career was the unprecedented success of his fifteen-minute 1983 triptych, *Dimensions of Dialogue* (*Moznosti dialogu*), generally considered to be his most accomplished work. This macabre allegory about communication and violence won the Grand Prix and FIPRESCI Prize[9] at the prestigious Animation Film Festival in Annecy, France, and a number of other distinguished prizes and awards, including the Golden Bear and Jury Award (short film category) at the Berlin Film Festival, Main Prize at the Sydney Film Festival, and several awards at the Melbourne Film Festival.

The suggestive gruesome imagery of this short is also an excellent example of the implicit horror favored by Švankmajer. The film involves three independent "stories" illustrating different kinds of flawed communication ending in violent confrontation. In the second story, titled "Passionate Dialogue," a male and a female head, both made of unbaked clay, engage in a passionate encounter. The result is a tiny clay "baby" who tries to cling to the one or the other but is rejected by both "parents," eventually triggering a mortal struggle ending in mutual destruction.

Švankmajer's first feature film was *Alice* (*Něco z Alenky*, 1987), winner of the Best Film Prize in the Animated Feature category at Annecy. *Alice* presented to the English-speaking world the familiar and widely cherished subject of Lewis Carroll's book, albeit through Švankmajer's unfamiliar, dark vision.[10] After *Alice*, the director made three more features with macabre themes: *Faust* (*Lekce Faust*, 1994), *Conspirators of Pleasure* (*Spiklenci slasti*, 1996), and *Little Otik* (*Otesánek*, 2000). This shift from the director's earlier focus on shorts signals a change in his philosophy, probably reflecting the fact that it is easier for feature-length movies to find their way to cinema screens around the world. His full-length films and some of the shorts have been released internationally, including in North America; in Asia, they have found positive reception mainly in Japan.

Švankmajer's gloomy subjects and mannerist techniques are unlikely to become blockbusters or prime-time television draws, but this has never been their creator's main intention. Looking realistically at the economic structure and priorities of existing global theatrical distribution and commercial television programming, independent films like those of Jan Švankmajer will, even in the future, remain consigned to the festival circuit, repertory cinemas, film societies, and "art television" channels. Nevertheless, the Czech animator has kept his freedom, shooting in his own animation studio converted from a defunct local cinema in the village of Knovíz, near Prague. Moreover, his films are now appearing on videotape, laserdiscs, and, more recently, on DVD. This new medium may become the most efficient means of delivering Švankmajer's remarkable film art to international audiences.

Švankmajer's signature appears to be a combination of animation and live action. "I don't like the cartoon and I prefer to place my imaginary world into reality," stresses the director.[11] This technique links him with the rich traditions of Czech folk puppetry of the seventeenth to nineteenth centuries,[12] as well as the post–World War II Czech puppet films and experimental animation of Karel Zeman (*An Invention for Destruction*, 1958; *The Fabulous Baron Münchhausen*, 1961) and Jiri Trnka (*A Midsummer Night's Dream*, 1958; *The Hand*, 1965).[13] Zeman's *The Invention for Destruction*, for example, based on the eponymous novel by the French nineteenth-century sci-fi writer Jules Verne, combines live actors with animated backgrounds recalling the period illustrations of Verne's books. However, Švankmajer's concept of the puppet film differs from that of both Zeman and Trnka; unlike the traditionally poetic-lyrical approach of these two artists, he explores the dark and the bizarre, the horror and the absurd.

In Švankmajer's early short *The Last Trick of Mr. Schwarcewalld and Mr. Edgar* (*Poslední trik pana Schwarcewalldea a pana Edgara*, 1964), the two main characters are live actors wearing large wooden masks covering their heads and shoulders: the person and the effigy blend together almost seamlessly. In *Punch and Judy* (*Rakvickárna*, 1966), two hand puppets share the stage with a live guinea pig; in *Don Juan* (*Don Šajn*, 1970), live actors are fitted with strings and special harnesses and trained to move mechanically so as to simulate life-size marionettes. In *Alice*, the little "live" heroine inhabits a fantastic world of animated images. Over the years, the artist has perfected this technique of mixing the real with the unreal, which has become an indispensable component of his oeuvre. In his recent films, especially the four features, the live-action element has become increasingly important.

This tendency was emphasized in Švankmajer's most recent (and longest) film, the 127-minute feature *Little Otik*, a contemporary horror-comedy based on a popular Czech fairytale in which live action clearly prevails over animated scenes. *Little Otik* is not the director's first film dominated by real-life action; he has used such an approach more than once before, including in the shorts *The Garden* (*Zahrada*, 1968), *The Flat/The Apartment* (*Byt*, 1968), and the "proto-*Alice*" short *Down to the Cellar* (*Do pivnice/Do sklepa*, 1983). In *The Garden*, for example, the director fuses a realistic story about a man visiting his friend's home with a fantasy epitomized by the presence of a "human fence" (a line of people stretched around the house and garden, imitating a fence with a gate). *Down to the Cellar* presents an almost documentary tale about a little girl sent to the cellar of her flat to bring up a basket of potatoes; only a small part of the film—the child's fears and fantasies—are animated.

The blending of reality with animation is achieved through editing, particularly the technique of rapid montage introduced by the avant-garde film. However, Švankmajer gives this technique his own spin by combining it with extreme close-ups.[14] In *The Garden*, the viewer is repeatedly assailed by extreme close-ups of the characters' body parts, for example, the Adam's apple. These fleeting inserts cause an otherwise harmless conversation to appear menacing and disquieting.[15] The viewer perceives these details as unnatural and expects something gruesome to happen—a technique frequently used in the horror genre. The juxtaposition of live images with animated action has become a characteristic element of Švankmajer's visual style, producing a disorienting and shocking

The White Rabbit
surrounded by some
skeleton friends in
Alice (1987)

effect on the audience. In *Dimensions of Dialogue*, for example, a clay head
sticks out its tongue, not one made of clay as one would expect, but a realistic, and scary, "flesh and blood" tongue instead.

   The satirical shorts *Virile Games* (*Muzné hry*, 1988) and *Food* (*Jídlo*,
1992) include violent demolitions of the characters' faces and body parts,
but it takes a moment before the viewer realizes that the live actor's face
has been swiftly replaced by a clay figure or paper cutout. The director
plays with audience expectations like a cat with a mouse: in *The Death of
Stalinism in Bohemia* (*Smrt stalinismu v Cechách*, 1990), a white gypsum
bust of Stalin is placed on an operating table; a scalpel slowly cuts into it
revealing *real* bowels within. A gloved hand reaches in and pulls something out of the bloody mass. A *real* umbilical cord shown in extreme
close-up is severed—but the object extracted out of this head/womb is
another gypsum bust, that of the Czech communist president of the Stalinist period (Klement Gottwald). It is carefully washed, placed upright on
a table, and given a slap, to which it replies with the cries of an *actual* baby.

More Horror and the Macabre

The alternation between animation and live action helps to create an
ambiguity between reality and fantasy. Sometimes Švankmajer will make
his human characters act like robots (for example in *Don Juan*) while

investing his inanimate objects with a considerable degree of anthropo-morphism. They create humanlike mischief, get involved in fights, and display savagery, including decapitation, infanticide, suicide, and canni-balism; the "penknife hara-kiri" in *Jabberwocky* (1971) is a perfect exam-ple of an ordinary object behaving like a living being. This ingenious scene of beauty and subtle tension shows a small penknife jumping and twist-ing like a ballet dancer on a table covered with a white-laced cloth. Sud-denly it freezes and falls flat, its switchblade vehemently closing onto itself with an audible snap; a dark red trickle slowly pours out of the knife's "body." Initially, this seems like an homage to the "Oceana Roll" dance in Charlie Chaplin's *Gold Rush* (1925)—but the haunting conclusion is unmistakably Švankmajer. In the same film, an idyllic Victorian scene with innocent-looking children's dolls cutely dining at a toy table, turns disquieting as soon as the viewer realizes that their meal consists of other "cute" dolls, who have just been minced in a (real) meat grinder.

By substituting live actors with dolls, puppets, or figurines, Švank-majer is able to submit his characters to forms of violence that would be impossible to depict in live-action films without risking censorship and the viewers' emotional endurance. Conversely, as observed by British film critic Leslie Felperin, "[t]he use of live actors adds a menacing realism to these rituals which would never be possible in the all-cartoon world films of the similarly sadistic Tex Avery."[16]

Evidently the Czech animator offers a different perspective on the classical conventions of the horror genre; although horror has been mar-ried to suspense practically from the beginnings of the genre,[17] there is lit-tle emphasis on suspense in his films. One reason is that the director rarely conceives his films in terms of a traditional plot; in more conventionally constructed narratives, such as *Little Otik,* he reduces the suspense ele-ment through distancing techniques. One of the few exceptions in his corpus may be *Down to the Cellar.* This almost entirely live-action short includes moments when the viewer becomes worried about the safety of the child heroine descending into the dark subterranean corridors of an old building to bring home a basket of potatoes.

A closer look at Švankmajer's work reveals that he does not threaten the viewer with what he shows. There are no screaming people, lurking chainsaw murderers, ghosts, zombies, or Draculas with pointy teeth; no killer bees, man-eating sharks, or dinosaurs running amok. One is less scared by what is presented than by what these images represent in the real world: murder, oppression, war atrocities, childhood fears, greed, and avarice. The two wooden characters from *Punch and Judy* hitting each other relentlessly until they smash each other to pulp, or the Arcimboldo-like collages from *Dimensions of Dialogue* each having a turn at devouring the other, may recall the endless violence in the Middle East or Northern Ireland. Horror in Švankmajer's films is not visceral horror but rather horror by association, where the audience is invited to play an active role. Moreover, there is no comforting redemption to be found. The decapitated, demolished, chopped-to-pieces effigies never rise again, unlike the Sylvesters or Tweety Birds of the explicitly violent, conventional animated slapstick in North America. The Czech director's portrait of human folly and destruction is permanent and unyielding.

Echoes of a Dark History

Jan Švankmajer has spent most of his life in Prague, a city with a long, rich, and dark history. Among the more mysterious and culturally stimulating periods of the Czech capital was the sixteenth century, particularly its second half during the reign of the eccentric Hapsburg Emperor Rudolf II (1575–1611). Unlike the enlightened Emperor Charles IV of the Luxembourg Dynasty (1346–1378) who made Prague a showpiece of his Holy Roman Empire, the moody Rudolf II was not a great ruler. Nevertheless he was an enthusiastic lover and supporter of the arts and sciences. At the time, the "sciences" included alchemy and astrology. Emperor Rudolf invited famous astronomers such as Tycho Brahe (1546–1601) from Denmark and artists from all over Europe to his Prague court: among them was the Mannerist genius Giuseppe Arcimboldo (1527–1593), whose haunting paintings have provided significant inspiration for Švankmajer's work.

In the Rudolphine period the ideas of the Renaissance were blending with the receding Middle Ages and waxing baroque sensitivity; great discoveries were being made at home and on the new continents. Magic was turning into science and Prague became the European melting pot of creativity. In this fertile multicultural soil, imagination flourished. Popular fantasy and many archetypal horror tales arose from this period, such as the story about Dr. Faustus, the scientist who signed a pact with the Devil to obtain ultimate knowledge; another tale was about the venerable Rabbi Loew who, in order to protect his Jewish community from imperial abuse, mustered his magic powers to breathe life into Golem, a clay colossus that eventually turned destructive—like many robots of the sci-fi literature and film of later centuries. Vampire-related tales about the sadistic Hungarian Countess Báthory also originated during this epoch.[18]

Even today much of Rudolf's spooky Prague remains alive in the city. Tourists line up to visit the old Jewish cemetery, especially the grave of Rabbi Loew. Švankmajer and his wife and collaborator, the surrealist painter Eva Švankmajerová, live in a narrow winding lane under the ancient Prague Castle in a Caligari-like house occupied by alchemists centuries ago. His films provide a wealth of references to the mysterious Rudolphine period,[19] while their collagelike style reflects the profound influence of Arcimboldo—displayed most succinctly in his twenty-second video *Flora*, made for MTV in 1989.[20] The atmosphere of the historical Prague is tangible in Švankmajer stories such as *Faust, Down to the Cellar*, and *Little Otik*, which take their viewers into old, scruffy apartment houses, scenes of mysterious happenings.

Švankmajer has also successfully exploited one of his country's most unusual and bleakest monuments, the Sedlec Monastery Ossuary, which became the subject of *The Ossuary* (1970), a unique "horror documentary."[21] The Sedlec Ossuary contains the bones of some 50 to 70,000 people buried there since the Middle Ages. After a decade of work in 1870, they were fashioned by the Czech artist František Rindt into fascinating shapes and objects, including skull pyramids, crosses, monstrance, and a chandelier containing every bone of the human body. These artifacts have been placed in the crypt of the Cistercian chapel ever since as a memento mori for all visitors to see. Švankmajer filmed this extraordinary exhibit in black-and-white stock, using distancing techniques such as a nervously moving camera and rapid editing.[22]

According to the Czech Surrealist and Švankmajer's friend František Dryje, *The Ossuary* is "realistic Gothic[23] par excellence": "Against the background of a macabre interior, which could in other circumstances quite easily become the stage for a ghostly encounter, the author allows everything to unfold that is dark and which the human character has been carrying with it since time began, and which makes itself icily clear in the face of rigidly encoded contemporary stupidities."[24] The Ossuary includes two subtle references linking its macabre subject matter with present-day reality, giving the film an added dimension: one is the silly, and unintentionally ironic, commentary of the official tourist guide (removed by the communist censors); another lies in the "I was here" initials scratched into the skulls and bones by visitors—some would say vandals—highlighted in the concluding shots of the film.

Breast-feeding the
tree-stump baby in
Little Otik (2000)

Surrealism and Horror

The Rudolphine period is justifiably one of the two most powerful
sources of inspiration of Švankmajer's work; the other is surrealism,
which, like the former, embraces horror, fantasy, and the macabre.
Švankmajer has also explored historical works related to surrealism, particularly those of the literary horror genre master Edgar Allan Poe
(1809–1849), the French novelist and playwright Villiers de l'Isle-Adam
(1838–1889),[25] Lewis Carroll, and Horace Walpole (1717–1797).[26]
From the ranks of earlier filmmakers, he has particularly admired Luis
Buñuel and Federico Fellini, both icons of surrealist cinema.[27]

But even in the realm of surrealism, it is once again Prague that has
given Švankmajer a creative stimulus worth mentioning: Franz Kafka
(1883–1923), a German-speaking Jew who lived an inconspicuous life in
the midst of the Czech cultural element, who has become an icon of
alienation, absurdity, and other distinctly twentieth-century anxieties. It
was Kafka who introduced in his novel *The Trial* a powerful archetypal
character of modern horror—the "wrong man," an innocent individual
accused of a crime or involved in it by mistake, a theme later popularized
by Alfred Hitchcock who owes to it a lion's share of his fame. In Hitchcock's films, the unfounded suspicion is usually dispelled in the end and
his protagonists' innocence reestablished. The hero of *The Trial*, however,
is executed, as were millions of Jews during the Holocaust. This link with

reality is one reason why Kafka is so important. As the Polish critic Roman Karst has stated, Kafka's nightmare ceased to be a purely "aesthetic" experience when the nightmare conformed to reality.[28] The American film critic Roger Ebert sees *The Trial* as "one of the best stories ever written about the Innocent Man, and all the better because there is a sense that Josef K., its hero, secretly suspects that he must have done something wrong to deserve such cruel treatment from the authorities."[29]

Kafka's influence on Czech culture, and on Švankmajer in particular, is profound. It is reasonable to assume that the writer inspired the animator to discover that "[i]n our civilization, the dream, that natural wellspring of the imagination, is constantly blocked, and in its place we find absurdity which grants precedence to our 'scientific, rational system.'"[30] Kafkaesque absurdity was already a key theme in Švankmajer's early work, *The Garden*. The film's narrative is constructed around a subtle confrontation between two male characters. One of them appears to be a political conformist who managed to build a comfortable life for himself in an agreeable country home. The other man is apparently an old friend who did not do so well. Švankmajer reveals the manipulative nature of the former in an explicit and highly original finale: the "fence" around his home and garden consists of a human chain—people stand next to one another holding hands, silently obeying their master's orders. The film's political implications can hardly be overlooked. Although conceived during an oppressive totalitarian regime, it transcends any concrete historical period, country, or system of government.

The last decade of Švankmajer's work brought a new theme indicating the director's growing interest in food abuse: his *Virile Games* and the one-minute videoclip *Meat Love* (1989) introduced the theme; the short triptych *Food* was even more explicit in commenting on the problem of gluttony, a subject to which the director returns in *Little Otik*. The problem of overeating in affluent societies has two major consequences, individually and socially: physically, it presents a serious health hazard to those living in plenty; it is also disturbing morally as it highlights the depressing poverty of a significant portion of this planet's population. The Italian director Marco Ferreri had already raised the problem of overeating in his provocative horror-grotesque feature *Blowout* (*La grande bouffe*, 1973), in which four gourmets gorge themselves to death. In the same year, the Canadian National Film Board produced the computer-assisted animated short *The Hunger*, directed by Peter Foldes, focusing on the same problem. The latter film contains nightmarish images of literally hungry eyes—eyes with teeth—attacking the obese protagonist.

Švankmajer's images in *Food* are equally disturbing, with characters devouring practically everything around them, and finally each other. In *Virile Games* the main character continuously stuffs himself with sausages, cookies, and beer while watching a soccer match on television. Otík, the baby boy from *Little Otik* fashioned out of a tree-trunk, cannot control his appetite, thereby gobbling up everything he can. His yearning for red meat extends to people, including his human father. Even the officer at the police station is preoccupied with his meal, totally oblivious to the woman reporting a missing person. The neighbors of Otík's family are also obsessed with food. One of the film's most haunting moments comes when Otík attacks the hefty social worker who has come to check on the perceived problem in the family. The assault can only be observed as a shadow play through a translucent glass pane that eventually gets splattered with blood while screams can be heard in the background. This is reminiscent of Hitchcockian horror, including the famous shower scene in *Psycho* (1960).

For almost four decades now, Jan Švankmajer has sought to expand the traditional definition of film animation beyond the restricted concept of mainstream cartoon aesthetics. His concern for the human condition, his pessimism, and his dark humor mirror the historical experience of his own country and that of Central Europe. Working with horror but remaining outside the strict conventions of the genre, he does not attempt to shock or scare his audience by assaulting their emotions; instead, he uses indirect, implicit horror to stimulate the viewers' mind, forcing us to contemplate the darker side of reality beyond the film screen.

Notes

1. Editorial introduction to "Dossier Animation 1," *Positif* 345 (1989): 36.
2. Jan Poš, *Výtvarníci animovaného filmu* (Prague: Odeon, 1990), 138.
3. Julian Petley, *Monthly Film Bulletin* 53, no. 629 (1986): 188.
4. The American-born twins Steven and Timothy Quay (b. 1947) have acknowledged the important influence on their work by Švankmajer. Their films include the *Street of Crocodiles* (1986) and *Institute Benjamenta* (1995); their *The Cabinet of Jan Švankmajer* (1984) is a tribute to the Czech animator.
5. After his script for *Down to the Cellar* was rejected by Prague's Krátký Film Studios, the director shrewdly exploited the personal rivalry between the Czech and Slovak studio management groups, and the (Slovak) Bratislava Studios eventually accepted the project. The Czechoslovak authorities refused the initial request from

the Oberhausen Festival organizers to enter the film into competition, but they reluctantly gave up. *Down to the Cellar* won the Prize of the Critique there.

6. Peter Hames mentions *Dimensions of Dialogue, Down to the Cellar,* and *The Pendulum, the Pit and Hope.* See Peter Hames, ed., *Dark Alchemy: The Films of Jan Švankmajer* (Westport, CT: Praeger, 1995), 41.

7. Unrealized scripts include *Palebluebeard (Bledomodrovous), Insects (Hmyz),* and *Nobody Nowhere (Nikde Nikdo); Palebluebeard* was incorporated into the 1996 feature *Conspirators of Pleasure (Spiklenci slasti).*

8. The post-1968 repression fell hardest on the prominent directors of the Czech New Wave of the 1960s, including Miloš Forman, Ivan Passer, Vojtech Jasný, Jan Nemec, Evald Schorm, Jiří Menzel and Vera Chytilová. Forman (now a famous American director), Passer, Jasný, and Nemec chose exile; Schorm was entirely banned from the film studios; Menzel and Chytilová were allowed a slow, controlled comeback before the weakening regime's downfall in 1989.

9. The International Federation of Film Critics.

10. See Brigid Cherry, "Dark Wonders and the Gothic Sensibility: Jan Švankmajer's *Něco z Alenky (Alice,* 1987)," *Kinoeye* 2, no. 1 (1997), online at http://www.kinoeye. org/02/01/cherry01.php, accessed September 3, 2003.

11. Michel Ciment and Lorenzo Codelli, "Entretien avec Jan Švankmajer," *Positif* 345 (1989): 45.

12. Švankmajer studied puppetry at the AMU (School of Dramatic Arts) in Prague from 1954 to 1958. He also worked with avant-garde stage productions such as the *Semafor* theater and the internationally known *Laterna Magika,* which successfully combined stage and film techniques.

13. The Polish-Lithuanian filmmaker Wladyslaw Starewicz (1892–1965), who invented the 3-D stop-motion animated film, may have influenced Švankmajer. Starewicz used real (dead) beetles and puppets in his films, which include *The Cameraman's Revenge* (1913). His *Voice of the Nightingale* (1923) combines animation with live action.

14. The emotional power of close-ups has been well known to filmmakers since D.W. Griffith. The extreme close-up amplifies the shot's aggressive potential, often crossing the threshold into the bizarre and grotesque. See Per Persson, "Towards a Psychological Theory of Close-ups," *Kinema* 9 (Spring 1998): 24–42.

15. The Polish-born Walerian Borowczyk is one of the few directors known for using the technique of extreme close-up flashes intercut with the action. This technique is noticeable in his feature *Blanche* (1971).

16. Leslie Felperin, "Conspirators of Pleasure/Spiklenci slasti," *Sight and Sound* (February 1997): 39.

17. Robert Weine's *The Cabinet of Dr. Caligari* (Germany, 1920) is frequently credited as being the first horror film. Contrary to popular belief, *Caligari* was preceded by several German proto-expressionist movies, including *The Student of Prague* (1913) and *The Golem* (1915). The earlier of the two films is a doppelganger tale involving a diabolical character named Scapinelli who looks very much like Caligari. The stories of both films are set in Prague, *The Golem* in the sixteenth century.

18. Over a number of years, Countess Báthory and her associates tortured and killed over 600 girls; seeking immortality, the Countess would bathe in their blood.

19. Švankmajer's early short *Historia naturae, suita* (1967) was dedicated to Rudolf II.

20. *Flora* is one of Švankmajer's most explicit tributes to the work of Giuseppe Arcimboldo, whose painting *Flora*, which depicts a woman constructed from flowers, was clearly the film's inspiration. *Flora* is possibly Švankmajer's most disturbing film.

21. The Sedlec Monastery is located about seventy km/forty miles east of Prague. Its ossuary and the neighboring historic town of Kutná Hora are now listed as UNESCO heritage sites.

22. *The Ossuary* exists in two versions featuring different soundtracks. The subversive irony of the original one, involving the commentary of a local guide, was held to be politically unacceptable in 1970, so the filmmaker was forced to replace it; he chose piano music with a girl singing (in Czech) the poem by Jacques Prévert, "Pour faire le portrait d'un oiseau" ("How to Draw the Portrait of a Bird").

23. The term "realistic Gothic" was coined by the French literary critic Maurice Heine (1884–1940), remembered for his fine research on the writings of the Marquis de Sade.

24. František Dryje, "The Force of Imagination," in Hames, ed., *Dark Alchemy*, 155.

25. The principal works of Count Philippe Auguste Villiers de l'Isle-Adam include *Cruel Tales* (1883), *Axel* (1885–86), and *New Cruel Tales* (1888).

26. Confirmed in personal conversation with the director in 1985.

27. Švankmajer was inspired by Poe in his shorts *The Fall of the House of Usher* (*Zánik domu Usheru*, 1981) and *The Pit, the Pendulum and Hope* (*Kyvadlo, jáma a naděje*, 1983); by Carroll in *Jabberwocky*, *Alice*, and *Down to the Cellar*; and by Walpole in *Castle of Otranto* (*Otrantský zámek*, 1977).

28. Roman Karst, in an interview with Antonín J. Liehm, "Franz Kafka in Eastern Europe," *Telos* 23 (Summer 1975): 73.

29. Roger Ebert, "*The Trial*," review of the film by David Jones in "Roger Ebert on the Movies Online," *Chicago Sun Times* (April 8, 1994), online at http://www.suntimes.com/ebert/ebert_reviews/1994/04/914072.html, accessed June 1, 2001.

30. Amos Vogel, "Hallo Berlin," *Film Comment* 24, no. 3 (1988): 63.

15

Egypt:

A CINEMA WITHOUT HORROR?

Viola Shafik

Not the horror but its absence is one of the most striking characteristics of Egyptian cinema. Considering the importance of mummies and Ancient Egyptian magic to the Western fantasy and horror film, it may seem astonishing that they were never pictured in Egyptian productions, at least not as a source of mystery. Yet even more surprising is the fact that current remnants of popular magic and the traditional belief in demons have rarely been addressed, or if so, primarily to be mocked and denounced. To give you an idea of the genre's marginality: among the more than 2,500 full-length feature films produced so far in Egyptian cinema, it seems that only three films deserve to be classified as horror.

If we put aside for a moment the basic question of generic definition, we are caught from the beginning in an analytic as well as a political problem: how to describe something that is absent in a national cinema if not by referring to another cinema in another place. It is impossible to examine this absence in Egyptian film production without discussing the presence of horror in Western, or more precisely in American, cinema. Consequently, the following considerations cannot avoid referring to and concerning themselves with the West as much as with Egypt. And they will likely call attention to another instance when this absence-presence in question does not amount to a difference so much as a sign of cultural and political interdependence between East and West, former colonized and its colonizer. In fact, the so-called difference turns out, at a certain point, to be the product of their mutual interaction far more than inscribed in a rooted cultural context.

To return to my initial question: a whole range of reasons suggests itself when one considers the eclipse of the demonic in Egyptian cinema. And all of them need to be discussed in order that we may distinguish the truly decisive ones. For example, it would be easy but too simplistic to emphasize the economic factor. It is certainly true that some developments in early U.S. horror films and thrillers were made possible by the high production costs necessary for designing beasts, monsters, and extravagant sets—something that a poor film industry such as Egypt's simply cannot afford. But of what that category of American horror known as "B-pictures," including films such as *Mother's Day* (1980) or *The Texas Chainsaw Massacre* (1974)? Works such as these would meet with a major obstacle in the Egyptian context, since their transgressive violence and sadistic notion of sexuality—or, to speak with Rick Altman, their temporal "denial of cultural values"[1]—could never pass official censorship in Egypt. As a general rule, lowbrow or subcultural cinematic expressions have difficulty seeing the light, not only because of the censors hampering (even if not preventing) their distribution but also because of the lack of funding available for such endeavors.

Another, rather orientalist, explanation for the absence of horror in Egypt points to the missing literary tradition similar to the European *Schauerroman* and ghost tales—something along the lines of an Edgar Allan Poe or an E. T. A. Hoffmann—which could have facilitated the adaptation of horror to the big screen. Although fairy tales that include genies are very familiar in Arab and Egyptian storytelling, no particular literary movement developed these tales in modern times. Thus, the local cinema had neither a strong tradition nor a modern literary model to rely on for creating the horror movie. Nevertheless, there were other genres (such as realist drama and the detective story) that also lacked predecessors in Arab literature but were nonetheless able to be adapted, and to make it to the higher echelons of mainstream cinema.

Rational Horror

Before I dig any deeper in order to identify the more accurate causes I need to clarify my notion of the horror film in the Egyptian context. To begin, I would like to distinguish between the horror film and the thriller even though I am fully aware how problematic any such attempt at generic definition may be—not least because of the fluidity and constant shifts in meaning discussed by Altman.[2] For the moment at least, I will employ Robin Wood's handy characterization of the horror film as normality threatened by monsters.[3] Now to a certain extent, imperiled normality is the meeting point between horror films and the thriller. But if the latter relies on quasi-natural and objective causes in order to incite fear, the former draws primarily on the animalistic, monstrous, supernatural, or quasi religious to create its sensational effects.

According to Egyptian scholar Ali Abu Shadi, crime appeared in Egyptian movies as early as the 1930s and 1940s. Shadi attributes the first true thriller to director/editor Kamel El-Cheikh in the early 1950s, however.[4] In fact, it is remarkable that thriller and police films did not appear before then, for the genres that founded Egypt's national film industry were first of all melodrama and comedy, mostly in combination with musicals. Crime remained relatively harmless, bound into melodramatic plots. Eventually, in 1952, Kamal El-Cheikh (al-Shaykh), who was first trained as an editor at Studio Misr, made his successful debut with *al-Manzil raqam 13* (*House #13*), which immediately installed him in the Egyptian context as an extraordinary thriller director. During the 1950s he directed some of Egypt's best psychological thrillers, such as *Tujjar al-mawt* (*Death Traders*, 1957), *Sayidat al-qasr* (*The Lady of the Palace*, 1958), and *al-Layla al-akhira* (*The Last Night*, 1963). All of them were interestingly contrary to many police films, situated as they were in a middle-class surrounding. *House #13*, for example, tells a *Dr. Caligari*–type of tale in which hypnosis is used in order to incite a successful young architect to commit murder on behalf of his doctor.

Crucial to this kind of Egyptian thriller is the preoccupation with crime and the evil nature of human (but not any occult, demonic, or supernatural) forces. Hence, the rationality and psychological sophistication characterizing El-Cheikh's films can be seen as well in *The Last Night*. Its plot relies on a recurrent thriller motif, lost personal identity, but it does not touch on abnormality so much as construct itself as a claustrophobic marital drama. The claustrophobic effect is generated by the narrative structure and also by black-and-white imagery. Set entirely at night, the second half of the film grows increasingly darker and is dominated by low-key lighting, while the action as it approaches the final showdown—the attack on the heroine's life—is underscored by dramatic orchestral music.

Fatin Hamama, petite and girlish star of melodrama, here features as a woman who wakes up one morning to discover herself a wife and the mother of a grown up daughter. Yet all she can remember of her past is her preparation to get married to a totally different man. In the course of the film, she tries to regain her memory of how this mysterious change occurred. Meanwhile, her strict and unfriendly husband suspiciously observes her. Gradually she grasps her true identity and discovers that her husband is an imposter. In response, he attempts to murder her, but her sympathetic doctor is able to save her life at the last minute. What she learns is that she lost her memory on the eve of her own wedding during an air raid on Port Said, which killed her entire family including her married sister. Her brother-in-law simply declared her his wife and moved with her and his little daughter to another town.

El-Cheikh's narrative presents itself as a typical tale of familiar horror, or in the Freudian sense as a typical manifestation of the scary unfamiliar (*das Unheimliche*) operating within the familiar (*das Heimliche*). In fact, our heroine encounters the deadliest threats in the shelter of what is supposed to be the most intimate relationship possible. The horror of her marriage, however, is not simply that of physical violence or male domination (which may be experienced in any marriage); rather, what is at stake here is the manipulation and male domination of female identity. The heroine is not only deprived of her original love and twenty years of her youth but is also deceived into entering a false marriage and forced to lead the life of another person—possible complaints of any woman who gets pushed into an arranged marriage.[5]

The underlying concepts that enable this drama to function are the antagonizing of individual identity and the nuclear bourgeois family. The latter is considered, in contrast to the traditional extended (but partly segregated) family, to have isolated women from the shelter of female solidarity, diminished their power in the home, and reinforced male dominance.[6] It is precisely this focus on the dynamics of modern nuclear family life that brings the narrative close to psychological drama. The husband's control—not only over his wife's body but also over her very soul—is what destabilizes her, and this translates into a psychic problem as well. Yet unlike Alfred Hitchcock's *Psycho* (1960), for example, where horror is triggered by real insanity, *The Last Night* makes a sincere effort to view psychic aberration as something that can be objectified and understood through analysis. Whereas *Psycho*'s finale offers an ironic and quite evident anti-climax in which the psychologist "explains" in retrospect the main character's abnormal development, in *The Last Night* a comparable role is played by the doctor, who realizes that his patient is not sick and who helps her to look for the true reasons for her uneasiness. What this character signifies, in brief, is that horrifying experiences are in fact explainable, and may be objectified with no questions left open. That is what brings this kind of thriller away from horror proper and close to the standard detective or police investigation film. Metaphysics are excluded, and rationality confirmed.

The Demonic Human

Normality's encounter with the supernatural or irrational does not suffice as a description of the few existing Egyptian horror movies. The stress must lie on the frightening existential threat that is exercised by these forces. For magic and ghosts as such already made appearances in relatively early productions, for example, in *Taqiyat al-ikhfa'* (*The Hiding Cap*, 1944), *'Afrita Hanim* (*Lady Ghost*, 1949), and *'Afritat Isma'il Yasin* (*Isma'il Yasin's Ghost*, 1954), yet in a harmless or profoundly comic way. Bound in an overall joyful context, and without the necessary sensationalistic audiovisual effects, the *'afrit* or ghosts in these films may create confusion and scare the film's characters, but not the audience. In *Isma'il Yasin's Ghost*, for example, the ghost of a murdered belly dancer haunts the comedian Yasin until he finds the culprit responsible for her death.

In contrast, the crucial innovation of El-Cheikh's work in the 1950s was the introduction of a more effective mise en scène and editing style that could function to create suspense, although the emphasis here was on a Hitchcockian notion of psychological (quasi-rational) horror. The more irrational, supernaturalistic approach has been spared until the 1980s. The few—I have not been able to discover more than three—clearcut Egyptian horror films, Muhammad Shebl's (Shibl) two features, *Anyab* (*Tusks*, 1981) and *al-Ta'wiza* (*The Amulet*, 1987), and Muhammad Radi's *al-Inss wa-l-jinn* (*Humans and Demons*, 1985), were all produced in that decade. Contrary to earlier works that touched on ghosts and demons, these three films make a serious attempt to apply not only the motifs but also the familiar technical and visual repertory of the genre (such as low- and wide-angled shots, dark lighting, mobile camerawork from the point of view of the unseen monster, and other typical special effects, including fire, smoke, and moving objects).

However, Shebl's films may just as easily be placed in the category of social drama, as they comply at the level of plot and character development with new realist social criticism of the time, as exemplified in the work of plainly realist directors such as Atef El-Tayeb ('Atif al-Tayyib), Mohamed (Muhammad) Khan, and Khairy Beshara (Bishara).[7] *Tusks*, which the director also co-scripted, was inspired by *The Rocky Horror Picture Show* (1975). Although by no means as transgressive as its model,

The abnormal
Norman Bates
(Anthony Perkins) in
Psycho (1960)

Tusks too is a musical and horror film parody, and it exhibited a slight flair for the vulgar by starring Ahmad 'Adawiyya, a very popular singer at that time. *Tusks* was not held in high esteem among Egypt's elite who considered it appropriate only for the taste of citizens in the Gulf States, whose active role as consumers of Egyptian entertainment products became strongly felt during the period in question. But the film still works to affirm 'Adawiyya's lowbrow reputation by conferring on him the negative role of the vampire. Hence, instead of undermining bourgeois ideology, *Tusks* voices its basic fears and biases. Moreover, it reveals that new realist commitment was in part not as much socialist oriented but submitted to a large extent to the perspective of a materially cornered petty bourgeoisie.

In brief, the plot is framed by a character who doubles as the narrator, and begins with a couple whose car breaks down on the road one night. They search for help in a remote palace inhabited by Dracula and his retinue. The visitors attend the party and are invited to dinner. While the girl feels herself attracted by Dracula's flirtation, her fiancé is troubled by their strange surroundings. Meanwhile, the narrator reveals some of Dracula's general characteristics by linking him to the outside world. The prince of darkness features in a series of successive scenes in which he represents various corrupt and greedy characters who attempt to suck out the

The Rocky Horror Picture Show (1975), inspiration for Muhammad Shebl's *Tusks* (1981)

money of the helpless couple. Examples include the plumber who drives a Mercedes, the taxi driver, the butcher, the trader, and the schoolteacher, all of whom hoard commodities and demand excessive compensation for their services. Eventually, the couple manage to vanquish Dracula by opening the windows of the palace, letting in the sunlight that disintegrates the prince and his companions.

The plot contains several musical numbers that create on the sonic level an opposition between 'Adawiyya's popular music and the songs of the young bridegroom (performed by the singer 'Ali al-Haggar). Whereas the former spices his colloquial lines with urban lower-class slang wrapped in relatively rough tunes, the latter has a more polished performance style, be it in text or sound. The contrast also has a visual component, one that manifests itself in the skin color of the two singers. Slim al-Haggar, with his light complexion complemented by the blondeness of his bride, is strongly opposed by 'Adawiyya's stout darkness and frizzy hair. 'Adawiyya's looks are also mirrored in the Negroid features of his first assistant, with whom he competes at the end for the girl's blood.[8] Thus the bourgeois couple here is threatened not only with getting their pockets emptied but also with being swamped by supposedly "gross" lowbrow art and the ascendant aspirations of the lower classes. This in turn makes for an interesting contrast with *The Rocky Horror Picture Show*, which seeks to mock bourgeois sexual morality and ideology. Doubtless, *Tusks'* message must be seen in the light of the 1970s Open Door Policy or *infitah* launched by president Anwar al-Sadat, who officially terminated Egypt's socialist experiment.

Al-Sadat was later criticized for opening things up to consumerism, and for bringing a new class of import-export entrepreneurs to the fore, a number of whom were accused of illegal and corrupt business practices at a time when the middle class was threatened materially by all kinds of deprivations (such as inflation, curtailed public services and subsidies, and a shortage of available housing). In fact, al-Sadat's policy was not the sole reason for the deep changes in Egyptian society during this period; another was the increased immigration of Egyptian laborers to the Gulf region, many of whom returned with money and goods and with different, often more conservative attitudes.

The so-called *infitah* ideology—that is, materialism spreading at the expense of the educated but materially deprived middle class—is also tackled in *The Amulet,* a film scripted entirely by director Shebl. Mahmud and his wife Rawya are victims of the general housing crisis in Egypt, and so are forced to share an old house with Mahmud's mother and siblings. A broker tries to lure them into selling it with a large sum of money and the offer of a new, modern apartment. When Mahmud refuses to let his father's house go, the broker resorts to spell casting. A demon takes possession of the house, moves furniture, destroys inventory, and sets it on fire. Eventually, Mahmud's younger sister has a nervous breakdown. The police are called in, but to no avail. At the end, Mahmud's wife and mother are able to get rid of the demon by reciting Qur'anic verses.

It must be noted that the monsters here do not behave all that badly. Actually, those who seem far more monstrous are the humans, which is in line with the popular pragmatic saying quoted in the film: "ma 'afrit illa bani adam" ("man is the only ghost"). Traders, brokers, and others who are accused of enriching themselves at the expense of the normal middle-class citizen are the ones equated with true evil. Supernatural powers are only called in to facilitate the already-existing abuse, thereby rendering demonic possession into a social allegory. What is addressed in these narratives first and foremost is social change and class struggle. Not the proletariat, however, but the petit bourgeois is the positive agent here. It is s/he who is portrayed as obviously repressed by current social conditions. Unlike the thriller, though, his or her psyche is not at stake in the least. The peril depicted in these narratives is that of imminent social ascent, a motif addressed countless times throughout the long history of Egyptian cinema.

The Amulet is concerned not only with the existing social order, but also with modernity, notably the complex relationship between metaphysics and rational thinking. This is expressed through the various strategies adopted by different characters in order to counter the demonic invasion. Mahmud, the male head of the family, launches a criminal investigation, and receives support from his future brother-in-law and a sympathetic police officer. Mahmud's mother, in contrast, secretly proposes to her daughter-in-law Rawya that they visit a shaman who is known to have the power to break spells. After a frightening visit, the two women invite him to hold a *zar*, an exorcism celebration. However, the ritual gets violently interrupted by Mahmud and the officer. The latter denounces the shaman and his companions as crooks and threatens them with further procedures. After her daughter passes out, Mahmud's mother tries a final strategy, asking a Muslim *shaykh* to come and see her. The *shaykh* recites the Qur'an until the girl recovers. Yet Mahmud pleads to have his sister sent to the hospital. Later, the *shaykh* pays a visit to Rawya, who has just been frightened by a vision of being showered in blood. He asks her to show strong faith and provides comfort by repeating the line: "ma 'afrit illa bani adam." Quoting the Holy Scripture eventually proves to be the proper cure for the malediction. While Rawya and her mother-in-law incessantly recite the Qur'an, the soundtrack reinforces their recitation with a loud call for prayer. Meanwhile, the broker's own monstrous features are revealed: he transforms into a huge billy goat with long horns, which he uses to gore his human assistant. The film ends with prayer and a low-angled shot of an imposing mosque.

Characters employ similarly disparate strategies in *Humans and Demons,* directed by the mainstream filmmaker Muhammad Radi and starring the Egyptian king of comedy, 'Adil Imam, as a demon. Rather than allude to the existing social order, however, this film focuses on female psychology. Moreover, it presents a clear picture of the ideal modern bourgeois religious identity and sexual morality. Dr. Fatima, a highly successful specialist, returns from a mission abroad to join her mother and sister. Her professor and colleague, Dr. Usama, awaits at her former research institute to propose both a job and marriage. However, Fatima is haunted by a *jinn* (demon) called Galal, in remembrance of her first fiancé who was killed in a car accident. Initially seeking out psychological treatment, Fatima becomes more and more convinced that she is dealing with a very powerful force who wishes to marry her. Her mother asks a shaman for help, and after several disgusting procedures (such as stepping over corpses in a graveyard at night), Fatima experiences a nervous breakdown. Eventually, Dr. Usama confronts the demon in order to win the hand of his beloved. His final and most powerful weapon is to quote the Qur'an.

On this occasion both characters express their firm belief in the existence of demons and state that they are mentioned in the Holy Scriptures. Thus, the latter is again installed as the sole means of combating the *jinn*.

Rejected Traditions

Just like *The Amulet, Humans and Demons* reserves exclusive rights for orthodox scriptural belief. The fact that the couple in question are both highly educated scientists is even more crucial in affirming the compatibility of Muslim faith with modern knowledge and science, while simultaneously scapegoating popular quasi-religious practices. This policy of excluding aspects of popular tradition is fundamental in the repackaging of cultural values, which serves to cement the image of a unified and exclusive scriptural (and modernist) Islam.

Here we are approaching one possible answer to my initial question of why magic and supernatural powers were not able to sneak into Egyptian cinema in the same way—transgressive and undermining, at least in part—as in the West. Motifs of horror cinema were largely ignored, or else were not taken seriously, in order to confirm a strongly modernist and/or scriptural Muslim ideology. In other words, they were not allowed to function as a temporal denial of dominant values. In a film like *Demons and Humans,* these motifs are instead bound, right from the beginning, into a negative discourse. Although the existence of demons is admitted, any strategies for dealing with them that belong to popular religious traditions such as sorcery and *dajal* (humbug) are dismissed and are evaluated as clear signs of ignorance, backwardness, and underdevelopment—in sharp contrast to the orthodox belief. Such a view includes any and all representations of traditional popular religious practices, including folk medicine, the veneration of saints, spell casting, and the conjuring up and appeasing of demons.[9] Their possible therapeutic effect is of course never mentioned or admitted.

The most negatively depicted practice is the quasi-religious institution of the *zar,* as can be seen in both *The Amulet* and *Demons and Humans.* At its core, this therapeutic celebration is comprised almost exclusively of women who gather under the guidance of a female *shaykha,* and who eat, drink, sing, dance, fall into trances, and sacrifice an animal. The *shaykha* calls on the demons who have presumably caused the illness and tries to appease them in order to relieve the patient.[10] The sources of these practices are possibly ancient, and have, among others, East African origins.[11] They continue to be put into use by Christians as well as Muslims.[12] The belief in demons is not necessarily opposed to Islam (nor Coptic Christianity), as demons are not regarded as gods, despite the fact that orthodox Muslim belief has tended to dismiss it, along with veneration of the saints, as *shirk,* that is, polytheism.[13] Corresponding to this, in the late nineteenth century the *zar* started to be evaluated in critical terms by the modern-educated elite. In 1903 for example, Muhammad Hilmi Zain al-Din published a book titled *The Negative Effects of the Zar* (*Madarr al-zar*). Another even more critical title, *Kitab bida 'al-fujjar fi haflat al-zar* (*The Book of the Debauches' Heresies in the Sear-Celebrations*), appeared in 1911.[14] Following these disapproving judgments, Cairo's authorities made it compulsory in 1964 to license any *zar* celebrations.[15]

In accordance with these developments, Egyptian cinema has (to the present day) mocked and denounced the *zar* as either foolishness or fraud. Such negative representations have not only been disseminated through the horror film but also have surfaced in numerous other works as well. Stereotypical characters are often made to embody the practices in question, such as the madman in *Darb al-Mahabil* (*Fool's Alley,* 1955) who dresses up like a traditional shaman and lives by hassling shop owners and people on the streets. He is explicitly depicted as an imbecile. In Salah Abou Seif's *Raya and Sakina* (1953), one of the early Egyptian police films, two women and their gang perform *zar*-like activities as a means of duping well-to-do women, killing them, and stealing their jewelry. In *al-Halfut* (*The Imbecile,* 1985), by Samir Saif, the comedian 'Adil Imam dresses up as a woman and sneaks into a *zar* celebration in order to watch women while they are at ease. And in *'Atabit al-sitat* (*The Ladies' Threshold,* 1995), a *shaykha* uses magic and the *zar* ritual in order to trick infertile women into spending their money.

Thus, it is apparent that popular demonology has been negatively inscribed within the Egyptian discourse of modernism, a discourse that holds up the binary concept of enlightenment and objective science (as introduced by the Occident) as the key to progress and modernity, in opposition to local ignorance and superstition. Such a binary concept was utilized in the West as well, yet as the colonizer and initiator of modernity the latter had less need to develop a similar discourse of apologetic rejection. If monsters and black magic are dismissed as trivial by white bourgeois education, there is (nevertheless) still enough subcultural freedom to allow such triviality to surface—even to make it a highly successful form of entertainment. Not so in Egypt, where the cultural elite evidently feels obliged to prove its so-called civilized and modern convictions, and so employs both official and unofficial tools in order to reinforce them.

In Search of the Repressed

One of the most highly controversial points needing to be negotiated during the process of modernization concerns the status of women. Reviewing our Egyptian horror films according to this hypothesis we are able to make a crucial observation. In all three examples, the weak points through which the demon gains access to the world are women, be it the bride in *Tusks,* Rawya in *The Amulet* (the most haunted member of her family), or Dr. Fatima in *Demons and Humans.* They are all very easy to impress, and are quicker than men in resorting to the popular *dajal.* This depiction appears to comply with the popular saying that regards women as *naqisat 'aql wa din* (lacking mind and religion).[16] Moreover, it is the mothers in particular who here seem to be "deemed 'ignorant,'" to use Omnia Shakry's expression, as it is always they who suggest the shaman's useless intervention.[17]

Dr. Fatima, equipped as she is with sufficiently contradictory traits, is in this respect the most interesting character. At first she is suspected by the psychoanalyst to be suffering from a guilt complex insofar as she believes that the demon Galal desires to marry her. According to popular superstition, cohabitation with a *jinn* is a common (though not exclusive) motif in cases where a woman is possessed by a male demon. In fact, as Enno Littmann argues, legendary stories date the whole development of the *zar* back to this particular theme. A sultan of *jinn,* or king demon, is said to have entered a princess after her father, the pharaoh, refused to let him marry her. It took a magician priestess named Zara to exorcise him by organizing a celebration in line with his wishes. Needless to point out the psychological connotations of this image, whereby a male demon is envisioned as wanting to possess a woman sexually when transposed into a modern yet patriarchal family context: doubtless it refers (among other things) to repressed female sexuality.

The fact that such a motif is employed in *Humans and Demons* deserves comment. Dr. Fatima is represented as a woman with a scientific education who for the sake of her career refuses to be dominated by a man. The way she is approached by her male colleague is highly rational, reminiscent of two contractors or business associates. They never flirt or touch; his feelings are expressed though his respect for her professional achievements. He visits her at home only once, and this because of an emergency, whereas the demon sneaks into Fatima's bedroom at will—usually at night when she is in bed. Moreover, through several crosscuts the *jinn* is linked to a black cat, which has a more female than male connotation in the Egyptian vernacular, but which certainly embodies an animalistic component in this context. The symptoms Dr. Fatima develops after several encounters with the increasingly possessive demon are clearly hysterical and result in a nervous breakdown followed by hospitalization. In all of this the allusion to repressed female sexuality seems quite clear; even her prospective bridegroom suggests that immediate marriage would be the best cure. Final appeasement is achieved via submission to the law of orthodox religion and to the concept of a bourgeois but strangely rational and desexualized marriage.[18] The indirect message sent by this film's narrative and depiction of female character traits is that despite speaking in favor of women's education and contribution in the workplace, a woman's career may well conflict with her emotional life. Moreover, traditionally female-dominated forms of healing are here rejected as inappropriate and backward.

A Dispensable Genre

Apart from the three examples discussed here, horror cinema has remained a dispensable genre for the Egyptian film industry. One explanation for this is the obvious discomfort with which modernist discourse in Egypt was met by popular religion and syncretistic, transgressive, and female-oriented practices. But if we consider those well-known theories that relate the horror film to what is psychologically repressed in a particular culture, the question remains why—if said theories are true—there was not a similar development in Egyptian cinema.

The horror film as locus of repressed psychological material certainly applies to *Humans and Demons,* but this formula is much less visible in *Tusks* and *The Amulet* where the monstrous is quite plainly thrown back onto the social order, social change, and its representatives. In fact, the manifest fears of Egypt's middle class—to be seen as uncivilized, to be swamped by lower-class culture, to be unable to meet certain material standards—are openly expressed in the country's few horror films and in other genres as well.

By way of contrast, while social change and the negotiation of modernity are crucial to Egyptian horror cinema (to the extent that such a cinema exists), such concerns are of little interest to horror films in the West. What has necessitated it there, rather, is the complex psychology of the over-controlled and over-informed, presumably "normal" WASP-citizen. That is, if we follow Wood's argument that horror film monsters and beasts may be viewed as the "return of the repressed"—as personified fears and anxieties surrounding everything that is different (foreigners, people of color, women, children, etc.), anything that stands as aberrant or "other" to white male Christian bourgeois normality.[19]

Indeed, the notion of repression does not suggest freedom but firm control. In Freud's view, the place where this control is first exerted and internalized is the family, more specifically the nuclear bourgeois family. But this particular type of social organization is still relatively recent in Egypt and its implementation dependent on class as well as region. Nonetheless, the narratives of bourgeois-oriented Egyptian cinema have, since its introduction in the late 1920s, been filled with familiar stories of oppression and rebellion against it, stories that herald and confirm the Freudian view. This fact should not be too surprising given the predominantly middle- and upper-middle-class affiliations of Egypt's early producers, filmmakers, and scriptwriters. Moreover, on a more structural level, Timothy Mitchell has argued that along with colonialism, Egyptians were exposed to Michel Foucault's "new disciplinary power."[20] Thus, they have come a long way through colonization, in other words through the process of internalizing power through public institutions such as schools and the military.

Yet the patriarchal bourgeois family is not coherently settled, the rate of illiteracy remains quite high, and even if the state gained the means to supervise every last inch of the country, traditional strategies of subverting the highly centralized and remote means of control would likely still be at work. As well, the most visible state authority is complemented and contradicted by the powerful structure of clientelism, be it rooted in kinship or in other forms of personal or professional relationships. Official control and power may be diverted and subverted by means of personal connections to those in command; this holds even with respect to public censorship, where certain prohibitions can be circumvented by these very means. Of course there are limitations here, limitations that increase the higher you climb the pyramid of power. Even if you can get sexual or political allusions past the censors you still cannot touch God or the president, for example, nor the latter's direct representatives.

Thus, I would argue that social reality in Egypt is demarcated in a way that is more visible than in the West by the struggle for and against disciplining. Accordingly, we find that Egyptian cinema, including horror cinema, has been primarily concerned with reflecting structural rather than psychological dynamics. In other words, this helps to explain why Egyptian horror films have been more concerned with rationalizing than in demonizing, or more precisely, in depicting "social reality" rather than its people's psyche.

This leads to another question. Does the American horror film function only as a cathartic outlet for that which has been repressed? Or is it not the case that "daily life" as such—safe, tidy, and well organized—conjures the need for its opposite, not necessarily on the symbolic level, but in a directly reflexive manner, if only for the sake of feeling "painfully" alive? Rhetorically speaking, I would ask whether a deprived African American living in Harlem is likely to develop the same attachment to a horror film like *Mother's Day* as a New Jersey youth who lives in a *Halloween* safe, clean, and guarded middle-class neighborhood. I am not claiming that the visualization and experience of certain bourgeois fears in everyday life invalidates the repressed—I am only suggesting that it could render its symbolic representation less necessary.

If this is so, then is it not possible that frequent exposure to actual violations of values and order in an environment that overtly contains vast social discrepancies can function to preserve an individual's so-called (in Freudian terms) psychic energy, thereby rendering the horror film experience for such an individual more or less dispensable?[21] Moreover, would this experience not require a constant affirmation of order in the cinematic text as a means of appeasing the fears of at least middle-class viewers?

Admittedly, the evidence in favor of such considerations remains speculative. Even considering Egypt's nearly incoherent internalization of power, it cannot be denied that the middle class—whose representatives are filling the ranks of Cairo's movie theaters—must have come the furthest in that process. And it may well be the case that other cinematic genres have functioned as outlets for repressed fears and anxieties. However, I do not think that the repressed material as described by Wood and others can be detached from the specific cinematic form through which it has been most obviously and successfully mediated. The preference of the Egyptian film industry and its largely urban middle- and lower-class audience for the melodramatic social drama, for comedies, musicals, and the action film (even more topical during the time in which our three horror films were produced)—or for a hybridized mix of all of these genres—speaks again to the dispensability of the horror thrill in favor of the condensed and sublimated emotional gestures of melodrama, the carnivalesque catharsis of farce enacted in comedy.

In conclusion, the lack of interest shown by the Egyptian film industry toward the horror genre can be understood for structural reasons, reasons that go a long way toward explaining why the three horror films discussed in this essay evince but little of the repressed material found in Western cinema and are moderate (at best) in their employment of spectacular effects. Thematically, these films focus largely on existing fears of the proletariat and of female sexuality. They set out first of all to construct a modernist but still conservative and uniform urban middle-class image of normality, and this by eclipsing, dominating, or simply dismissing lower-class and/or traditional cultural expressions (which are often far more polyphonic and syncretistic). The perils depicted in *Tusks, The Amulet,* and *Humans and Demons* are almost entirely linked to the perspective and problems of the former group. Indirectly, however, these films express an apologetic position, one that could only develop as a result of the colonial experience to which the region was exposed, and which is still perpetuated through the new world order.

Notes

1. Rick Altman, *Film/Genre* (London: BFI Publishing, 1999), 155.
2. Altman, *Film/Genre*, 62.
3. Robin Wood, "An Introduction to the American Horror Film," in *Movies and Methods*, vol. 2, ed. Bill Nichols (Berkeley: University of California Press, 1985), 204.
4. Ali Abu Shadi, "Genres in Egyptian Cinema," in *Screens of Life: Critical Film Writing from the Arab World*, ed. Alia Arasoughly (Québec: World Heritage, 1996), 125.
5. Arranged marriages are still common in Egypt, at least within the poor rural population, although the practice has been harshly criticized and contested since the 1930s (not least by Egyptian cinema) and has been eclipsed by love marriages among the more educated strata of society.
6. Timothy Mitchell, *Colonising Egypt* (Cambridge: Cambridge University Press, 1988); Lila Abu-Lughod, ed., *Remaking Women: Feminism and Modernity in the Middle East* (Cairo: American University of Cairo Press, 1998), 12.
7. See, by way of comparison, Viola Shafik, *Arab Cinema: History and Cultural Identity* (Cairo: American University of Cairo Press, 1998), 142.
8. Note that black-African features may still invoke in the Arab context the word *'abd,* or "slave."

9. In Yahya Haqqi's 1944 novelette, *Qandil Umm Hashim* (*Umm Hashim's Lamp*), popular healing methods, embodied by the blessed oil of a female saint, are put into opposition to enlightened modern medicine, showing a European-trained doctor rebelling against the tradition that almost cost his uneducated cousin her eyesight.

10. See, by way of comparison, Enno Littmann, *Arabische Geisterbeschwörungen aus Ägypten,* series Sammlung Orientalischer Arbeiten, 19 (Leipzig: O. Harrassowitz, 1950).

11. Littmann, *Arabische Geisterbeschwörungen aus Ägypten,* 50.

12. Ibid., 57.

13. F. De Jong, "Die Mystischen Bruderschaften und der Volksislam," in *Der Islam in der Gegenwart,* ed. Werner Ende and Udo Steinbach (Munich: C. H. Beck, 1984), 495.

14. Littmann, *Arabische Geisterbeschwörungen aus Ägypten,* 5.

15. De Jong, "Die Mystischen Bruderschaften und der Volksislam," 495.

16. Although this is not suggested by the Qur'an itself, if we believe Leila Ahmed.

17. Omnia Shakry, "Schooled Mothers, Structured Play," in Abu Lughod, *Remaking Women,* 157.

18. It might be objected here that, in an ethnographic context, the *zar* ritual is not employed so much to exorcise the *jinn* as it is to talk with them and thereby ease their cohabitation with the women they possess (the possession is believed to be incurable). Janice Boddy, in *Wombs and Alien Spirits: Women, Men, and the Zar Cult in Northern Sudan* (Madison: University of Wisconsin Press, 1989), describes a whole range of *jinn* possessing woman in her ethnographic study of the Sudan. Both male and female *jinn;* lots of foreign figures. Boddy suggests that the *zar* state actually functions to enable women's transgressiveness. Repressed female sexuality was very much a part of the equation, but the *zar*—pointedly including possession by male *jinn*—was a means for resisting it. According to Boddy, "They [*zayran,* a type of *jinn*] move her from a monological (monolithic) world where other voices—alien cultures, feminine perspectives—are disclaimed, exist only 'in absentia,' to a polyphonous world where others may speak, may enter into dialogue with her ... self. ... Here the *zar* as an aesthetic genre resembles the novel as described by Mikhail Bakhtin ... where social heteroglossia, the existence of multiple expressive worlds, is not muted but incorporated into the 'text' itself, effectively decentering hegemonic truths." However, while all of this may be true within the ethnographic context, in the films here under discussion there is an obvious urge for exorcism (as still practiced, it should be noted, by priests and shaykhs today), and not for mere appeasement. On the contrary, the liberating transgressiveness Boddy describes is effectively *silenced* in Egyptian horror cinema. Thanks to Walter Armbrust for bringing this potential objection to my attention.

19. Wood, "An Introduction to the American Horror Film," 199.

20. Mitchell, *Colonising Egypt,* 176.

21. Altman introduces this idea as an explanation for the viewing pleasure generated through a specific, generic economy that is defined by the difference between actual values and their temporal denial in genre cinema (*Film/Genre,* 155).

16

Burn, Witch, Burn:

A First Look at the
Scandinavian Horror Film

Rebecca A. Umland and Samuel J. Umland

> Whenever Scandinavian cinema has five minutes to fill, it burns a
> witch.

British film critic Dilys Powell, noted for her sometimes harsh assessments of Ingmar Bergman's oeuvre, made the above remark in a review of the latter's *Det sjunde inseglet* (*The Seventh Seal,* 1957). We quote it because it so clearly suggests her discomfort with Bergman's famous art film set in the Middle Ages, not because we find it to be a particularly accurate observation about Scandinavian films in general. Why of all possible features would Scandinavian films be associated in her mind with the practice of burning witches? At the time of her review, 1957, by "Scandinavian cinema" she could only mean films from Denmark or Sweden, the two Scandinavian countries with a rich cinematic tradition and an international reputation. Likewise, we intend to focus here on (art) films from these two countries, with some references, later on, to recent trends in the Norwegian cinema.[1]

Powell's comment predates the 1960s increase, in the Anglo-American cinema at least, in films about Satanism and witchcraft. Certainly there had been a few such films made in Classical Hollywood: Edgar G. Ulmer's *The Black Cat* (1934), whose character with a Scandinavian name, Hjalmar Poelzig (Boris Karloff), was allegedly modeled on The Great Beast himself—Aleister Crowley—immediately comes to mind.[2] So too does Val Lewton's *The Seventh Victim* (1943), about a young girl who becomes entangled with a group of devil worshippers. Yet these two Hollywood films feature contemporary locales, unlike Bergman's *Det sjunde inseglet,* for example, with its medieval setting.

The Scandinavian film closest in time to Bergman's *Det sjunde inseglet* that includes a scene in which a witch is burned is Danish director Carl Theodor Dreyer's *Vredens dag* (*Day of Wrath*, 1943). Set in the early seventeenth century, *Vredens dag* is intertextually related to *Det sjunde inseglet*, especially in its use of the biblical book of Revelations, in which the opening of the seventh seal heralds Doomsday. A mere two films that include the burning of a witch in a fourteen-year time span would not seem to suggest that witch burning had become a common feature of Scandinavian cinema. (Benjamin Christensen's *Häxan* [*The Witch*, 1922] was rereleased in 1941, and while the film explores the phenomenon of witchcraft, there is no actual burning depicted.) Yet what makes Powell's observation so provocative is that she seems to have intuited a singular feature that recurs—almost exclusively—in Scandinavian horror films, and is so clearly expressed in the act of burning a witch: the confabulation of (pagan) superstitions and Christian belief.

In contrast to their American and Japanese counterparts, Scandinavian horror films do not readily invoke stereotypical images of marauding monsters or supernatural creatures. In Dreyer's *Vampyr* (1932), for instance, the titular vampire is a white-haired old woman, not a creature hissing at his crucifix-bearing persecutors through bared, sharply fanged teeth.[3] Film historians such as Kristin Thompson and David Bordwell have observed that at an early stage Swedish cinema became distinctive because of its "dependence on northern landscapes" and its "use of local literature, costumes, customs, and the like," noting also that Danish cinema had an "international standing" during the 1910s.[4] But neither Swedish nor Danish cinema is identified with a specific artistic movement such as, for example, German Expressionism, an avant-garde tradition identified by a nation as well as a style and sensibility. This tradition produced one renowned horror film, Robert Wiene's *Das kabinett des Dr. Caligari* (*The Cabinet of Dr. Caligari*, 1920), even though expressionism, ironically, may have had its roots in Norwegian Edvard Munch's pictorial art. Thus, although no distinct horror film tradition has been identified in Scandinavian cinema, decades of auteur criticism have championed certain strong directors—Swedes such as Victor Sjöström, Mauritz Stiller, and Bergman, for instance, or Danes such as Christensen,[5] Dreyer, and recently, Lars von Trier—exploring the defining features of their idiosyncratic films without necessarily scrutinizing the underlying premises of the films that might suggest common themes.

Powell's remark that Scandinavian cinema's defining feature is its penchant for burning witches therefore seems comically absurd. Yet, as we remarked earlier, her observation contains a rather important insight struggling for expression. Why indeed would Bergman include in his film a segment about burning a witch? Was it merely because of the loose association in the popular imagination of witch burning with the Middle Ages? The act of persecution confabulates pagan superstition and medieval Christian fear of it into one single image—witches are by definition pagan, even as their persecutors have punished them in the name of Christianity. The act of witch burning, then, exemplifies this conflict, one that is certainly peculiar (even if not exclusive) to Scandinavian cinema, and indeed, some of that cinema's greatest artists have employed it.

Peter Cowie, one of Bergman's strongest champions, holds that critics such as Jörn Donner see Bergman's historical films as merely taking on "the trappings of the past" in order to "disguise the questions and assertions of modern man."[6] Under the terms imposed by such a reading, contemporary audiences might be compelled to identify with the disillusioned, spiritually confused Knight (Max von Sydow), who looks on in horror as a mute girl, about to be burned at the stake, submits to her terrible fate. This sort of reading suggests that Bergman is employing the device of dramatic irony: as beneficiaries of the Enlightenment, modern viewers, freed of our ignorance and superstition, look on in horror at a reenactment depicting the unspeakably cruel and barbarous acts of our medieval ancestors.

Yet perhaps Scandinavian cinema's supposed predilection for burning witches is only a particular instantiation of a tension, with roots deep in the history of the culture, between pagan and Christian virtues. Under the terms of this alternative interpretation, Bergman's film expresses not merely the director's own religious doubt or confusion (the auteur critic's reading) but also his culture's as well, as the Scandinavian countries were the last in Europe to be Christianized.

Bergman's Pagan Paradigm

In our view, the paradigmatic Scandinavian horror film is Bergman's *Jungfrukällan* (*The Virgin Spring*, 1960), for precisely the reason stated above: the severe tension between pagan codes and Christian virtues. Like his earlier work, *Det sjunde inseglet*, *Jungfrukällan* is set in the Middle Ages. The story is about a naïve virgin, Karin (Birgitta Pettersson) who,

while riding alone to deliver candles to the church for a feast day, is brutally raped and murdered by two brothers who have in their care a younger
brother, still a child. What ensues is a story of revenge, as the girl's father
Töre (Max von Sydow) reverts from his adopted Christian faith to an
older, pagan ethos, slaughtering his daughter's tormentors without
mercy.[7] Karin's rape and ensuing murder is graphic and revolting; the
brothers are crude and repulsive, forerunners of the backwoods predators
of John Boorman's *Deliverance* (1972), and as demented and callous in
their cruelty.[8] This is augmented by its juxtaposition to Karin's adolescent
sense of her own self-importance and mistaken belief that she is unas-
sailable, invulnerable. When the brothers murder her it is violent and
swift, made all the more shocking by the fact that we see it from the point
of view of another child, their younger brother, who is traumatized by
what he witnesses. Also despicable is when the brothers unwittingly
attempt to sell items of Karin's clothing to her own family, which is what
implicates them in her murder.

The later parallel scene, in which Karin's father issues a retribution
equally swift and brutal, is made truly horrible by his murder of the abused
and innocent younger brother, whom Töre kills even though his wife
implores him to show mercy. Despite this, the film lacks the usual presence of monsters (unless one sees the otherwise human murderers as
monsters) and the supernatural elements are minimized: there is the miracle of the virgin spring that appears at the end, but otherwise in
Jungfrukällan we see Bergman's insistence on portraying the Middle Ages
in a quotidian light, with attention to historical accuracy. The result is a
realistic effect not often associated with horror, in contrast to the director's use of a naturalistic landscape and symbolic drama in *Det sjunde
inseglet*.

Jungfrukällan is a paradigmatic Scandinavian horror film for two
reasons. First, what distinguishes Scandinavian horror from that of other
nationalities is the tension between paganism and Christianity, revealing
a deep-rooted cultural fear, or at least preoccupation, with the opposition
between a Norse heroic code of life and the Christian values that drove
this ancient system of belief underground, culturally and psychologically.
The repressed pagan code that survived aggressive Christian efforts to
supplant it—frequently, but not always, presented as a form of witchcraft—continually threatens to break through the veneer of its successor,
and sometimes does just that, with startling results.[9] Second, *Jungfrukällan* insists on de-emphasizing the sensationalism often associated with

horror in favor of a more realistic mode of expression: a preference for narrative rather than spectacle, and complexity of character rather than special effects. Indeed, the horror in this film resides in the light of common day, and, ironically, on a Sunday as well.

It has been widely acknowledged that Wes Craven's *Last House on the Left* (1972) is a remake or adaptation of *Jungfrukällan,* but our argument that *Jungfrukällan* is a horror film does not rest on the fact that Craven used it as source material.[10] Indeed, the differences between the films only bring our claims into sharper relief. *Last House* expurgates the entire religious conflict—the clash between pagan and Christian values—that drives *Jungfrukällan,* thus underscoring by its absence how essential it is to Bergman's film. In preparation for the slaughter of his daughter's murderers, Töre engages in an ancient (pagan) ritual of purification, selecting with care the proper birch tree for his self-flagellation, followed by a cleansing bath. Michael Brashinsky characterizes Töre's dilemma in concise fashion: "He is torn between the pagan god he has renounced and the Christian god he does not understand. . . . A hero of a classical tragedy . . . he kills because the god he has chosen has not only left him but has also left him no choice."[11] Bergman's film dramatizes with pristine accuracy the repeated fear of the return of the repressed paganism that serves as a distinguishing feature of Scandinavian horror films. Amidst a quotidian reality and Christian calm, subterranean pagan impulses rise up, violently and unexpectedly disrupting the façade of tranquility and acceptance.

We thus find a profoundly deep irony in Märta (Ingrid Thulin)'s line to the pastor suffering from a loss of faith in Bergman's *Nattvardsgästerna* (*Winter Light,* 1963): "A Sunday at the bottom of Thor's Valley." According to Cowie, Bergman characterized *Nattvardsgästerna* as "certainty unmasked,"[12] a description that could also be applied to *Jungfrukällan.* This and other features of Bergman's film art appear in that of other directors, revealing a pattern that helps to move toward a definition of typical shared features that make Scandinavian films unique.

Dreyer and the Witch

At this point we are compelled to raise what would seem to be an obvious question, which is why a non-Catholic, Danish as opposed to French director would have been so strongly interested in making a film about

Joan of Arc. We are referring, of course, to Dreyer, and his 1928 film, *La passion de Jeanne d'Arc*. Certainly we can't discount the director's own comments, including the short statement written at the time of the first release of *La passion de Jeanne d'Arc*, in which he claimed, "The virgin of Orleans and those matters that surrounded her death began to interest me when the shepherd girl's canonization in 1920 once again drew the attention of the public-at-large to the events and actions involving her—and not only in France."[13] Dreyer had previously published an article praising what he saw as a revival in French filmmaking, which included some strong words of praise for director Abel Gance, whose epic *Napoléon* was being filmed at the time Dreyer met him.[14] Indeed, it was Charles Pathé's Société générale de films, producers of *Napoléon*, who would produce Dreyer's film on Joan of Arc and hire him to direct it. Pursuing this line of argument, Dreyer's desire to make a film about Joan of Arc stemmed from several reasons: there was popular interest in Joan of Arc (i.e., "box-office appeal"); he was strongly interested in her story; the international success of Dreyer's comedy, *Du skal ære din hustru* (*Master of the House*, 1925) had established his reputation in France; and he could work in France, where financiers and technicians would be sympathetic toward an art film about one of that country's cherished historical figures.

Even if these assumptions are correct, a thorough knowledge of Dreyer's oeuvre reveals that there had to be other factors, and we do not simply mean certain religious reasons (e.g., perhaps a presumed non-Catholic, Protestant belief of Dreyer's that Jean of Arc did indeed receive individual messages sent directly from God). First of all, Dreyer did not film Joan of Arc's entire life—only her trial and execution. The historical record shows that the trial itself lasted for five months, from early January 1431 to late May 1431. Dreyer compressed this time period to one day—the day she is burned at the stake—in a closed environment reminiscent of the Kammerspiel, relying on the records taken during Joan of Arc's 1455 trial of rehabilitation.[15] During the actual historical trial, several accusations were made against her, among them (perhaps the most revealing of all) the charge of witchcraft.[16]

Witchcraft had been explored in films before *La passion de Jeanne d'Arc*, especially in Christensen's *Häxan*—a particularly idiosyncratic film for which Dreyer had admiration—and in Dreyer's own *Blade af satans bog* (*Leaves of Satan's Book*, 1919). Moreover, he was to return to the subject again; as in *La passion de Jeanne d'Arc*, in *Vredens dag* a woman is wrongly accused of witchcraft and, after a false confession is extracted, is burned at the stake. Clearly this was a theme to which Dreyer returned for reasons that are both complex and varied.

Written by Edgar Høyer, *Blade af satans bog* was substantially rewritten by Dreyer. The film consists of four episodes depicting the role of evil during different periods of human history, built loosely around the notion of betrayal. Widely acknowledged to have been influenced by D. W. Griffith's *Intolerance* (1916), *Blade af satans bog* is, however, thoroughly anti-modernist in its style. Dreyer eschews Griffith's crosscutting technique for a static visual style composed of a series of tableaux vivants. The first section, "In Palestine," tells the story of Judas's betrayal of Christ but is heavily dependent on the gospel of John because it links the Pharisees' desire to kill Christ to Jesus's raising of Lazarus. Although not accused of witchcraft, Christ is nonetheless persecuted and betrayed by Judas, with, remarkably, Satan sorrowed by his own culpability in the perpetration of such evil.

More important is the second episode of the film, "The Inquisition," with Helge Nissen again as Satan, here playing the role of the Grand Inquisitor.[17] We are not the first to point out that this episode strongly anticipates *La passion de Jeanne d'Arc,* but as we shall see, it also apparently influenced *Häxan.* This episode is set in sixteenth-century Seville at the height of the Spanish Inquisition. Various intrigues in the spirit of Poe ensue, culminating in the persecution of a beautiful young woman, Isabella (Ebon Strandin), taken away to be burned at the stake. Just as the torture chamber was used for dramatic effect in *La passion de Jean d'Arc,* Dreyer uses the torture chamber for similar effects in *Blade af satans bog.* Isabella is spared torture by throwing herself at the lustful mercy of Don Fernández (Johannes Meyer), her father, but Don Gomez (Hallander Hellemann) is shown being tortured, and indeed dies as a result of the trauma.

The central three episodes of *Häxan*—a film in which Dreyer took a strong interest[18]—culminate in the printer's wife being falsely accused of witchcraft by a group of Inquisitors and being led away to be burned at the stake. Christensen elicits great sympathy for the victim by showing us that she is entrapped by the wily, zealous inquisitors—here the gothic villains. In 1927, while making *La passion de Jeanne d'Arc,* Dreyer would in turn take from *Häxan* this same gothic device, the entrapment of an innocent, defenseless woman. After the first trial scene, Jeanne (Maria Falconetti) is taken to her cell, where British guards harass her. One of them pulls her ring from her finger, intending to steal it, but the ring is returned by the sinister Nicolas Loyseleur (Maurice Schutz, who would later appear in *Vampyr* as the old man whose daughter has been bitten by the vampire) who thereby hopes to dupe Jeanne into confiding in him as a friend. As Loyseleur tries to gain Jeanne's sympathies by showing her a (counterfeit) letter from King Charles, Pierre Cauchon (Eugène Silvain) secretly approaches and spies on them from behind a small opening in the wall—in his original script, Dreyer refers to this aperture as "a judas, or chink in the wall," through which Cauchon can eavesdrop.[19] In *Häxan*, this collusive strategy is precisely how the inquisitors dupe the frightened woman, wrongly accused of witchcraft, into giving false testimony suggesting she knows witchcraft in order to save her infant child. The sadism portrayed in these films is readily apparent, but also an essential ingredient of the stories.

Thus, in the Inquisition episode of *Blade af satans bog*, Dreyer introduced into film imagery instruments of torture, used by the inquisitors to coax confessions from those accused of witchcraft. Perhaps the imagery is not as byzantine as that in *Häxan*, but one of the sets in the Inquisition sequence is the "torture chamber." The torture chamber reappears in both *La passion de Jeanne d'Arc* and *Vredens dag*, when Herlof's Marte (Anna Svierkier), a defenseless old widow, is tortured into confessing that she is a witch. In addition to instruments of torture, Dreyer included sequences that contain what might be called "the machinery of death." In his essay on *Jungfrukällan* and *Last House on the Left*, Brashinsky notes that one of Craven's trademarks is the "elaborately schemed and painstakingly executed . . . variety show of vengeance," consisting of imagery including "murderous hammers, chain saws, short circuits, etc."[20]

While it is true that Dreyer's imagery does not consist of murderous hammers, chain saws, and the like, it is rather startling to consider that precisely the same observation can be made about Dreyer (and, as we shall see, Bergman). Think of the elaborate, detailed preparations for the burning of Herlof's Marte, or the sophisticated architecture of Joan of Arc's funeral pyre, the traveling guillotine in the third episode of *Blade af satans bog*, and the grotesque punishment inflicted on the doctor at the conclusion of *Vampyr*, in which the flour mill is used to entrap and asphyxiate him (anticipated by the torture chamber sequence in *La passion de Jeanne d'Arc*).[21] It may be that "elaborately schemed and painstakingly executed" acts of vengeance originated in Scandinavian cinema, an outgrowth of the detailed preparations needed to burn a witch. Is not the driving of a massive metal rod through the chest of the female vampire in *Vampyr* the first such instance of the actual driving of a stake in vampire cinema? In Tod Browning's 1931 *Dracula*, the driving of the stake—into a male vampire—occurs offscreen. Perhaps the hammer wielded by David Gray (Nicolas de Gunzburg, billed as "Julian West") indicates a distant trace of Craven's murderous hammers? (A painstaking labor it is indeed to use a heavy hammer to drive a metal stake through the chest of a vampire.) No such elaborate act occurs in F. W. Murnau's *Nosferatu* (1922), for instance, in which the rays of the sun destroy the vampire.[22]

While certain of Dreyer's film have elaborately conceived acts of violence, this is not to say that Dreyer found no important lessons in *Nosferatu*. We have argued that a feature of Scandinavian horror is that it opts for a realistic mode of expression, and thus the mist-shrouded landscape and disjointed plot of *Vampyr* would seem to violate our own premise. Yet as S. S. Prawer observes:

> It was Murnau who had shown . . . how much the fantastic film would gain from using real settings: streets and interiors in Lübeck, Wismar, Lauenburg, and Dolni Kubin; Oravski Castle in the Carpathians; the waves and shores of the North Sea. It was Murnau who had shown, once and for all, how such "real" settings could be suffused with poetic, imaginative, subjective elements; and . . . how even within the closed genre of the terror-film the scene could be opened out, could point beyond itself, through an imaginative treatment of space.[23]

Vampyr's elaborate violence may have inspired the violence of vengeance in Bergman's *Jungfrukällan*, here captured in all its fury by Cowie:

> The eldest brother meets his death. Töre stabs him through the heart and leaves him in a crucified stance at the far end of the hall. The thin brother almost escapes by dodging Töre's first lunge and scrambling up the pole that supports the vent in the roof, using the same grip as Ingeri did when invoking Odin. This association is made even more significant when Töre crushes his victim in the flames of the fire that Ingeri has blown alight. Finally, the boy is snatched from Märeta's arms, where he has fled for protection. Töre gathers him up in a fireman's lift and flings him against the wall.[24]

In this passage, Cowie encapsulates the conviction that drives Töre to his act of vengeance, undertaken with the commitment of a warrior dedicated to a sacred code. Töre's earlier ritualistic preparation, dramatized by an act of purification before battle, underscores the notion that in his murder of the three brothers he reverts to an earlier heroic code that is antagonistic to the New Testament emphasis on forgiveness. Additional examples of such violence in Bergman's work abound. Albert Emanuel Vogler (Max von Sydow)'s elaborate act of vengeance against Dr. Vergérus (Gunnar Björnstrand) during the autopsy sequence in *Ansiktet* (*The Magician*, a.k.a. *The Face*, 1958) is one such example, a sequence that also includes references to the horror genre.

Both Dreyer and Bergman make use of the vampire, although a study of Bergman's cinematic art reveals a more persistent presence of the figure. His films frequently focus on vampirism and art, offering various configurations of the "exchange" between the artist and his audience and also between the artist and his subject. As we shall see, Bergman's artists are commonly vampiric in their relentless efforts to prey on human subjects, which they transform in their art; on occasion, however, the artists are, in turn, preyed on by their audience. Vampirism also appears metaphorically in his films when some secret trauma or guilt from the past (often a broken taboo) returns to prey on an individual. This return of the repressed serves as a microcosm of the larger cultural clash between a vanquished paganism and a Christianity antithetical to it that is so pervasive in Scandinavian film.

Vampirism, Art, and Horror

In his insightful 1981 study of the vampire in romantic literature, James B. Twitchell explores the concept of vampirism as an "exchange" that takes place between the artist, his object of art, his audience, and/or the subject of his art, a concept that emerged fully with the high romantics and continues in contemporary art. His chapter, "The Artist as Vampire," features a scheme that uses examples from romantic art illustrative of this relationship. For example, Coleridge's "The Rime of the Ancient Mariner" involves a positive gaining of energy for the Mariner—a taboo breaker and artist who tells the tale of his own guilt—at the expense of the Wedding Guest, whom the Mariner detains with his hypnotic "glittering eye." Against his will, the Wedding Guest must listen to the tale, departing afterward "a sadder but a wiser man." By extension, according to Twitchell, the reading audience provides energy for the artist, Coleridge himself. In the case of Poe's short story, "The Oval Portrait," the object of art (the painting of the artist's beloved) gains life as it is drained from the subject of art, the beloved, who sits for the painting but dies doing so. The reverse is true in Oscar Wilde's *The Picture of Dorian Gray*, in which the subject of the painting, Dorian himself, derives strength from the object, Basil's portrait of him. These cases, and others Twitchell cites, feature an artist who either breaks a taboo or carries a guilty secret within him, one who preys on others and/or is preyed on. This notion of the relationship between the artist, his subject, his object (or artifact), and his audience, is helpful in understanding how prevalent the concept of vampirism is in Bergman's films.

Såsom i en spegel (*Through a Glass Darkly*, 1961) employs the Kammerspiel in that it features only four characters, all of the same family, in an environment that is decidedly claustrophobic. Bergman renders explicit the theme of the predatory artist and the devastating effects of pursuing his art at any cost. The father, David (Gunnar Björnstrand), is an ageing novelist who has garnered enormous popular fame although true greatness has eluded him. His schizophrenic wife had died years before the film opens, apparently bequeathing her disease to her daughter Karin (Harriet Andersson), who is entering the final stage of this degenerative, crippling disorder, despite the vigilant care of her loving husband Martin (Max von Sydow). The fourth character, Minus (Lars Passgård), is Karin's seventeen-year-old brother who is experiencing the sexual frustration of adolescence and the loneliness of life with a neglectful and distant artist father.

The family has gathered to await David's arrival at the ubiquitous summer retreat found in so many of Bergman's films—on a remote island that affords privacy but also augments its inhabitants' isolation. David attempts to finish his latest novel even as Martin updates him about the seriousness of Karin's illness. The siblings, Minus and Karin, share some tense scenes together, alternately filled with affection and fits of ill temper. David is troubled because he knows that ultimate success has eluded him, so when Martin tells him of Karin's condition and prognosticates that her madness will soon be permanent, the vampiric artist emerges. This is evident when Karin reads an ensuing entry in her father's diary in which he confesses that he wants to study her descent into madness, grist for the mill for his art. Naturally, this is devastating for Karin, serving as the impetus that finally results in her entry into the delusional, nightmare world she has imagined.

David's desire to "study" his daughter's demise obviously represents a pattern in his life, one that his family resents and also one for which he ultimately reproaches himself. This urge is, indeed, vampiric. Here, the proposed object of art (a future novel) preys on the subject of art (the mentally ill Karin), an arrangement made even more despicable because the artist uses his own daughter. This fits the vampiric mode, too, because, as Twitchell observes, the vampire's initial victims are almost always family members or close acquaintances, whether the hunger is for love or revenge.[25] In this case it also suggests an incestuous pattern, one that is realized in the incest between Karin and Minus just before she loses her lucidity. That both Karin and Minus "confess" their incest to David, who is not surprised but only saddened by it, indicates that it has been lurking under the surface for a long time.

This camaraderie between Karin and Minus, formed by their resentment toward their selfish father, takes its final expression here, but earlier it had been dramatized in a short skit written by Minus and performed as a "present" for David on his return to the island. In this skit, an artist (played by Minus) refuses to join in death his beloved, a princess played by Karin. To a true artist such a sacrifice should not matter: his art renders him immortal and indifferent to death, but here the artist cannot relinquish his life to join his beloved, suggesting that, in reality, he knows he has not achieved greatness. Clearly, this is intended to show David that his family is aware of the fact that it is continually being sacrificed to his art. And yet the mask of affection continues until Karin succumbs to her madness, which, significantly, she envisions as a room filled with expectant people awaiting the arrival of *Him*, God. God, it turns out in the last moment of horror, is only a predatory spider who attempts, unsuccessfully, to mate with Karin, to "penetrate" her. Her notion that God is not the loving, forgiving deity of Christian myth, but rather a devouring predator who inflicts great suffering, demanding sacrificial victims to satisfy his own appetite, is repeated in the spiritual crisis of Pastor Ericsson (also played by Gunnar Björnstrand) and the nonbeliever whom he vainly tries to help in *Nattvardsgästerna*.[26]

Såsom i en spegel, then, portrays the predatory artist, a type of vampire. A passage from dramatist George Bernard Shaw's *Man and Superman* is applicable to this film, showing why all of the family members reproach David as he ultimately reproaches himself:

The true artist will let his wife starve, his children go barefoot, his mother drudge for his living at seventy, sooner than work at anything but his art. To women he is half vivisector, half vampire. He gets into intimate relations with them to study them, to strip the mask of convention from them, to surprise their inmost secrets, knowing that they have the power to rouse his deepest creative energies, to rescue him from his cold reason, to make him see visions and dream dreams, to inspire him, as he calls it.[27]

Vampires, it seems, need not wear black capes and bare their fangs. They need not exist only in the night, although it is significant that David cannot sleep, nor can Karin, who preys sexually on Minus, herself becoming the victimizer (though he finally seems willing enough) as she is also victim. Instead, vampires can be those to whom we are most closely attached, those we entrust with our lives, those to whom we look for guidance, solace, joy. This theme Bergman revisited repeatedly, suggesting that he attached a personal as well as cultural significance to it.

Bergman's only overt horror film, *Vargtimmen* (*Hour of the Wolf*, 1968), also focuses on the connection between art and vampirism.[28] In some sense, this film functions as a revised, more complex version of *Såsom i en spegel*, with the two works enjoying a number of common features: a predatory artist who keeps a diary, the presence of a progressive madness, guilty secrets and transgressions that haunt the characters, a setting on a remote island, and images of insects or animals as predators and/or vampires. In *Vargtimmen*, Johan (Max von Sydow), a popular painter, retreats with his pregnant wife, Alma (Liv Ullman), to a remote island because a mental affliction has impeded his ability to work. The film is told in flashback form based on what Alma has told the narrator and on Johan's own diary. Alma identifies two revealing "symptoms" of Johan's illness: an increasing agoraphobia and insomnia, caused by his fear of the dark, which is ultimately a fear of himself. In his diary and sketches, Johan records his fears, the latter of which he shares with Alma, and the former of which she reads—as Karin had read her father's diary—without permission.

Johan has sketched "them," his persecutors whom Alma assumes are imaginary. One, whom he labels "ordinary," appears to be homosexual; another is an old woman whose face comes off with her hat (harlot/mother); the "Bird Man" Johan claims is the "worst," and the "others" he fears are carnivores ("cannibals"), insects and, especially, "spidermen"—yet another connection with Karin's illness. He pleads with Alma (which means "soul") to stay awake with him, as he is particularly terrified of the "hour of the wolf," that last hour before dawn when, Johan claims, "most people die and most children are born, when nightmares come to us, and if you are awake you are afraid."

At first we are sympathetic to Johan and to his wife, whom he loves because she reminds him that he once told her: "God had made me all of one piece" and "I had whole feelings and whole thoughts." It is important to note here that while the titular allusion would seem to belong to another element of the horror genre—the werewolf—it is closely allied to, and often interchangeable with, vampire lore. As Twitchell explains, "The vampire myth in the West has always had animalistic overtones; in fact, in certain languages like Slavic and Greek, the word 'vampire' also meant 'wolf,' and lycanthropy, or the human-wolf transformation, is often part of the vampire myth."[29] Moreover, there is considerable overlap between the werewolf and the vampire: "In both cases the human victim appears normal by day but then metamorphoses at nightfall,"[30] as some werewolves, when killed, become vampires. Perhaps this is why Alma remarks that Johan was upset when he discovered the "footprints outside the kitchen window" shortly after their arrival on the island.

The quotidian reality amidst which this horror unfolds only increases its effect. Alma's sanity, her simple affection for her husband and their unborn child, stands in sharp contrast to Johan's delusions. As she hangs clothes on the line, darns socks, and fetches water from the pump, Johan slips more and more into his madness, which is not unlike Karin's in its paranoia. The film's disjointed, elliptical narrative makes it difficult to distinguish between Johan's dreams and delusions from objective reality. The film is, finally, a psychodrama: we soon discern that various characters who appear out of nowhere belong to Johan's guilty past, and that, although they appear to be great admirers of his art, they are privy to his transgressions and have returned to persecute and consume him—a conflation of vengeful Furies and parasitic vampires.

Even Alma experiences the supernatural quality of some of the characters, especially the old woman with the hat (Naima Wifstrand), whose face peels off like a mask that Johan had drawn in his sketch book. She appears suddenly, tells Alma she is 216 years old, then quickly corrects herself, stating she is 76, and instructs Alma to read the diary that accompanies the sketchbook.

Key characters from Johan's past appear, evidently as they are recorded in his diary that Alma reads: a previous lover, Veronica Vogler (Ingrid Thulin), and a young boy. Veronica, an alluring blonde with whom

Johan had had a five-year illicit affair, appears to him on the beach. She shows him a bite mark on her breast[31] and then confesses that she received a cryptic letter that read, "You can't see us but we see you. Awful things can happen. Dreams can be made known. The end is near. The springs will dry up. And other fluids will moisten your white thighs." The two embrace, and Johan undresses her. His next "visitor" on the beach is a man with a beret and glasses, Curator Heerbrand (Ulf Johansson), who dogs Johan, taunting him: "One returns to the scene of the crime, they say," as he boasts, "I turn souls inside out." Johan, angered and unnerved, knocks him down and shouts "Shut up!" Out of the blue appears one Baron von Merkens (Erland Josephson) who explains that he occupies a castle on the island, that he is an admirer of Johan's art, and then issues a dinner invitation. The castle's Archivist Lindhorst (Georg Rydeberg) is consciously modeled on Dracula, and bears a striking resemblance to the most famous of Dracula actors, Bela Lugosi. It is Lindhorst who at last "feeds on Johan" in a scene that explicitly portrays a violent bite, as the other predators— those who are all connected with the Baron's castle and are present at his dinner party—encircle him in the ritualistic murder, one that appears in Johan's mind but is nonetheless real.

Other explicit vampiric elements lead up to this: a puppet show at the dinner party that dramatizes a scene from Mozart's *The Magic Flute;* the bite on her thigh that the Baron's wife displays to Johan and Alma, given to her by a lover; the scene in which Johan is summoned back to the castle for an assignation with Veronica. Bats abound, the jealous Baron walks up the wall and across the ceiling, and Veronica—who appears to be dead— suddenly comes to life when Johan embraces her. However, at this climactic moment of wish fulfillment in which he is reunited with her, she and those who have directed and then witness the scene begin to laugh and ridicule him, which makes him start to age rapidly. In a lucid moment, Johan says: "The limit...at last has been reached and I thank you. The glass is shattered...but what do the splinters reflect? Can you tell me that?"

In this cathartic moment Johan, the artist, is shown to be vampiric in that he has fed off the emotions of others to create his art. He has carried on an illicit affair with a married woman he still desires, immortalizing her in a portrait owned and displayed proudly by the Baron's wife. The "scene of the crime" alluded to by Heerbrand is, as it turns out, one that is recorded in Johan's diary, the most shocking of all. It shows a pubescent boy who accompanies Johan when he is fishing on the shore. Suddenly Johan attacks the boy, who bites him in apparent self-defense. Johan beats the boy mercilessly, then attempts to dispose of the body in the water. Cowie sees this as a possible homosexual relationship, the struggle rife with erotic overtones: "Even the mortal struggle between the two has the rhythm of a violent orgasm. And the ominous reappearance of the body after it has been tipped into the water suggests that the boy's significance cannot be so easily dismissed."[32] To us, it seems that this is arguably an encoded molestation scene.[33]

The characters at the castle literally feed on Johan in his delusion, one that hurls him into permanent madness and then, presumably, death (possibly suicide). Thus, if he feeds on others to create his art, he also becomes a victim of an audience that consumes him, gathering energy in their exchange with Johan and his art. Using Twitchell's scheme, in *Vargtimmen* the artist feeds on his subjects, while the audience gains positive energy from both the artifacts, or objects of art, and from the artist himself.

Aside from his loss of a firm grip on reality, a subtler element of horror occurs in a defining episode from his childhood, which Johan recounts to Alma. This incident is based on Bergman's own experience. Johan recalls that once, as a child, his father locked him in a closet, claiming that a little man who lived there would gnaw off his toes. (Bear in mind that Twitchell states vampires in folklore might even bite toes.) He howled with terror and begged to be forgiven—for a transgression that is never specified. At last the door opened and the young Johan was allowed to see daylight. He was subsequently caned on a green sofa, his father asking, "How many strokes do you deserve?"—to which the guilty and chastened boy replied, "As many as possible." Afterward, oddly, Johan asked his mother to forgive him; she wept and extended her hand, which he kissed. Although the mother's role in this punishment seems peripheral, in actual fact it must have been important since he had begged her forgiveness, which she granted through her regal gesture of the extended hand, cold and comfortless. It is worth noting that the aged harlot who dwells at the castle entices Johan as he returns to search for Veronica, coaxing him to "kiss her foot" with the promise that she will then reveal Veronica's whereabouts. One could read the foot as a fetishized object, but it may be an example of displacement, as Johan remembers kissing his mother's hand as a child. If this is the case, both parents, not just the father, are implicated in the trauma that drives his art.

The true element of terror can scarcely be missed here: this, quite plainly, is a story of child abuse. This is perhaps why Johan confesses to his "persecutors" (the people in the castle) that his art is nothing more than "compulsion," that he is driven to create. Indeed, the only art we see him produce on the island are the sketches of his nightmares and an unsuccessful portrait of Alma. As Cowie correctly notes, Johan is hardly innocent.[34] His transgressions include excessive alcohol consumption, deception, adultery, jealousy, possible bisexuality, and attempted murder. Yet the episode from his childhood so clearly indicates the returned of the repressed, as do the ghosts who haunt him from his past. Guilt brings them to life, as guilt created his art.

The Child as Victim

The themes of vampirism and child victimization, of the vampire preying on children, clearly haunted Dreyer's imagination as well as Bergman's. In the original screenplay for *Vampyr*—which, incidentally, appeared in Germany the year before Fritz Lang's *M* (1933)—Dreyer included a chilling sequence in which David Gray enters an old, cluttered, dirty laundry room. As Gray looks around the junk-filled room, the thing that utterly "astonishes" him "is a collection of children's clogs standing neatly in rows. They are not quite as dusty as the other things in the old laundry room."[35] Backing out of the room, Gray goes "back to the spot where a door leads out to the staircase." He stops there, and hears, "in the quivering stillness of the old house . . . hounds baying and a child weeping. Then a scream, a half-suppressed child's scream, as if a hand had closed over the mouth of the screamer."[36]

As Prawer notes, in the actual film (at least the most complete version of the film presently available) the image of the children's clogs is absent.

> and though the sound-track includes what sounds like barking, baying, and whimpering dogs, a child's weeping cannot be clearly distinguished on it. Instead, we have shots of a tiny skeleton, a cross between an atomized baby and a voodoo doll. David Gray's enquiry after the weeping child is, however, retained (he, obviously, has heard a child, even if the viewer has not) and so are the doctor's negative answers: "There is no child here," and again: "Here there are neither children nor dogs."[37]

In our view, *Vampyr* is the distant precursor to Lars von Trier's *Forbrydelsens element* (*The Element of Crime*, 1984) and to certain of the sub-

David Gray (Julian West) staring out of his own coffin in *Vampyr* (1932)

plots in von Trier's 1994 TV mini-series, *Riget* (*The Kingdom*). Both of these films—*Forbrydelsens element* a hybrid mixture of the horror and post-apocalyptic science-fiction genres, *Riget* a horror comedy—are centrally concerned with children as victims of violent crimes.

Forbrydelsens element, von Trier's feature film debut, is about a Detective Fisher (Michael Elphick) who returns to Germany to solve a series of "lotto murders," in which a mysterious figure by the name of "Harry Grey" (an allusion to David Gray of *Vampyr*, as is the setting in Germany, where *Vampyr* was made) is suspected of stalking, killing, and horribly disfiguring children who sell lottery tickets.[38] Fisher returns to Europe after thirteen years of exile in Cairo. He has been contacted by his aged former mentor at the police academy, Osborne (Esmond Knight), author of a controversial book of theoretical criminal psychology titled *The Element of Crime.*

Osborne's book details "a series of mental exercises designed to improve our understanding of the behavioral pattern of the criminal." Although it is implied that the investigative method outlined by Osborne has since been discredited, Fisher begins to think and act like Harry Grey in order to retrace Grey's route and in so doing anticipate the scene of the next crime. Fisher is befriended by a prostitute, Kim (Meme Lai), who he takes with him on his journey, urging her to address him as Harry Grey. Soon, Fisher intuits what he believes to be the geometrical pattern that Grey is using to choose his murder sites—not the geometric figure of the square, as Osborne had believed, but the alphabetic glyph "H"—and hastens to Halle, the city where he believes the next murder will occur. There, an elderly man, "grandfather" (Preben Lerdorff-Rye, who had played leading roles in Dreyer's *Vredens dag* and *Ordet*), allows his grand-daughter to serve as bait in a trap Fisher sets to capture Grey. A mysterious figure appears, casting a shadow; when Fisher draws his handkerchief to hand to the small girl to dry her tears of fright, a talisman falls out of his pocket identical to those left at the murder scenes by the killer. The girl panics, thinking Fisher is Grey, and begins to scream as she breaks the glass out of a window in an attempt to escape. Overreacting, Fisher grabs the girl and in attempting to stifle her screams, he suffocates her. (Recall the passage from Dreyer's script to *Vampyr:* "[I]n the quivering stillness of the old house . . . a child weeping. Then a scream, a half-suppressed child's scream, as if a hand had closed over the mouth of the screamer."[39])

Von Trier has said that at the beginning of his career he typically used "people who're very sure of what's right and what action to take," adding, "You can be sure that when they've done the right thing, it's gone wrong and they also did it badly."[40] This is certainly applicable to the protagonist of *Forbrydelsens element,* Detective Fisher. Although the frame narrative suggests that Fisher is urged by the therapist (Ahmed El Shenawi) to recount his story out of expiation of guilt (the allusion to Coleridge's *Rime of the Ancient Mariner,* "Water, water everywhere," that begins Fisher's narration is highly suggestive), at times there are contradictory suggestions that he himself is Harry Grey's doppelgänger, as emphasized by the repeated references to Fisher's severe headaches. At one point, during a boat ride down a mysterious tunnel that is referred to as "the tunnel of love," prior to performing oral sex, Kim gives him a bottle of pills designed to intensify his sexual pleasure; after the effect of the pill(s) wears off Fisher suffers an excruciating headache. As Fisher claims to be closing in on Harry Grey, he acknowledges that the headaches have become more frequent. When he and Kim check into the Elite Hotel after leaving Halberstadt, the desk clerk claims to remember Harry Grey (Fisher?) because he had asked for the anti-psychotic medicine, Thorazine. Does the desk clerk remember Fisher or Grey? Is Fisher following his own tracks, assuming that they belong to someone else, like Winnie the Pooh following his own tracks around the big oak tree? And when he is waiting with the little girl for Grey to arrive, Fisher is shown wincing in pain and rubbing his forehead, a sign that he is suffering a severe headache, as if he is "splitting" or morphing into Harry Grey—which, in some sense, he does, during his act of "silencing" the screaming girl.[41]

Fisher (Michael Elph-
ick) grabs the girl in
The Element of Crime
(1984)

Yet, like the Congo River in Joseph Conrad's *Heart of Darkness,* or
the Mopu Palace in Michael Powell and Emeric Pressburger's *Black Narcissus* (1947), the dark, eerie, rain-drenched (*Blade Runner*-ish) Europe to
which Fisher returns functions as an "excessive signifier." In *The Melodramatic Imagination,* Peter Brooks theorizes that the melodramatic form
creates an asymmetrical relationship between signifier and signified;
more precisely, a signified in excess of the signifier, "making large and
insubstantial claims on meaning."[42] As Priya Jaikumar observes, settings
such as the Congo River and Mopu Palace are "places where things happen far in excess of explicable causes. The incommensurabilities among
word, intention, and their meanings or consequences are inexplicable and
therefore attributed to the place."[43] The haunting imagery of the location—the vague, ill-defined sense of menace, of some unspecified eco-
logical and economic collapse (the buses stopped running three years
earlier), the oppressive effect of perpetual rain and darkness (as Kim says
to Fisher, "it's always three o'clock in the morning"), the child murders—
all contribute to Fisher's psychic and emotional disintegration.

In *Riget* (*The Kingdom,* 1994), von Trier's horror comedy that was
originally a four-part Danish television series, the Kingdom Hospital
likewise functions as an excessive signifier, as the hospital's very location
promises effects over and above that which can be attributed to (rational)
explicable causes. The Kingdom Hospital, although it had been dedicated
to the belief that superstition and ignorance would never again "shake the
bastions of science," in fact rests on ancient, primordial marshland, enig-
matically alluded to by a voice-over at the beginning of the film. Thus, the
Kingdom's literal foundations on ancient marshland reflect a figurative

truth, that its principles of Enlightened reason and science have replaced, but not in fact eradicated, earlier systems of belief. In the words of Lao Tzu, "High rests on low." This layering, or stratification, is a sort of figurative restatement of our thesis that Scandinavian horror films dramatize a deep-seated cultural fear that paganism, which was driven underground but never vanquished, threatens to (re-)surface and (re-)assert itself at any time.

Although *Riget*'s four-hour-plus running time allows for several engaging and interconnected byzantine plots, for our purposes the most revealing is the one concerning Mrs. Drusse (Kirsten Rolffes), a spiritualist who feigns a neurological disorder in order to gain entrance to the hospital and conduct séances with the patients she has befriended. Mrs. Drusse is apparently drawn to the Kingdom because she believes that contact with the spiritual world is increased where death is near—in this case, the hospital. Her nemesis, Dr. Stig Helmer (Ernst Hugo Järegård), is a Swedish neurosurgeon unhappily exiled to Denmark—and hence the Kingdom Hospital—because of unspecified irregularities in his surgical practices. A champion of the Enlightenment, Stig makes it a point to discredit and mock superstition in all its forms.

During a recent visit, Mrs. Drusse hears a small child crying, and with the help of her son Bulder (Jens Okking)—an employee of the hospital—she uncovers a murder that had occurred in the early decades of the twentieth century. Through the help of various patients (one of whom dies and communicates with her from the other side), Mrs. Drusse is able to learn the identity and tragic story of the weeping child, Mary Jensen, whose spirit cannot rest until the mystery is solved and her body is put properly to rest. Mrs. Drusse's investigative efforts comprise a standard murder mystery plot, but the true element of horror occurs when the murderer is identified. As it turns out, Mary Jensen was the illegitimate daughter of Aage Krüger (Udo Kier); he kept Mary incarcerated at the hospital under the pretext that he was treating her for tuberculosis. With the help of Bulder, Mrs. Drusse uncovers Mary's patient records, which indicate that while she officially died of TB, she also had signs of acid damage, caused by the possible inhalation of chlorine gas. In addition, Mrs. Drusse learns the curious fact that Mary was never buried; indeed, in a rather startling turn, her body is discovered in a pathologist's office, preserved in a large clear glass tube. With the help of Bulder, Mrs. Drusse inters the body on the site of the old hospital chapel, saying, during a burial ceremony that invokes certain Christian funereal practices ("Ashes to ashes"), that she hopes her "tormented little soul will thus find peace." The burial scene consists of a confabulation of superstition and Christian beliefs.

Such is not the case, however. Although her body is interred, Mary cannot yet find peace, her spirit apparently still wandering in the realm of "Swedenborg's angels." Mrs. Drusse concludes that she must conduct an exorcism of the hospital, again enlisting the help of Bulder and another hospital employee. She orders a hole to be knocked open in one of the hospital's basement hallways, through which Mary's ghost can pass, and when the ghost appears they conduct an exorcism that is yet another marvelous instance of the confabulation of various religious beliefs. The series concludes with the revelation that while the ghost of Mary Jensen may have been exorcised from the hospital, other ghosts have gained entrance.

In conclusion, we'll return to Prawer, who observed, "Whoever seeks to trace the development of a genre in the art of film will inevitably come up against the principal difficulties that beset genre-studies in any medium."[44] Prawer identifies four such difficulties: films that modify a genre's formulaic practices and conventions; hybridized, borderline cases; borderline cases that reference or cite devices from other genres; and radical variations in quality and value. In our own efforts to arrive at some understanding of what constitutes Scandinavian horror films, we have provided examples that fit all four of these categories. Horror can take many forms, some more subtle yet certainly not less frightening than the stereotypes we associate with the genre. It may seem that we have strayed far from the film we have identified as paradigmatic, Bergman's *Jüngfrukällan*, yet its dramatization of the conflict of two opposing codes and the fear that the earlier may once again rise to challenge its usurper does indeed suggest that it is time to rethink our definitions about the horror genre.

Notes

1. A few studies of the Finnish cinema have been written (one by Peter Cowie, *Finnish Cinema*, was published in 1976), but we have chosen to not include a discussion of that national cinema here, largely because Finnish is more closely related to the three Baltic languages than it is to Danish and Swedish. Moreover, Finland is a relatively isolated language and culture, but we suspect that the Finnish Cinema might be best studied in the context of the Russian cinema.

2. One of the great Swedish writers of the twentieth century was Hjalmar Bergman, whose widow, Stina Bergman, was instrumental in gaining Ingmar Bergman

entrance into the screenwriting division at Svensk Filmindustri (see Peter Cowie, *Ingmar Bergman: A Critical Biography* [New York: Scribner's, 1982], 21–22). Apparently Bergman was fascinated by the connection, although he found no familial connection between himself and Hjalmar Bergman.

3. In *The Vampire Film* (South Brunswick, NJ: A. S. Barnes, 1975), James Ursini and Alain Silver observe, "The very idea of the undead woman as a white-haired crone borrows more heavily from the lore of witchcraft and sorcery than that of vampirism—the figure in the film closely resembles the witch who is burned at the stake in Dreyer's *Day of Wrath*—and, excepting such secondary characters as the Baroness in *Brides of Dracula*, is without parallel in film," 118.

4. David Bordwell and Kristin Thompson, *Film History: An Introduction* (New York: McGraw-Hill, 1994), 65, 448.

5. A retrospective of Christensen's films was held at the Museum of Modern Art in 1999. The catalog, *Benjamin Christensen: An International Dane*, was written by Jytte Jensen.

6. Cowie, *Ingmar Bergman*, 141.

7. Recall that Antonius Block, the knight played by von Sydow in *Det sjunde inseglet*, has returned from the Crusades with profound doubts about the value of slaughter in Christ's name.

8. A sex criminal and murderer had appeared in Alf Sjöberg's *Hets* (*Torment*, 1944), scripted by Bergman, in the figure of the sadistic Latin teacher students have nicknamed "Caligula" (Stig Järrel).

9. In *Lords of Chaos: The Bloody Rise of the Satanic Metal Underground* (Venice, CA: Feral House, 1998), Michael Moynihan and Didrik Søderlind explore the widespread appeal of pre-Christian religion to Scandinavian youths, including the revival of Odinism: "In Norway and Sweden there has also been growing general interest in the indigenous religion of their forefathers, to the point that at least one heathen group, Draupnir, has been recognized as a legitimate religious organization by the Norwegian government. Along with them, other Aacutesatrú [Odinism] organizations such as Bifrost also hold regular gatherings where they offer *blot*, or symbolic sacrifice, to the deities of old," 181. For a narrow band of extremists seeking inspiration from ancient European traditions, this has led to the burning of churches (some national landmarks) in homage to the Viking warriors who descended on the monasteries of Britain, and to embracing principles of fascism and National Socialism—emphatically *not* in any way a feature of the films we discuss in this essay.

10. See Michael Brashinsky, "The Spring, Defiled: Ingmar Bergman's *Virgin Spring* and Wes Craven's *Last House on the Left*," in *Play It Again, Sam: Retakes on Remakes*, ed. Andrew Horton and Stuart Y. McDougal (Berkeley: University of California Press, 1998), 162–71. We have also greatly profited from Steven Jay Schneider, "The Legacy of *Last House on the Left*," in *Horror at the Drive-In: Essays in Popular Americana*, ed. Gary D. Rhodes (Jefferson, NC: McFarland, 2003).

11. Brashinsky, "Spring, Defiled," 164.

12. Cowie, *Ingmar Bergman*, 197.

13. "Realized Mysticism," in *Dreyer in Double Reflection*, ed. Donald Skoller (New York: E. P. Dutton, 1973), 47.

14. "French Film" (1926), in Skoller, ed., *Dreyer in Double Reflection*, 36–46.

15. Paul Schrader's *Transcendental Style in Film: Ozu, Bresson, Dreyer* ([1972] New York: Da Capo, 1988) contains a valuable discussion of Dreyer's style from someone who has carefully studied his films. In *La passion de Jeanne d'Arc*, says Schrader, "expressionism and transcendental style vie for control of the Kammerspiel," 114, and later, "Dreyer weights the style heavily with Kammerspiel and expressionism," 122, insights with which we do not disagree.

16. Mark Nash, in his monograph *Dreyer* (London: BFI Publishing, 1977), argues that the theme of witchcraft was for Dreyer "an exemplary site where the discourses of religion, art, and the feminine intersect," 19. We find this a rather imprecise formulation as it can be applied not only to witches but also to angels as they appear in Dreyer's work as well: for instance, the good mother, Inger (Birgitte Federspiel), in *Ordet* (1955), who dies during childbirth and is resurrected during the film's uncanny conclusion.

17. With his deep-seated, piercing eyes, pale complexion and pronounced widow's peak, Nissen's Grand Inquisitor (i.e., Satan) may well have been the model for the appearance of Karloff's Hjalmar Poelzig in *The Black Cat*.

18. Months before the actual premiere of *Häxan*, on New Year's Day, 1922, Dreyer wrote an article in *Politiken* praising Christensen's high artistic ambitions. See "New Ideas about the Film: Benjamin Christensen and His Ideas," in Skoller, ed., *Dreyer in Double Reflection*, 31–35.

19. Carl Theodor Dreyer, *Four Screenplays*, trans. Oliver Stallybrass (Bloomington: Indiana University Press, 1970), 41.

20. Brashinsky, "Spring, Defiled," 170n5.

21. S. S. Prawer, in *Caligari's Children: The Film as Tale of Terror* (New York: Oxford University Press, 1980), argues that *Vampyr*'s evil doctor may be the among the first of such figures in horror cinema, 149.

22. In *The Living Dead: A Study of the Vampire in Romantic Literature* (Durham, NC: Duke University Press, 1981), James B. Twitchell remarks that "'porphyria'... was a disease in which the victim became very sensitive to sunlight. A person with porphyria can look terrifying, for his teeth and nails take on a strange fluorescent glow," 99.

23. Prawer, *Caligari's Children*, 157.

24. Cowie, *Ingmar Bergman*, 187.

25. Twitchell, *Living Dead*, 8.

26. The notion of God as a spider might have been suggested from the great Russian novel, *Crime and Punishment* (1866), in which its tortured protagonist, Raskolnikov (the name means "split" or "schism" in Russian) is told by his devil, Svidrigaylov, that eternity may well be best represented by spiders lurking in every corner of a dark, small room, perhaps a bathhouse.

27. Quoted in Twitchell, *Living Dead*, 142.

28. Prior to *Vargtimmen*'s filming, Bergman completed *Persona* (1966), a Kammerspiel also depicting the vampiric attraction the artist (here an actress, Elisabet Vogler [Liv Ullman]) has for the subject of her art (Sister Alma [Bibi Andersson], her nurse/muse). The vampiric relationship is strongly suggested; at one point, Elisabet pays a nocturnal visit to Alma's room. John Simon, in *Ingmar Bergman Directs* (New York: Harcourt Brace Jovanovich, 1972), claims: "There are publicity stills

extant showing Elisabet avidly gluing her open mouth to Alma's neck. In the film, Bergman lets the image dissolve before we get to anything so explicit," 290. In *Mindscreen: Bergman, Godard, and First-Person Film* (Princeton: Princeton University Press, 1978), Bruce Kawin also invokes vampirism in connection with Elisabet Vogler, 109. See, by way of comparison, Daniel Shaw, "Woman as Vampire: Ingmar Bergman's *Persona* (1966)," *Kinoeye* 2, no. 15 (October 7, 2002), online at http://www.kinoeye.org/02/15/shaw15.html, accessed September 6, 2003.

29. Twitchell, *Living Dead*, 20.

30. Ibid.

31. Marks and bites are afflicted in a number of places on the body in this film. Of the vampire, Twitchell writes: "Although he can puncture any part of her, after *Dracula* the neck became *de rigueur*. In folklore, however, he may just as easily bite the arm or the breast, or, in some cultures, even the toes!" *Living Dead*, 10–11.

32. Cowie, *Ingmar Bergman*, 245.

33. Cowie suggests that Johan is bisexual and that this is a possible rape/humiliation scene, citing as evidence Alma's allusion to "your boy" for whom Johan had purchased a gift. Moreover, in the castle, the image of the boy's head in the water returns, and Cowie also notes the ambivalent painting of Johan's face with makeup as he prepares to meet Veronica.

34. Cowie, *Ingmar Bergman*, 245.

35. Dreyer, "New Ideas about the Film," 88.

36. Ibid.

37. Prawer, *Caligari's Children*, 148.

38. In Stig Björkman's highly informative documentary about von Trier, *Tranceformer: A Portrait of Lars von Trier* (1997)—thus preceding the release of the highly feted *Dancer in the Dark* (2000)—Ernst Hugo Järegård recounts a highly revealing anecdote about von Trier's relation to his artistic precursor, Dreyer. Järegård tells of being with von Trier at the Cannes Film Festival. Von Trier was late for an engagement. When he finally arrived, he was, according to Järegård, wearing the tuxedo Dreyer had worn in 1928, which von Trier had previously purchased at an auction.

39. Dreyer, "New Ideas about the Film," 88.

40. Quoted from Björkman's documentary, *Tranceformer,* included on the Criterion DVD *The Element of Crime* (Criterion #ELE090, 2000).

41. In *Lost Highway* (1997), director David Lynch signals Fred Madison's (Bill Pullman) morphing into Pete Dayton (Balthazar Getty) by the horrible headache Fred gets prior to becoming Pete. Pete's subsequent amnesia is coded by the terrible bruise he has on his forehead.

42. Peter Brooks, *The Melodramatic Imagination: Balzac, Henry James, Melodrama, and the Myth of Excess* (New Haven: Yale University Press, 1976), 199.

43. Priya Jaikumar, "'Place' and the Modernist Redemption of Empire in *Black Narcissus* (1947)," *Cinema Journal* 40, no. 2 (2001): 62. The West Texas setting of Victor Sjöstrom's Hollywood film *The Wind* (1928), for instance, also functions as an excessive signifier.

44. Prawer, *Caligari's Children*, 37.

17

Man Bites Dog and the Critical Reception of Belgian Horror (in) Cinema

Ernest Mathijs

> Some reviewers call it gore cult, others a reflection on cinema. That's good!
>
> André Bonzel on the reception of *Man Bites Dog*
> Belgian Film Criticism and References to Horror

It almost seems like Belgian horror cinema does not exist. Although it has produced several acclaimed cult favorites, of which Harry Kümel's *Le rouge aux lèvres* (*Daughters of Darkness*, 1971) and Rémy Belvaux, André Bonzel, and Benoît Poelvoorde's *C'est arrivé près de chez vous* (*It Happened in Your Neighborhood*, a.k.a. *Man Bites Dog*, 1992) are well-known examples, its reputation is still far from enviable. Belgian critics seldom discuss these films as *horror* films, and rarely compare them to internationally acknowledged members of the genre. Moreover, Belgian film criticism has never developed a tradition of interpreting horror films (or films with horrific elements); neither reviews nor analyses pay much attention to issues of horror in relation to the country's cinema.[1] So instead of recognizing horror as an important political, thematic, and stylistic influence on Belgian film, the critics tend to limit their remarks to intrinsic "artistic values," discussing horror in relation to a well-established film canon and thereby reducing its social function, disallowing considerations of the genre's cultural role.

Yet much Belgian film writing does employ arguments that belong to the international vocabulary of horror criticism. Isolating moral issues, discussing plots and stories as originating in reality but bordering on the supernatural in their development, and questioning the broader cultural aspects of representations of "the Other" are well-established practices in Belgian film criticism.[2] They have previously been applied to several other genres, including comedies, documentaries, and realistic "heimat" films.[3]

Why then, have the critics never gone the final step? Why has the horrific largely been ignored in Belgian film writing?

Any attempt to explain this situation must operate on a level that combines close interpretation of cultural texts with a materialist approach to the actual situations governing the reception of Belgian films. Janet Staiger's model of a "contextual and materialist approach" to the reception of specific films provides such a level.[4] In fact, Staiger argues that it is exactly this combination of textual interpretation and contextual materialism that makes it possible to understand the reception of films in specific contexts. In this essay I will first oppose historical Belgian criticism (on Belgian "horror" films) with international criticism in order to identify the horrific in Belgian cinema and how it has traditionally been perceived. Next, I will analyze the reception of one Belgian film, *Man Bites Dog* (hereafter *MBD*), that both synthesizes the representation of horror in Belgian cinema and symptomatically illustrates the practices of Belgian film critics and reviewers when confronted with a movie that unavoidably evokes references to horror. *MBD* provides a good example since it stands out as a horror film, while it also generated some controversy concerning its "metaphorical" use of violence. I will discuss issues of realism, the use of references, and reflexivity to explain how *MBD* has been received. Finally, I will offer a general perspective on the reception of Belgian horror cinema

I am aware that this approach may not fully explain why Belgium seems to approach horror films differently from other cultures. Although a much broader comparative analysis is warranted, I contend that Belgian culture is not unequivocally "against" or "for" horror. The indifference with which this country's horror films are sometimes met, as well as the exuberant celebration of horror cinema in festivals such as the Brussels International Festival of Fantastic Film, indicate the complexity of Belgian attitudes toward horror. This essay seeks to identify the rhetorical patterns of Belgian film criticism and, to some extent, film culture—patterns that allow for specific opinions and arguments concerning horror to surface time and time again in Belgium's public sphere.[5]

The Historical Reception of Belgian Horror Cinema: Magical Realism, Sex, and Violence

Since Belgian film criticism has no tradition of discussing Belgian horror cinema, the first problem is to identify just what represents the horrific in

Belgian film.[6] I will do this by comparing national and international critiques of films that are said to employ or reflect horror-related themes and motives.

Only a few critical texts on Belgian cinema deal with the horrific at all. General newspapers, magazines, and even the film press usually avoid the genre. There have only been two specialist journals in Belgium devoted to fantastic cinema: *Le Journal de Jonathan Harker,* which published eight issues between 1967 and 1968, and *Fantoom,* which published six issues between 1975 and 1979. Book-length works are even more rare. One significant exception is Francis Bolen and Danny De Laet's study of Belgian fantasy and science fiction cinema.[7] Although they do not explicitly deal with horror, the authors connect the horrific in Belgian cinema to the well-established tradition of magical realism. Introduced by Franz Roh in 1925, magical realism originally referred to a painting style that adhered to surrealist principles (notably in the paintings of René Magritte, Paul Delvaux, Pierre Alechinsky, and Christian Dotremont).[8] In Belgium, the term also came to denote a literary concept, one found in the works of authors such as Jean Ray, Hubert Lampo, and Johan Daisne. Magical realism signifies a combination of realist/naturalist and fantastic influences in which the emphasis is shifted from social reality to the psychological aspects of perception, often culminating in alienation. Later analyses often stress magical realism's connection with offbeat "heimat" and genre literature (with highly symbolic representations of social oppositions, as in the works of Louis Paul Boon and Hugo Claus). In cinema, the term first appeared in reference to the debut features of Kümel (*Monsieur Hawarden,* 1968) and André Delvaux (*The Man Who Had His Hair Cut Short,* 1965), both of which were based on magical realist literature. According to Adolphe Nysenholc, magical realism in Belgian film is typified by "an interest in the representation of the split between the real and the imaginary, or a dialectic between life and illusion."[9]

De Laet identifies E. G. De Meyst, Norbert Benoît, and Marcel Jauniaux's *La maudite* (*The Damned,* 1949) as one of the earliest Belgian films with references to magical realism that can be seen as preceding representations of the horrific.[10] De Laet also attempts to draw similarities between Belgian films on the one hand and international horror/fantasy films on the other. For instance, he calls *L'homme à l'armure brisée* (*The Man with the Broken Armor*), a 1964 television series that adapted short stories of fantasy literature (magical realist literature in particular), the

"Belgian Twilight Zone."[11] However, despite Bolen and De Laet's efforts to situate Belgian cinema within a framework of fantasy criticism, references to pre-1966 horror films are virtually nonexistent. Even the connection to magical realism hardly appears in reviews of the time.

All this changes by the end of the 1960s. With the growth of both state-funded and commercially financed film production in the middle of the decade the emphasis on magical realism increased and was combined with (sometimes explicit) depictions of sex and violence.[12] Kümel's *Monsieur Hawarden* is a perfect example of how the "use of chiaroscuro," "atmosphere," "Freudian symbolism," and restrained "ambiguous sexual implications" generated a new aesthetic akin to horror styles and themes.[13] And Kümel was not the only example. Pierre Laroche's *Il pleut dans la maison* (*It Rains in My House*, 1968), Roland Lethem's and Jean-Louis Van Belle's short films, and even Guy Nijs's more sex- than horror-oriented *In Love with Death* (1970) employed violence, sexuality, and magical realism to create a style that bears much resemblance to international horror of the period.

This combination of magical realist influences and depictions of sex and violence brought Belgian film critics one step closer to mentioning horror, but they still refused to make explicit reference to the horrific. When Philip Mosley identifies Lethem, director of notorious shorts like *La fée sanguinaire* (*The Sanguine Fairy*, 1968) and *Le sexe enragé* (*Sex Rage*, 1969), as just another "experimental" artist "exploring provocative, uncompromising approaches," he synthesizes how critics of the time generally discussed such films.[14]

Two films from the early 1970s finally put Belgian horror on the critical agenda: Kümel's *Daughters of Darkness* and Jean Brismée's *Au service du diable* (*The Devil's Nightmare*, 1972). Both films contain explicit references to sex, violence, and magical realism, and both succeed in integrating these references into their plots. *Daughters of Darkness* tells the story of a vampire countess who, along with her female servant, seduces an American couple, while *The Devil's Nightmare* also focuses on a predatory female vampire, this one seducing seven young travelers in her chateau. The aesthetic of these productions, perfectly in accord with contemporary horror films from (e.g.) Hammer Studios and Jess Franco, meant that critical attention to their nature as "horror films," dealing with "the horrific," was inevitable. The use of established settings (gothic Ostend and the Black Wood) and literary source material (the legend of Countess Elizabeth Báthory and *La plus longue nuit du diable* [*The Longest*

Night of the Devil], original author unknown) also invited such connections. However, most Belgian critics reached the conclusion that these were horror films only with great reluctance. As reviews in *Film & Televisie* and *Le Soir* demonstrate, the national reception of both pictures was far from favorable. Mosley notes that each one "gained cult status" and "topped in the US, UK and France" but "not in Belgium."[15] Frédéric Sojcher writes that *The Devil's Nightmare* "was fiercely attacked by critics," who considered many of its scenes too "daring."[16] Ironic phrases such as "Dracula à Marienbad" (referring to *Daughters of Darkness*) and "Grand Guignol with the production quality of Petit Guignol" (referring to *The Devil's Nightmare*) accompanied these negative evaluations.[17] Apparently, Belgian critics at the time could not combine a positive evaluation with an interpretation of a film as a member of the horror genre.

This negative attitude toward horror stands out even more when the international reception of *Daughters of Darkness* and *The Devil's Nightmare* is taken into account. As Mosley describes, *Daughters of Darkness* was an enormous success in America, France, and Britain,[18] a fact that is often cited in works on Belgian film history. René Michelems writes that "the film went on to enjoy an enormous success, in Paris as much as in Britain and the States,"[19] and Sojcher calls the film's box-office results in Paris "unsurpassed by any other Belgian film up until now."[20] *The Devil's Nightmare* was also a moderate critical success in several European countries, including France and Germany. More importantly, both films received praise because they transgressed/transcended mainstream generic boundaries, *not* because they fitted so well into already existing frameworks. Both Joan Hawkins and *The Encyclopedia of Horror Movies* note that *Daughters of Darkness* was "unsuccessful in finding a generic niche," falling outside the domain of "established audiences for art cinema, horror or camp movies."[21] Clearly, however, this did not prevent critics from praising the film, *Daughters of Darkness* even gaining quickly a measure of academic and intellectual attention.[22] So, contrary to its national reception, contemporary international criticism of Belgian horror was much more willing to see the films' main characteristics—sex, violence, and magical realism—either as signifiers of horror film status or as elaborations on (rather than failures to comply with) conventional horror cinema.

The reception of *Daughters of Darkness* and *The Devil's Nightmare* is paradigmatic for practically all Belgian films with horrific elements up until 1992. Whenever critics were able to avoid using references to horror that is what they did, as was the case with the receptions of Maurice

Rabinowicz's *Le Nosferat* (*Nosferatu*, 1974), Luc Veldeman's *The Antwerp Killer* (1983), and Johan Vandewoestijne's *Lucker* (1986).[23] When such references were inevitable, as with Boris Szulzinger's *Mama Dracula* (1980) and Emmanuel Kervyn's *Les mémés cannibales* (*Rabid Grannies,* 1988), they were downplayed as much as possible and generally combined with very harsh evaluations.[24] Again, several of these films did in fact receive critical appreciation and favorable receptions outside Belgium, with *Lucker* achieving commercial success in France and Switzerland, and *Rabid Grannies* being described as both a "success on the international market" and "a gorefest for aficionados" in *Variety,* winning awards at several international festivals.[25]

There are several reasons why Belgian film criticism has failed to embrace horror. Generally, Belgian critics display an aversion to the horror genre in its entirety, inspired by the strong national tradition of making moral judgments about films.[26] As Gilbert Verschooten put it in 1983, horror has always been "dismissed by the film press and . . . 'right-minded' public opinion" because of its "challenge to morality."[27] Significantly, Verschooten's essay appears in *Film & Televisie,* published by the Catholic Film League, where it stands as the magazine's (Belgium's largest) first-ever appreciative essay on fantastic film. In a market dominated by moral criticism it is no surprise that horror cinema has not been positively received. Moreover, the many references to sex and violence in Belgian horror films have provided critics the opportunity to condemn them, without having to make distinctions between those films that challenge traditional morality and those that reinforce it.[28]

Another important reason is that Belgian critics have typically considered horror films culturally irrelevant. This has various explanations. First, it is a symptomatic consequence of Belgian criticism's refusal to embrace new trends in international film interpretation, trends influenced by psychoanalytic, (post)structuralist, and even feminist theories that explicitly link film texts to contemporary culture.[29]

Second, Belgian film critics have always focused on the economic, political (policy-making), and literary/stylistic aspects of national film culture, discussing these in relation to cinema's high-art aspirations. As a result, they have consistently dismissed or ignored the more popular aspects of genre and commercial filmmaking to which many horror directors aspire.[30]

Third, and perhaps most important, Belgian critics (sometimes unintentionally) have employed practices that hinder connections being drawn between horror cinema and its cultural function. This becomes clear when one looks at the reviews' references to magical realism.[31] In every single case, these references are gradually eliminated in favor of separate mentions of either realism (*Nosferat, Rabid Grannies*) or surrealism (*Mama Dracula, Daughters of Darkness, The Devil's Nightmare*). Through this process of replacement, the initial positive connotation of magical realism as a constitutive feature of Belgian film culture is lost, together with the possibilities it offers for rendering Belgian horror cinema culturally relevant. Instead, the references to realism invite (usually simplistic) comparisons between film and reality, and hence function as an incentive for moral arguments that mostly condemn the horror film. The references to surrealism are used to explain (and approve of) a deviation from reality, a step toward "pure fantasy," so that the reviewer can dismiss the film (or parts of it) as irrelevant for contemporary cultural analysis.

A final practice Belgian critics employ to avoid making their country's horror cinema culturally relevant is to emphasize its reflexivity. *Daughters of Darkness* has more than once been referred to as a "Sternbergian" reflection on the horror genre rather than an exponent of it.[32] *The Devil's Nightmare* is frequently characterized as a synthesis of lesbian vampire themes and motifs. *Nosferat* evokes references to "remaking *Nosferatu*," while *Mama Dracula* has been called a savvy remake of *Daughters of Darkness*.[33] And *Rabid Grannies* is often described as an homage to Troma Studios' American exploitation horror movies. With the exception of Kümel's films, such reflexivity is not viewed by critics as providing intertextual commentary, but instead is regarded as a form of frivolity absent any further meaning.[34]

The Reception of *MBD*

Prior to the 1990s, almost all writing on Belgian cinema used the term "horror" only in reference to films dealing explicitly with the supernatural. *Daughters of Darkness* and *The Devil's Nightmare* are obvious examples, but even reviews of *In Love with Death* mention horror solely during discussions of the film's "ghost sister"; such references do not occur when the film's depictions of sex and violence are the topic of interest.[35] Even 1980s films like *Lucker* and *The Antwerp Killer*, which do invite *some* references to horror without its being connected to the supernatural (since these pictures deal with serial killers rather than vampires), are generally received through the same descriptive framework. Instead of using the term "horror" in their discussions of these films, critics frequently revert to words like "exploitation," and "cult," and only reluctantly use those such as "gore" or "splatter."[36]

This changes with the 1992 release of *MBD*. Here, references to horror and the horrific suddenly became culturally relevant since these were the only concepts critics could use to explain the relationship between the film's elements of magical realism, surrealism, and black humor. In *MBD*, self-made serial killer and local gun-for-hire Ben (Benoît Poelvoorde) agrees to let a documentary camera crew follow him around on his assignments, and he discusses his murder methods with them as if talking about the size of his latest catch. As the killings mount, the crew becomes increasingly implicated in Ben's activities, going to dinner with him, catching a child that is trying to escape, and holding his things while he disposes of a corpse. These activities escalate until it is obvious that, his sense of humor and philosophical musings aside, Ben is nothing but a murderer and a rapist. Finally, after escaping from the police, Ben and the crew are shot by anonymous gangsters in a decrepit warehouse.

Made on a budget of 2 million Belgium Francs (approximately USD $50,000),[37] *MBD* enjoyed its international premiere at the 1992 Cannes Film Festival, where it captured several awards. From there it quickly became a national and international commercial success, attracting about 400,000 viewers in Belgium (4 percent of the population), and earning huge profits worldwide. In Brussels alone, where it played for thirty-seven consecutive weeks, it ended up making more than 20 million BF (approximately USD $500,000).[38]

MBD also received a great deal of critical acclaim. Its national and international receptions were very positive, with many reviewers calling it one of the year's most "authentic" films.[39] More importantly, the critical reception in Belgium and abroad clearly identified *MBD* as a horror movie, with references to horror and the horrific frequently appearing in reviews. These references were made up of the same components as before (surrealism, magical realism, sex and violence, reflexivity, humor), but contrary to previous Belgian film reviews, they were now linked to positive overall appraisals. In the Belgian press, only three reviews of the film were negative. Internationally, positive evaluations also prevailed, although they tended to be a bit more tempered than in Belgium.

There were, of course, several differences between the national and international receptions of *MBD*, especially regarding the composition of

Ben (Benoît Poelvoorde) discussing his murder methods in *Man Bites Dog* (1992)

the reviews. Most remarkable is the regularity and explicitness with which international reviews referred to the film as "horror." Virtually every one used the term repeatedly, especially near the end of the review. The Belgian press, in contrast, usually used the term "horror" only once or twice per review, replacing it with synonyms elsewhere. Furthermore, Belgian critics typically situated the term in the middle of their reviews without returning to it at the end. These differences may indicate how uncomfortable Belgian critics are using the word "horror"—a sign of their lack of experience writing about the genre. This is also revealed in the critics' mention of other films. Both the international and Belgian reviews of *MBD* referred to a wide range of other titles, including *Twin Peaks* (1992), *Bad Lieutenant* (1992), *Henry: Portrait of a Serial Killer* (1990), *Wayne's World* (1992), *Reservoir Dogs* (1992), *Benny's Video* (Austria, 1992), and *Bob Roberts* (1992). While the international press bunched these titles together as a means of supporting their positive evaluations of *MBD*, Belgian critics usually mentioned them separately, as loose ends.

Apart from these significant differences there are also many structural similarities between the national and international receptions of *MBD*. Besides the references to similar titles for the sake of comparison, these similarities include an emphasis on budget, reception (always describing *MBD* as a "surprise hit"), and the film's dynamic style and pacing. There are also numerous references in both sets of reviews to *MBD*'s violence, sex, black humor, and realism (including documentary realism, magical realism, and surrealism).

As noted, these four references have been used frequently with respect to Belgian horror. Thus, it should come as no surprise that critics used them to discuss and describe *MBD* as well. Their presence here, however, indicates that the national and international receptions of Belgian horror cinema are converging, leading to a more stable framework from which to approach the films. Moreover, the very term "horror" no longer functions in the Belgian press solely as an identifying label, but rather as a crossroads in the argumentation. Reviewers of *MBD* took care to connect it with other arguments about the horrific, indicating a kind of awareness of the several levels of horror present in the film. For example, critics tended to distinguish between the obvious "horror" of Ben's life (and death) as a psycho-killer, the "horrific" elements of his profession— a contract killer who actually enjoys his job—and his cultural status as an outsider with respect to the world he believes he is a part of. Critics also distinguished between Ben's "horrific" worldviews (racist, sexist, and demagogic), his "horrific" relation to the film crew (over whom he holds almost absolute power, but to whom he also, as one critic puts it, has a homoerotic attraction), and the "horrific" explosiveness and arbitrariness of his actions (he lets some people live, and kills others, without any particular or apparent reason).

Finally, critics distinguished between different types of murder. Ben's assassinations, for example, were rarely compared to the killings the crew participates in, suggesting that these latter are of another order. Many of *MBD*'s horrific elements were linked to the explicitness of what is depicted (not just showing, but even zooming-in on the sex and violence), and to the film's bleak style. Even while the handheld camerawork, quirky editing, and location shooting reveal an obvious affinity with cinéma vérité, these techniques also brought to reviewers' minds the often-disturbing subject matter of mondo films, as well as the motivation behind realist horror cinema generally. For the first time in Belgian film criticism, reviewers seemed to have a sense that it matters *what kind of horror* they are analyzing, and how their analysis connects up with and explains other aspects of the film's overall meaning.

References to sex and violence, prevalent in all the reviews, played a central role in establishing these connections. Given the film's explicit attitude toward these story components, this should not be surprising. What is noteworthy is the fact that Belgian reviews no longer concealed their presence and no longer combined their mention with a moral condemnation. Instead, references to sex and violence now appear in the middle of critical discussion. In some cases this led to letters from readers complaining about the "explicitness of the references."[40] There has been some speculation as to why the presence of references to sex and violence in *MBD*'s reception was not subjected to the same prudence as before. Sojcher suggests that sex and violence must be involved in critical arguments about the film because the narrative focuses precisely on the impact of these activities. If references to sex and violence were left out, even simple retellings of the film would have been impossible.[41] Others refer to *MBD*'s metaphorical use of sex and violence for reasons of criticism and redemption, which effectively forced reviewers who wanted to explain the film's meaning to refer to these elements. Interestingly, though not unexpectedly, references to sex and violence almost always appeared alongside references to horror, indicating that the practices originating after *Daughters of Darkness* and *The Devil's Nightmare* were still at work.

Many of the references previously used to downplay the implications that mentions of horror, sex, and violence carry with them still appeared throughout reviews of *MBD*. However, they now served to *enhance* rather than *reduce* the impact of the latter. This is particularly the case with references to humor and reflexivity. Most discussions of humor in *MBD* stressed the film's "ironic," "satirical," "parodic," and "cynical" elements, but because the filmmakers self-consciously employ these elements, references to them functioned in the reviews primarily as explanatory rather than evaluative instruments. Many critics also noted that *MBD*'s use of humorous devices actually adds to the film's horror rather than detracting from it. Retrospectively considering the film's "mockumentary" qualities, Mosley wrote that "though deliberately shocking and deemed 'irresponsible' by objectors, the film had a serious side in its uncompromising examination of the spectator's ambiguous relationship to the representation of violence on the screen."[42] Moreover, the presence of humor was seen as reinforcing *MBD*'s reflexivity: the manner in which the film text comments on its own status as a film.[43]

By portraying the adventures of Ben and the camera crew through the very cameras they use, thus invoking a layered (though seemingly direct) mode of representation, *MBD* invites considerations of reflexivity from the start. This fundamental reflexivity is complemented by numerous passing references to film and the mass media, some playful (as when a drunken Ben sings a song about French film stars Jean Gabin and Michèle Morgan), some shocking (as when Ben compares his bashing of someone's head in a bathroom to the acting style of France's toughest film star, Philippe Noiret). A particularly reflexive moment that many reviews picked up on is the making of a "Pétit Grégory" cocktail—a mixture of gin, tonic, and "la pétite victime," an olive. As reviews in *Télérama, Le Soir, Libération,* and *La Libre Belgique* all testified, this "sick joke" refers to a real-life "sensational French child-murder case in the 80s."[44] Such references in the film and in the reviews invited critics to make comparisons between *MBD* and real life, and hence to consider the film's horror in relation to reality. This in turn forced critics to address the relationship between horror cinema and culture generally.

A striking feature of the Belgian reviews of *MBD* is that they brought together all of the elements that until then had appeared separately in reviews of horror films. For the first time, reviewers combined individual references to horror on the one hand, humor (and reflexivity) on the other, into larger arguments in which the various terms no longer contradicted each other's meaning, but instead served to reinforce one another. Indicative of this is Philippe Rouyer's remark in *Positif* that *MBD* "surpasses the laws of genre by offering a vibrant reflection on the representation of violence in cinema."[45] Through its synthesis of elements, *MBD* invited discussions that joined together references to humor, horror, sex, violence, and reflexivity. And this resulted in a framework that invited both favorable reviews and connections with contemporary culture.

MBD and the Cultural Relevance of Horror

Probably the most important feature of *MBD*'s reception, but also the most difficult one to demonstrate, was its linking of the film (*as* a horror film) to the culture from which it came, and its recognition of the film as representing that culture. This was most evident in the references to reflexivity. Many of these references concerned television programs and documentary techniques used to record everyday life that the diegetic camera crew also use and/or refer to. The Belgian reality TV show *Striptease* was frequently mentioned in reviews, but other reality television programs such as *Jambers, NV de wereld, Faits divers,* and *Het eenzame harten buro* were also regularly referred to. The appeal of these shows is that they purport to depict real life, inviting comparisons between the show and everyday culture and allowing people to treat the former as if it were a truthful representation of reality. Although most of the reviews did not engage in debates on representation, they did point to the cultural implications of *MBD*'s reflexivity, stating that the film becomes a commentary on media practices, thereby rendering its theme culturally relevant.

One of Ben's (Benoît
Poelvoorde) brutal slay-
ings, early in *Man Bites
Dog* (1992)

In several reviews the above observation was then connected to the
film's representation of horror, sex, and violence. In some cases (e.g., in *De
standaard*) the references to horror led to moral arguments that were then
used to discuss the ethics of reality TV shows. In most cases, however, the
references to horror helped to explain these shows' ambiguous appeal:
through representational practices and techniques, people (and their stories) are isolated from their respective contexts and presented as outsiders,
abnormal and freakish. This is an argument that perfectly fits the tradition of horror interpretation, and it allowed for connections to be drawn
between reality shows and horror films, even leading in some cases to the
favoring of horror cinema (which is at least straightforward in its intentions) over reality television. The argument thus rendered *MBD* culturally
relevant and also granted horror cinema and the horrific as such cultural
relevance, if only by criticizing the relative insincerity of reality TV.

But there is more. Discussions concerning the cultural relevance of
horror in *MBD* occurred on three levels. The first level, dealing with the
impact of the first brutal murders committed by Ben, could be dismissed
as culturally irrelevant fairly easily, because these murders are staged as
slapstick humor. Still, even on this level, several critics noted that the horror here is closely related to cultural commentary, for example, by pointing out the caricature-like representations of minorities (elderly people,
migrants) who are Ben's victims in these scenes.

The second level unearths a more general thematic cultural relevance. As the film progresses, the humorous veil covering many acts of
horror, sex, and violence disappears, at the same time making the depictions more realistic and disturbing. When Ben kills a man in a bathroom

and remarks that this reminds him of Philippe Noiret in *Le vieux fusil* (*The Old Gun*, 1975), it can be considered (as several critics suggested) either a frivolous or a reflexive moment. But when, later on, Ben ruthlessly murders an entire film crew to provide his own crew with new material, his assaults can no longer be "redeemed" by reflexive references to other movies. They have become too horrifying and realistic. The gradual intensification of the depictions, from frivolous murders to horrific assaults, enables *MBD* to ingeniously combine horror, realism, and cultural relevance by implying that the more realistic and horrific the film gets, the more it becomes like the shows it is criticizing. In fact, almost every critic writing about *MBD* picked up this suggestion, arguing that it is the intensification of horror that makes the film more culturally relevant.

The third level considers *MBD*'s reception context. In a majority of the reviews, critics would shift from discussing the story's meaning to discussing the audience's reaction to particular screenings, whenever they deemed the film's depictions of horror to be too graphic. The key sequence typically held to introduce this shift occurs when Ben and the film crew break into a house one night and assault a couple who lives there (raping the woman, then killing both husband and wife). This scene is just too violent and disturbing to fit into the frame of cultural commentary that the critics initially aimed for. Rather, it makes it apparent that, until now, audiences have been accepting so much depicted violence precisely because it can be seen as cultural commentary or satire. When the film text makes this point explicit, many critics argued that Belvaux, Bonzel, and Poelvoorde overstepped their own mark and that the real horror that follows in *MBD* can no longer be justified by the clever disguises of humor, reflexivity, or cultural criticism.

Ironically, however, this scene also constitutes the point at which the film actually does become culturally relevant. As several critics noted, up till now, the audience (themselves included) has been assuming it is aligned with the filmmakers, enjoying a horrific but rather entertaining story that reflects on the practices of reality representation. When, in the last ten to fifteen minutes, *MBD* becomes a genuine horror movie, presenting no cultural smokescreen for its gratuitous depictions of horror, audiences become aware of this and have to change their attitude.[46] This awareness and change in attitude on the part of viewers led most critics to discuss the film as an event rather than as a story with encoded meanings, a shift in level that occurs in the middle portion of almost every review. In introducing this shift, critics also displayed a remarkable attention to the audience's reaction of laughter. As many of them argued, laughter is an appropriate way of acknowledging both the film's relevance and its intensity. After the rape scene, however, hardly any laughter occurs,[47] not because the audience no longer grasps what the film is about but because they are forced to reconsider their own previous reactions. Although such reflexivity concerning audience reaction is not new to horror scholarship,[48] it does contain new elements for the consideration of horror film reception.

References to magical realism apparently disappear from the agenda when horror becomes culturally relevant. Yet they still continue to play an important role in reviews of *MBD*, especially on this third level. Admittedly, most critics referred to documentary realism, particularly when developing comparisons between the film and reality television.[49] However, on closer examination of these references, it turns out they are not so different from the traditional magical realist references. For starters, Belgian film historiography only draws a thin line between documentary realism and magical realism.[50] They are considered to be mutually influential, and canonized filmmakers such as Henri Storck and Paul Delvaux often cross back and forth between them, for example, by introducing unusual characters in realistic locations or by stretching scenes in time so that they begin to take on dreamlike features.[51] Both traditions are also widely held to be of equal importance when it comes to the cinematic representation of Belgian cultural reality.

In a few exceptional cases, critics invoked the differences between magical realism and documentary realism to make moral evaluations. But usually they were referred to in tandem. Whenever critics discuss documentary realism in relation to Belgian horror, as they did for the first time with *MBD*, magical realism cannot be far away. Symptomatic of this strategy is the way Ben's role in the film is discussed. Although Ben is a realistic character, he also evinces features of the typical horror-movie monster, particularly what Steven Jay Schneider identifies as the psychopath.[52] This is arguably the most realistic type of monster since it possesses no actual supernatural characteristics. But Ben still acts a bit "supernatural" in his bragging and self-positioning. Almost every review dealing with Benoît Poelvoorde's acting style referred to this attitude, which is typical for the psychopath. It serves to bracket the documentary realist context within which most of the above remarks are made, and demonstrates the film's debt to magical realism and its correspondence with "traditional monster theory."

Together, the three levels of humor, cultural commentary within the text, and cultural commentary about the text, give *MBD* a multidimensional cultural relevance. Many critics recognized this fact. For instance, the cultural relevance issue is perfectly evoked in Antoine de Baecque's *Cahiers du cinéma* review of *MBD*.[53] De Baecque devotes an entire paragraph to the description of several crimes committed (and subsequently resolved) in the region near Mouscon—a region similar to the one depicted in the film. The fact that *MBD* was shot partly near Mouscon serves, for de Baecque, not just as a reference, but also as a cue for viewers who can pick up the connection and use it to address the real-life issues this brings to mind. Significantly, de Baecque begins his review of the film by describing the first transmissions of the Belgian reality TV show *Striptease,* a show to which Poelvoorde, Belvaux, and Bonzel also constantly refer in interviews. He then introduces the themes and styles of these shows, eventually moving to a discussion of the film itself, dealing not so much with its content as with its significance for the representation of Belgian culture.

Many other reviewers adopted similar approaches. Sojcher, for instance, writes that in *MBD*, "Belgicism is to be found on several levels," for example, in Ben's accent, the film's title—which refers to a well-known regional newspaper and gossip section (most notably in *Le Soir*)—and "a spirit of abrasive anarchy that could well be described as a national tradition."[54] Louis Danvers refers to this tradition as a Belgian "version of reality (or, why not, a surrealism)."[55] Although the international reviews were of course unable to reference the same topical and regional issues as the Belgian press, they used other means to suggest *MBD*'s cultural relevance. And so, in *Cineaste,* comparisons were made with both *Cops* and *Rescue 911* to make a point about reality representations, while London's *The Guardian* newspaper made an argument about the universality of the film's horror, asserting that it has to do "with the true banality of evil."

In sum, it seems evident that with *MBD*, Belgian horror cinema and criticism has, at least formally, entered its realist phase, the film rapidly becoming the country's *Night of the Living Dead* (1968) both in fame and fortune, forcing critics to place the horror not outside but inside their own culture.

Conclusion

Belgian film criticism has long failed to adequately deal with the horrific elements present in its national film culture, for several reasons. First, such criticism overemphasizes, even today, "traditional" and "official" aesthetics and ethics, stemming from a historical desire to construct a national film culture and to defend cinema as "good" art, meanwhile ignoring alternative, subcultural, or countercultural films. The horror genre suffers even greater disdain. With literally every textbook history of Belgian cinema emphasizing the dual construction of the country's film culture (with separate financing systems for French-speaking and Flemish films), genres like horror, which do not address this construction, are typically left unmentioned or else dismissed as irrelevant. It is not surprising, therefore, to find that *Daughters of Darkness* is held to evince no trace of "vindicating or affirming, through cinema, the historio-cultural particularities of the people to which it belongs."[56]

Second, Belgian film criticism has tended to focus on elements that downplay the contemporary social relevance of fiction cinema, avoiding arguments that would invite mentions of horror. For example, references to magical realism are either reduced to realism (and then treated in moral terms) or else transformed into references to surrealism, allowing critics to stress the fantastic and avoid connections to the real. Discussions of humor and reflexivity are used to counter the possible relevance of references to sex and violence, disassociating them from the main argument about the meaning of the film in question. And when references to horror and the horrific are inevitable, they are flanked by moral condemnations or negative assessments that hold that horror films are simply "bad." As a result, up until quite recently Belgian film criticism has refused to firmly link Belgian cinema to contemporary culture, or to regard films as reflecting on and dealing with (whether consciously or not) real horror in society.

I have argued that films like *Daughters of Darkness* and especially *MBD* challenged this state of affairs, introducing—even forcing—new perspectives on both Belgian horror cinema and Belgian film criticism, thereby leading to more complex considerations of what constitutes horror, how it could be discussed, and what it represents from a cultural standpoint. Since *MBD*'s release, however, there has been no continuation of these new perspectives. Belgian horror film production has remained too fragmented to encourage an ongoing debate concerning its function in Belgian film culture.[57]

Although references to the horrific now appear more frequently than ever before in Belgian film criticism, Belgian horror remains an often-ignored genre. Moreover, ongoing international discussions concerning, for example, the metaphorical representation of abjection in horror cinema remain rare in Belgium.[58] Thus, it is still both possible and acceptable for Belgian film studies and criticism to neglect horror.[59] Although Belgian cinema apparently possesses a horrific potential, its critical reception remains highly problematic.

Notes

1. See Ernest Mathijs, "Referentiekaders van hedendaagse filmkritiek" (PhD diss., Free University of Brussels, 2000).
2. Mathijs, "Referentiekaders van hedendaagse filmkritiek," 196–201.
3. See Frédéric Sojcher, *La kermesse héroïque du cinéma belge,* 3 vols. (Paris: L'Harmattan, 1999). These genres belong to the classical typology of Belgian cinema. "Heimat" films are rural dramas symbolizing the opposition between high-culture French-speaking bourgeoisie and low-culture Flemish or Walloon working-class and peasant communities. Specifically, many films from the 1930s and 1970s are considered to be "heimat" (or "patoisan" = peasant, as Sojcher calls them). For elaboration, see Sojcher, *Kermesse héroïque,* vol. 1, 102–10, 129–35; and Paul Geens and others, eds., *Naslagwerk over de Vlaamse film* (Brussels: CIAM, 1986).
4. See Janet Staiger, *Interpreting Films: Studies in the Historical Reception of American Cinema* (Princeton: Princeton University Press, 1992); "Taboos and Totems: Cultural Meanings of The Silence of the Lambs," in *Film Theory Goes to the Movies,* ed. Jim Collins, Hilary Radner, and Ava Preacher Collins (New York: Routledge, 1993), 142–54; and *Perverse Spectators: The Practices of Film Reception* (New York: New York University Press, 2000).
5. For specific research into how Belgian audiences deal with the horrific, see Dirk Van Extergem, "A Report on the Brussels Festival of Fantastic Film"; and Ernest Mathijs, "Alternative Belgian Cinema and Cultural Identity: S. and the Affaire Dutroux," both in *Alternative Europe: European Exploitation and Underground Cinema,* ed. Ernest Mathijs and Xavier Mendik (London: Wallflower, 2004).
6. To avoid tumbling into a discussion of what constitutes horror cinema and the horrific as such, I refer to Steven Jay Schneider's introduction to *The Horror Film and Psychoanalysis: Freud's Worst Nightmares* (Cambridge: Cambridge University Press, 2004) and to Robin Wood's introduction to *The American Nightmare* (Toronto: Festival of Festivals, 1979) for descriptions of the horror genre. I also use Noël Carroll, *The Philosophy of Horror; Or, Paradoxes of the Heart* (New York: Routledge, 1990); Carol Clover, *Men, Women, and Chainsaws: Gender in the Modern Horror Film* (London: BFI Publishing, 1992); and Mark Jancovich, *Horror* (London: Batsford, 1992) as points of reference. See also Ernest Mathijs, "Cultuur en het beest: Filosofie van de horror," in *Het eigene en het andere,* ed. J. Baars and R. Starmans (Delft, Netherlands: Eburon, 1999), 215–26; and Mathijs, "Cut & Copy: Lichamelijkheid en reflexiviteit in de horror film," in *Film, genre en publiek,* ed. D. Biltereyst and Ph. Meers (Ghent, Belgium: Academia Press, 2004).
7. Francis Bolen and Danny De Laet, *Science-fiction et fantastique dans le cinéma belge, (1913–1974)* (Brussels: Skull-Kosmopolis, 1979); see also De Laet, *Fantasy and Science-Fiction in Belgian Film* (Brussels: Pey Mey Diffusion, 1995).

8. This use of the term predates its connection with Latin American literature, and as a literary style worldwide. See Lois Parkinson Zamora and Wendy B. Faris, eds., *Magical Realism: Theory, History, Community* (Durham, NC: Duke University Press, 1995), and the *Grove Dictionary of Art* (London: Macmillan, 2000).

9. Nysenholc and Delvaux identify Pirandello, Borges, Hoffman, and De Maupassant as predecessors of filmic magical realism. See Nysenholc, "André Delvaux ou les visages de l'imaginaire," in *Special Edition of the Revue de l'Universitee de Bruxelles,* ed. Adolphe Nysenholc (Brussels: Editions de Université de Bruxelles, 1985); and Nysenholc, *André Delvaux* (Brussels: Editions de Université de Bruxelles, 1995), 221.

10. De Laet, *Fantasy and Science-Fiction in Belgian Film*; Marianne Thys, *Belgian Cinema—Le cinema belge—De Belgische film* (Ghent, Belgium: Ludion, 1999), 314.

11. De Laet, *Fantasy and Science-Fiction in Belgian Film,* 78.

12. See Ernest Mathijs, "Ploegen in de droom: Historische poetica van de Vlaamse film" (working paper); and Philip Mosley, *Split Screen: Belgian Cinema and Cultural Identity* (Albany: State University of New York Press, 2001).

13. Thys, *Belgian Cinema,* 450.

14. Mosley, *Split Screen,* 124–25.

15. Ibid., 120.

16. Sojcher, *Kermesse héroïque,* vol. 1, 238.

17. Thys, *Belgian Cinema,* 483; Sojcher, *Kermesse héroïque,* vol. 1, 238.

18. Mosley, *Split Screen,* 120.

19. Thys, *Belgian Cinema,* 483.

20. Sojcher, *Kermesse héroïque,* vol. 1, 69.

21. Joan Hawkins, *Cutting Edge: Art-Horror and the Horrific Avant-Garde* (Minneapolis: University of Minnesota Press, 2000), 25.

22. See, for example, David Soren, *Unreal Reality: The Cinema of Harry Kümel* (Columbia, MO: Lucas Brothers, 1979); Bonnie Zimmerman, "*Daughters of Darkness:* Lesbian Vampires" (1981), in *Planks of Reason: Essays on the Horror Film,* ed. Barry Keith Grant (Metuchen, NJ: Scarecrow, 1984), 153–63; Gilbert Verschooten and Jan Van Genechten, *Harry Kümel* (Grimbergen-Brussels: Fantasy Films / Vlaamse Gemeenschap, 1985); Carol Jenks, "*Daughters of Darkness:* A Lesbian Vampire Art Film," in *Necronomicon: The Journal of Horror and Erotic Cinema, Book One,* ed. Andy Black (London: Creation, 1996), 22–34.

23. Thys, *Belgian Cinema,* 550, 678, 750; Mosley, *Split Screen,* 140.

24. Thys, *Belgian Cinema,* 638, 770; Sojcher, *Kermesse héroïque,* vol. 1, 239; Mosley, *Split Screen,* 169.

25. Thys, *Belgian Cinema,* 725, 770.

26. See Mathijs, "Referentiekaders van hedendaagse filmkritiek," 196–201.

27. Gilbert Verschooten, "De fantastische film: Op de drempel van de erkenning?" *Film & Televisie* 318 (November 1983): 24–25.

28. Arguably, it is virtually impossible to make firm distinctions between Belgian horror films that challenge morality and those that confirm it. All of the pictures mentioned have been attacked for their explicit depictions of violence and sexuality as well as for their "horrific" content. Belgian critics seem incapable of separating one from the other.

29. Mathijs, "Referentiekaders van hedendaagse filmkritiek," 457–60.
30. See Mosley, *Split Screen;* Jan-Pieter Everaerts, *Film in België: Een permanente revolte* (Brussels: Mediadoc, 2000); Sojcher, *Kermesse héroïque,* vol. 1.
31. All review information comes from the press guides that the Royal Film Archive keeps for each film released in Belgium. The guides for *Daughters of Darkness, The Devil's Nightmare, Nosferat, Mamma Dracula, Lucker,* and *Rabid Grannies* contain twenty-one, thirteen, seven, nine, five, and six reviews respectively. I thank the staff of the Royal Film Archive for allowing me to use their materials, and for their assistance in finding further information.
32. See, for example, Thys, *Belgian Cinema,* 483.
33. Sojcher, *Kermesse héroïque,* vol. 1, 69.
34. Reflexivity, or the degree to which horror films refer to or comment on their own premises (as a genre, or as one film in a series or cycle), is widely considered to be a crucial feature of contemporary horror cinema, by no means restricted to the Belgian tradition. See, for example, Noël Carroll, *Interpreting the Moving Image* (Cambridge: Cambridge University Press, 1998), 265–73; Hawkins, *Cutting Edge;* Mathijs, "Referentiekaders van hedendaagse filmkritiek"; and Steven Jay Schneider, "Kevin Williamson and the Rise of the Neo-Stalker," *Post Script* 19, no. 2 (2000): 73–87.
35. Thys, *Belgian Cinema,* 470.
36. Ibid., 687, 725.
37. The film's production costs have been disputed. Sojcher states 2 million BF, but in an interview for *Film & Televisie,* the directors claim it was 6 million BF. Still another review lists 4 million BF, while according to *Knack* magazine the film cost only one-half million BF. Sojcher's figure seems most reliable.
38. Sojcher, *Kermesse héroïque,* vol. 1, 233.
39. This analysis of MBD's critical reception incorporates reviews from all of Belgium's major newspapers and magazines. Internationally, I have analyzed reviews from a total of thirty-four different newspapers and magazines. I will only refer to specific reviews when quoting or when specific statements are emphasized. When a journal or newspaper published more than one review of the film, I indicate the issue number and date.
40. Le Soir-MAD dossier.
41. Sojcher, *Kermesse héroïque,* vol. 1, 124–25.
42. Mosley, *Split Screen,* 184.
43. In *Film Theory: An Introduction* (Oxford: Blackwell, 1999), Robert Stam argues that reflexivity is an important feature of contemporary cinema (303). As noted in note 32, numerous scholars link reflexivity explicitly to the horror genre.
44. *Variety.*
45. Quoted in Sojcher, *Kermesse héroïque,* vol. 1, 123.
46. Thys, *Belgian Cinema,* 824.
47. Ibid. See also the interviews with the filmmakers in *Film & Televisie* and *Humo.*
48. See Staiger, *Perverse Spectators,* 179–87.
49. See, for example, Julia Hallam with Margaret Marshment, *Realism and Popular Cinema* (Manchester, UK: Manchester University Press, 2000); and Frank Lafond,

"The Life and Crimes of Ben; Or, When a Serial Killer Meets a Film Crew in *Man Bites Dog*," *Post Script* 22, no. 2 (2003).

50. Mathijs, "Ploegen in de droom."

51. Nysenholc, "André Delvaux ou les visages de l'imaginaire"; Nysenholc, *André Delvaux*.

52. Steven Jay Schneider, "Monsters as (Uncanny) Metaphors: Freud, Lakoff, and the Representation of Monstrosity in Cinematic Horror," in *Horror Film Reader*, ed. Alain Silver and James Ursini (New York: Limelight Editions, 2000), 183.

53. *Cahiers du cinéma* 461 (1992): 62–63.

54. Sojcher, *Kermesse héroïque*, vol 1, 123.

55. *Le Vif/L'Express*, n.p.

56. Sojcher, *Kermesse héroïque*, vol. 1, 69 [my translation].

57. One exception is the reconsideration of the reputation of Johan Vandewoestijne, director of *Lucker* and producer of *Rabid Grannies*, Harry M. Love's *Maniac Nurses* (1990), and Reginald Adamson's *State of Mind* (1992). He received some critical recognition when a national newspaper devoted an entire article to his company, Desert Productions, christening him "the father of Flemish horror." See "Desert: Vader van de Vlaamse griezel," *De Morgen*, April 6, 1997.

58. See Mathijs, "Niemand is onschuldig," in *Waarheid & Werkelijkheid*, ed. Ernest Mathijs and Wouter Hessels (Brussels: VUB Press, 2000); and Ernest Mathijs and Wouter Hessels, "Film en 'het middenveld': S. en Film 1 tussen kunst en commercie," in *Kunst te Koop? Over bruggen en breuken tussen kunst en economie*, ed. Bert Mosselmans (Rouselare, Belgium: Roularta, 2001).

59. Jan-Pieter Everaerts's study of Belgian cinema, for example, contains no mention of *Daughters of Darkness* and discusses *MBD* only in relation to its use of documentary techniques. See Everaerts, *Film in België*, 105.

18

Exorcising the Devil:

RUSSIAN CINEMA AND HORROR

Josephine Woll

Russian cinema and Soviet cinema are not synonymous: Russian cinema both pre- and post-dates the Soviet Union, and the Russian screen showed horrors in the conventional Western sense in both periods: in the decade before the establishment of the Soviet Union, when imports competed with domestic products for a largely middle-class urban audience, and in the last decade or so, when filmmakers have essayed a variety of genres, including horror, hoping to compete effectively with foreign films. However, for most of its history, Russian cinema excluded horror films. From the creation of a Soviet film industry, which occurred soon after the creation of a Soviet state, virtually until the dissolution of that state and, in some ways, the demise of the industry, Soviet studios produced many sorts of films, but no *Cabinets of Dr. Caligari*, no *Nosferatus*, no *Psychos*, no *Diaboliques*, *Rosemary's Babys* or *Exorcists*, no *Nights of the Living Dead* or *Invasions of the Body Snatchers* or *Carries*. No vampires, no zombies, no multiple-personalities, no werewolves, no sociopaths with angelic faces, no terrifying hypertrophies of natural forces, no malevolent but mesmerizing flesh-eaters, no "crawling hands" or "murderous greenery."[1] In this essay I discuss both: the films that were made before and after the Soviet Union, and the absence of such films during the state's lifetime, examining the circumstances and politics that affected this area of film production.

I begin by outlining some of cinematic horror's most salient and consistent themes and conventions. Horror emphasizes individual psychology, relying on a general feeling of isolation and claustrophobia,[2] on a fear of the "uncanny"[3] and the supernatural, and on the perception that chaos is imminent (or immanent) and about to take over.[4] Horror films of every provenance and time period typically involve the penetration of personal space, usually envisioned as houses, where staircases may separate safety from danger, sanity from madness—but also admit their entrance.[5] Violence frequently invades basements, dark and womblike; bathrooms, the most intimate domain; and bedrooms, the private haven where one can, theoretically, safely bare oneself physically and psychologically. As Barry Keith Grant writes, "The horror evoked by . . . images of monstrous penetration of the bedroom also articulates, on one level, the generalized fear, at least in western culture, that monsters are bred by the sleep of reason. To be in the state of sleep is, in effect, to surrender one's identity . . . and hence to be in a position of extreme vulnerability."[6]

In the classic horror films of the 1920s and 1930s, outward physical monstrosity typically represented suppressed aspects of human personality; later, propelled by fear of bombs and radiation, postwar Western and Japanese cinema incorporated science-fiction elements in films depicting "the horror of personality" and the "horror of Armageddon."[7] Later still, in American films of the turbulent 1960s and 1970s, a horror of the demonic returned. If movies like *Psycho* (1960) posited insanity to account for a violently horrible world, and movies like *Night of the Living Dead* (1968) proposed that horror derives from man's inhumanity against his fellow man as well as from the inherent malevolence of the universe, movies like *Rosemary's Baby* (1968) and *The Exorcist* (1973) suggested that evil forces—witches, demons, devils, spiritual presences—constantly undermined the quality of existence.[8]

These features, by no means exhaustive, form contours recognizable to any Western filmgoer as characteristic of horror films. Now let us see how Russian and Soviet filmmakers accommodated or adapted those characteristics to their own peculiar circumstances and history.

Pre-Soviet Cinema

During the decade before the upheavals of 1917 established a new state on the territory of the Russian empire, movies had become a commonplace entertainment for residents of every major city, particularly the more affluent residents who belonged to the official caste known as *meshchanstvo* (petty bourgeoisie).[9] Despite a certain amount of snobbish resistance on the part of intellectuals toward the upstart medium—the same sort as occurred in European capitals—movies in Russia belonged to the culture of the time, creating a "much-needed synthesis of high culture, entertainment, and technology as well as drawing on Russian folk motifs."[10] Whether imported (mainly from France, America, and—until the onset of World War I—Germany) or homemade, melodrama was the most popular film genre, often imbued with mysticism or satanic overtones and not infrequently tinged with decadent eroticism. "The characteristics of excess, sensation, spectacle, and affect, so closely associated with melodrama, are ... deeply ingrained in Russian cultural history, suggesting ... fertile ground for the reception of melodrama there."[11] The movies resembled the popular literature of the day, the "boulevard" and quasi-pornographic fiction by writers like Mikhail Artsybashev and Anastasia Verbitskaya that "began to flood the book-stalls after the easing of the censorship in 1905."[12] The early Russian directors often adapted literary classics to provide their movies with irreproachable credentials and to get onto the screen images—including frightening images—that might, without such a "high culture" imprimatur, offend or anger. Gogol and Pushkin, who drew heavily on folk material for their fiction and poetry, proved particularly rich sources: Gogol's fiction yielded two "horror" stories, "The Portrait" and "Viy," plus a "satanic" spoof, "Christmas Eve," all of which were adapted for screen during the teens, and Pushkin's oeuvre provided his folkloric mermaid (Rusalka), the spurned-woman-turned-vamp, a figure that, slightly adjusted for melodramatic emphasis, readily morphed into a ruthless female predator of weak, passive men.

From Pushkin, too, came the ghost from "The Queen of Spades." Indeed, in an age when "tales of the supernatural were especially popular ... regardless of the medium,"[13] "Queen of Spades" spawned two prerevolutionary screen versions, one in 1910 (by Pyotr Chardynin) and a second in 1916, when Iakov Protazanov, one of the most prominent directors in the business, cast Ivan Mozzhukhin as German, the Napoleonic protagonist whose growing obsession turns him into an accidental murderer. Both films exploited the scary ghost-image of German's victim, the Countess, who gets her revenge on her murderer by driving him mad.

Satanism in Silver Age Russia (roughly 1890–1914) grew out of a general revival of the occult in Europe, and the fin-de-siècle rediscovery of Lucifer and Mephistopheles as Romantic heroic figures. "A shift to the occult as subject matter for literature and art is symptomatic of disaffection from orthodox belief," writes Kristi A. Groberg, "and is often accompanied by a sense of remorse, as if the intellectual had dispensed with a God in whom it was impossible to believe, but whose absence was also disconcerting. The turn to Satan as a cultural hero can then justify the existence of evil in the world and explain why human beings and the societies they create are imperfect and limited."[14]

In Russia politics and aesthetics overlapped: the failed revolution of 1905 enhanced the appeal of the Satanic, "often colored by apocalyptic ideas engendered by the Russian sociopolitical crisis and by visions of the Nietzschean *Übermensch* (Superman), or of the Antichrist, who reversed 'good' and 'evil,'"[15] but so did a less politicized fascination with decadent motifs. Art historian John Bowlt notes that images of sex and violence constitute "a protest against the taboos of a given society,"[16] and such images filled the literature, music, painting, and movie screens of the day.

Movies easily integrated the supernatural and the perverse, as is evident in films by the industry's most gifted directors, Iakov Protazanov and Evgeny Bauer. In 1917, Protazanov directed a peculiar hybrid of eros, Satanism, and possession, *Satan Triumphant*. Set in Scandinavia, *Satan* epitomizes both the decadence of late Russian imperial society and its fascination with Satanic possession. Protazanov's use of superimposition and dissolves enlivens the banal story in which a mysterious stranger finds his way to a house where the virtuous Esfir and her painter-husband dwell. Despite Esfir's unease and the stranger's bizarre manner, the righteous pastor Talnoks welcomes him warmly and urges Esfir to do the same. . . . The predictable upshot involves corruption of the pastor and Esfir alike, and, in the second part of the film (set years later), the ultimate corruption of Esfir's son, born of her adultery with Talnoks. In Bauer's *Daydreams* (1915), corpses rise up from coffins and the protagonist turns into a kind of monster; in *The Dying Swan* (1916), the artist-protagonist, intent on capturing death on canvas, ends by breaking his model's neck. Although Bauer sometimes features vampire-women who destroy their men—most famously in *Child of the Big City* (1914)—he and Protazanov typically portrayed women as victims, consistent with melodrama's paradigm; as Louise McReynolds notes, "melodrama traffics in secrets, threats, and repression, and when these undercurrents endanger the heroine, who was presumed to be more vulnerable to external forces than a man would be, evil would seem easier to identify."[17]

These pre-revolutionary films mingle elements of horror with elements of melodrama and, occasionally, the thriller, though their mélange of "blended cues" (to use Rick Altman's term for "bricolage, pastiche and intertextuality"[18]) is common to all genres. Pre-revolutionary Russian audiences, members of a society in transition, felt strongly a sense of what Paul Coates considers the key component of horror, the disquieting entrapment of the uncanny (*Unheimlich*), when "the other emerges within the same" and "one grasps that one's failure to penetrate the essence of the apparently human being or seemingly friendly situation has allowed the Other to gain power over one."[19] But the luxury of meditating pleasurably on lurking dangers from the safety of a theater seat vanished with the Bolshevik revolution. From about 1918 until 1922, during the years of revolution and Civil War, nearly all domestic cinema production except newsreels and "agitki" ceased, and imports disappeared. When the industry revived and feature films resumed their place in the repertoire, the genre of horror had essentially disappeared from Soviet screens, remaining "in the closet" until the late 1980s.

The Early Soviet Period

To borrow a term from psychiatry, the absence of horror films from Soviet cinema can fairly be called an "overdetermined" phenomenon. Ideological reasons account for it in the first place, followed by broadly cultural reasons and, finally, by practical-cum-aesthetic reasons.

The Bolsheviks in positions of authority—Lenin first of all, but also Trotsky and Commissar for Enlightenment Anatoly Lunacharsky—saw cinema first and foremost as a tool of education and propaganda. Nevertheless, they recognized the earning potential of the medium. In January 1922, with the domestic industry in disarray and in dire need of financial support, Lenin "authorized the Commissariat of Foreign Trade to import large numbers of feature films which were slated for commercial exhibition in the USSR."[20] He specified that film programs combine propagandist films (e.g., on the "colonialist policy of the British in India, . . . the starving in Berlin, etc.") and "entertainment films, especially for publicity purposes and their receipts (without, of course, any obscene or counterrevolutionary content)."[21] Soviet movie houses, back in more or less full-scale business by 1923, typically showed a program consisting of "a feature film, usually an import, a comedy short, a low-budget Soviet-made educational or propaganda film, and sometimes even a political lecture."[22]

In the silent era of the 1920s the Germans dominated horror film production, followed by the United States (Lon Chaney) and Scandinavia (Victor Sjöstrom, Carl Dreyer). Those pictures, however, rarely reached the Soviet Union.[23] Rather, the Soviets imported action pictures, comedies, and melodramas. Audiences adored the German adventure-film star Harry Piel; they adored even more swashbuckling Douglas Fairbanks. In 1922, for instance, Moscow's biggest theater, seating more than 1,000 patrons, showed new American movies every week, and Fairbanks's *Robin Hood* played in fourteen of Moscow's fifty theaters simultaneously.[24] Viewers loved Hollywood's physical dynamism, its believable characters, and its routinely "kheppi end" (often scornfully transliterated into Russian rather than translated). And although critics spurned that happy ending as "alien to the Russian cultural tradition,"[25] they found American films of all genres save horror relatively acceptable ideologically, because of their "cheerful" and "life-affirming" qualities.

Horror as a genre was perceived—whether rightly or wrongly—as inherently reactionary,[26] one that would not serve the need to create a totally new Soviet cinema designed to abet in the creation of a totally new Soviet citizen in a new Soviet society. Whatever audiences really wanted—and they usually "preferred escapism to realism, however unreal that realism might in fact have been"[27]—by the mid-1920s three-quarters of cinema installations in the Soviet Union were housed in workers' clubs, and the Soviet industry increasingly produced the kind of films the Party wanted those workers to see. "In as far as the new way of life is still an abstract concept," wrote one critic, "we must show it in the process of creation. We must depict the sprouting shoots of the new way of life, the new relationships between people. We must romanticize the struggle between the birth of the new and the death of the old."[28]

As for filmmakers, they too spurned horror. The leading avantgarde directors of the time—Eisenstein, Dovzhenko, Vertov—"believed that their obligation to society was fulfilled by creating the art of the future," and that audiences, transformed by socialism, would learn to enjoy and appreciate "hitherto 'inaccessible' art."[29] Horror's emphasis on individual psychology over social and class phenomena ill-accorded with the revolutionary messages they wished their films to convey.

The directors who chose to make entertaining movies, and who often adapted American generic paradigms to do so, mainly avoided horror, preferring melodramas, adventures, and comedies, all of which could easily be situated within the emerging Soviet society. They still incurred critical and official wrath, especially from the "proletarian watchdogs" who considered this kind of cinema "tantamount to counter-revolution and . . . no less dangerous than the 'Formalist' heresies preached by Eisenstein, Vertov and many others."[30] But at least Boris Barnet, Abram Room, Protazanov, and a few others managed to make movies that people actually paid money to see.

Lunacharsky, less doctrinaire than many of his colleagues, consistently advocated a revitalized form of melodrama as the best way to combine entertainment and propaganda.[31] He co-authored the script for one of the few "horror melodramas" of the 1920s, the sensational and enormously popular *The Bear's Wedding* (1926). Based on a Prosper Mérimée story, with a hero who metamorphoses into a prowling bear and mutilates his bride in their wedding bed, *The Bear's Wedding* is a defiantly apolitical variation of a vampire story. (One of the two directors, Vladimir Gardin, had worked with Protazanov on *Satan Triumphant*.) Its "emphasis on perversion places it squarely in the pre-revolutionary tradition"[32]; indeed, because of scenes depicting a nineteenth-century feudal lord raping peasant women, it was deemed "too risqué for village people," and was banned from the countryside.[33]

The Stalin Years

From the late 1920s until the early 1950s, imports fell drastically. Practical as well as ideological reasons played a role: the early talkies could not be exhibited in the USSR because of lack of facilities and equipment, and by the end of the 1920s foreign films "had served their initial economic function by providing a large share of the capital used to finance the Soviet industry's expansion."[34] The strident rhetoric of 1927–29 officially condemned "stupid, trashy and profoundly harmful" foreign films, made in order to bolster Western capitalist states, and late in 1928, foreign films were purged from film libraries.[35] The attacks targeted American films in particular, since America—source of most imports—epitomized the worst capitalism could offer. Thus, the wave of horror films Hollywood released after the introduction of sound (*Dracula, Frankenstein, White Zombie, King Kong*, all 1931), the time when "a distinctive national mythography and commodity [were] born simultaneously,"[36] did not penetrate Soviet borders.

Neither did the British pictures made just before and during World War II. During the wartime alliance, although a more relaxed cultural milieu prevailed, audiences saw relatively few Western films, mainly ones—like *Sun Valley Serenade*, first shown on Soviet screens in 1944— that provided relief from all-too-real horrors. And after the iron curtain descended, at a time when Hollywood and the British studios grappled with "end-of-the-war, atomic-bomb anxieties,"[37] Stalin's final cultural pogrom effectively eliminated nearly all imports, save for the "trophy" films confiscated from the Germans and captured American films.[38]

With the partial exception of the war years, the parameters of possibility in domestic Soviet cinema narrowed and ideological requirements multiplied throughout the 1930s, 1940s, and early 1950s. After the centralization of the Soviet film industry in 1930, and under the leadership of film "czar" Boris Shumiatsky, each Soviet studio had to produce an annual "thematic plan," outlining forthcoming projects. Scriptwriters and directors continued to adapt to their own needs and circumstances both the narrative structures and visual patterns of several genres from the West, as they had in the 1920s, but perforce they avoided horror. Shumiatsky, who reviewed every "thematic plan," favored commercial cinema. He called for "a cinema for the millions" and at one time hoped to create a "Soviet Hollywood" on the Black Sea capable of turning out 300 movies annually.[39] During his tenure (1930–38) he tried to ensure what he considered a desirable balance of genres, favoring in particular musical comedies and science fiction.[40] The most popular films of the 1930s—*Chapaev* (1934), the *Maxim Trilogy* (1935–38), and the string of musical "comedies" made by Grigory Aleksandrov (*Jolly Fellows* [1934], *The Circus* [1936], *Volga-Volga* [1938], and *Radiant Path* [1940])—emulated Hollywood's adventure films and its Busby Berkeley–style musicals, albeit with a distinct ideological twist.

Genre per se did not trouble the Soviet authorities, but with the exception of melodrama (which lost much of its sexuality and unconscious neuroticism when adapted to the Soviet screen), the particular genres typically identified in Western cinema discourse have little relevance to the generic categories ("production" films, with zealous and inspirational factory-worker protagonists in industrial settings; historical films; films about the countryside; films about young people) used by the Soviet film industry to designate its products, and less still to the political organs that oversaw it. When Richard T. Jameson matter-of-factly writes that movies "belong to genres much the way people belong to families or ethnic groups," he really refers to the West. "Name one of the classic, bedrock genres—Western, comedy, musical, war film, gangster picture, science fiction, horror—and even the most casual moviegoer," he continues, "will come up with a mental image of it, partly visual, partly conceptual."[41] For Soviet viewers, images of stalwart officers and snarling villains whose conflict culminates in a shoot-out set against a landscape of open spaces and little human population, filmed in long shots and panoramic vistas, call to mind a specific genre as clearly as they do to a Midwesterner's. The Soviet version of that classic Western paradigm pitting clearly designated forces of good against forces of evil, however, took the form of the Soviet

Civil War film, a genre that produced many entries in the 1920s (including Pudovkin's masterful *Storm over Asia* [1928]) and 1930s, surviving into the 1950s. The Bolsheviks and their Red Army supporters, metaphorically wearing white hats, rode out against the evil White Army and treacherous civilian elements that supported the Whites. Conflict climaxed in violence, usually a battle, often physically situated in small towns or in the countryside rather than in urban or populous areas, and filmed in long, sweeping, panoramic shots.

Altman notes that genre films "typically depend on *symbolic* usage of key images, sounds and situations":

> Actual location matters less for the Western's incessant long shots of the landscape than the way the landscape is used to figure the simultaneous danger and potential that the West represents. Similarly, a train crossing the prairie..., a contested gun..., and the building of a church...or a schoolhouse...all carry a symbolic weight that outstrips the historical referent. Genre films also gain from their simplicity, for it is the very concentration derived from simplification that allows cowboys, gangsters, dancers, detectives and monsters to take on symbolic value so easily and systematically.[42]

The same, certainly, is true of Soviet Civil War movies: some of their specific images (though not all) differ from those of Hollywood westerns, but their symbolic importance far outweighs actual history.[43]

The horror genre, however, and the formulas that constitute its essence, contradict almost every major tenet of Marxist historical materialism, of Soviet doctrine, and of socialist realist dogma. The fears and anxieties underpinning horror films—of the uncanny or supernatural, of chaos, of the irrational—contravene a materialist philosophy that holds as self-evident the primacy of man as a social and rational being, who acts primarily out of motives of material interest, and whose alienation stems from specific economic and social conditions. Socialism would, in Marx's view, "liberate all the powers latent in every human being, and develop his personal abilities to the utmost *in the social context*."[44] There's not much room there for the murk of madness or for the "horror of personality,"[45] for Freud's conviction that human beings are essentially envious, and that growing up within any social system "is necessarily a repressive process," becoming more so as "the advancement of civilization lays an increasing burden of anxiety on the individual's sense of a guilty self."[46] The Soviet state had little use for the tragic view. Despite efforts by several Soviet

Marxists to unite Marx and Freud, Freud's writings ceased to be translated into Russian by the late 1920s, and "genuine discussion of Freudianism was swamped by one-sided denunciations."[47]

Nor does such a view accommodate the supernatural. The Party considered Russian peasant superstition—belief in, for instance, "dark forces" (*tyomnaia sila*)—no less retrograde than Russian piety, and the Party's official artistic doctrine of socialist realism demanded positive heroes, men of action and utter selfless devotion to (political) cause, not inward-looking neurasthenics.[48] "In the Soviet Union . . . masterful men knew that getting out of oneself, proving one's worth in progressive social activity, is the practical answer to the sickly self-absorption of quitters and losers."[49]

Soviet cinema had its moments of horror, even during the 1930s and 1940s. Eisenstein, who borrowed for his own purposes the aesthetics of German Expressionism and Kabuki drama's counterpoint of sound and image, deliberately shocked and provoked his viewers. In *Alexander Nevsky* (1938), for instance, he dehumanizes the Teutonic knights by replacing their human faces not merely with metal masks, but with particularly bestial masks, and he records the Teuton trumpets "so near to the microphone as to achieve an almost physically distressing feedback."[50] In his study of tyranny, *Ivan the Terrible* (1945/1958), Eisenstein transforms what is ostensibly a historical epic into something closer to a psychological horror film by blurring the lines between victim and victimizer, hero and monster, male and female. His use of extreme, even grotesque camera angles, memorably distorted and deformed shadows, vertical montage, and color all rely on effects relating to the supernatural and horror, and speak of (as well as to) the repressed fears underlying them—his own and his putative audience's.[51]

In general, however, the "monsters" that threatened the heroes and heroines of Stalinist cinema, that allowed viewers the luxury of feeling "safely frightened,"[52] belong outside the realm of the subconscious. Tangible and three-dimensional, the foes vanquished by stalwart Soviet citizens took palpable form: in peacetime, enemies of the people, foreign spies and their domestic accomplices, saboteurs and wreckers; in wartime, invaders, occupiers, and destroyers.[53]

The Thaw and "Stagnation"

Stalin's death in 1953 ended the *malokartin'e* years when Soviet film output from the major studios dwindled to a rusty trickle and the republican studios for all practical purposes ceased to exist. With the onset of the

Thaw, Soviet cinema slowly came back to life, supported by Party-mandated expansion and a cadre of young, well-trained professionals eager to get to work.[54] Filmmakers responded eagerly to every hint of relaxation in official policy, making movies about the past and—to the great pleasure of Soviet audiences—about the present. Beginning in 1956, studios released a substantial number of movies that revisited, and revised in significant ways, many of the national myths that had been so central to Soviet culture and society. At the same time, foreign films reappeared, though Western and Eastern European films preceded and outnumbered British and American ones. Thus, neither ordinary Soviet moviegoers nor the privileged members of the industry who had access to a considerably broader range of films were able to see Don Siegel's *Invasion of the Body Snatchers* (1956), or the movies made by Britain's Hammer Studios (e.g., *Curse of Frankenstein* [1957]), or American International Pictures' horror cycle beginning with *I Was a Teenage Werewolf* (1957), or Roger Corman's adaptations of Edgar Allan Poe.

Not that they particularly wanted to see such movies. After years of isolation, both filmmakers and film audiences thirsted for interaction with the outside world, but they sought movies with some connection to their own world, either to their cinematic traditions or to their Weltanschauung. Directors were eager to turn their cameras on their own society, to explore its dilemmas and represent it onscreen with a hitherto unthinkable degree of veracity, and found relatively little (technical sophistication apart) to borrow from grade B movies; when they did reach for American models, they preferred the allegorical possibilities of science fiction. Like many Russian and Soviet intellectuals they turned their collective noses up at Hollywood, instead voraciously watching the Italian neo-realist cinematic masterpieces of De Sica and Rossellini, the films of the French nouvelle vague, the work of idiosyncratic directors with distinctive visions and styles, like Bergman and Kurosawa.

Furthermore, the anxieties that fueled American and British horror films in the 1950s, 1960s, and 1970s had no real parallels in the Soviet Union. Despite the zigzags of the Thaw, the unpredictability and irregularity of its periods of relative tolerance, most Soviet citizens regarded the dozen years between Khrushchev's 1956 Secret Speech and the 1968 invasion of Czechoslovakia as a period of liberation. A liberation that artists had continually to defend and fight for, a liberation often threatened by renewed repressions, but still, compared to what had preceded it, a liberation. Rather than feeling the kind of alienation that expressed itself in much of American popular culture, Soviets felt for the first time in many years invested in their country and its evolution and during the initial part of the Thaw, until about 1961, quite hopeful about its future.

Consider the attitude toward science implied by U.S. horror films of the 1950s and early 1960s. Society, menaced by natural disasters or by technology run amok, cannot turn to science or scientists for help; indeed, scientists prove helpless in averting the danger, if they do not (at their worst) actively abet it. What defeats menace (though in later American films, such defeat is transient, a victory only over evil's current manifestation but not over its enduring essence) is what R. H. W. Dillard calls

> a working combination of reason and faith, of practical understanding and belief. Neither is properly efficacious without the other. Belief alone may save one's soul, but it will give him only the direction for any temporal and practical victory. . . . Reason, too, is ineffectual, because it denies the existence of any evil that does not fit the immutable laws of a logical and orderly universe. The myriad doctors, scientists, and believers in a rational world are baffled by occurrences which can fit in no possible way into their system; they examine the happenings of the night by daylight and cannot understand the mysteries of the dark. Theirs is a more foolish innocence than that of the superstitious peasant, for their scientific optimism often leads them to deny evil as an active force in human affairs altogether.[55]

Compare this with the cult of science that swept the Soviet Union in the late 1950s and early 1960s: by 1961, scientists had become the modern heroes of Soviet society, "a cross between magicians—modern alchemists—and cult-idols, 'tenors' of the twentieth century."[56] In the age of atomic energy, cybernetics, and space travel, poet Boris Slutsky wrote in 1960, science had surpassed the popularity of poetry and eclipsed literature in imagination; its language "resonated like contemporary music."[57] Most of Soviet society regarded the Soviet Union's scientific progress with uncritical and unequivocal admiration, eagerly buying Fermi's memoirs and rapturously welcoming back the cosmonaut Yuri Gagarin, whose April 1961 space flight turned him into an instant public icon. In the early 1960s, perhaps emboldened by Soviet success in space, Khrushchev felt sufficiently self-confident to demystify some of the USSR's top secret scientific research establishments, and to establish Akademgorodok, the extremely prestigious research center near Novosibirsk.

Movies expressed more ambivalence toward science and scientists, perhaps because filmmakers, like other Soviet intellectuals, understood the risks as well as the thrills of scientific progress. Mikhail Romm's *Nine Days of a Year* (1961) treats the destructive potential of splitting the atom. Yet one of its protagonists, unambiguously heroic, continues his experiments despite irradiation and certain death, unshakably convinced that scientific research is the best means to achieve long-term benefits for mankind; and his best friend, far more cynical about the possible perversion of science and about human beings' inability to change, remains in the end a dedicated scientist.[58]

In a more commercial and extremely popular film, *The Amphibian Man* (1962), directors Gennady Kazansky and Vladimir Chebotarev mix more or less equal parts science fiction, romantic adventure, and exotic underwater photography to produce a political allegory, an oblique comment on Soviet history.[59] Their film (based on a popular story by Alexander Belyaev) features a brilliant scientist, Dr. Salvator (Nikolai Simonov), who dreams of establishing an underwater society of equality and justice. The first and only citizen of his Utopia, his amphibious son, happily lives underwater; he knows no human except his father, until he rescues a drowning maiden and falls in love with her. Dr. Salvator is far closer to the Faustian scientist of political fantasy/science fiction "who pays too little heed to the consequences of his experimentation"[60] than to the obsessed scientist of horror films: he belongs to the same pantheon as Rotwang (Rudolf Klein-Rogge) in Fritz Lang's *Metropolis* (1927), Kubrick's eponymous Dr. Strangelove (Peter Sellers), and Dr. Persikov in Mikhail Bulgakov's 1925 novella *Fatal Eggs*. The film criticizes the political manipulation/perversion of science, but it never doubts science itself, just as it never doubts Salvator's idealism or his love for his child.

Until quite recently, Soviet life offered few of the accoutrements integral to the horror genre, most obviously those pertaining to space. As mentioned, the violence in horror films typically invades personal space, especially the domestic spaces of hearth and home. But as Barry Keith Grant writes, "one cannot fear the violation of the boudoir's privacy until one has attained the capital to acquire a room of one's own."[61] Few Soviet residents, rural or urban, had that luxury. In the traditional peasant house a family slept in one large room heated by a stove; its renovated or modernized replacement still gives precedence to a large common space, with sleeping areas often alcoves separated by curtains or small, purely functional

The underwater fantasy world of *The Amphibian Man* (1962)

bedrooms. Soviet city dwellers lived for decades in communal apartments, a circumstantial necessity turned into an "institution of social control" under Stalin.[62] One family occupied one or at most two rooms, and shared bathroom, toilet, kitchen, and corridor with neighbors. Even after construction of new housing and repair of old housing partly alleviated overcrowding, and families could move out of communal apartments into their own, they rarely had more than two rooms for living, dining, and sleeping.

In urban households, parents typically slept on a foldout sofa in the living room, allotting the second room to offspring; frequently they shared "their" space with a grandparent or a nanny, who would sleep in the same room, behind a screen. The notion of violating private space makes little sense in that context. As Boym, who grew up in a communal apartment in Leningrad, recalls,

> Once I was asked what were my earliest memories of growing up in the same room with my parents. The first thing I remembered was the texture of the curtain (*port'era*) that partitioned our shared room. The *port'era* of my childhood was heavy and dark yellow, with an ornamental appliqué. I remember overhearing the voices of my parents and their friends and the songs of Okudzhava and Vysotsky [two famous "underground" poet-singers of the 1960s], but most of all I remember the *port'era* itself. So much for the primal scenes.[63]

In the 1960s and 1970s, the USSR witnessed nothing like the social strife that wracked American society at the time, with assassinations, the polarizing Vietnam War, race riots, and fissures along fault lines of age, race, politics, gender, and class. American horror movies took on new life in these years, generally locating the source of horror inside the individual, sometimes in insanity or "possession," often in sordid, matter-of-fact and motiveless sociopathy, or in equally motiveless external forces of disaster, a malevolent universe whose "evil forces constantly undermined the quality of existence."[64] Brezhnevite Russia, by contrast, experienced material growth accompanied by ideological and cultural rigidity. Counter-systems to resist that rigidity arose: the black and gray markets in the economy, dissident intellectual and political undergrounds, and several varieties of youth countercultures. On the whole, however, it was a period of relative social stability. Its movies avoided ideology, preferring to examine "the realities of Soviet life"—including corruption—and personal destinies.[65] The "genre repertoire widened considerably,"[66] with the studios retaining melodrama as their mainstay but producing a large number of comedies, sci-fi, adventure pictures, and political thrillers; most, however, were at best undistinguished, and few attracted large audiences.[67] Only one movie from this period can even marginally be counted a horror film, Konstantin Ershov and Georgy Kropachev's adaptation of Gogol's *Viy* (1967), and although a dead girl rises from her coffin and summons all kinds of fantastic and wonderfully realized spirits and demons (no surprise, with the brilliant master Alexander Ptushko in charge of special effects and animation), *Viy*—with its dated look, its simpering seminarian hero, and its lethargic pace—is unlikely to have frightened anyone.

Post-Soviet

Filmmakers avidly welcomed Gorbachev's radical policies of perestroika and glasnost in 1986, seeing in them the opportunity to release creative energies stifled for nearly twenty years.[68] They formed a commission to investigate about 100 films that had been censored or withheld from distribution, eventually releasing nearly all of them. They restructured their professional union, replacing the conservative old guard with a group of liberals; they reorganized the economic structure of the industry so that studios and independent producers gained autonomy over production (including the right to negotiate directly with potential co-producers)

The wicked witch of
Viy (1967)

and concomitant fiscal responsibility for self-financing.[69] Yet after a brief euphoric interval, and for a complex mixture of reasons, the post-Soviet film industry found itself in a desperate situation. As critic Andrei Plakhov wrote, "the centennial of Russian film, in 1996, nearly went down as the year of its death. . . . Amid unprecedented inflation and the collapse of the state filmmaking and distribution system, the industry had spiraled downward to a historic low. It appeared making a movie in Russia had become an unaffordable luxury."[70]

Happily, that is no longer true, though conditions remain extremely difficult for Russian filmmakers and dreadful for filmmakers in most of the former republics. (Georgia's central studio in Tbilisi, for decades a source of outstanding films, has virtually ceased to function.) In the past five years or so a younger generation of filmmakers has sought—and occasionally found—innovative financing schemes, has capitalized on the growth of Russia's small moneyed class (the "new Russians") and their thirst for amusement, and has managed to make movies that find audiences in theaters and in the video shops that have proliferated in the former Soviet Union.

Although nobody has discovered the "magic formula of a universally marketable hybrid, made with Western money and Russian artistic sensitivity,"[71] genre pictures seem most appealing to domestic audiences. Russians may not flock to see, but at least they go to see movies like Aleksei Balabanov's *Brother* (1997) and its sequel *Brother 2* (1999), Valery

Todorovsky's *Land of the Deaf* (1998), and similar adventure pictures and gangster/thrillers, often with a political or national subtext and with a lone social avenger as protagonist. Melodramas remain popular, as do comedies.[72] And for the first time in about seventy-five years, Russian directors are making horror movies.

Back in the mid-1980s, when St. Petersburg was still Leningrad, a group of avant-garde directors based there made mainly short, low-budget taboo-breaking films they grouped under the designation "necrorealism." Yevgeni Yufit's *The Stretcher-Bearer Werewolves* (1985), Andrei Myortvy's *Mochebuitsy-trupolovy* (1988: the title plays on the words "urine," "corpse" and "catch," but doesn't actually mean anything, and the director's name is a pseudonym meaning "dead man"), and their successors, including Yufit's *Daddy, Santa Claus Died* (1992), supposedly inspired by the official "zombies" of the Brezhnev era, feature the "necrophiliacs and corpses" of post-Soviet life, a "world of walking dead."[73] These are cult movies, seen by very few people, and despite boasts of mutual support between "parallel" cinema and the mainstream industry, relations are tenuous at best.

Within "mainstream" commercial cinema at least three movies of the last few years can legitimately be categorized as horror films: Oleg Teptsov's *Mr. Decorator* (1989), Sergei Vinokurov's *Vampire* (1997), and Nikolai Lebedev's *Snake Source* (1997); Alexei Balabanov's *Of Freaks and Men* (1998), one of the best movies to come out of Russia recently, is not a horror film but uses many of the genre's conventions and themes.[74] Both *Of Freaks and Men* and *Mr. Decorator* take place in the twilight of the Russian empire, in the first years of the twentieth century, a period already noted for its interest in Satanism and the occult. *Vampire* and *Snake Source* situate their plots in contemporary provincial Russian cities: in the former, vampires infect nearly the entire town, and the "last man" (a thief) sends for a professional vampire-destroyer in order to cleanse the city; in the latter, a young teacher arrives in the provincial town and immediately falls under suspicion of having committed a string of murders.

Despite variations in plot, setting, and time frame, these films share certain characteristics. All involve images of doubling—a motif that has haunted the horror film "from *The Student of Prague* to *Solaris*"[75]—to portray a variety of tensions: between tradition and modernity, between art and consumerism, between classes.[76] All suggest a demonic universe in which nothing innocent can survive, most disturbingly in *Of Freaks and Men* because it involves the sexual exploitation of a blind woman[77] and the commercial exploitation and corruption of angel-voiced young

Siamese twins, one of whom dies as a result. All follow the horror paradigm of the disruption of natural order, the threat to domestic/familial harmony, and all manipulate the border between order and chaos visually and thematically (corpses come to life in *Santa Claus* and *Mr. Decorator,* dead creatures prey on the living in *Vampire* and *Snake Source*). All rely on repression, the "dominant strategy of the traditional horror" film, where "what is repressed returns in condensed and displaced form to threaten and challenge and disrupt that which would deny its presence,"[78] most obviously and derivatively (from Hitchcock) in *Snake Source,* whose villain, a prissy school secretary/psychopath, assumes the garb and outward identity of his next victim for each murder.

Snake Source and *Vampire* belong to a group of movies made on tiny budgets, each an attempt to adapt genre formulas to post-Soviet Russian cinema and "reconcile the specificity of a national culture with the requirements of a pan-European—or global—market."[79] It is not easy. National cinematic traditions differ: the Soviet preference for psychological camera, artificial lighting, and slow pace contrasts with American genre cinema's "tight story line, suspense building, location shooting, fast-paced editing, and the ability to reveal a character in one or two big strokes."[80] Moreover, the post-Soviet absence of consensus on values militates against successful genre pictures, since genre relies on "common topics, plots, key scenes, character types, familiar objects, recognizable shots and sounds," as well as "character relationships, image and sound montage."[81]

Russian critic Igor Mantsov believes Russian cinema cannot yet produce wholly successful genre films because such films require an emancipated hero capable of autonomous action; the screen cannot supply what the society still lacks. During the Soviet period, he notes, ideological and social markers differentiated friend, enemy, Party member, patriot, and traitor, categories out of which grew cinema's dramatic fabric. Even though the Soviet Union no longer exists, Russian cinema is unable to show two distinctly different private worlds: "Identity [in the same of 'sameness']," Mantsov writes, "dominates our cinema, when these genres demand differentiation. . . . Genre—detective, thriller, melodrama—begins precisely at the point where the individual succeeds in separating himself from the social mass. . . . In our context no full-fledged genre is possible, because the rule of identity [sameness] does not permit singling out the criminal and exposing the crime. Everyone resembles everyone else."[82]

Thus, in *Vampire* the vampires walking the streets seem like identical twins, and the hero lacks a clear character: he may be evil's enemy, he may be evil's embodiment. When the Destroyer finally meets his double, we don't know which of the two, Destroyer or Vampire, is less human and more awful; good and evil are indistinguishable from each other. Nikolai Lebedev, director of *Snake Source*, comments on the stifling atmosphere of the town (implicitly, the whole society) by presenting his killer as being much like the town's other residents, all of whom have passed through the local school and been "molded" by its terrifying director. Lebedev exposes a well-entrenched Soviet paradigm, that of the "wonderful school years": in this town, the school experience has deformed everyone, turned them into at least potential killers.

Mantsov points out that the sort of external detail that acts as a genuinely distinguishing marker in, for instance, Hitchcock films, is far less effective in a Russian movie. Jimmy Stewart can be forgiven for mistaking one woman for another in *Vertigo* (1958), given their unique clothing and hairdo. But outside of a handful of Russian cities, relatively little variation exists in Russian clothing even today. Thus it is absurd for *Snake Source* to suggest that the heroine's checkered dress suggests her guilt, as if only she could wear that dress: in a Russian provincial city, everyone walks around in the same dress. "What is a nightmare in Hitchcock," Mantsov concludes, "is a commonplace in the Russian context."[83]

Audiences want entertainment and filmmakers want viewers, a symbiosis that favors generic development. Without the restrictions that proscribed horror as a genre, Russian cinema is likely to continue to produce examples of horror films, though horror seems unlikely to displace melodrama or comedy, perennial Russian favorites. Still, as they did nearly a century ago, Russian filmmakers are once more using the conventions of horror to externalize some of the nightmares and address some of the fears and uncertainties that haunt their audiences, men and women living through one of the most difficult periods in what has been an exceptionally traumatic national history. What McReynolds and Neuberger highlight as melodrama's importance in Russian culture applies as well to its related genre, horror: "By dramatizing class tensions, urban-rural transformations, marriage politics, struggles over national memory, the nature of heroism, and the conflict between the worship of ideas and the accumulation of things, melodrama had the capacity to explore the most important cultural conflicts at the heart of the construction of both national and individual identity."[84] At a time when those questions of identity take a close back seat to issues of economic survival, horror films may be one avenue to understanding the metamorphosis in Russian consciousness, and in Russia itself.

Notes

My thanks to Joan Neuberger and Alexander Prokhorov, and to the editors of this volume, whose comments and queries on an earlier draft significantly improved this essay.

1. Ivan Butler, *Horror in the Cinema*, 3rd ed. (London: Tantivy, 1979), 58.
2. Butler, *Horror in the Cinema*, 15.
3. Paul Coates, *The Gorgon's Gaze: German Cinema, Expressionism, and the Images of Horror* (Cambridge: Cambridge University Press, 1991), 4.
4. Butler, *Horror in the Cinema*, 72.
5. Charles Derry, *Dark Dreams: A Psychological History of the Modern Horror Film* (South Brunswick, NJ: A. S. Barnes, 1977), 42–43.
6. Barry Keith Grant, Introduction, in *The Dread of Difference: Gender and the Horror Film*, ed. Barry Keith Grant (Austin: University of Texas Press, 1996), 5–6.
7. Derry, *Dark Dreams*, 17, 49.
8. Ibid., 85.
9. On pre-revolutionary Russian cinema, see Yuri Tsivian, *Early Cinema in Russia and Its Cultural Reception*, trans. Alan Bodger (London: Routledge, 1994) and Denise J. Youngblood, *The Magic Mirror: Moviemaking in Russia, 1908–1918* (Madison: University of Wisconsin Press, 1999). For information on early studios, production, etc., see Youngblood, 6–45.
10. Youngblood, *Magic Mirror*, 7.
11. Louise McReynolds and Joan Neuberger, Introduction, in *Imitations of Life: Two Centuries of Melodrama in Russia*, ed. Louisa McReynolds and Joan Neuberger (Durham, NC: Duke University Press, 2002), 4.
12. Richard Stites, *Russian Popular Culture: Entertainment and Society since 1900* (Cambridge: Cambridge University Press, 1992), 24.
13. Youngblood, *Magic Mirror*, 76.
14. Kristi A. Groberg, "The Shade of Lucifer's Dark Wing," in *The Occult in Russian and Soviet Culture*, ed. Bernice Glatzer Rosenthal (Ithaca: Cornell University Press, 1997), 101.
15. Groberg, "Shade of Lucifer's Dark Wing," 102.
16. John Bowlt, "Through the Glass Darkly: Images of Decadence in Early Twentieth-Century Russian Art," *Journal of Contemporary History* 17, no. 1 (1982): 98.
17. McReynolds and Neuberger, *Imitations of Life*, 127.
18. Rick Altman, *Film/Genre* (London: BFI Publishing, 1999), 141.
19. Coates, *Gorgon's Gaze*, 5, 7.
20. Vance Kepley Jr., and Betty Kepley, "Foreign Films on Soviet Screens, 1922–1931," *Quarterly Review of Film Studies* 4, no. 4 (1979): 429–42, quote on p. 433.
21. Cited by Richard Taylor, *Film Propaganda: Soviet Russia and Nazi Germany*, rev. ed. (London: I. B. Tauris, 1998), 35.
22. Kepley and Kepley, "Foreign Films on Soviet Screens," 435.

23. *The Cabinet of Dr. Caligari* (1919) was seen, as was *Dr. Mabuse, The Gambler* (1922). See Peter Kenez, *The Birth of the Propaganda State* (Cambridge: Cambridge University Press, 1985), 38.

24. Denise J. Youngblood, *Movies for the Masses: Popular Cinema and Soviet Society in the 1920s* (Cambridge: Cambridge University Press, 1992), 52.

25. Youngblood, *Movies for the Masses*, 55.

26. Robin Wood and others have demonstrated that horror has progressive as well as conservative potential insofar as it raises questions about the social construction of "evil" in Western societies. For Wood, horror films problematize the concept of the Other, refusing the "easy dichotomies of normality/abnormality associated with the construction of Self/Other in various popular genres" and refusing to see the monster "as aberration," whose destruction is necessary in order to "secure bourgeois normality" (cited by Christopher Sharrett, "The Horror Film in Neoconservative Culture," in Grant, ed., *Dread of Difference*, 253–54).

27. Taylor, *Film Propaganda*, 39.

28. Cited by Taylor, *Film Propaganda*, 39.

29. Denise J. Youngblood, "The Return of the Native: Yakov Protazanov and Soviet Cinema," in *Inside the Film Factory: New Approaches to Russian and Soviet Cinema*, ed. Richard Taylor and Ian Christie (London: Routledge, 1991), 110.

30. Youngblood, "The Return of the Native," 111.

31. Julie A. Cassiday, "Alcohol Is Our Enemy!: Soviet Temperance Melodramas of the 1920s," in McReynolds and Neuberger, *Imitations of Life*, 152–77, quote on pp. 155–58.

32. Youngblood, *Movies for the Masses*, 84.

33. Kenez, *Birth of the Propaganda State*, 222.

34. Kepley and Kepley, "Foreign Films on Soviet Screens," 440.

35. Youngblood, *Movies for the Masses*, 62.

36. Frank McConnell, "Rough Beasts Slouching," in *Focus on the Horror Film*, ed. Roy Gerard Huss and T. J. Ross (Englewood Cliffs, NJ: Prentice-Hall, 1972), 24–35, quote on p. 26.

37. Derry, *Dark Dreams*, 17.

38. See Stites, *Russian Popular Culture*, 116–26. For a list of the "trophy" films approved for release and the German ones actually released, see Taylor, *Film Propaganda*, 212–14.

39. Taylor, *Film Propaganda*, 47.

40. Ibid., 46.

41. Richard T. Jameson, ed. *They Went Thataway: Redefining Film Genres* (San Francisco: Mercury, 1994), ix; cited by Altman, *Film/Genre*, 13.

42. Altman, *Film/Genre*, 26.

43. See Katerina Clark's discussion of this phenomenon in literature in *The Soviet Novel: History as Ritual* (Chicago: University of Chicago Press, 1981), esp. 4–24, 108–13, 159–90.

44. Leszek Kolakowski, *Main Currents of Marxism*, vol., 1, trans. P. S. Falla. (Oxford: Oxford University Press, 1981), 307, emphasis added.

45. Derry, *Dark Dreams*, 17.

46. David Joravsky, *Russian Psychology: A Critical History* (Oxford: Basil Blackwell, 1989), 235.

47. Joravsky, *Russian Psychology*, 217.
48. See Rufus W. Mathewson Jr., *The Positive Hero in Russian Literature* ([1958] Stanford: Stanford University Press, 1975), for an analysis of this doctrine.
49. Joravsky, *Russian Psychology*, 237.
50. S. S. Prawer, *Caligari's Children: The Film as Tale of Terror* (Oxford: Oxford University Press, 1980), 30.
51. For new insights into *Ivan*, see essays by Herbert Eagle, Joan Neuberger, Alexander Zholkovsky, Yuri Tsivian, and Anne Nesbet, in *Eisenstein at 100: A Reconsideration*, ed. Al LaValley and Barry P. Scherr (New Brunswick, NJ: Rutgers University Press, 2001).
52. Prawer, *Caligari's Children*, 48.
53. Lars T. Lih offers a fascinating discussion of how melodrama formed the structure of party-nation relations, engendering a particular horror of deception and masks. See Lih, "Melodrama and the Myth of the Soviet Union," in McReynolds and Neuberger, eds., *Imitations of Life*, 178–207, esp. 189–94.
54. See Josephine Woll, *Real Images: Soviet Cinema and the Thaw* (London: I. B. Tauris, 2000), 2–13, 21–24.
55. R. H. W. Dillard, "The Pageantry of Death," In Huss and Ross, eds., *Focus on the Horror Film*, 36–41, quote on p. 40.
56. Lev Anninskii, *Shestidesiatniki i my* (Moscow: Soyuz kinematografistov SSSR, 1991), 96.
57. Neia Zorkaia, *Portrety* (Moscow: Iskusstvo, 1966), 248.
58. See Woll, *Real Images*, 127–33. Alexander Prokhorov (private correspondence) properly comments that terror sporadically surfaces in Soviet films that take as their subject man's struggle with nature, particularly in episodes where nature overwhelms human reason. Perhaps the best example of this is Mikhail Kalatozov's *The Unsent Letter* (1960).
59. Mikhail Romm's *Nine Days*, which won a number of awards in 1962, was seen by nearly 24 million viewers in its first year of domestic distribution. *The Amphibian Man*, released the same year, led all other films, with over 65 million viewers. See Sergei Zemlianukhin and Miroslava Segida, *Domashniaia sinemateka otechestvennoe kino, 1918–1996* (Moscow: Dubl-D, 1966).
60. Prawer, *Caligari's Children*, 39.
61. Grant, Introduction, in *Dread of Difference*, 5–6.
62. Svetlana Boym, *Common Places: Mythologies of Everyday Life in Russia* (Cambridge: Harvard University Press, 1995), 129.
63. Boym, *Common Places*, 145–46. See Boym's excellent discussion of "common places," 121–50. She points out that the entrances and interior courtyards of Soviet apartment blocks are "space[s] of fear, the dark limit of the house," a passage "to a dark corner of the Soviet unconscious" (141).
64. Derry, *Dark Dreams*, 85.
65. Stites, *Russian Popular Culture*, 169. To be sure, horror need not have a distinct supernatural dimension, and Western cinema produced a subgenre of "realist horror" films; see Steven Jay Schneider, "Introduction, Part 1: Dimensions of the Real," *Post Script* 21, no. 3 (2002): 3–7.
66. Anna Lawton, *Kinoglasnost: Soviet Cinema in Our Time* (Cambridge: Cambridge University Press, 1992), 3.

67. Stites, *Russian Popular Culture,* 169–74, gives an overview of Brezhnev-era films, as does Lawton, *Kinoglasnost,* 11–37.
68. See Woll, *Real Images,* 201–28, on renewed censorship in 1967–68.
69. See Lawton, *Kinoglasnost,* 70–107.
70. Andrei Plakhov, "Russian Cinema Reborn," *Moscow Times,* April 1998, 1–2.
71. Christina Stojanova, "The New Russian Cinema," *Kinema* (Fall 1998): 2.
72. For discussions of recent Russian films, see Stojanova, "New Russian Cinema," and Andrew James Horton's report on Russian entries at the 2001 Karlovy Vary Festival, "Rich Rewards in Simpler Forms," *Kinoeye* 1, no. 1 (September 3, 2001), online at http://www.kinoeye.org/01/01/horton01.html, accessed September 5, 2003.
73. Lawton, *Kinoglasnost,* 231–32.
74. Tony Williams (private correspondence) mentions in this connection Karen Shakhnazarov's *The Assassin of the Tsar* (1991), starring Malcolm McDowell, a "supernatural 'eternal return' thriller containing elements of the horror film especially relevant to the changes in post-Soviet society."
75. Prawer, *Caligari's Children,* 55.
76. See Steven Jay Schneider, "Manifestations of the Literary Double in Modern Horror Cinema," *Film and Philosophy* (Special Edition 2001): 51–62.
77. Linda Williams notes the frequency with which "good girl" heroines of cinema were either figuratively or literally blind. Blindness allows "the look of the male protagonist to regard the woman at the requisite safe distance necessary to the voyeur's pleasure, with no danger that she will return that look and in so doing express desires of her own." See Williams, "When the Woman Looks," in Grant, ed., *Dread of Difference,* 15–34, quote on pp. 15–16.
78. Vivian Sobchack, "Bringing It All Back Home: Family Economy and Generic Exchange," in Grant, ed., *Dread of Difference,* 143–63, quote on p. 144.
79. Christina Stojanova, "Russian Cinema in the Free-Market Realm: Strategies for Survival," *Kinema* (Spring 1999): 8.
80. Stojanova, "Russian Cinema," 8.
81. Altman, *Film/Genre,* 89.
82. Igor Mantsov, "Imitatsia Zhanra" (Genre Imitation), *Iskusstvo kino* 6 (1998): 3–4.
83. Mantsov, "Imitatsia Zhanra," 6–7.
84. McReynolds and Neuberger, *Imitations of Life,* 12.

CONTRIBUTORS

IAN CONRICH is senior lecturer in film studies at the University of Surrey Roehampton, England; an editor of the *Journal of Popular British Cinema;* and series editor for the Kakapo Books publications "Studies in New Zealand Culture." He is the coeditor of *Contemporary New Zealand Cinema* (Wayne State University Press) and *Horror Zone: The Cultural Experience of Contemporary Horror Cinema* (Verso).

RAIFORD GUINS is the principal editor of the Americas for the *Journal of Visual Culture* and is a senior lecturer in contemporary screen media at University of West England, Bristol. His work has appeared in *West Coast Line, Television and New Media, New Formations,* and *The Visual Culture Reader, 2nd Edition.* He is currently co-authoring two books with Sage Publications: *Popular Culture: A Reader* and *Popular across Culture,* and has begun work on a third entitled *Edited Clean Version: Censorial Procedures in the Age Digital Effects.*

STEFFEN HANTKE has written on contemporary American literature and film. He serves as area chair at the Southwest/Texas Popular Culture/ American Culture Association and recently guest-edited an issue of *Paradoxa: Studies in World Literary Genres* on horror. He currently teaches at Sogang University in Seoul.

JYOTSNA KAPUR teaches in the Department of Cinema and Photography at Southern Illinois University. She is currently working on a book-length study on the redefinition of childhood in contemporary American children's cinema, the public debate on children and television, and children's marketing.

ADAM KNEE holds a doctorate in Cinema Studies from New York University. He has taught at universities in Thailand, Australia, and Taiwan, and has written a number of essays on Thai cinema.

ERNEST MATHIJS is lecturer in film studies at the University of
Wales, Aberystwyth. He was formerly at the Free University of Brussels,
where this research started. His current interests include horror film, film
criticism, and the representational aspects of film. Essays have appeared
in *Literature Film Quarterly, Cinema Journal,* and local film journals (*Cinemagie, Plateau, Andere Sinema*).

BRIAN MCILROY is professor of film studies at the University of
British Columbia. He has published two books on Irish cinema, including *Shooting to Kill: Filmmaking and the "Troubles" in Northern Ireland*
(Steveston Press).

JONATHAN RAYNER is lecturer in film studies and English literature
at the University of Sheffield, England. He is the author of *The Films of
Peter Weir* (Cassell), *The New Zealand and American Films of Geoff Murphy* (Kakapo) and *Contemporary Australian Cinema* (Manchester University Press).

STEVEN JAY SCHNEIDER is a PhD candidate in cinema studies at
New York University. He is coeditor of *Underground U.S.A.: Filmmaking
beyond the Hollywood Canon* (Wallflower Press) and *Traditions in World
Cinema* (Edinburgh University Press); editor of *Horror Film and Psychoanalysis: Freud's Worst Nightmares* (Cambridge University Press), *Fear
Without Frontiers: Horror Cinema across the Globe* (FAB Press), and *New
Hollywood Violence* (Manchester University Press); and author of *Designing Fear: An Aesthetics of Cinematic Horror* (Routledge).

VIOLA SHAFIK teaches cinema studies at the American University in
Cairo and is author of numerous studies on Arab cinema, including *Arab
Cinema: History and Cultural Identity* (AUC Press). She is currently working on *Popular Egyptian Cinema: Gender, Class, and Nation.* She has
directed the following short films and videos: *Inside the Pomegranate*
(1987), *Iraqi Artists in Germany* (1991), *The Lemon Tree* (1993), *The
Mother of Light and Her Daughters* (1988), and *Planting of Girls* (1999).

CHRISTINA STOJANOVA teaches at Wilfred Laurier University in
Canada. She has published widely on historical, ethnic, and gender representation in the cinemas of Eastern and Central Europe, of German
interwar cinema, and the cinema of Québec. Her book, *Dual Vision: East*

European Cinema and the Totalitarian State, 1948–1989, is due out next year.

KEVIN W. SWEENEY is an associate professor of philosophy and teaches philosophy and film studies at the University of Tampa. An associate editor of the journal *Film & Philosophy*, he has published articles in *Film Criticism, Literature Film Quarterly, Film & Philosophy*, and *Wide Angle*. He is currently at work on a book about Buster Keaton and film comedy.

ANDREW SYDER is a doctoral student in the School of Cinema-Television at the University of Southern California. His dissertation focuses on issues of visual culture and psychotronic film from the 1960s and 1970s.

DOLORES TIERNEY is a lecturer in film and American studies at the University of Sussex, England. She has published on Spanish and Mexican horror film and Mexican melodrama and is currently completing a manuscript on Emilio Fernandez, the great auteur of classical Mexican cinema.

JAN UHDE is professor of film studies at the University of Waterloo, Ontario. His writings include *Latent Images: Film in Singapore* (co-author, Oxford University Press) and *Vision and Persistence: Twenty Years of the Ontario Film Institute* (University of Waterloo Press). He has contributed to periodicals in Canada, the United States, Germany, Holland, and the Czech Republic.

REBECCA A. UMLAND is professor of English and graduate faculty fellow at the University of Nebraska at Kearney. She has published widely on the Arthurian tradition in Victorian literature, focusing primarily on Tennyson, Morris, and Swinburne. With Samuel J. Umland, she authored *The Use of Arthurian Legend in Hollywood Film* (Greenwood Press) and several articles on the films of David Lynch.

SAMUEL J. UMLAND is professor of English and film studies and graduate faculty fellow at the University of Nebraska at Kearney. With Rebecca Umland he authored *The Use of Arthurian Legend in Hollywood Film* (Greenwood Press) and several articles on director David Lynch.

They are currently completing a biography and critical study of artist and film director, Donald Cammell (FAB Press).

TONY WILLIAMS is professor and area head of film studies in the English Department of Southern Illinois University at Carbondale. He is the co-editor of *Vietnam War Films* (McFarland), and author of *Jack London: The Movies* (Rejl), *Hearths of Darkness: The Family in the American Horror Film* (Fairleigh Dickinson University Press), *Larry Cohen: The Radical Allegories of an Independent Filmmaker* (McFarland), and *Structures of Desire: British Cinema, 1939–1955* (State University of New York Press). His essays have appeared in numerous anthologies and journals.

ANDREW WILLIS is a lecturer in media and performance at the University of Salford, England. As well as writing on Spanish horror films he has published a number of articles on martial arts movies. He is co-editor of *Spanish Popular Cinema* (Manchester University Press).

JOSEPHINE WOLL teaches at Howard University and writes about Russian literature and film. Her most recent book is *Real Images: Soviet Cinema and Thaw* (I. B. Tauris).

SUZIE YOUNG is associate professor in the Department of Film and Video at York University in Toronto, Canada. Her current research projects are David Cronenberg's flesh dances and films from the three Chinas.

Index